Bruce Lakofka

The People's Artist

Bruce Lakofka
The People's Artist

Joseph A. Bonelli

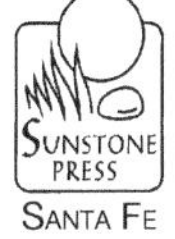

Sunstone books may be purchased for educational, business, or sales promotional use.
For information please write: Special Markets Department, Sunstone Press,
P.O. Box 2321, Santa Fe, New Mexico 87504-2321.

Book and cover design › R. Ahl
Printed on acid-free paper
♾

Library of Congress Cataloging-in-Publication Data

Names: Bonelli, Joseph A., 1942- author.
Title: Bruce Lakofka : the people's artist / by Joseph A. Bonelli.
Description: Santa Fe, NM : Sunstone Press, [2020] | Summary: "A book that explores the art of Bruce Lakofka with text by Joseph A. Bonelli"--Provided by publisher.
Identifiers: LCCN 2020013425 | ISBN 9781632933034 (paperback)
Subjects: LCSH: Lakofka, Bruce, 1946-2015. | Painting, American--20th century.
Classification: LCC ND237.L239 B66 2020 | DDC 759.13--dc23
LC record available at https://lccn.loc.gov/2020013425

WWW.SUNSTONEPRESS.COM
SUNSTONE PRESS / POST OFFICE BOX 2321 / SANTA FE, NM 87504-2321 /USA
(505) 988-4418 / FAX (505) 988-1025

Contents

Preface

So what is the best way to look at an artist's work over a lifetime? Start with his latest (and hopefully best work) or start with his early work and progress up to his last?

I like the historical or chronological approach and that is how I have organized it here. However, if you want to see the best of Bruce Lakofka's latest work turn to Chapter 3 (thirty-eight of his "best" oil paintings, with commentary). If you can wait for it, start with the Introduction, Biography, etc. in sequence and see how his paintings developed.

Now, here is a surprise for you. Bruce did some of his best paintings early in his career. You won't see the usual progression of improvement because he was spectacularly good to start with. The only progression is in his painting medium to the more complex and more difficult oil on canvas. Yet some of those will still be on someone's wall three hundred years from now looking as if they had just been painted. Even some acrylics I bought from Bruce forty plus years ago look as good today as they did then.

A useful word on titling and coding of painting images. Early paintings (1-158) Bruce had not titled, so the author did so posthumously. And later 105 oil paintings had titles by Bruce, but in the text, they are also identified by a simple letter/number code. For example, "Spirit of the Full Moon" is E-23. The letter part of the code refers to the category of subject matter. "E" stands for Indians, "C" stands for the category Indian Maidens, etc. This letter/number code is used as an alternate identifier to the painting's title.

If this makes no sense a quick look at Chapter 5, where all categories and paintings are listed, should clear it up.

Introduction

Why This Book and Title?

I have followed Bruce Lakofka's career as a friend and sometimes advisor for nearly fifty years until his death on October 21, 2015. I think Bruce was an undiscovered modern master painter. I hope you will agree when you see his paintings.

As a commercial artist his chances for exposure to a broad audience and opportunity to be remembered by posterity are limited. Mostly, only the most famous and financially successful get remembered in art books. And even those (think of the monumental talent of Norman Rockwell) are seldom accorded any respect by traditional art critics and art museum curators.

In 1998, I twisted Bruce's arm into entering two of his paintings in a juried art show and auction. One entry was disqualified (I don't know why), and the other was voted "People's Choice Best Painting." And it sold. A year later I met the buyer of that painting and she was still thrilled with it.

Few people ever passed one of his paintings without a visible positive reaction. That is why I chose the "People" title for this book. He earned it. He painted for himself and for others, but not for the art critics. And, people were his favorite subject. Bierstadt did mountain landscapes of the West. Bruce did people.

What Are My Qualifications to Write This Book?

I am not an art critic nor do I have formal training in the art field aside from a few undergraduate courses at UCLA in the sixties, some of them with the renowned professor Karl With. So call me an amateur art historian. I bet I have seen more of the world's greatest paintings than any trio of PhD art professors. How, you might ask.

I spent three months in the spring of 1966 traipsing about the U.S. visiting art galleries and museums using Greyhound's 99-day ticket offer (Anywhere for 99 days and $99). With my sheaf of dated tickets I crisscrossed the U.S. three times lengthwise.

The following two months I did the traditional "Grand Tour of Europe," a favorite of 19th century affluent college graduates upon completion of their studies. Since I was not born with a silver spoon in my mouth, I used Frommer's classic travel book, *Europe on Five Dollars a Day*.

For two months, I visited every major art gallery and museum in most of the major cities of Europe, including as a finale, one in East Berlin. With the assistance of a friend who was a knowledgeable West Berliner, we crossed through the Berlin Wall at Checkpoint Charlie into the Russian zone and through a devastated, bombed-out landscape of rubble to a lovely museum which housed the Pergamon Altar, the bust of Nefertiti, and other astonishing Assyrian and Egyptian pieces. There was only a handful of people inside this Greek-style temple of culture. The "Monument Men" did well in protecting this magic jewel of a place.

After two months, my eyes and brain were exhausted from looking at old masters and new, my wallet was empty and my American Express travelers' checks were gone. I took a metro to the airport and flew right home (in those days you didn't need plane reservations).

~ 1 ~

Biography of the Artist

Bruce was born Bruce Joseph Lakofka on October 23, 1946 in Chicago. The family moved soon thereafter to California. Bruce's father, whose ethnicity was German and Polish, was a postman, which was a walking job in those days. His mother Alice, who was of French descent, was a thin, frail lady with a nice sense of humor. Bruce came from a working class background and was proud of it and never forgot it. Bruce's first introduction to the arts was music, not painting—accordion lessons at age eight. He played multiple instruments: guitar, drums, piano, flute, and violin. He was multitalented, like Da Vinci.

His older brother, Dick, went to college and became a prison correctional agent. His younger brother, Bob, worked for the post office, as did his sister, Deb. She showed Bruce's same talent for drawing and painting.

Bruce started painting in high school in Pomona, California. He started his professional career at age nineteen by direct selling his early, large works at the famous Art Mart, a Saturday open-air parking lot operation on La Cienega and Melrose in Hollywood in 1965 which movie stars often frequented. These early, large works were usually acrylics or oils on 3'x4' or 4'x4' gessoed masonite panels which he worked on in his mother's garage.

In the summer of 1966 at the urging of his family, who wanted him to look into other possible career choices besides painting, he took a seasonal job with the National Park Service as trail crew worker. What better job than working far away from civilization in Sequoia and Kings Canyon National Park? He got interested in this work after taking a horseback trip with a packer who used mules to bring in supplies for the trail crews. It took three days on horseback to get into the back country where the work was done. Although he enjoyed it at first (and it was hard, physical work) by the end of the summer he knew he had made a mistake. He missed his painting desperately and was miserable. He knew then that art was his future and couldn't wait to get back to painting in his mother's garage.

In 1967, Bruce got a big break. The owner of Maggie's Clothing Store in Pomona, recognizing Bruce's skill and its commercial potential, bought eighteen paintings. Apparently, people didn't mind shopping for paintings as well as clothes, if the price was right.

His early works from this period are probably still extant and spread out over West Los Angeles and the greater L.A. area. It is possible that some of them have ended up in art galleries in the area. The Art Mart was a short drive away from Beverly Hills; maybe some of his works found a home there. It is also possible there are paintings out there that are true Lakofkas but are different images than the 158 images in Chapter 2.

Bruce used a roomy old van to transport his large paintings and set-up equipment for direct sales at the Art Mart. His operations were simple but effective. He made a living at it.

During this early period, he spent one and a half years taking art courses at Mt. San Antonio College in Walnut, California. He moved from that area before finishing the academic course requirements for his AA degree.

In 1967, at the La Cienega Art Mart I fell in love with Bruce's paintings and he liked some of the photographic work I had been doing, which I occasionally sold there as well. Our mutual friendship continued for nearly fifty years though our separate life paths wandered far from Hollywood and L.A.

Ironically, I met another artist around the same time I met Bruce, only she was at the end of her unusual career while he was just starting his. Irene Boucher was an "Old Masters" copyist. What's that? She typically painted in all the famous galleries where there was someone who wanted a specific painting copied or where she could copy on "spec." The Cezanne flower bowl she painted looked so much like the original photos I had seen it was scary. Additionally, she signed it "Irene Boucher after Cezanne."

Was she legit? Of course. The dimensions of a painting are carefully recorded information and the gallery guards simply measure the canvas routinely used by any copyist.

Bruce would always precisely measure the dimensions of his oil painting canvases and post that information along with the title of the work. People sometimes shop for paintings not only by image but by size. That way they will know if the painting will fit in the place they had planned for it. For purposes of this book, painting size was not included.

Bruce continued for some years to direct sell his artwork to the public through Art Mart, but also sold some paintings in a store/gallery in Hollywood.

Bruce was raised a Catholic, but in 1970 he experienced a personal conversion and became a Bible-reading born-again Christian.

For some years he continued painting and selling in L.A. but in a major life shift in 1975, he moved to a religious commune in Alma, Arkansas, not far from Fort Smith. This was the seventies and communes were a part of the evolving social landscape of the time. While a resident in the commune he began a series of thirteen portraits of country music stars that made guest appearances at the Alma Restaurant which was owned by Bruce's church. These portraits were usually done in advance and would hang behind each star as they performed on the stage in the restaurant banquet room. As portraits accumulated it became a sort of gallery of performers. You might look upon this as the Bruce Lakofka Art Gallery. But it is no longer there.

One of these thirteen performers was Tammy Wynette. Bruce remembered painting her portrait "under a parasol." This was back in 1975 (painting #135). He did not see that painting again for twenty-three years until it was splashed all over the newspapers and television because it was prominently displayed at her funeral. It was Wynette's favorite. She must have asked for it after her performance there in 1975 and taken it home. Bruce was unable to authenticate his claim because his business manager at the time it was painted asked him not to sign portraits. A national newspaper/magazine, *The Star* of Tarrytown New York, was contacted by Bruce after the funeral in July of 1998 and it was confirmed the painting was unsigned, and no artist's name had been made public. Tammy knew of Bruce's authorship; she asked that he do her album cover for the Tears of Fire 25th anniversary. The result is painting #148 in Chapter 2.

At the end of the 1970s, Bruce was doing montage paintings of celebrities, featuring portraits and scenes from the lives of stars and personalities such as Elvis Presley, John Wayne, Judy Garland, Dick Clark, Johnny Carson, and the cast of "Dallas." During this time period he also completed a monumentally-sized "Life of Christ" panel painting depicting numerous scenes from the life of Jesus. Bruce told me it reportedly sold for $15,000.

In the 1980s, Bruce did not do much traditional painting but worked in other areas of the complex art world. He worked in graphics, ad layouts, catalogs, brochures for businesses, fashion art, signs, window dressings, and murals for homes and businesses. He also did some video cassette boxes and album cover artwork and produced some of his own posters and postcards.

He married his sweetheart, Brenda, in 1983 and spent part of that summer doing street portraits of tourists on the river in Savannah, Georgia and on Music Row in Nashville. He also worked the Arkansas State Fair in Fort Smith. A snapshot of that operation is shown in the photographs after Chapter 1. Part of the reason Bruce liked doing street portraits is it enabled him to connect with and meet new people. He loved to capture the "light" in peoples' eyes; perhaps he found a clue there to their personalities.

Around 1987 he became involved in designing and producing glitzy entertainment jackets that became popular with celebrities and other flashy dressers. These were usually denim jackets that were painted over with air brushes and squiggle paint, then decorated with rhinestones.

After spending some time in the Nashville scene, where he is still remembered in the art community, he moved with his wife and two young children in the early nineties to Tampa, Florida. It was there he decided to get back into more conventional painting with traditional oils and brushes on panel or stretched canvas.

It was in Florida, of all places, that he conceived and painted the first of his Native American pieces. And the very first painting he completed was "Spirit of the Full Moon." However, it should be understood that his Indians are not like Remington's, George Catlin's, or Howard Terpning's who are realistically depicted down to every ethnologically correct detail. Bruce paints the Native American the way the general public perceives them, in a romanticized, dramatic and respectful manner. He had a lot of incentive to do that since his wife is part Cherokee and proud of it. Bruce's Indian themed paintings celebrate the Native American culture with special emphasis on spirituality and ceremony.

While in Florida, he signed up with a licensing agency and launched yet a new sub-career within the complex field of art. He was now a commercial artist. He did postcards, t-shirts, and fine art prints (18"x24") with The Creative Age, Inc. He signed on with a second agent in California.

Shortly thereafter in 1994, he moved back to Southern California and focused on Native American painting themes. Golden Turtle Press published two "Spirit of the Full Moon" calendars of his Indian-themed paintings in 1996 and 1997. Bradford produced a four plate Collectors

Series of his Indian images. F.X. Schmid produced a jigsaw puzzle of "Spirit of the Full Moon" and "Be a Clown" (which they renamed "Funny Face"). Then came crewel (stitching) sets, designer umbrellas, cups, etc. The Olympic Company bought numerous images for a line of t-shirt decals. An Australian company made a beach towel with the image of "Spirit of the Full Moon" (E-23) which was licensed for the 2000 Olympics in Sydney. Bruce was an international artist; his products sold in many countries. Bucilla made a pre-printed crewel of the same image. Both were spectacularly well done. Some time later, Impact Images of El Dorado Hills, California, did a batch of approximately eight of Bruce's images as small art prints (8"x10") on heavy board stock; they were quite impressive. This was the kind of business deal Bruce especially liked—getting his images to lots of people at low prices.

It was back in California where Bruce started seriously working in the oil painting on canvas medium. Part of the impetus for this came as a result of his new commercial career, but partly he wished to explore this ultimate test of the painting field to paint like the Old Masters.

As Bruce got deep into oil painting, he became affiliated with or at least interested in an organization called OPA (Oil Painters of America Representational). Its goal was to promote representational oil painting on canvas, in reaction to recent trends in "Modern Art" that have promoted abstract non-representational art.

Commercial artists today sell or license the use of their images in the multiple fields of commercial art. However, the artist is then free to sell the original painting if he or she is able to.

In order to record his painting images and provide his agent with images to sell to various commercial enterprises, Bruce used, for many years, an old Nikon F 35 mm camera which produced terrific 3x5 or 4x6 color prints.

The numbered photographs (158 of his early works) are mostly derived from Bruce's old Nikon. He made it a habit early on to take photos of his paintings. A few of the photographs are my own taken with a Petriflex or Konica; some are even closeups made with slides (converted to prints). Despite the uneven quality of reproduction, a slow perusal of these images will show you Bruce's early artistry and maybe even take you down memory lane. Bruce painted what he saw and what he liked.

How exactly did Bruce make photos of his paintings? He photographed them in his back yard using full sunshine and got great color saturation using low ASA (25) color print film. Sometimes he used a tripod, sometimes not. When that specific film was no longer available, he moved to 100 ASA then 200. For a short time he even developed his own color film, something only serious photo-bugs ever tried.

One day in 1993 or 1994, Bruce came across a specialty photo store that made large (8x10) transparencies (color slides) of paintings as well as other art "flatwork." Such slides would give a superior projected image (for large auditorium lectures or possibly even classroom teachers). In pure theory such slides might also give a superior printed image but it is difficult to be sure that is so because there is no obvious simple way to tell (without conducting a controlled experiment with a printing operation). My thought was the projection and printing technologies might not easily mesh.

Bruce fell in love with this new technology, partially because his paintings were like his children to him. He spent so much time on them that he felt they deserved the best. Generally, he sought a sale using the Nikon color prints first, then if a potential buyer signed on, he sent the 8x10 transparencies. Information about whether a transparency or plain color print were used to achieve the final product was never transmitted. I conjecture that some businesses might have had the technology to use the transparencies, but others not.

The effort Bruce put into his paintings shows in his meticulously crafted artwork; his dazzling use of colors stun the eye and brain. But, even an exceptional photograph of one of Bruce's paintings does not convey the reality of seeing it in person. Serious photographers know the limitations of their medium and accept this truism. Even after a photo of a painting had been taken, Bruce took pains to obtain a proper color balance and quality in the print sent to his agents.

As the price of making one of these specialty transparencies climbed to forty dollars per painting, I cautioned Bruce about using them. He was trying to make transparencies even for unsold paintings on spec. I suggested he stop using the transparencies entirely so he could drastically reduce his production costs. Then, over time, something happened that made my unpalatable and ignored business advice redundant. The specialty store went out of business, apparently with the advent of the digital revolution.

In 2007, Bruce became interested in a digital camera as a replacement for the loss of the transparencies. His family members were also interested in the new technology. Bruce bought a multiple-use digital camera, one the family could use for family photos, etc. and he could use for his work. About a year later he confided to me that he was finally able to obtain color digital prints that were almost as good as the Nikon prints. He explained that people doing serious artwork with digital cameras had to purchase expensive top of the line units and was told by a photographer that 12 mega-pixel capacity was needed.

To understand another aspect of Bruce's art career, it is necessary to backtrack. In October of 1998, Bruce entered two paintings in an art show and auction in Las Vegas. Generally, to enter these types of shows an art juror has to "accept" as appropriate the paintings an artist wishes to enter. The art juror that year turned down one of Bruce's entries. The other one was voted "People's Choice—Best Painting." And a Nevada Governor's Award. This was for the First Annual New Horizons Art Show and Auction. The New Horizons School (for children with learning differences) was the beneficiary of a percentage of all painting sales. In October of 1999, the second annual show was held and both of Bruce's entries were accepted, and both sold at the auction. I don't remember all the numbers but one of his paintings sold for $2,800 which was the most he had ever received for one painting.

For a time in early 1999 some of Bruce's paintings were exhibited at Art Encounter, an art gallery in Las Vegas which was run by Ron Maly, his wife, and son, Brett.

As can be seen by looking at his images of the 1990s and beyond, they are painted with infinite care and detail. His technical procedures now include "underpainting" in acrylics but mostly "overpainting" in oils. Sometimes he applied a finish afterwards which imparts an even brighter, glossier look. Sometimes he uses poppyseed oil (instead of linseed oil) to slow the drying time so he can use brushes to blend the paint into the color shades that form a face, animal, flower, etc.

His paintings can best be appreciated, I think, in a bright sunny location where their colors radiate. Lighting each individual painting properly is often neglected even by galleries. I once talked to a person at an art auction who only decided to bid on a Bruce painting at the extreme last moment when it was carried to a strong light at the front of the stage, preparatory to the formal bidding.

Many of Bruce's paintings are done with "studio wrap." The top, bottom and two sides of a wooden painting frame are ordinarily not painted by most artists working with canvas, even though the canvas is stretched over these points to secure it. Bruce sometimes felt like filling up that "empty" canvas. This takes great skill to do right, but when successful the effect is to give the painting a bit of a 3-D effect. And it is certainly ecological. The buyer has only to attach hooks and hanging wire and the painting is both framed and ready to hang on the wall. Bruce often attached the hooks and wire himself.

The owners of art galleries and framing shops, of course, do not care for this approach. The sad truth is beginning artists often get paid less for their paintings than it costs to frame them. You can't escape the economic reality that the cost of the framing is part of the purchase price for the buyer. This could make owning an original painting beyond the reach of those buyers with limited means.

The use of the studio wrap and his painting "The Last Reservation" (E-8) together, make a good case for nominating Bruce as outstanding painter/ecologist of the year. In "The Last Reservation" there is an image of our blue earth as seen from space to the right of the Old Indian Chief. The message is clear: "Earth is our last chance, let's not screw it up." It is a pictorial rephrasing of world renowned biologist Edward O. Wilson's writing (*Half Earth: Our Planet's Fight for Life*) that we have only one planet and one chance to make things right.

The intelligent "titling" of this painting is typical of Bruce's sharper use of titling during this period to convey and amplify the effect of his painting imagery. Of course, most of his titles appear merely descriptive, e.g. "Under Silent Stars" (E-2). However, "Native Cathedral" (E-16) gets more complex. Indians did not build cathedrals. Their cathedrals were the giant trees of the forest. An even more complex and thought-provoking title is "Southern Cross" (H-20). Robert E. Lee and Stonewall Jackson were military pillars of the Confederacy. The "Southern Cross" is a famous and esteemed star constellation in the Southern Hemisphere beloved by all world travelers. The Confederacy was also the cross the Union had to bear. This is a title with multiple possible meanings and interpretations especially in view of its origin (See Chapter 3). Politics of political correctness be damned, it's a great painting. And a great title.

Into the new millennium, Bruce continued his career as a commercial artist. As with most commercial artists he continued to stockpile his original paintings. Commercial artists decorate things or help to sell them. Both tasks are necessary in our complex society. And of course gallery or studio artists produce paintings to hang on our walls. Around this period I worked for Bruce as an informal (unpaid) business manager and advisor.

My efforts about this time focused on helping him get into a gallery so he could have an outlet for his paintings. I even went to a number of galleries myself as his representative with photos of his recent paintings. It proved almost entirely futile. Of course, the economy was in a slump at the time. However, on one such visit a prestigious gallery owner thumbed hurriedly through Bruce's photo pile until he got to "The Tire Swing" (I-5) and suddenly said, "I wish I had painted that." Another gallery owner liked only "Bouquet of Kittens" (F-7).

Galleries were not interested in seeing painting diversity; they wanted dependable "formula" artists, artists with a constructed persona, a consistent and dependable look, and paper credentials in the Fine Arts. Although many admitted that Bruce's work showed considerable talent, they just did not feel they could market that talent. Of course, most self-owned galleries represent their own work or that of their friends.

Under the above constraints, I doubt that Monsieur Monet, whose mediocre seascape/ landscape painting recently sold for $110 million dollars, could have gotten gallery representation. That painting was not even "one of a kind" as there were seven or eight duplicates in various museums. In Bruce's career I know of only four or five paintings that he repeated because they were so popular. He quickly tired of doing 'assembly line' paintings. The Monet sale was not really about art but the power of fame, money, and Veblenian extravagance.

Despite my failed expeditions to some upscale galleries, Bruce continued to seek gallery representation by direct mailing photocopies of his work. A few galleries showed an interest but to my knowledge nothing came out of this. Some gallery owners (by mail) were not stingy with their praise but no one signed on.

Bruce never got gallery representation. I do not pretend to understand the complex sociology of art marketing. My only afterthought was that successful artists must spend as much time on their marketing as on their painting. Bruce did not want to do that and I can't blame him for it. It suggests to me there might be a place for a new niche profession in the art field of Gallery Representation Agent. This would be someone who could match up studio artists and galleries by knowing the types of paintings that certain galleries favor and has a large stable of painter clients they can use to make such a match. Bruce had an agent for his commercial work. She was very good at selling his images to potential business customers. Unfortunately, she died of cancer at the height of her career. There was no one available with her talent to fill that gap. Such circumstances are probably not too unusual when you run a small business of your own.

Although Bruce never got gallery representation, he participated in various charitable shows, such as at the New Horizons School in Las Vegas. He also exhibited paintings at various venues including the Cheyenne Frontier Days Old West Museum, Art Center of Estes Park (Colorado), and San Bernardino County Museum Wildlife Art Festival.

Bruce was an accomplished imitator of other painters, their subject matter and their styles. A few of his paintings could be considered Kinkade imitations ("Village Lights" and "Peace Be Still"). I have been told that Bruce's newer paintings ("Snowfall" and "Cry of the Wolf") imitate the style and subject matter of a painter named Maya. If Maya is a very young person, I might wonder whether she is imitating Bruce who has been painting Indian maidens for the last twenty-five years. Bruce as imitator of Rockwell is discussed later.

Bruce and the Jigsaw Puzzle Market

Bruce's intricate craftsmanship and detail work, interesting images, montage work, and use of bright colors were a hit with jigsaw puzzle companies. Eighteen of his paintings that I know about have been made into puzzles:

Spirit of the Full Moon	FX Schmid	1993
Funny Face (Be a Clown)	FX Schmid	1994
Night Eyes	Express Gifts Ltd.	2000
Night Riders	Sunsout	2000
In the Shadow of the Wolf	Sunsout	2000
Ride the Wild Wind	Express Gifts Ltd.	2001
Wild Earth	Sunsout	2002
Eagle Dance	Sunsout	2002
Meow: The Cat Family	Sunsout	2003
Eagle Princess	Sunsout	2003
Thundering Herd	Sunsout	2003
Back in the Fifties	Masterpieces	2003
One in Spirit	Masterpieces	2004
World of Imagination	Sunsout	2004
Heavenly Welcome	Sunsout	2004
My Guardian Angel	Sunsout	2009
Sweet Dreams	Sunsout	2010
Native Tapestry	Sunsout	2010

The Subject Matter and Style of Bruce's Paintings

There are traditional sorts of subject matter: still life, landscapes, portraits, people, nudes, famous people, and in the 20th century abstract inner "mental landscapes." There is also non-representational abstract art which allows people like me who can't even draw a "stick man" to consider ourselves potential artists.

In their school training or early apprenticeship most artists, assuming they can draw, will try some or most of these traditional categories of subject matter.

As time goes by, artists usually settle into painting the kinds of subjects they like or that they find easy to paint, or ultimately the subjects they think the public would like to buy. An obvious case in point is Thomas Kinkade and his deftly-painted lighthouses and cottages

Throughout his career, Bruce painted anything and everything that interested him. He was not afraid of a broad range and chose what he wanted, whether it was hippies, Vietnam soldiers, the Beatles, street people/people on the street or Bob Hope. He even painted unorthodox subjects (such as doing paintings of other painters) not favored by other painters. (See paintings #50, 90, and 97)

I once asked Bruce, "What is the secret of success in the art world?"

He replied, "Artists find a niche in subject matter or style and then repeat variations of it over and over to create a name identity."

Many people have a stereotype of painters as bohemian free spirits and libertines. This is probably due to a number of 19th century Impressionist painters who seemed to fit that mold. However, today the financially successful top painters such as those in Jackson Hole galleries work not freely but with rigid regimentation in what and how they paint. These folk are undeniably excellent but must continue to rigidly paint "in their persona." They are also rich and certainly not bohemian; but free spirits they are not.

There is a related stereotype that all great artists are lascivious libertines like Gauguin (going out to the isles of the Pacific) or Toulouse-Lautrec because of the kind of ladies he liked to paint. Francisco Goya painted "majas" with and without clothes. Other painters stayed home and made a living while others had to die first before people looked at their paintings and finally noticed they were great painters. I have known one painter very well and three others superficially. All were sober, serious, and disciplined, so I dispute the libertine stereotype.

Be assured the current art world does not encourage diversity and catholicity of subject matter. Diversity is much praised but seldom practiced. The art world of today really doesn't want any more Leonardo Da Vinci's, people who spread their talent in many directions. An artist has to have a persona or recognizable and stable and consistent image and style. Reliability supersedes spontaneity and creativity.

Not only is there a rigidity in choice of subject matter that is usually considered "serious art" but there is also accepted or preferred styles of painting to accompany it. There are abstracts, surrealistic, realistic, impressionistic, etc. and of course there has to be a "fit" between the style and the subject matter. Kincaid's success lies not just in his choice of soul-soothing images, but in his colorful, slightly fuzzy, romantic, and not quite photo-realistic style. Two other comparable artists would be Terry Redlin and Charles Wysocki.

The breadth of Bruce Lakofka's subjects and painting styles is astonishing particularly in his early works. As with subject matter, he appears to have made a systematic exploration of most styles of painting, perhaps merely to see if he could. He has systematically tried most categories, even some semi-abstract ("Boat Village Red" #67), minimalist ("Sun on the Water" #20), and some semi-abstract interior landscapes.("Red Demon Lion" #18 and "The Scream" #43).

Some of his regular landscapes ("South Seas Color" #69 and "The Blooming Tree" #103)

are nearly impressionistic. Bruce however didn't do repetitive images, Campbell soup cans, or purely abstract stuff. After all there is too much competition in that area of art. The Jane Goodall Institute's chimpanzee painting therapy class has turned out stuff that looks better than Jackson Pollock's. I've even heard of an elephant being coached to produce good stuff with his trunk.

This amazing variety continued throughout the 60s, 70s, and 80s. In the 1990s it narrowed somewhat and a complex but definable style emerged. What is the Lakofka style of the 90s? It includes use of intensely bright colors painted in oil on canvas, giving a realistic portrayal with infinite care and craftsmanship, almost like Bob Byerley's prints which look better than most artists' originals. It includes "montage" painting (multiple images painted realistically but with a romantic or imaginative, or even metaphorical, configuration or treatment) and often colorful and almost luminous blotches of impressionistic color, or sometimes colorful symbols creating a decorative background.

His occasionally humorous paintings such as "The Rival" (G-1) and "The Competitor" (G-2) tell a story, i.e. they are narrative or illustrative (like most of Norman Rockwell's) upon which they are obviously patterned. Bruce changed their titles (from "Cowboy Mail" and "Cowgirl Mail") because those titles clouded the "one-horse joke." The horse loved his rider and the mail was the competition. If Rockwell's output wasn't so well documented, they could well pass at first viewing as "lost Rockwells." Because in these two, Lakofka captured not only Rockwell's visual style but his optimism and romanticism. And Rockwell, of course, in response to critics carping that he didn't paint the world the way it was, responded, "Why should I? I prefer to paint it better than it is." So did Bruce, with optimism and a sweet air of childlike innocence. This is particularly true for his paintings of Native American Indians.

Among his earlier paintings there is a humorous one titled "Beatles as Bullfighters" (#95) and possibly another, "The Scream" (#43).

Twice, Bruce "revisited" an early painting with a later "conceptual revision" of the same painting idea. That takes an encyclopedic and historical memory. Look at "Vietnam War—Mourning the Fallen" (#123), then at "Fallen Comrade." (B-8) Look first at "Lady at the Rainy Day Window" (#105) then scan "Rain, Rain, Go Away." (I-4)

People interested Bruce more than landscapes (a very traditional subject area for painters). He only did a Monument Valley, a Sedona, a Grand Canyon and a Big Sur. He did lots of high mountain scenery, mostly as props for Indians or horseback riders, and lots of green pastoral scenes. None with the attention to detail of his people paintings. His "Back to the High Country" (E-5) reminds me of the paintings of Mark Ogle of Kalispell, Montana.

One traditional area of painting—portraits—Bruce seldom did. His portraits in Alma of country western stars were made from photographs as were his other paintings of famous people. He did tourist portraiture in Savannah by the river in 1983, which in its own way is very demanding. One exception in the older group was "Portrait of Brenda" (#145) and in the newer group a striking "A Teacher Lady" (H-21). For "Desert Sunshine" (H-19) he was given photos of three people to work into a painting. Only the "Grandma" was available for Bruce to meet in person. So he did. Despite his success with celebrities Bruce felt a really good portrait could only be done by eyeballing the subject in person (even if they did not do a long sitting session).

Paintings, like people, can also have adventures. Here is the story. In May of 2005, Bruce wrote me that one of his paintings had been "found" in a gallery, Emory's Fine Arts Gallery in Murfreesboro, Tennessee, the site of a famous Civil War battle. Since I didn't know it was lost, I was taken aback by this news. (The back story comes later.)

The gallery owner had phoned Bruce with this good news. Bruce had bad news to tell him—the painting was stolen. I suggested that Bruce rush documentary proof to the gallery owner confirming that he owned this valuable painting.

Someone just walked into the gallery saying the painting, which was a stunner, was theirs, but they needed to sell it. For all those crime story fans—scofflaws are not that easy to spot in real life, and certainly the provenance of a painting is hard to figure out. Perhaps Mr. Emory got suspicious when this person was willing to part with the painting for only $1,500. How he eventually found Bruce, I don't know. Perhaps he researched Bruce on the Internet and got his phone number that way? Bruce often wrote his name and the painting size on the back frame.

Bruce had no money to offer a reward for his lost painting nor even enough to pay for its return. Yet Mr. Emory returned it to him.

Anyone willing to do the right thing, even if it hurts them in the pocketbook is a gentleman of the old school and I salute him.

Thus ended the adventures of "Spirit of the Full Moon" (E-23), Bruce's most famous and perhaps most valuable painting.

The back story mystery was solved. How did that painting get to Tennessee? Bruce delivered the painting to an art gallery in Nashville belonging to a friend of his who was going to try and sell it for him. The gallery was broken into and the painting and other valuables were stolen. This unfortunate adventure reinforced Bruce's ambivalence about selling his paintings. He felt the time and effort he put into these later paintings precluded his getting an acceptable market price. He wanted his art reproduced—used more than once. He only sold paintings when money was needed for family.

A year later in 2006, Bruce got a call from the owner of a gallery in North Hollywood. He sounded out Bruce about having a showing of Bruce's paintings. However, soon thereafter Bruce got a call-back. His friend's gallery had gone bankrupt because of the recession. The deal was off.

Book illustration is one of those little known areas of art that few artists ever try. Bruce did once and the result was a colossal success. I had written a book in 2007 and asked him to provide me a color cover and a passel of black and white drawings and illustrations, various characters and scenes. At first, he was dubious about taking on this project but as I told him about the book and its screwy plot he warmed up to the idea.

The result was the oil painting "Iloni" (A-6), which made a great color front cover for the book which was entitled "Congo Ape Kitabu: Sirius Business." There was a passel of lovely illustrations in black and white (nineteen as I recall) to buttress this wacky crossover genre of African adventure paired with old-fashioned, funny sci-fi.

A couple of these illustrations are located after the oil painting list at J 1 and J 2 in Chapter

5. This book was published in 2008 by Rose Dog Books and is currently out of print. Occasionally pricy copies sold by book dealers are available on E-bay.

Bruce continued to do paintings for his commercial art career past his 65th birthday and onward until 2014. Then he was gone. He died on October 21, 2015 and I never had the chance to say goodbye. He was luckier. See Chapter 6 for this story.

To illustrate Bruce's early days as a painter, I dredged up eleven of my old slides and converted them to prints. The first five depicted activities at the famous Art Mart with Bruce waiting for customers and talking and interacting with them. The next two were of Bruce's studio (his mother's garage) with his massive easel (an upended ping-pong table). The next four were of a private art sale for our friends and neighbors held at a private home (the author's apartment). The dog on Bruce's shoulders was Janet (Protectoress of the author's household), who picked her human friends wisely and well. Bruce had earned her paw of approval.

I had already completed my narrative outline of Bruce's entire painting career, which had sparse information regarding his Nashville period, when I acquired at the last minute a treasure trove of new material including lots of photos. These will follow the photo pages of the early period (after Chapter 1).

In addition, I will present the new information that will "fill in" the Alma, Nashville, and Tampa-Miami period.

In Nashville, Bruce befriended an architect who sought his assistance. Bruce learned to do architectural renderings which were used in plans for the renovation of historic buildings; first in Nashville and later in Miami. Bruce was the artist on the Committee for Restoration of Old Downtown Nashville.

Ultimately, in Nashville Bruce did architectural renderings and interior design layout work and decorating for a number of buildings including a recording studio, two restaurants, Wild Childs, Inc., the Tavern on Music Row, the Take This Heart Gift Shop, Amusement Parks of America, Hartford Advertising, Gruhn's Guitars, and various schools.

For Alamo Designs he did drawings for custom fashions including ladies clothing, hats, dusters, leathers, t-shirts and an extensive line of 159 jackets, including the glitzy rhinestone ones.

For a musician friend he decorated his guitar. He did advertising artwork for local businesses. For the Music Square Church in Nashville, Bruce painted a massive wall mural of "The Ascension" (B-10) in the rear of the church. The "Ascension" is the final panel of his "Life of Christ" painting.

In 1982, Music Square Church, Inc. produced a 22"x32" art print of "The Life of Christ" (#130 of the early paintings). This was a superb print with tremendous color quality and fine images.

Bruce was an artistic guru and "jack of all trades" at Alamo Designs. One of his special projects there was decorating reception rooms (boutiques or salons) where stars were entertained (and sold high-end fashions). For this, decorations and wall murals were done. "The French Lady" (H-23) is a lovely example. Custom clothing by Alamo Designs was also sold "off-site" such as special trade shows at the Jacob Javits Convention Center in New York City and elsewhere.

Bruce also did a number of paintings of Nashville stars for which he did not make photographic records. Those paintings are all in private homes.

He also designed boots, furs, embroidered jewelry, and furniture.

The church that Bruce belonged to owned the famous Alamo Designs in Nashville (as it had owned the Alma Restaurant in Alma, Arkansas). This "commune" was more sophisticated than most. Church members lived in housing units (some of them together) owned by the church and worked in commercial buildings also owned by the church, receiving room, board, and when necessary, medical care.

Bruce's work, particularly in Alma, Nashville, Tampa and Miami brought him into contact with dozens, if not hundreds, of celebrities of the music and movie world as well as many ordinary people.

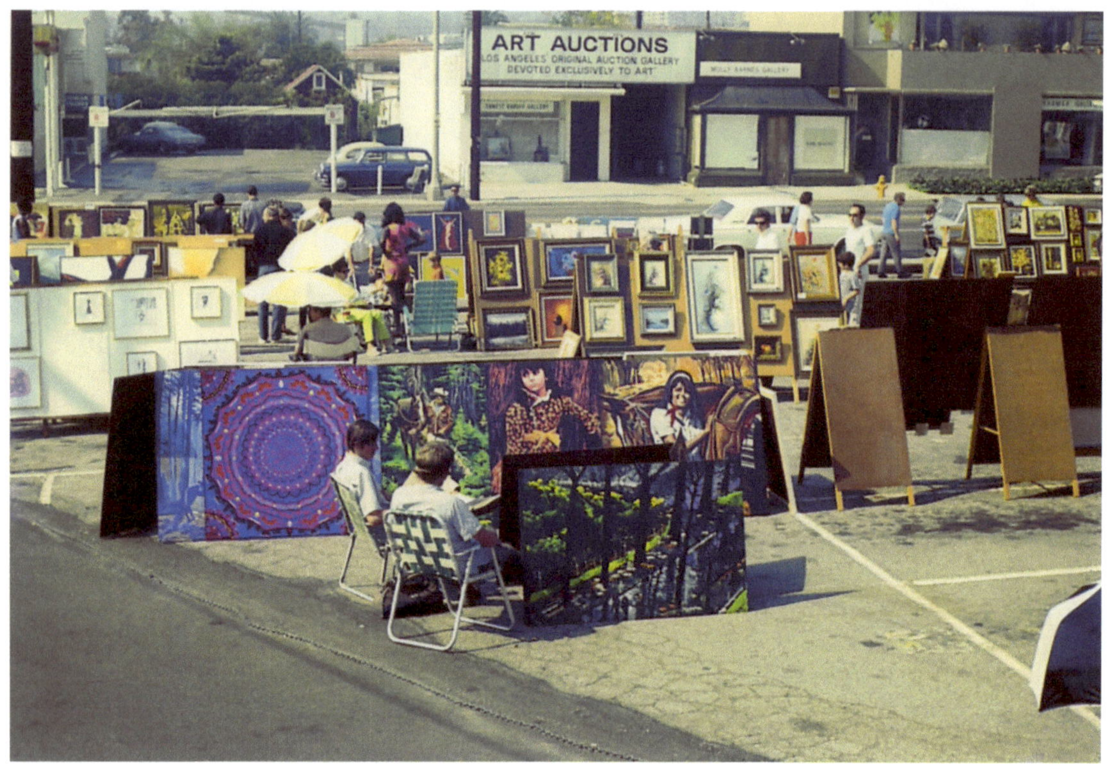

The famous Hollywood Art Mart in La Cienega and Melrose.

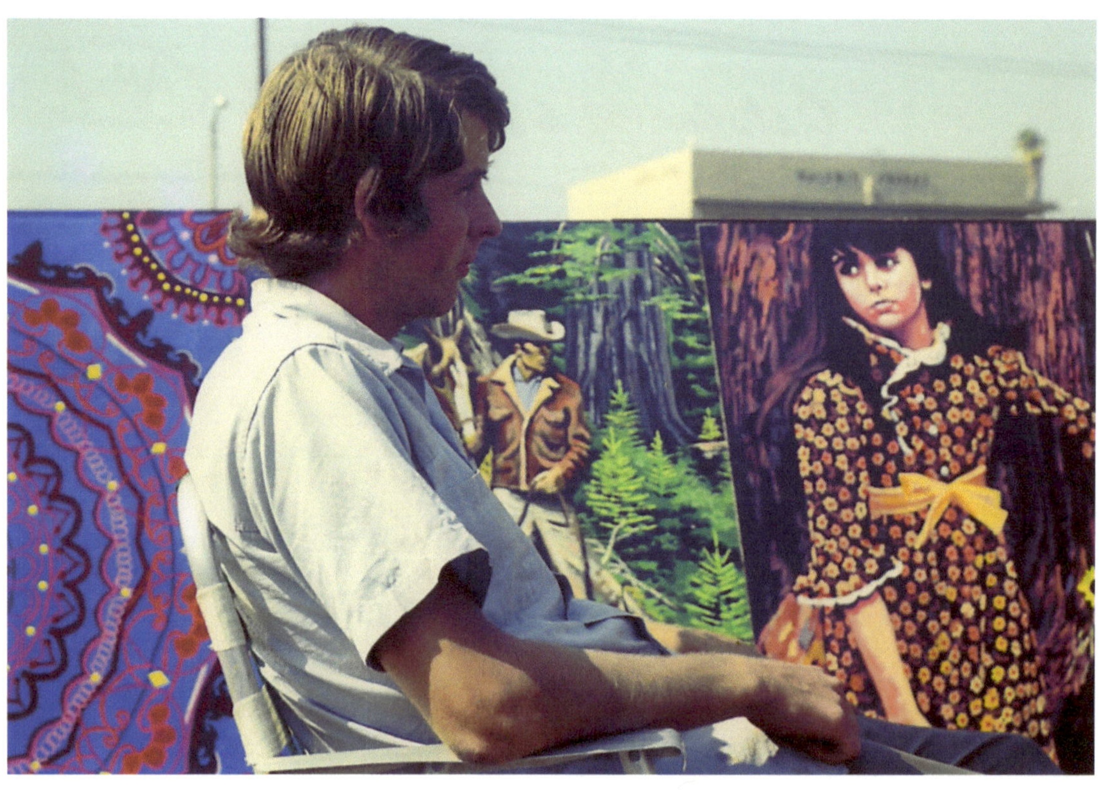

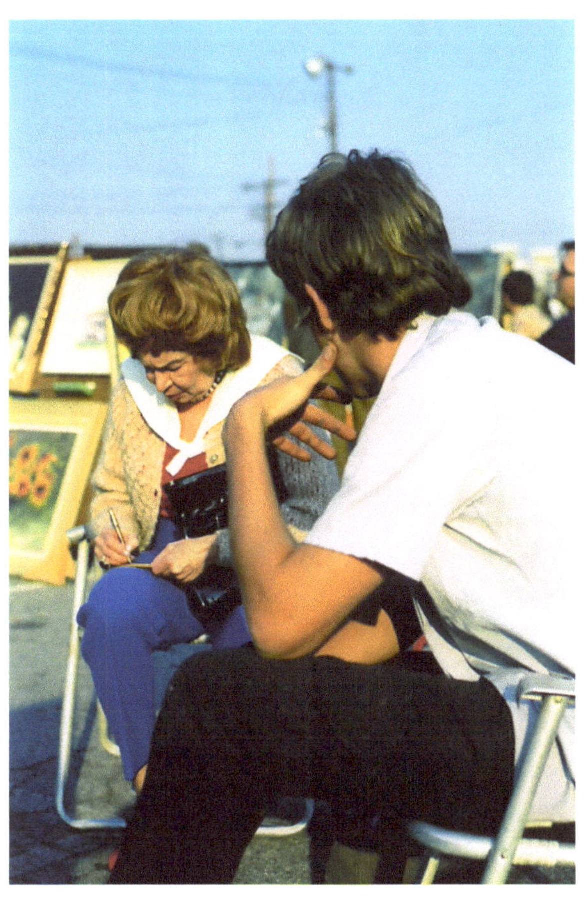

Negotiating at the Art Mart.

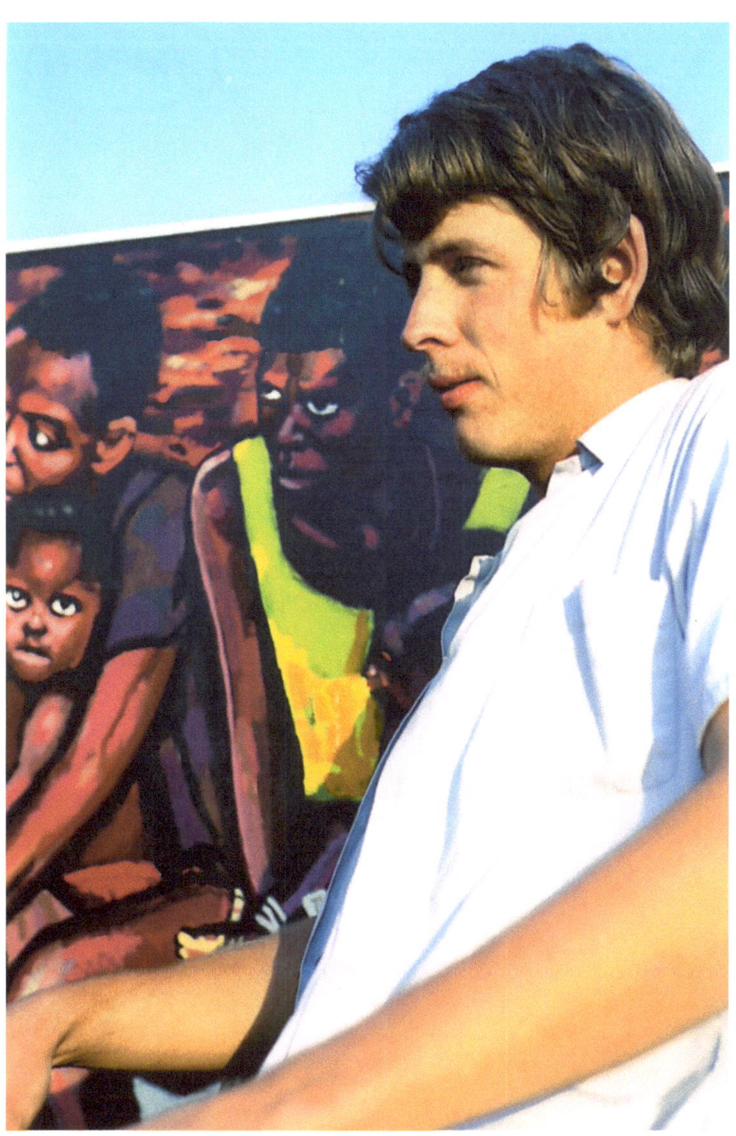

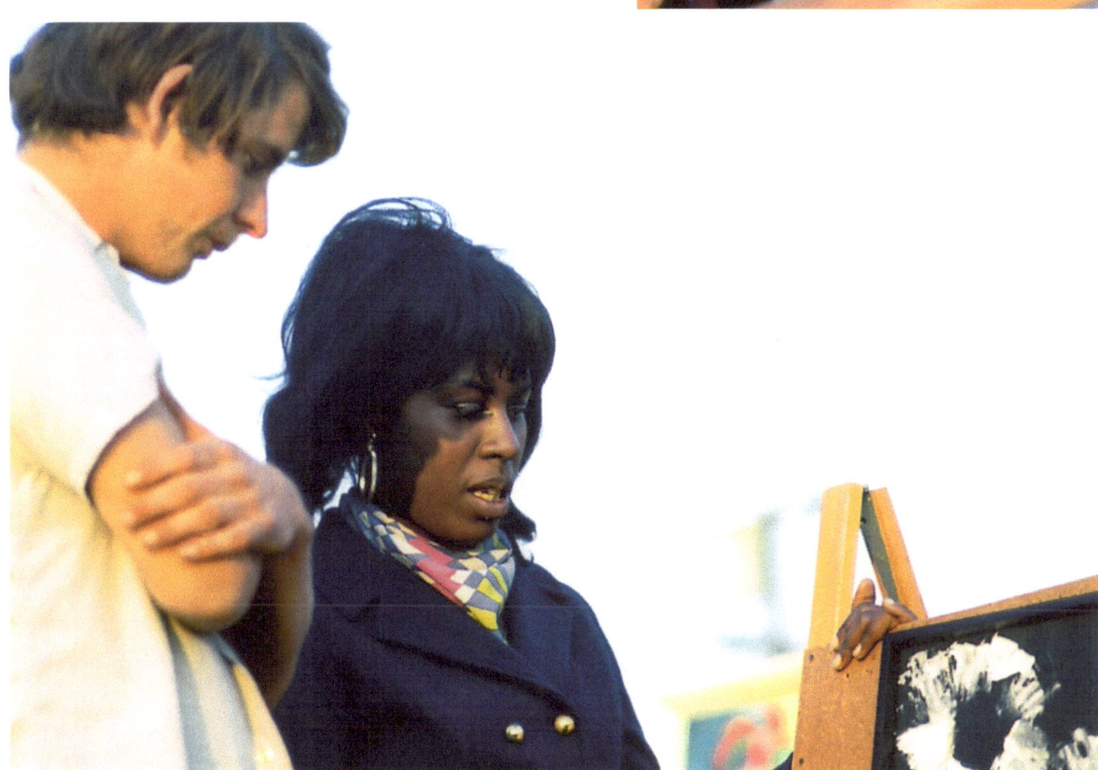

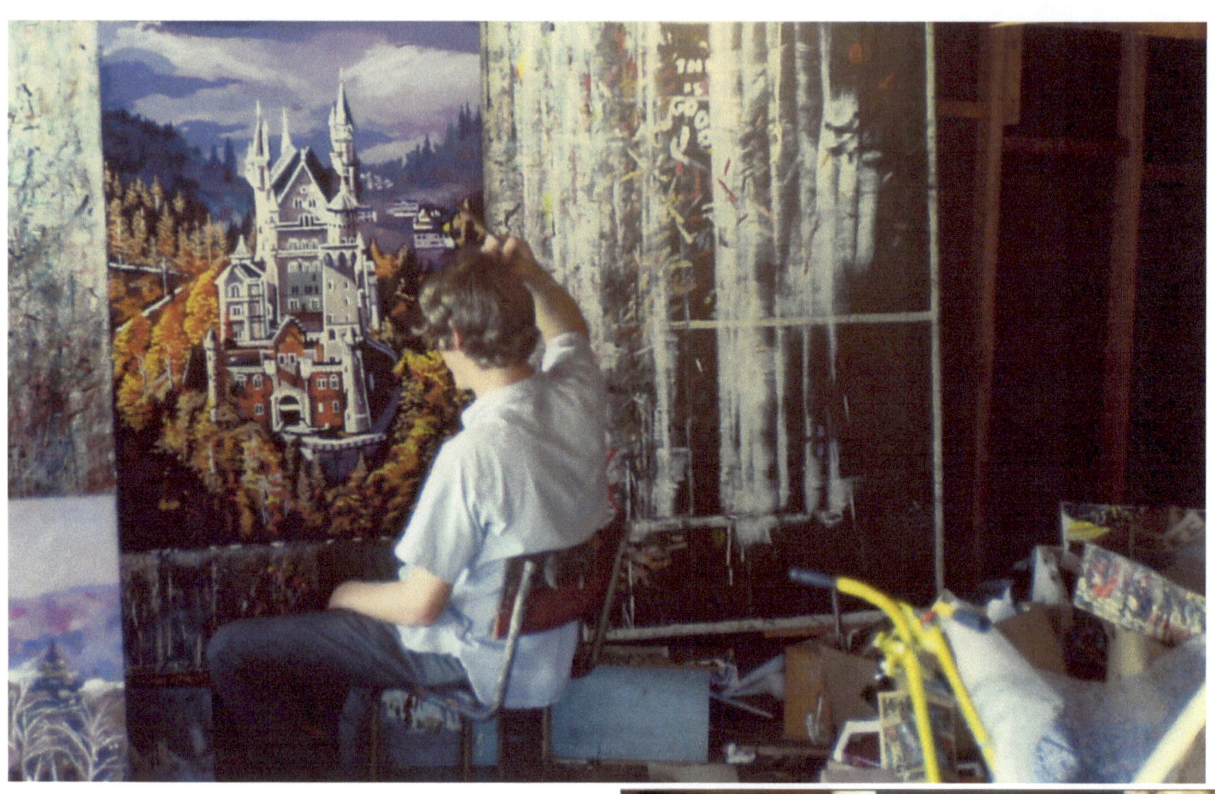

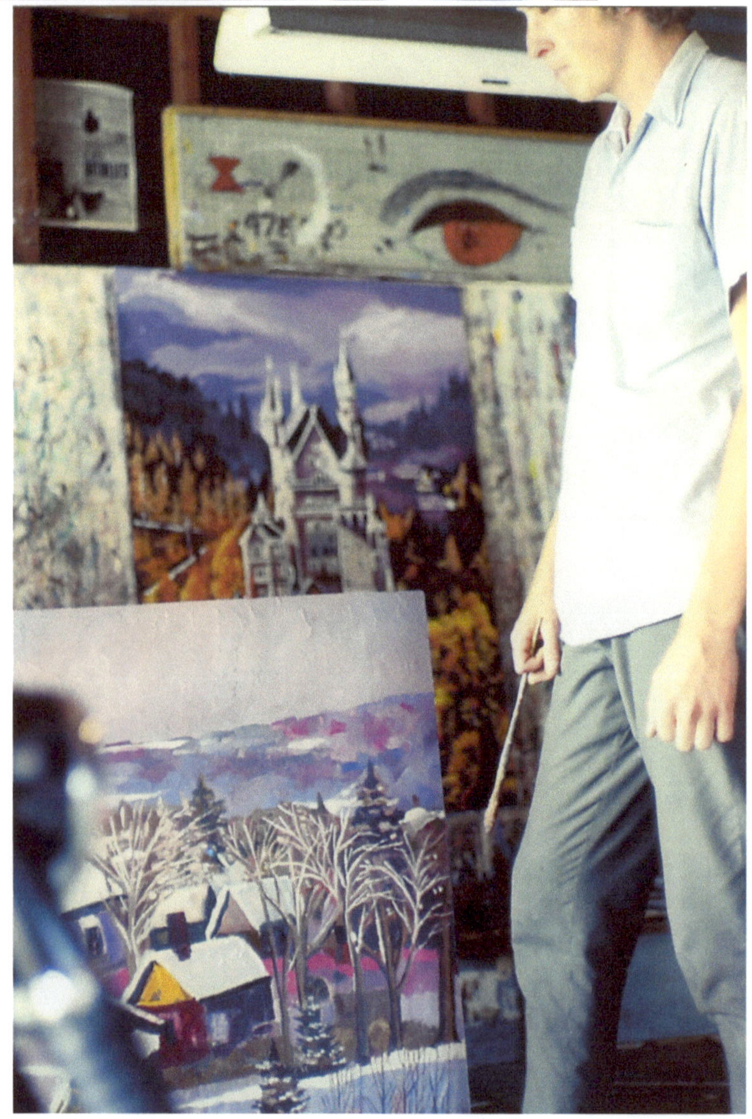

Bruce's first studio (his mother's garage).

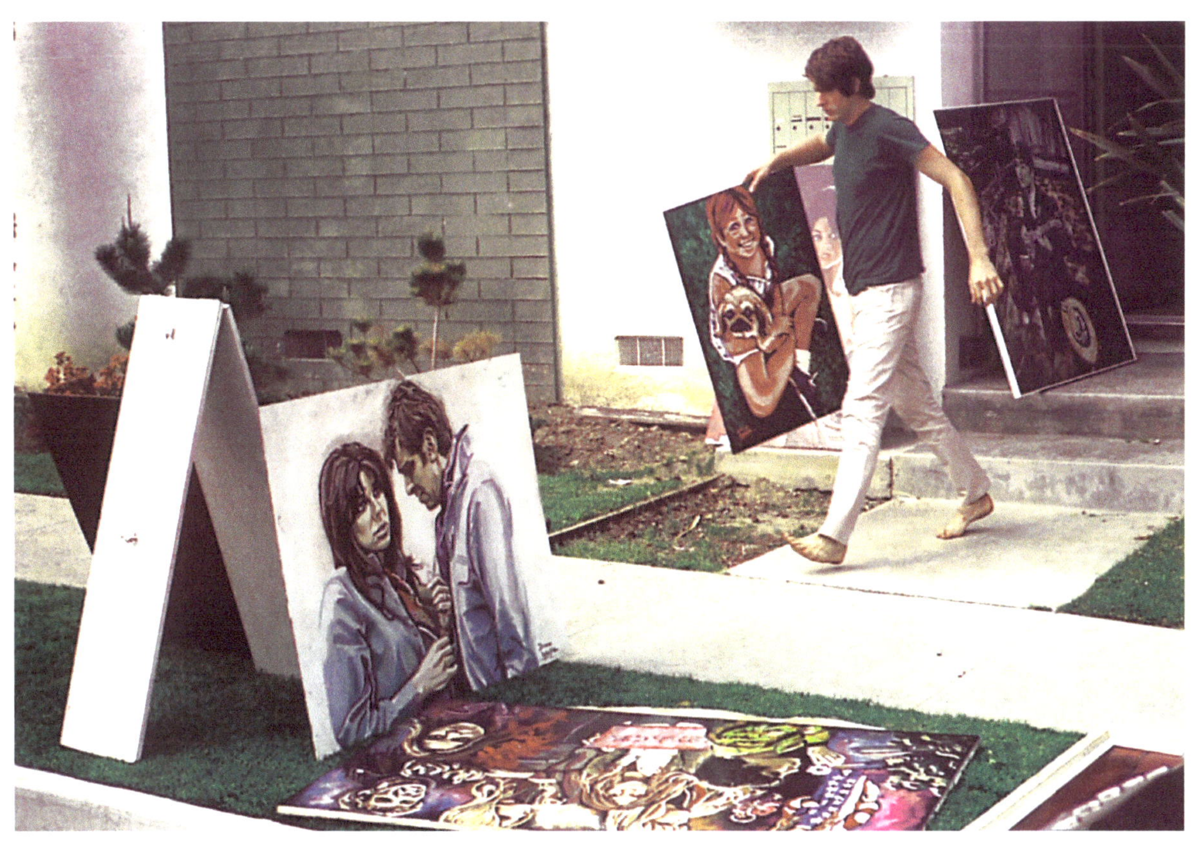

Private sale in Author's apartment.

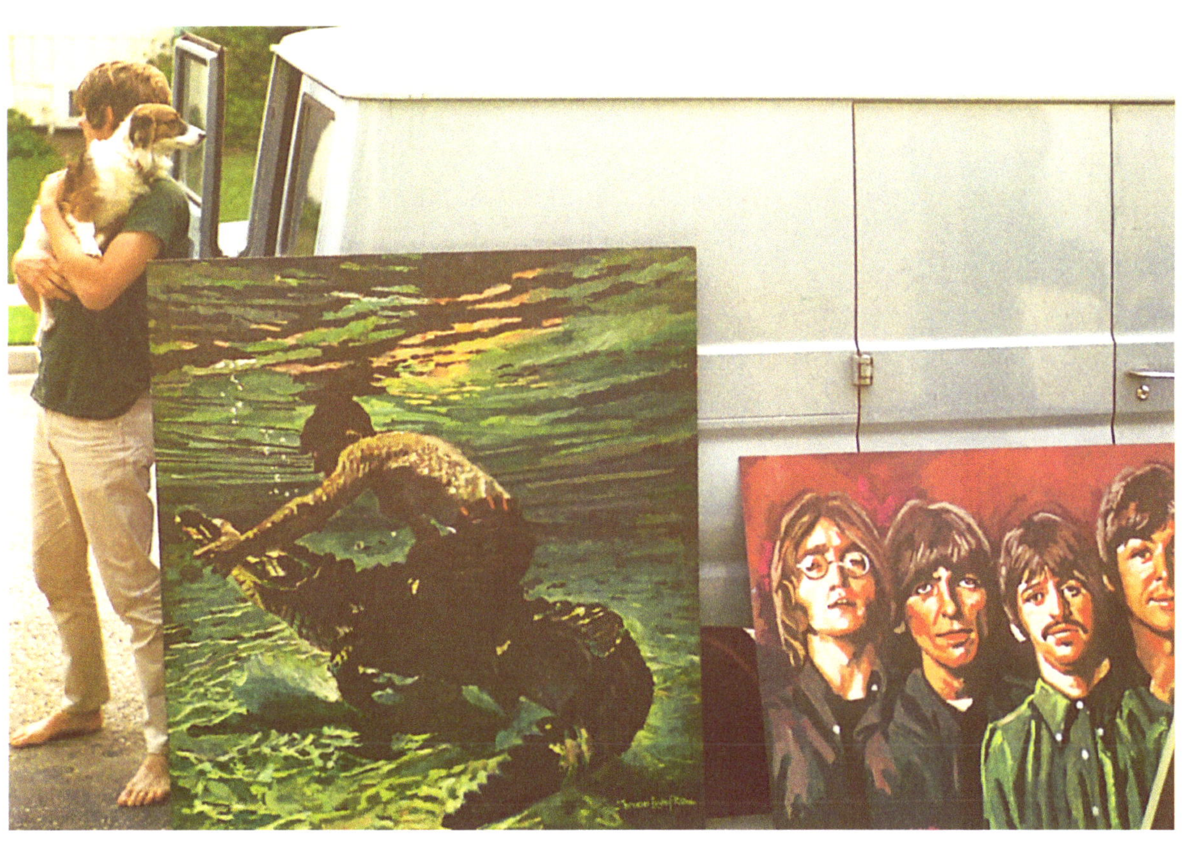

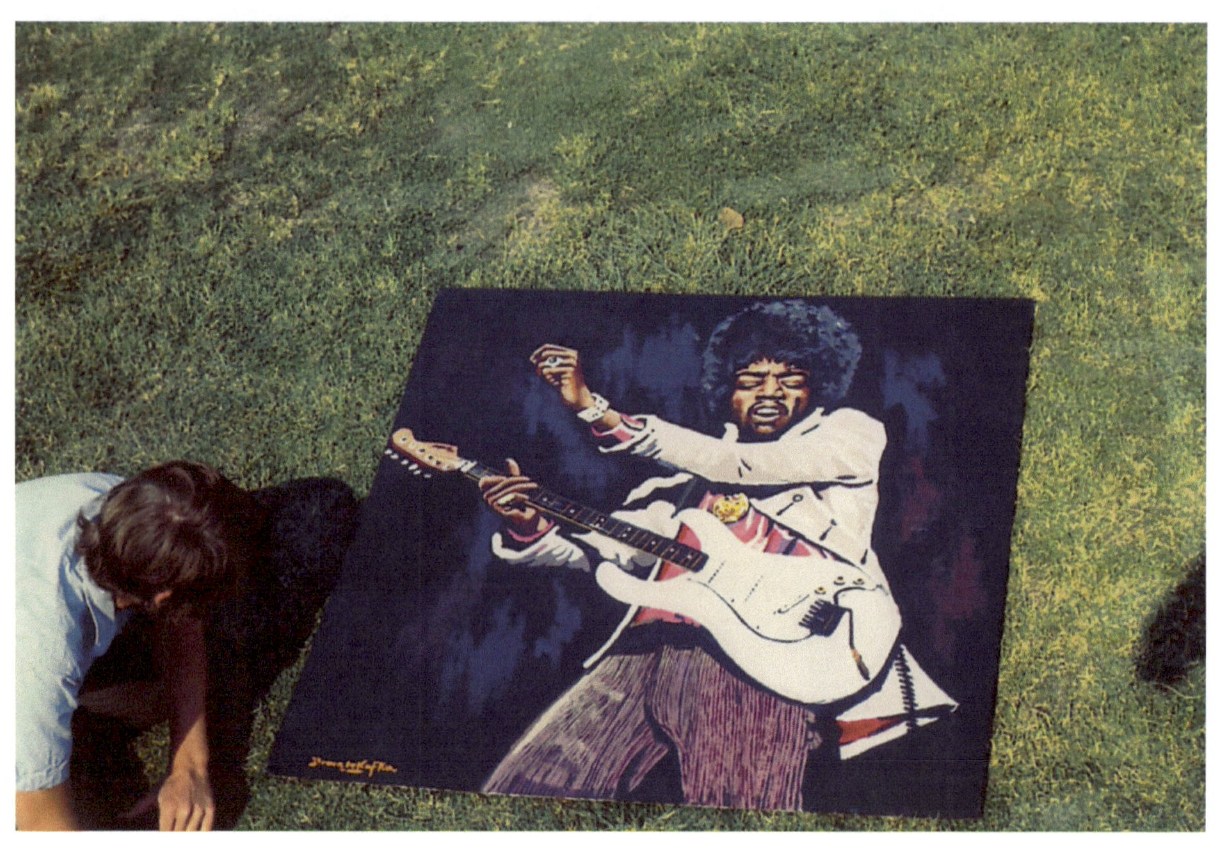

Loading up after the sale.

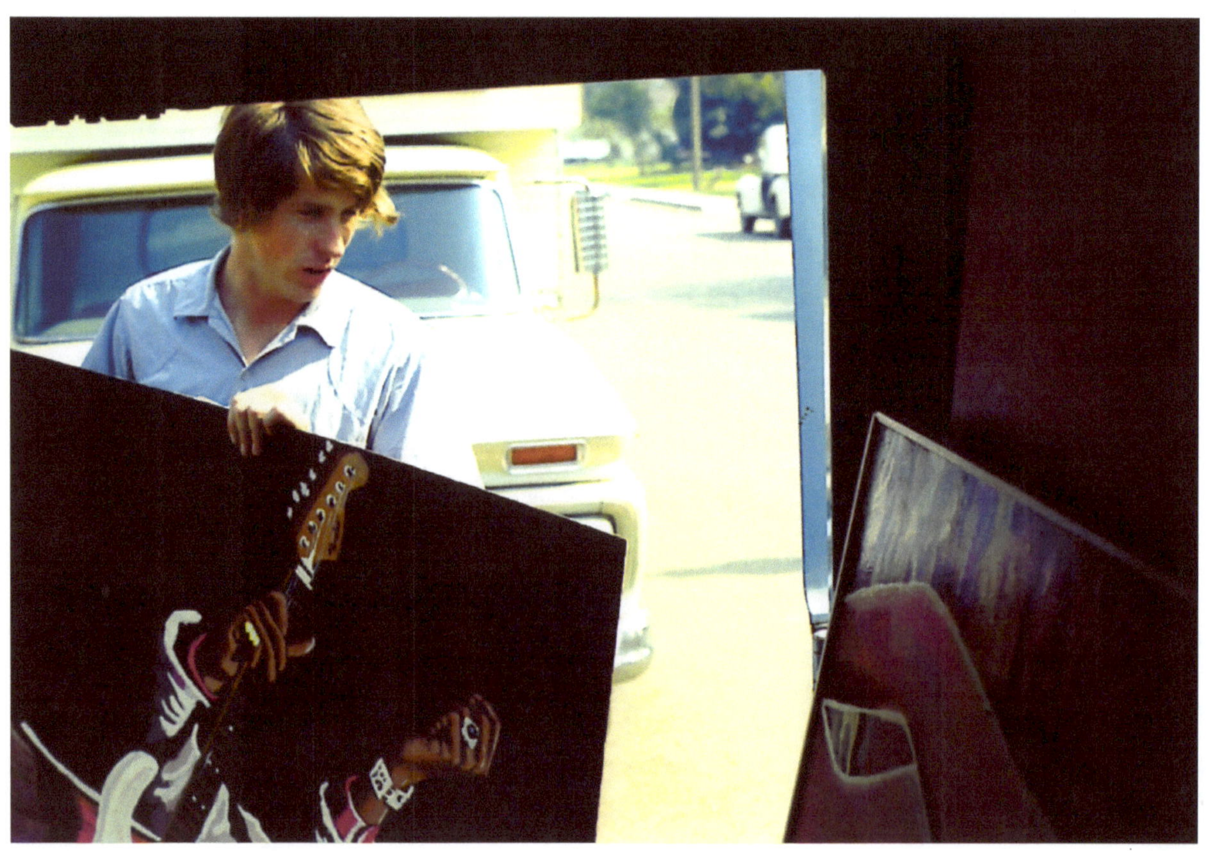

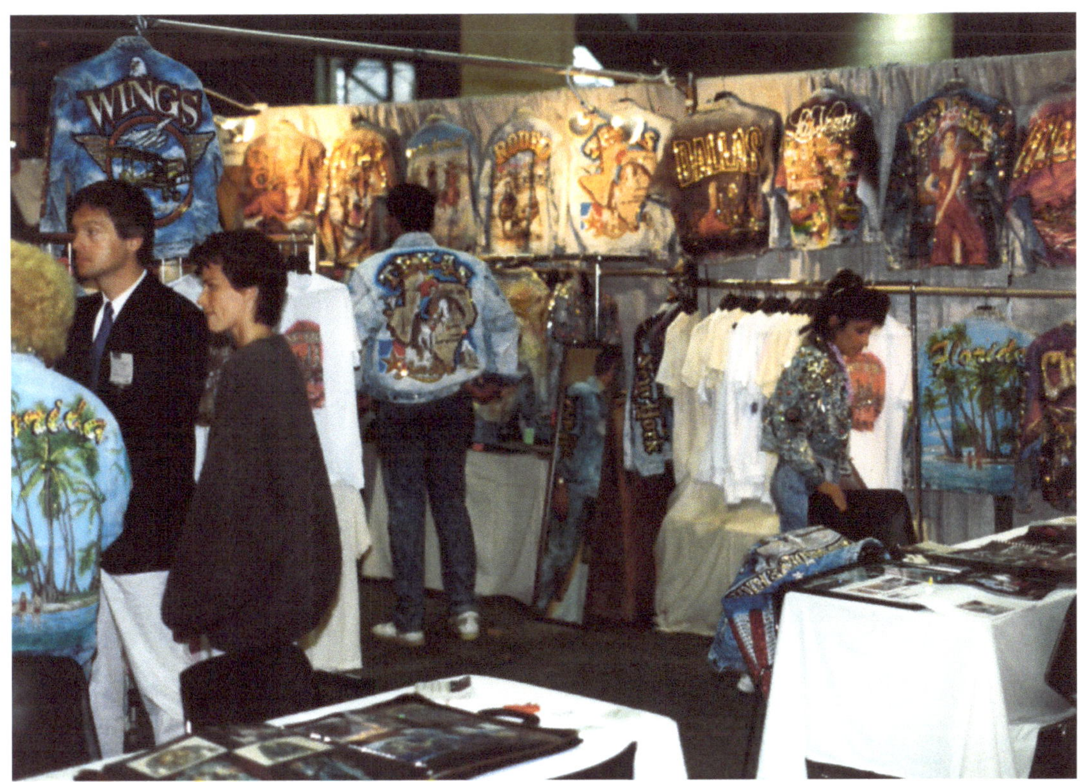

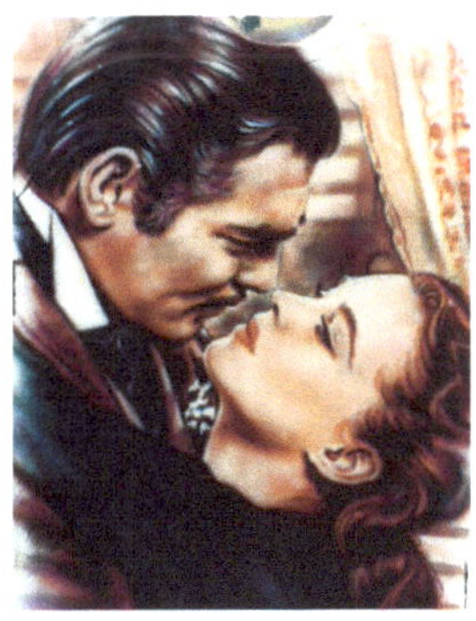

Alamo Designs, Jacob Javits Center, New York City

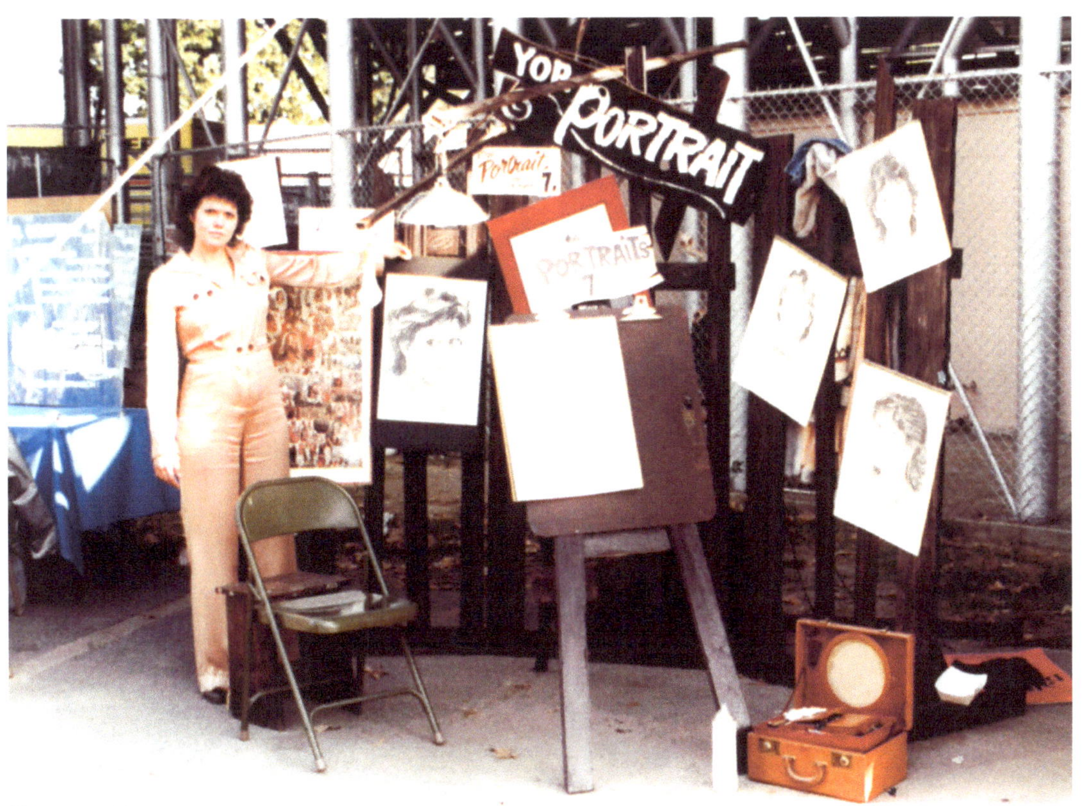

Arkansas State Fair, Fort Smith Street Portraits

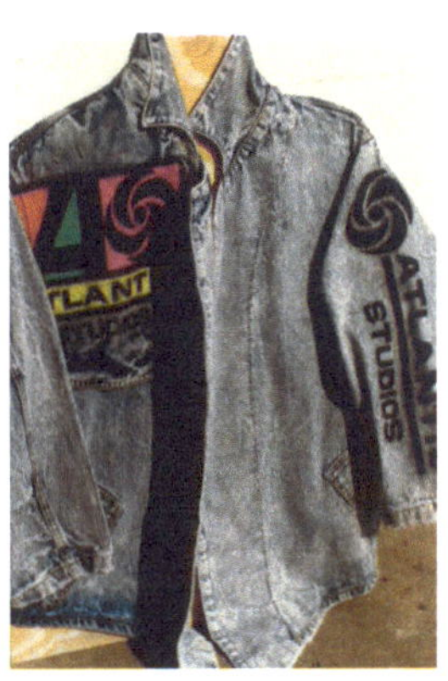

Spirit of the Full Moon Calendars

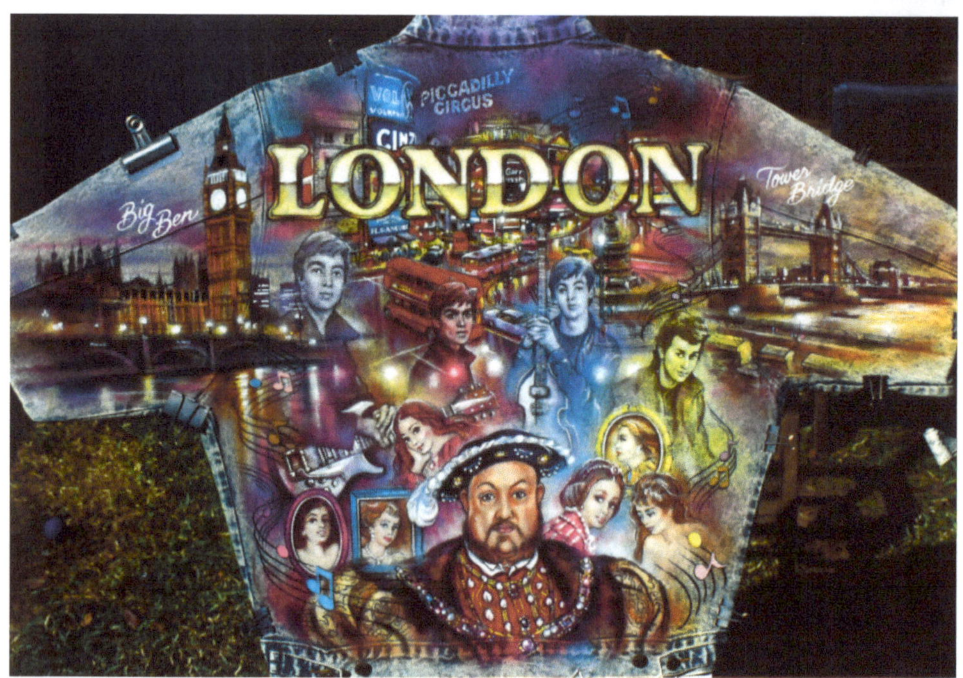

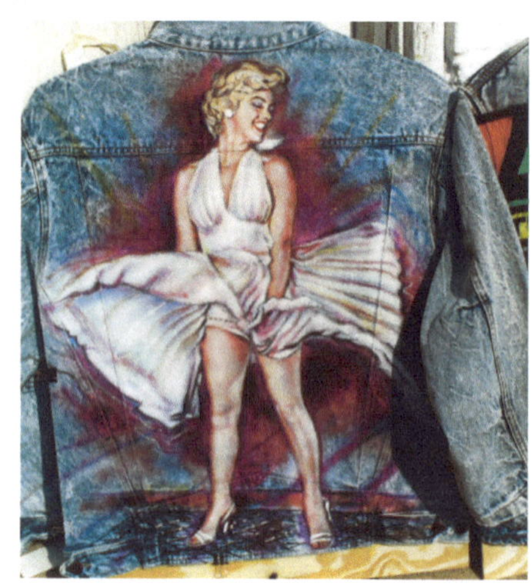

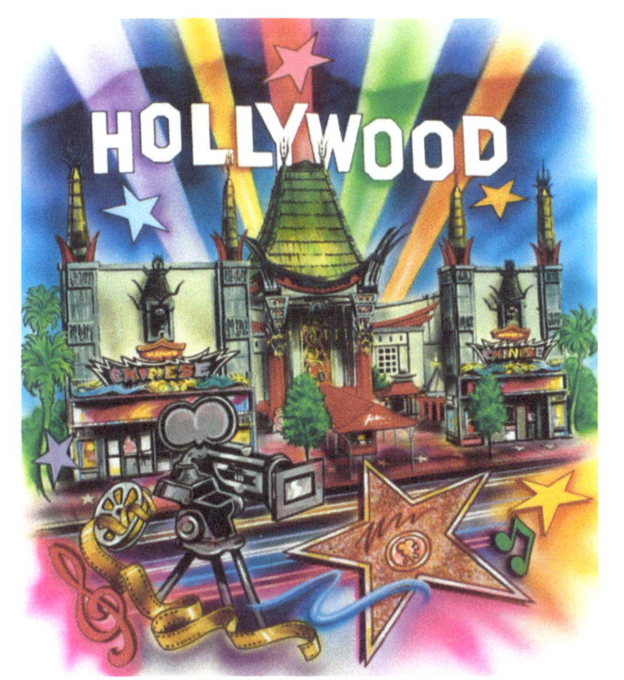
HOLLYWOOD

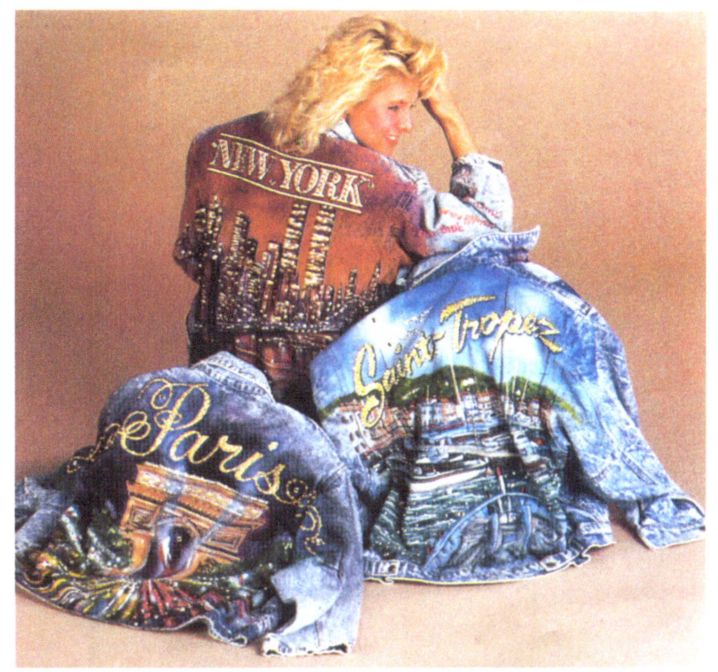
NEW YORK
Paris
Saint-Tropez

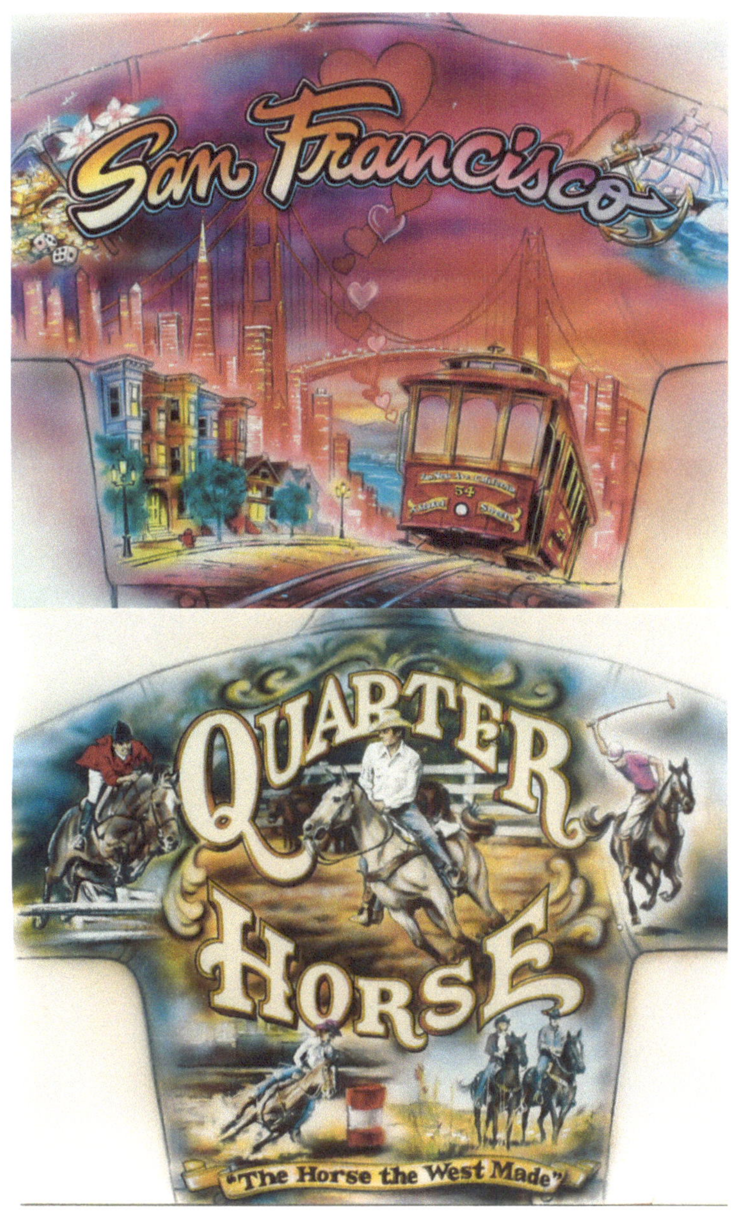
San Francisco
QUARTER HORSE
"The Horse the West Made"

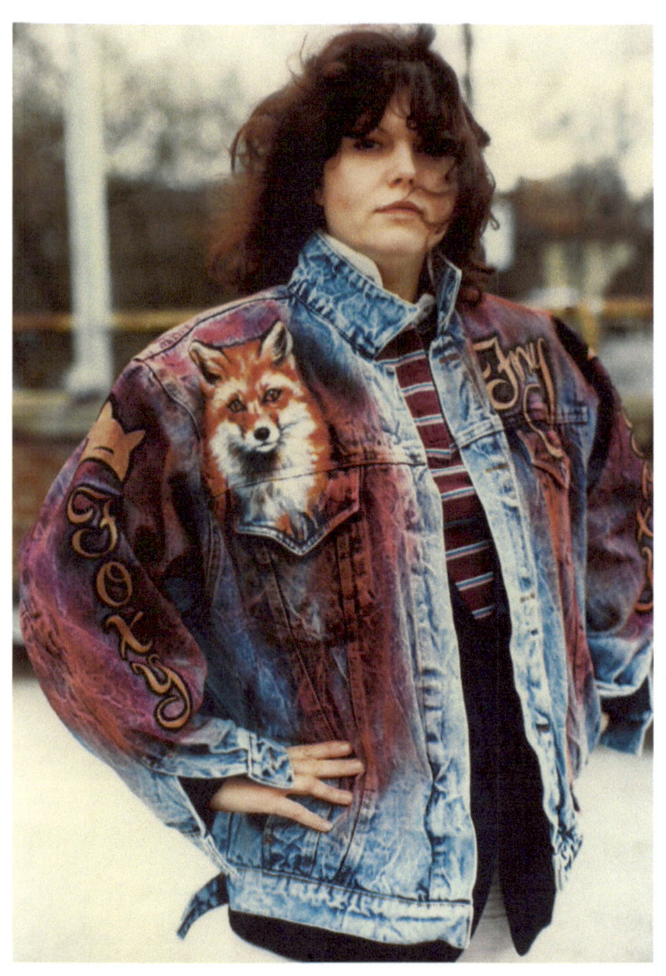
Foxy

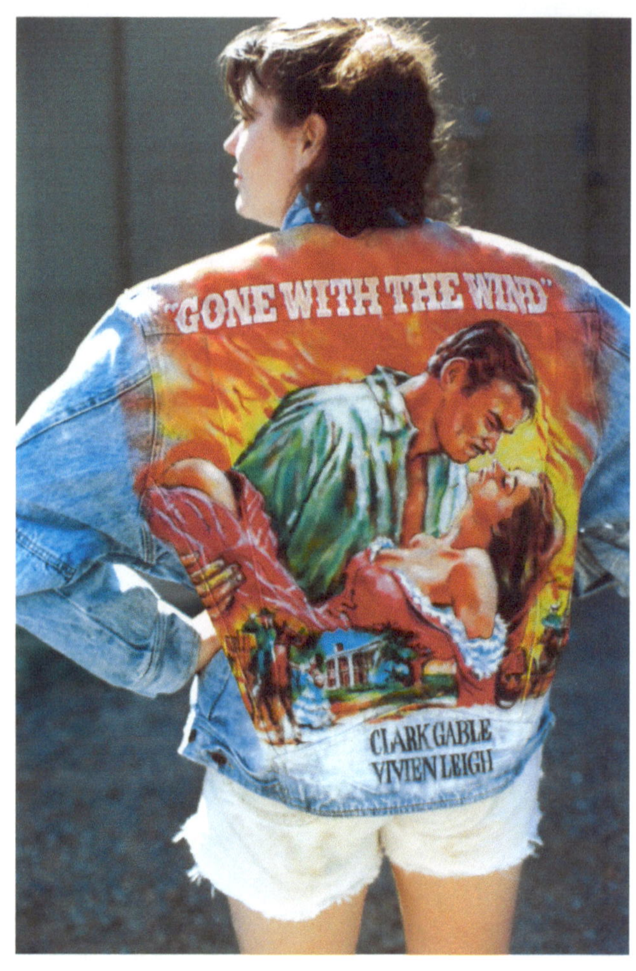
"GONE WITH THE WIND"
CLARK GABLE
VIVIEN LEIGH

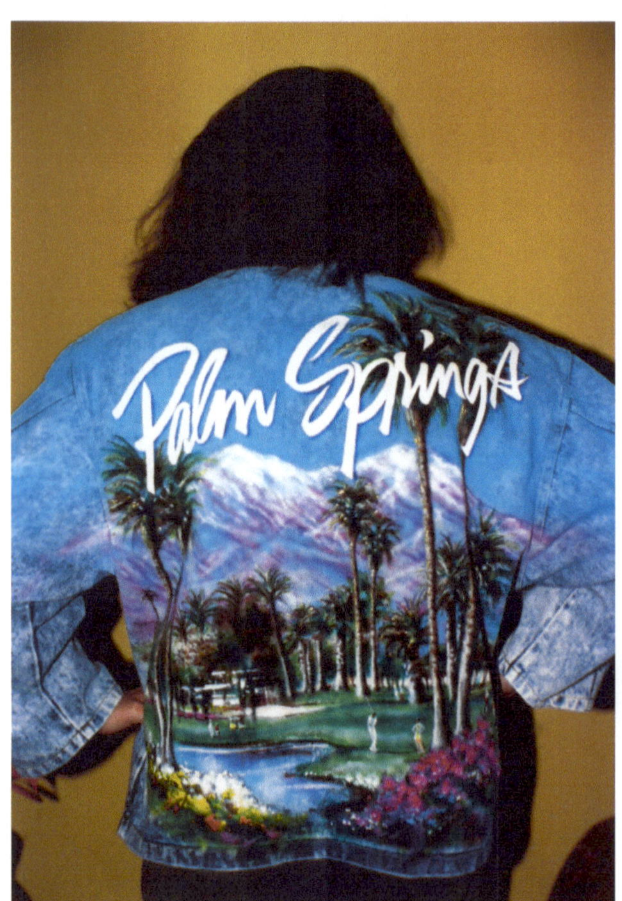
Palm Springs

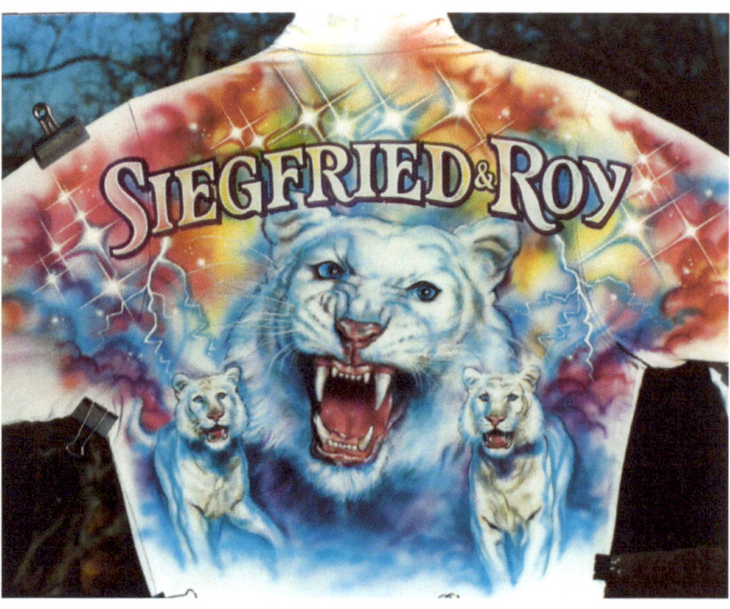
SIEGFRIED & ROY

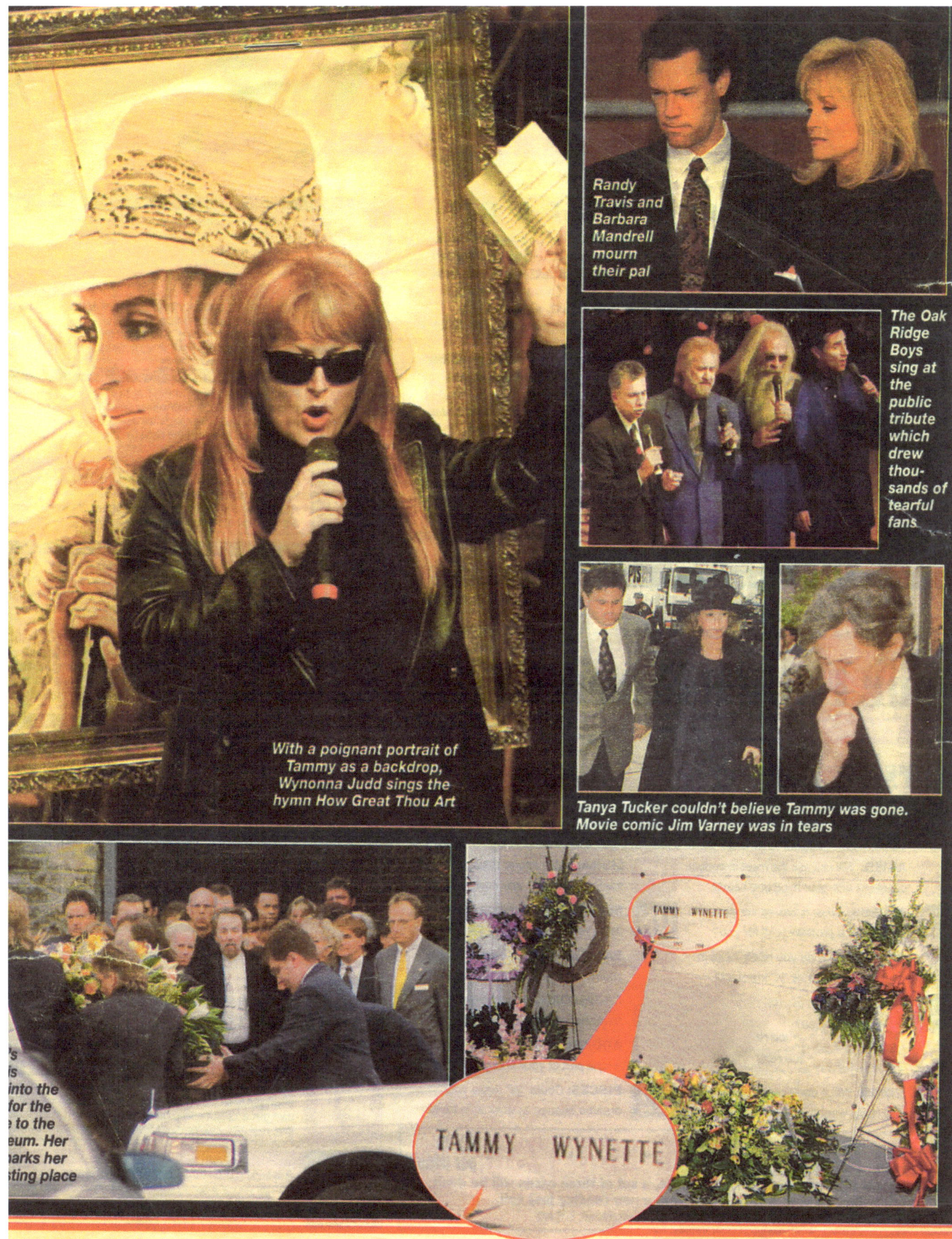

Randy Travis and Barbara Mandrell mourn their pal

The Oak Ridge Boys sing at the public tribute which drew thousands of tearful fans

With a poignant portrait of Tammy as a backdrop, Wynonna Judd sings the hymn How Great Thou Art

Tanya Tucker couldn't believe Tammy was gone. Movie comic Jim Varney was in tears

's
is
into the
for the
to the
eum. Her
arks her
sting place

~ 2 ~

Bruce's Early (Numbered) Paintings

Bruce never titled these paintings; titling here was added posthumously by the author. The author's choice of 38 "Best" paintings are marked with an asterisk.

*1 Big-Eyed Gal with Red Flowers

*2 Alligator Wrestler

3 Fall Country Scene

4 Barrio Boys on the Stoop

5 Girl and her Beau

*6 Family with Flower Child

*7 Young Lady in a Bonnet

8 Blonde Lady

9 Smile

10 Lady at a Love-In (from a photo of author)

11 Autumn in Red Rock Country

*12 Kids on Carousel

*13 Flamenco Guitarists

*14 Kid on the Beach

*15 Montage of the Sixties and Seventies: Beatles, Maharishi, Donovan, Love-In Couple (from a photo from author), Vietnam Soldier Mourning a Fallen Bud

16 Girl with a Love-In Kitten (from a photo of author)

17 Golden Horse Woman

*18 Red Demon Lion

19 Row Your Boat

*20 Sun on the Water

*21 Christmas Caroling in Days of Yore

22 Love-In Child, with Friend (from a photo of author)

23 Pretty Lady

*24 Jimmy Hendrix

25 Couple in the Trees

26 Horse Party in High Mountains

27 Close-up of "The Hippy Family"

*28 Blonde Girl on the Red Bike

29 Heavy Discussion (from a photo of author)

30 Man on a Beach

31 Nude on a Bed

32 Green Scene

33 Vietnam War Protestors (close-up)

*34 Love-In Couple (from a photo of author)

35 Young Lady with a Coffee Cup

*36 Boat Village #1

*37 Cowgirl with a Smile

*38 Blue Bonnet Girl with a Mile-long Smile

39 Vietnam War Protestors (close-up)

40 First Communion

*41 The Beatles on Purple

42 Costume Party with Rubber Duck

*43 The Scream

44 The Cook Who Fell Asleep

*45 Yellow Flower Girl

46 Party Scene

47 Country Church Scene

48 Love Poster Child

49 Mute Swan

50 Lady Artist

51 Ferns Among the Birches

52 Green Meadow Scene

53 Lady in Blue

54 Biafra (close-up)

*55 Blonde Lady

56 South Seas Adventuring

*57 Vietnam War Soldiers: Mourning the Fallen

58 Big Ben

59 Happy Lady with Pretty Flowers

60 Istanbul

61 Bob Dylan

62 Party Girl

63 Blonde in Black

64 Girls' Night Out on the Town

65 Sorrow with Pigeons

66 Girl and Apples

67 Boat Village Red

*68 Pretty Lady in White Shoes

69 South Seas Color

70 Smiling Lady

71 The Eternal Shore

72 Black-Haired Nude

73 Color on a Church Steeple

74 Big City Street Scene

75 Lion Monster Head

76 The Beatles on Purple (close-up)

77 Young Girl with a Smile

78 Sun and Ocean

79 Mother and Child: Love-In (from a photo of author)

*80 Consultation at the Candy Store

81 Surfer

82 San Francisco Street Scene

83 Soldiers of the Queen

84 Deer in the Forest

85 Nice Digs

86 Pensive Lady in White

87 A Nice Profile

88 Young Girl in Costume

89 Hay Loft Nude

90 Young Painter at Work—With an Audience

*91 Pouting Nude

*92 The Hippy Family

93 Cossacks in the Forest

94 Sonny and Cher

*95 The Beatles as Bullfighters

96 Hanging Out

97 Lady at the Easel

98 George Harrison

99 Tiger in the Grass

100 Nude in the Woods

101 Sailing Ship on Heavy Seas

102 Cowboy in the Forest

103 The Blooming Tree

104 The Fawn

*105 Lady at the Rainy Day Window

106 Elk in Snow

*107 Vietnam War Protestors

108 Tete a tete

109 Walking in the Woods

110 Brown Nude

111 Donovan on the Pond

112 Looking Good from Any Angle

113 Golden Muse

114 Blonde Baby Doll

115 Neushwanstein

116 Fagin and the Boys

117 Canyon Sunset

118 Light in the Forest

119 London Bridge

*120 Biafra

121 Sedona

122 Sun in the South Pacific

*123 Vietnam War—Mourning the Fallen

124 Man with Lots on His Mind

125 Las Lavanderas (The Washerwomen)

126 Rocky Mountain Scenery

127 High Mountain Lake

128 The Young Beatles

129 Sailing Ship on a Sunny Day

*130 The Life of Christ

*131 Two Sisters in a Rocker

*132 Big Sur

*133 Elvis—Montage #1

134 Ronnie Milsap

*135 Tammy Wynette

136 Brenda Lee

137 Crystal Gale

138 Hank Williams, Jr.

139 Dolly Parton

140 Judy Garland Montage

141 John Wayne Montage

142 Cowboy Cabin

*143 Elvis Montage #2

144 Saguaros

145 Portrait of Brenda

146 Horsepower

147 Monument Valley

148 Tammy Wynette—Tears of Fire 25th Album Cover

149 Copy of Rockwell's "Saying Grace"

150 Copy of Rockwell's "After the Prom"

151 Mother Love

152 Voodoo Man

153 Mom and Kid in Flowers

*154 Face in the Sand

155 Gondolieri

156 Chaplin

157 The Amish Man

158 Sailing the Pond

I thought I would have a lot to say about some of my favorite paintings in this big grouping but I decided to make my comments minimal. Why? *Res ipse loquitor*. That's legalese (just Latin) for "The Thing Speaks for Itself." Bruce's paintings speak for themselves. But mainly for the people who didn't live through those times, I've thrown in a bit of historical context.

Some lucky party has painting #15, a panoramic snapshot of the sixties and seventies. Painting #24 is of Jimmy Hendrix, an icon of that age. Number 34 "Love-In Couple" is my favorite image of the love-in culture. Number 36 is my favorite of the two "Boat Village" paintings. This semi-realistic painting image seemed to have caught on with people so Bruce did a few until he tired of them. "The Blue Bonnet Girl" (#38) has the nicest smile I've seen anywhere. I believe #43 is Bruce's parody of the famous painting of Edward Munch's "The Scream." The photo of #92 "The Hippy Family" does not do it justice. It is a spectacular painting and highly representative of the time.

"The Beatles as Bullfighters" (#95) is a really funny painting—just look at their expressions. And very good. Some lucky person has the moody "Lady at the Rainy Day Window" (#115). What a lovely painting. "Vietnam War Protestors" (#107) is a historically apt and important painting reflective of that time and place. "Biafra" (#120) is a striking painting of the aftermath of strife and civil war in Africa late in the 20th century. "Vietnam War Mourning the Fallen" (#123) is a part of our painful past history.

It took Bruce 2½ years to paint "The Life of Christ" (#130); completed 8/2/82. If this had been the only painting Bruce ever did in his life, he would still deserve a place among the finest painters of the twentieth century. It reads like a book, starting in the top left corner proceeding left to right until it ends in the bottom right corner with the Ascension, a total of 80 separate biblical panels.

Two paintings "Two Sisters in a Rocker" (#131) and "Big Sur" (#132) are just great paintings.

"Elvis—Montage #1" (#133) resides in the Country Music Hall of Fame and Museum in Nashville. As you can see by the photo, copies of Bruce's "Elvis" are for sale in that gift shop for all the fans of the King of Rock 'n Roll. To the right of "Elvis" is a print of Thomas Hart Benton's famous "The Origins of Country Music" so Bruce is in the best of company.

Painting #135 (Tammy Wynette) was discussed in the text of Chapter 1 (along with "Tears of Fire" (#148).

"Elvis—Montage #2" (#143) is at Graceland.

Somebody once said, "Imitation is the sincerest form of flattery." Bruce looked up to Rockwell and his copies of two of Rockwell's famous paintings, "Saying Grace" and "After the Prom" (numbers 149 and 150 respectively) expressed that regard. With a magnifier you can see on "Saying Grace" he signed it "Bruce Lakofka after Rockwell," the appropriate signature for a copyist. Bruce must have sent photos of these two paintings to the Rockwell family because for many years he received cards and Rockwell Christmas ornaments from them. Bruce never copied any other painter's work.

One final technical note: There are less than 158 discrete paintings. Technically what we are counting is painting photographs. For a few of the paintings closeups were taken for their dramatic appeal.

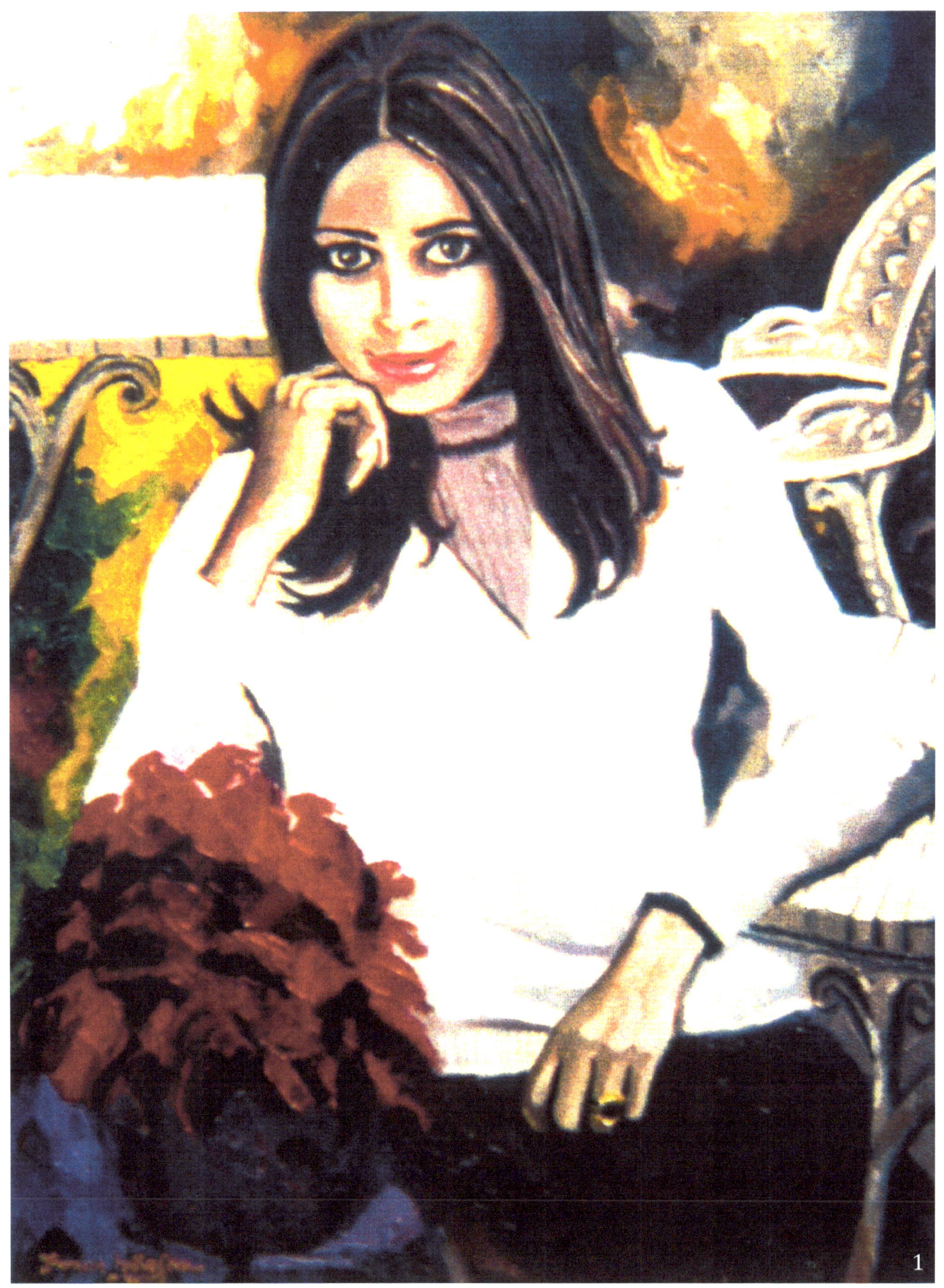
1

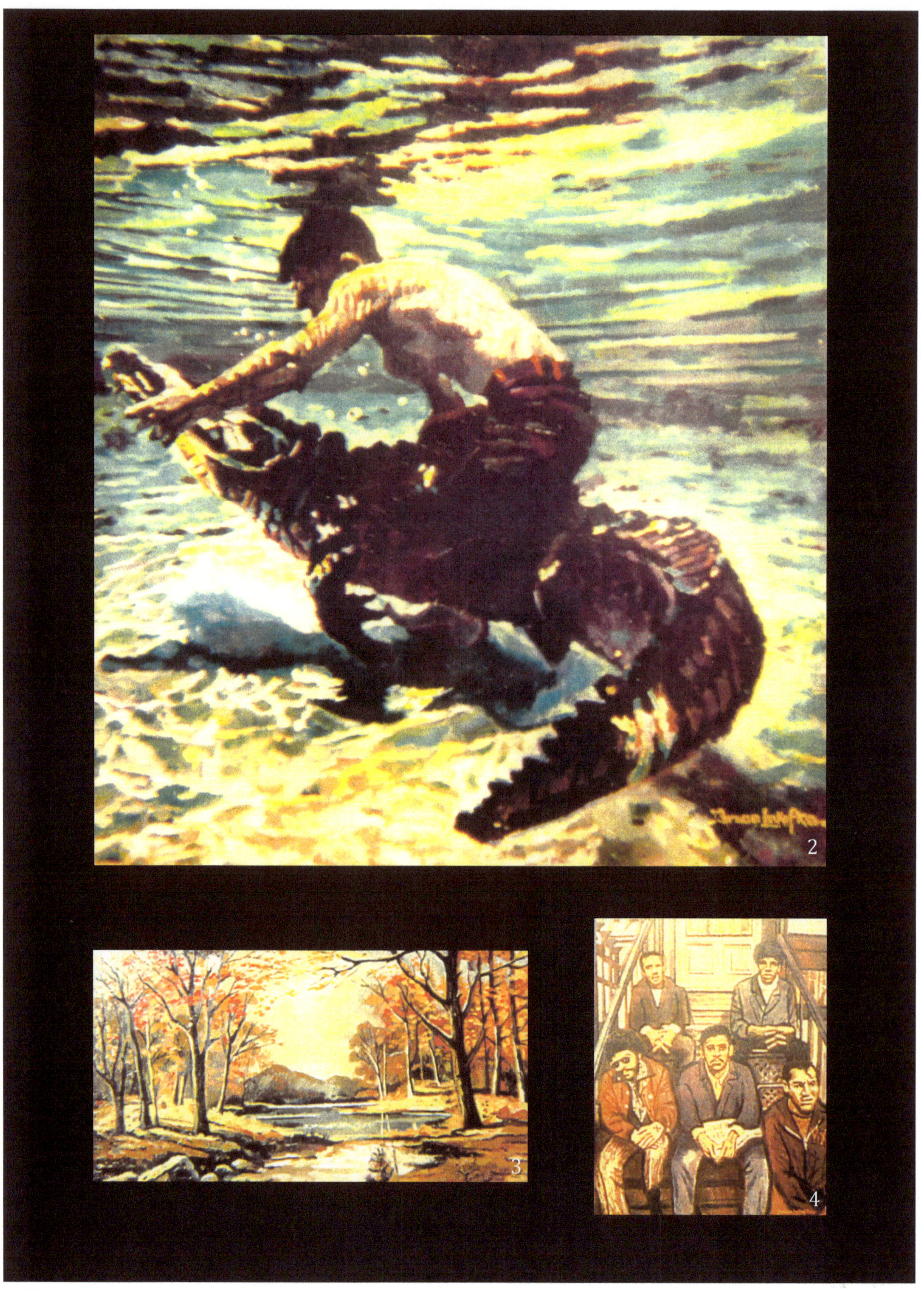
2
3
4

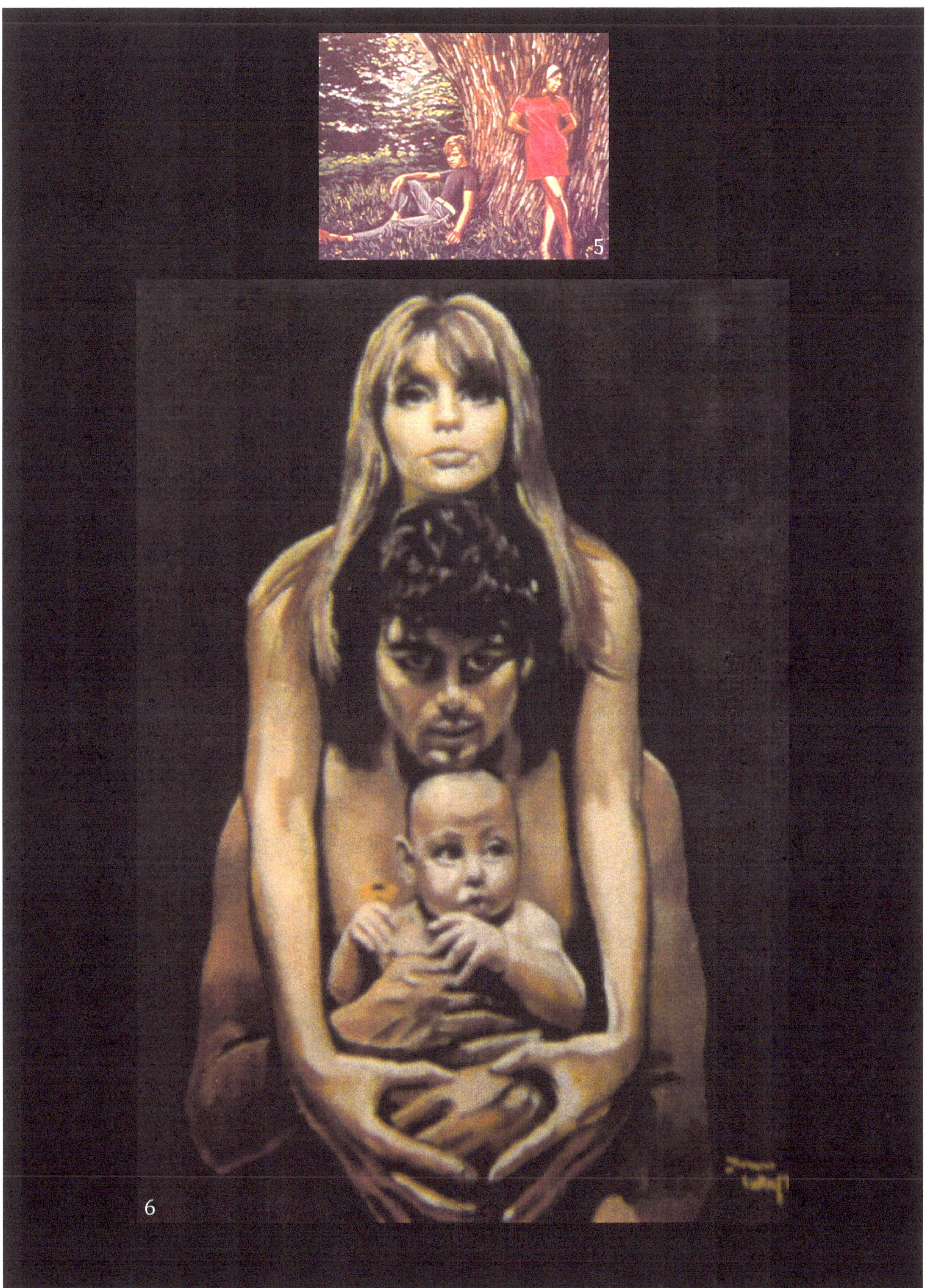
5
6

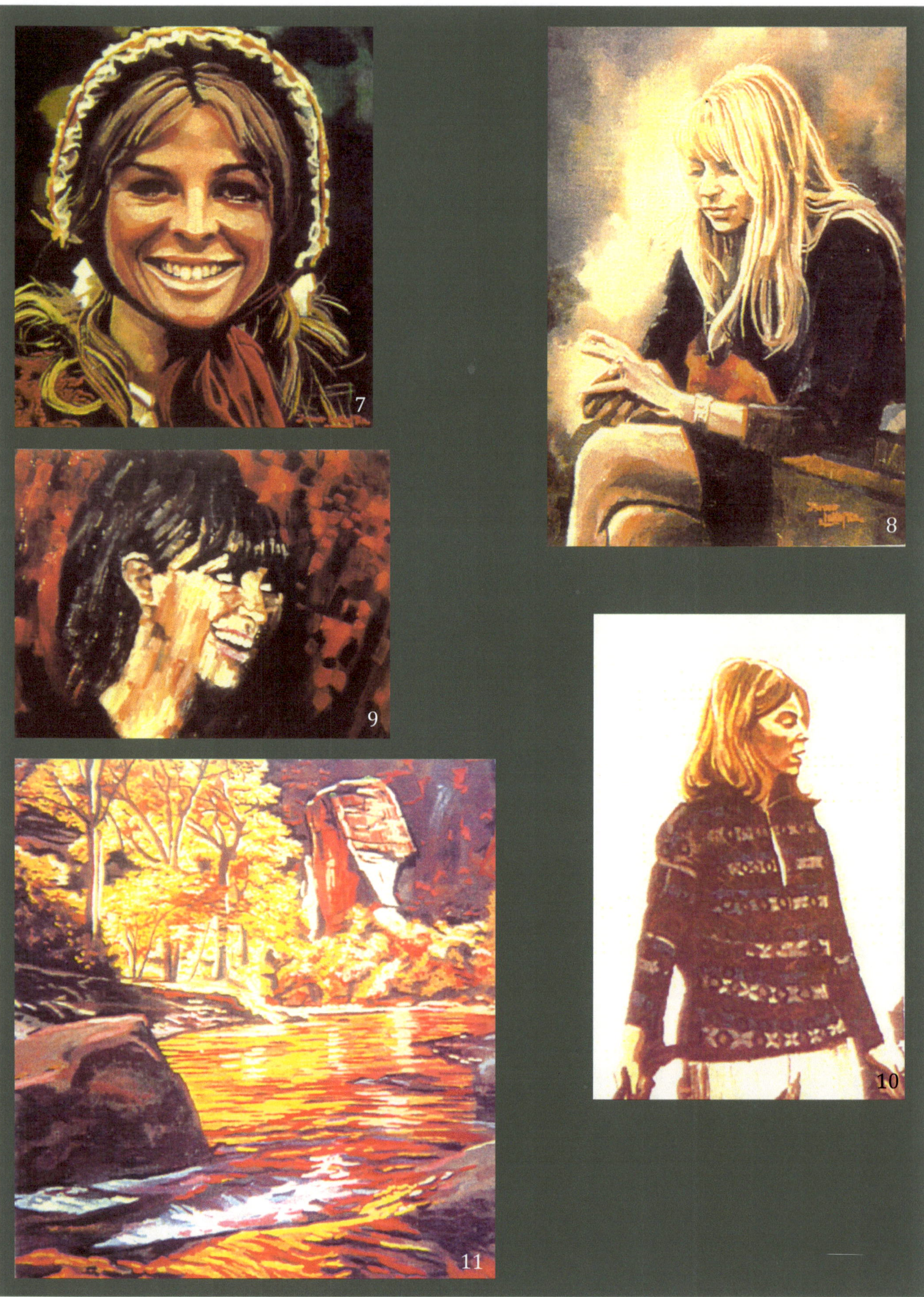
7
8
9
10
11

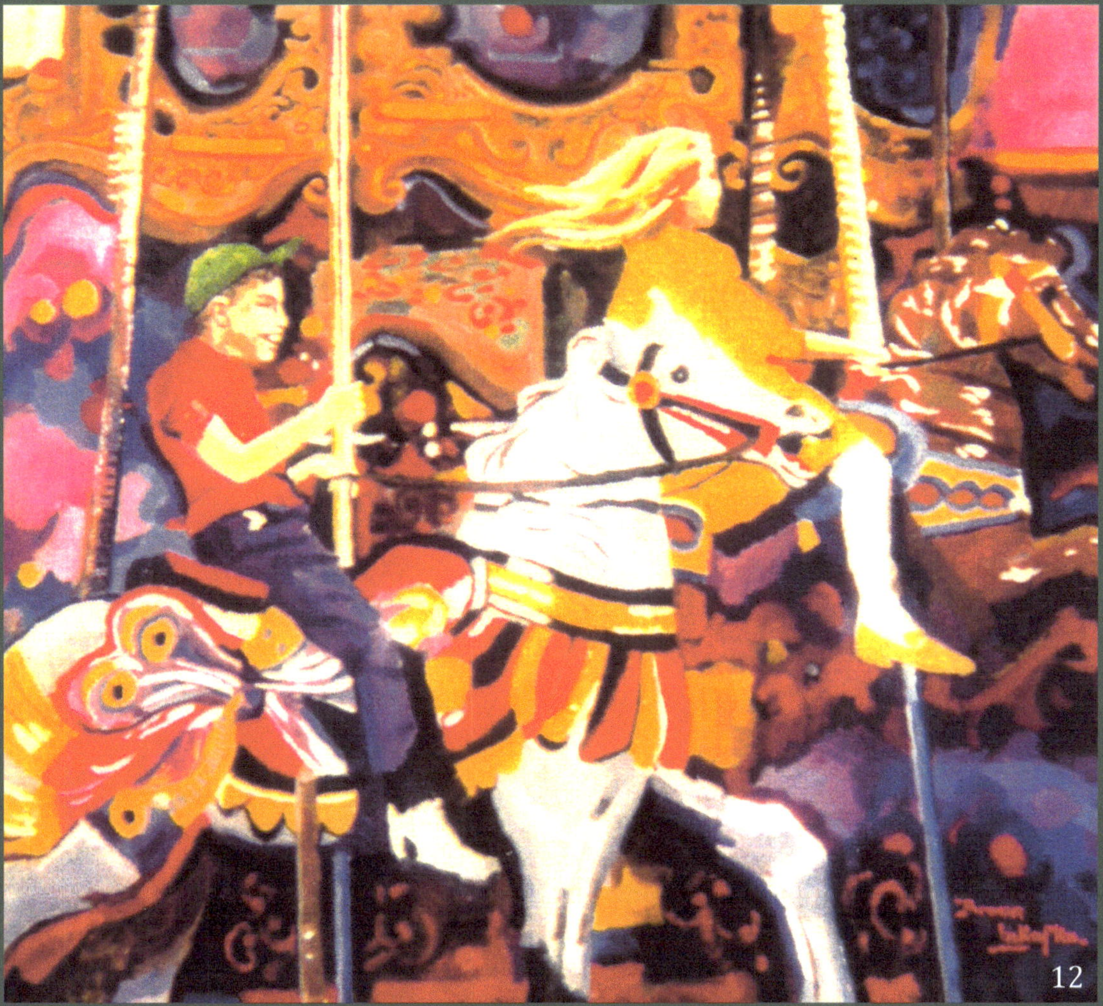

12

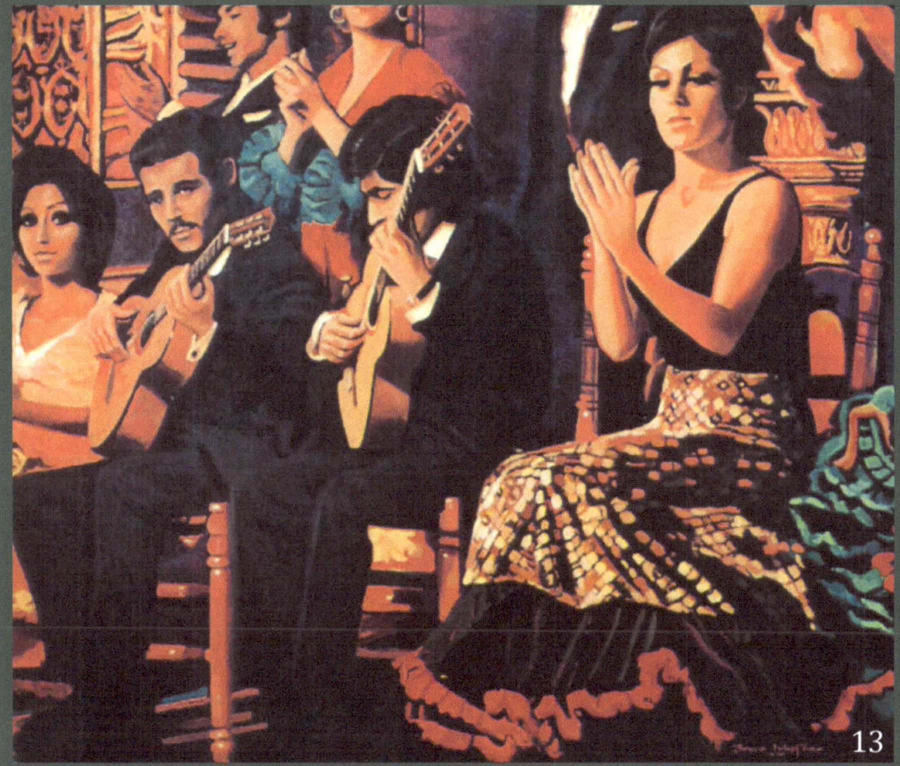

13

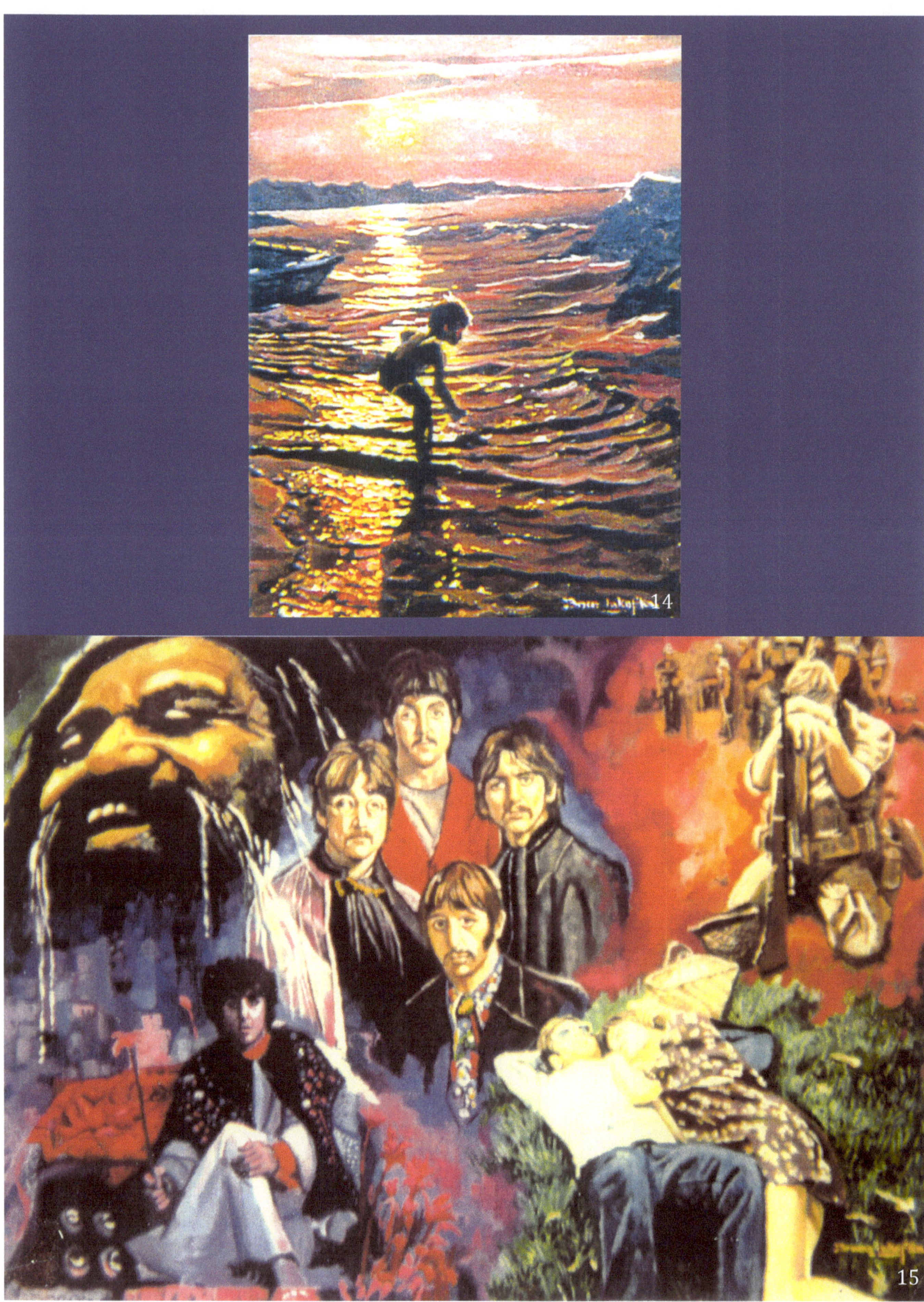
14
15

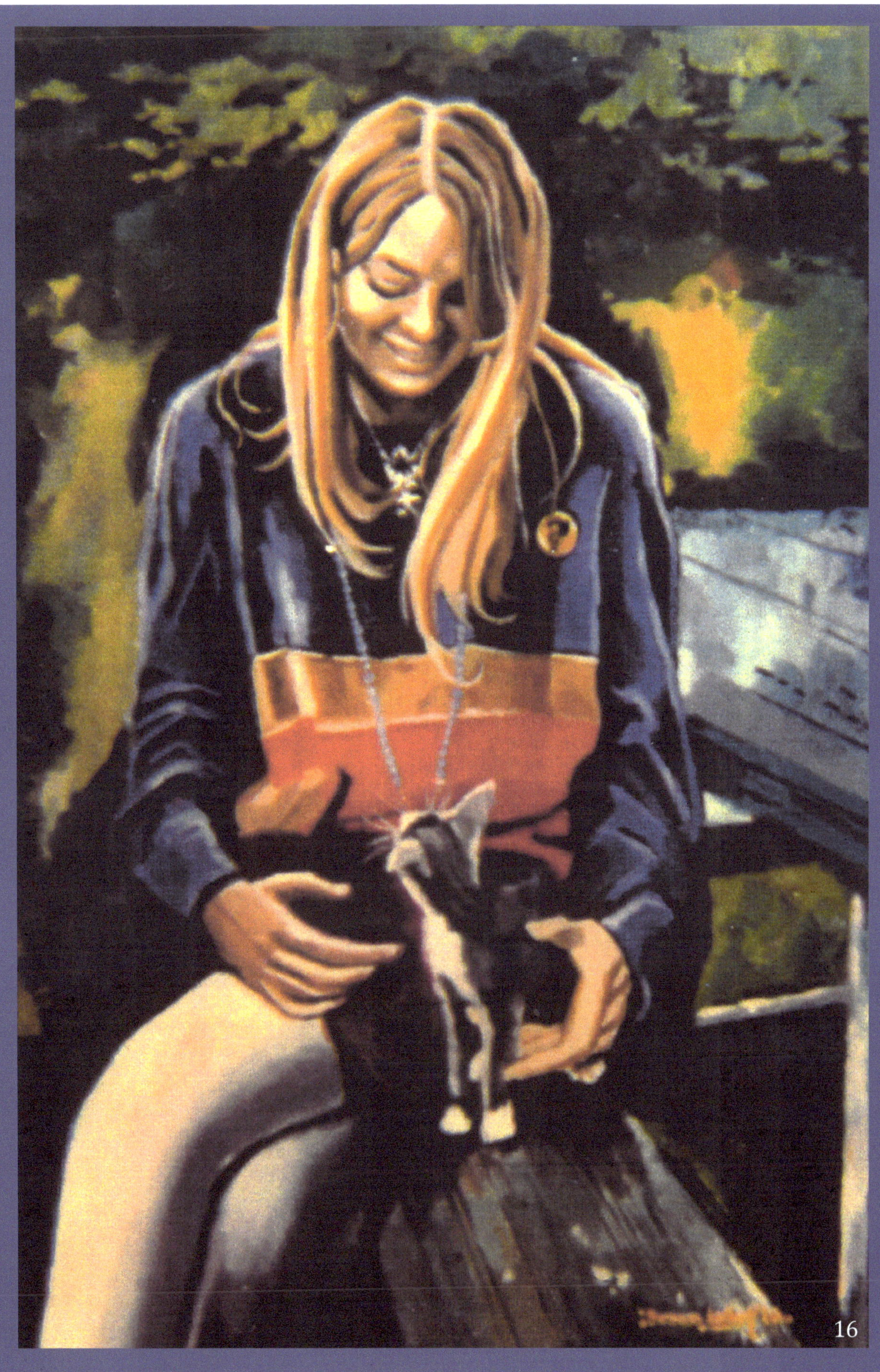

16

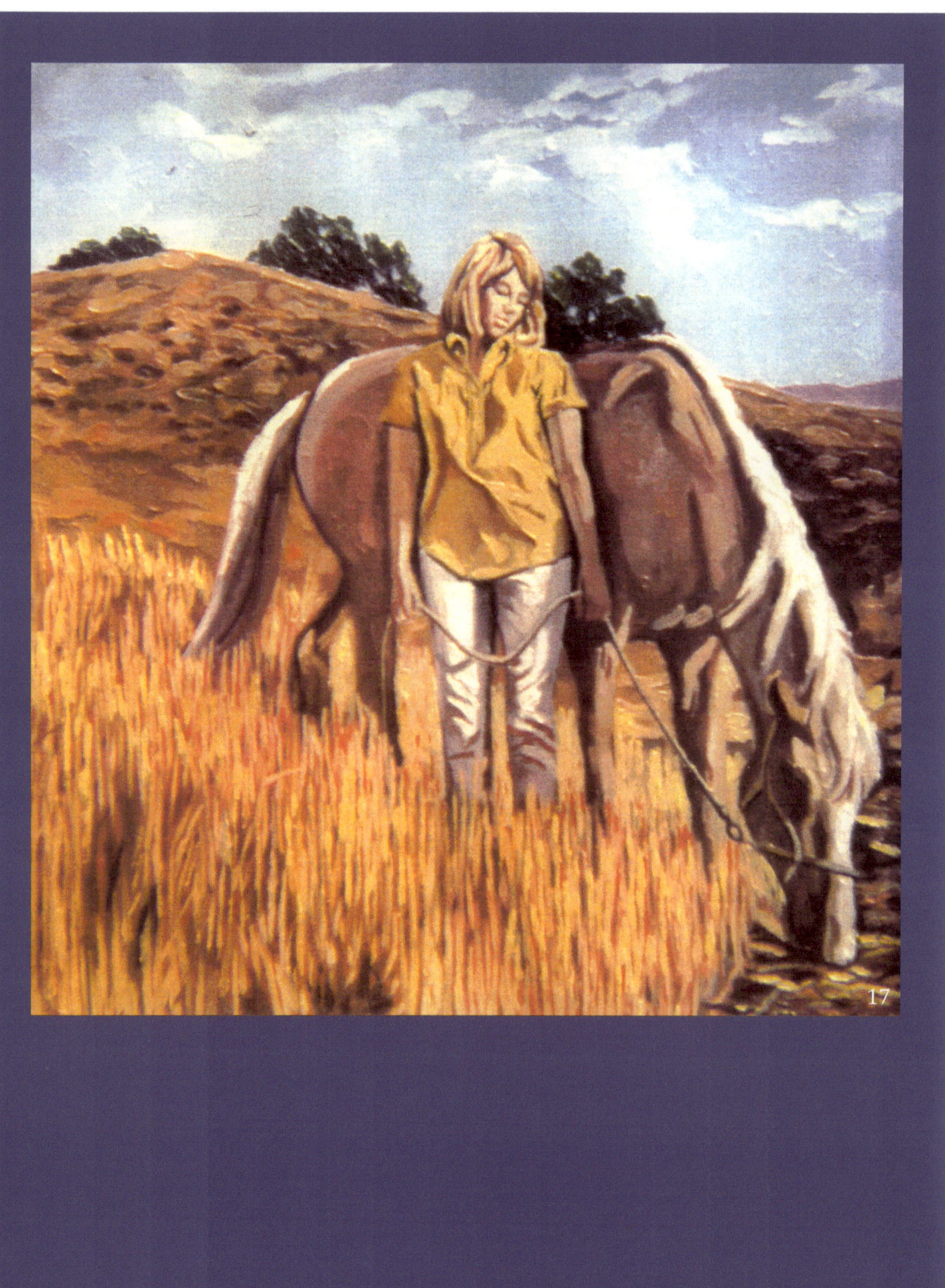
17

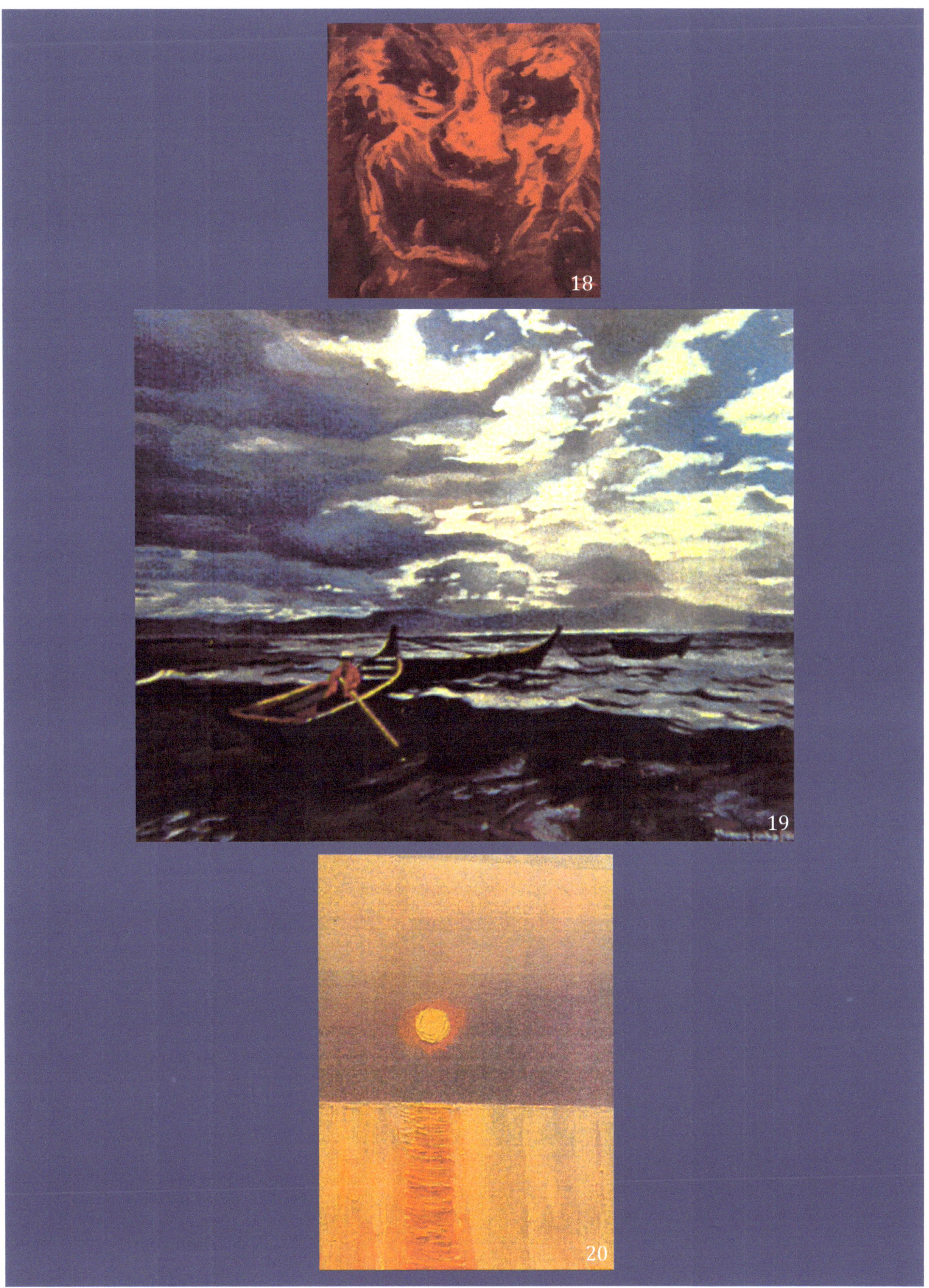
18
19
20

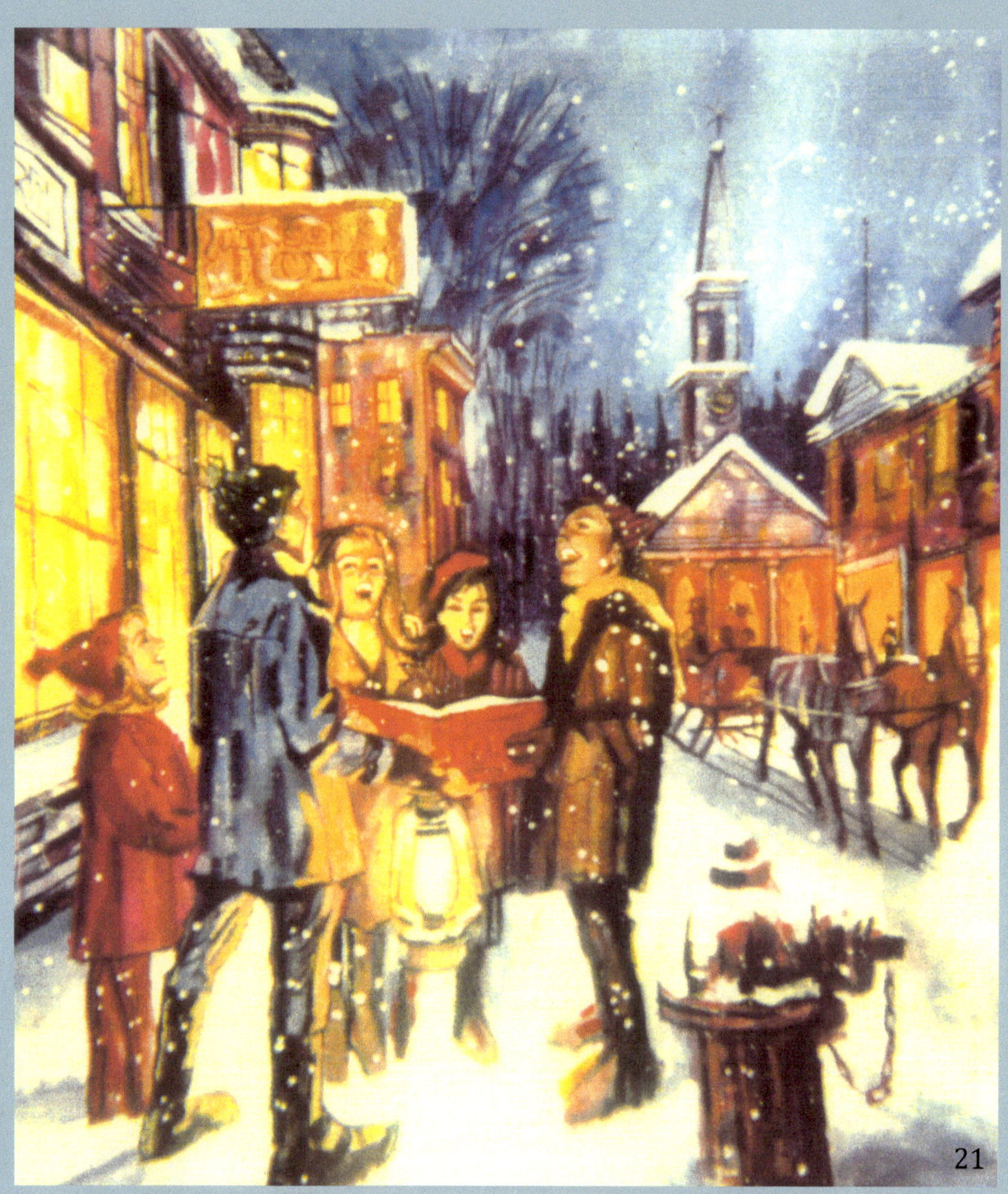
21

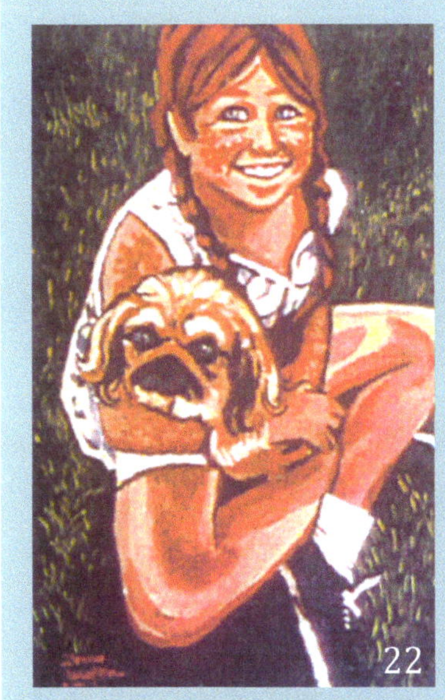
22

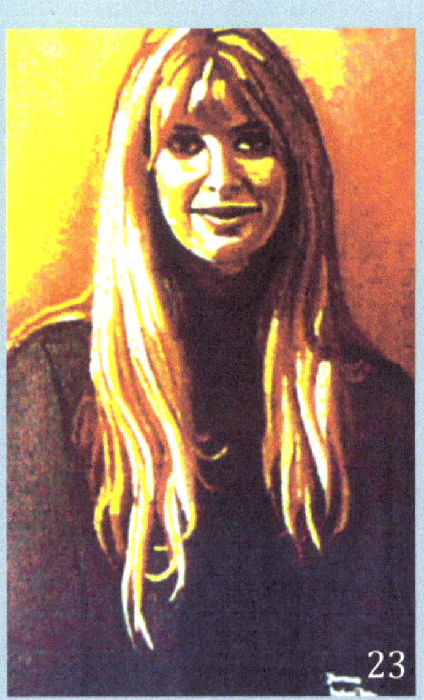
23

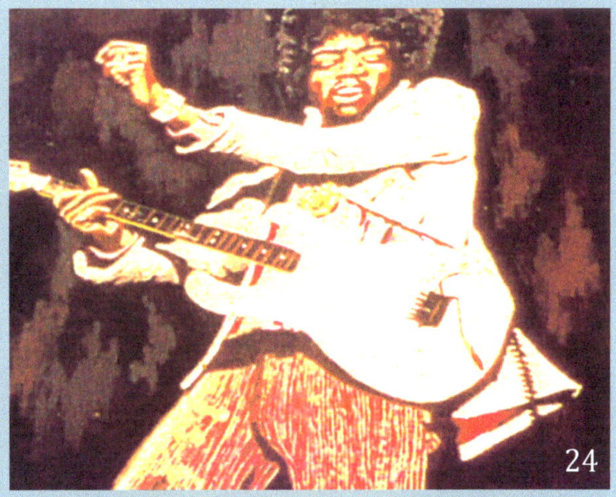
24

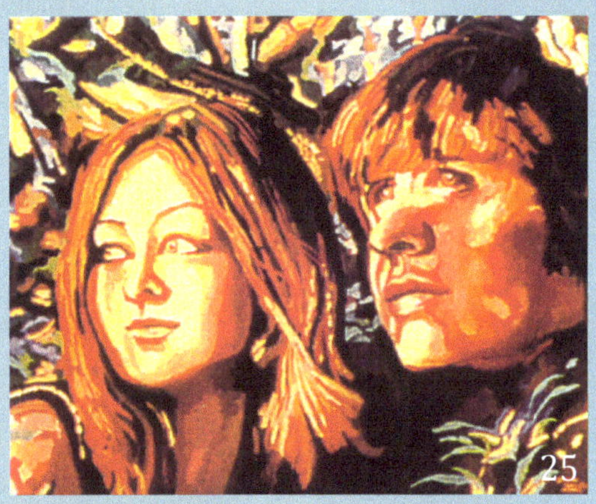
25

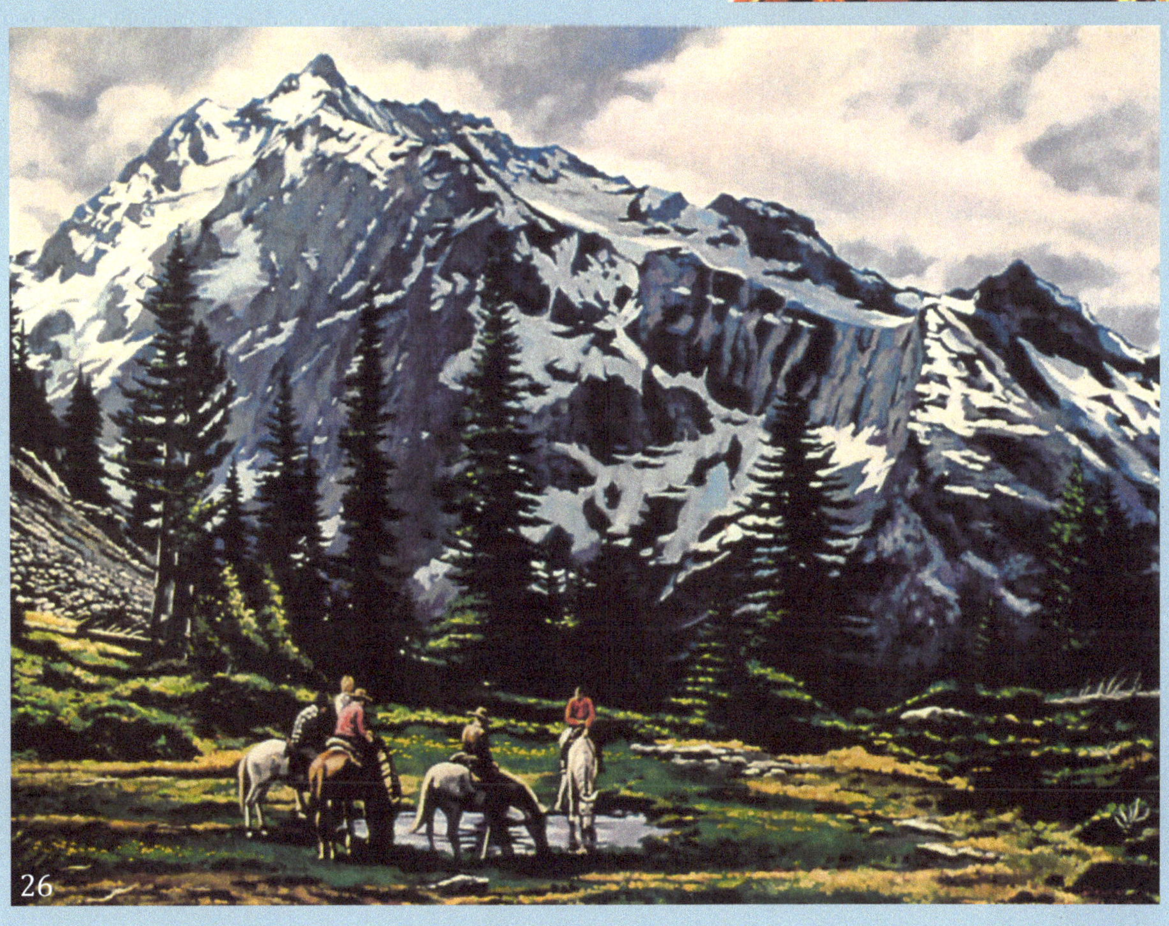
26

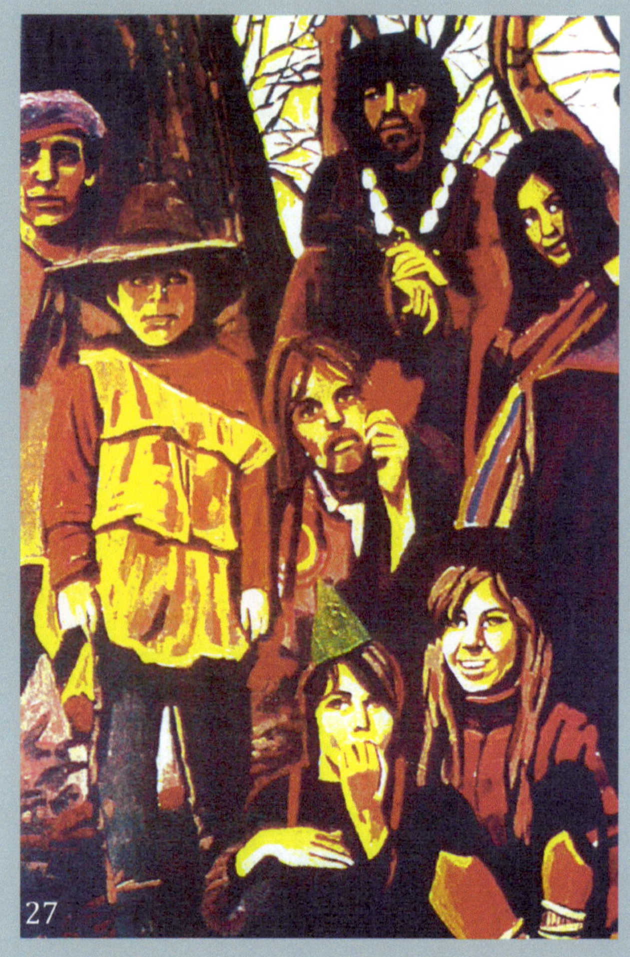
27

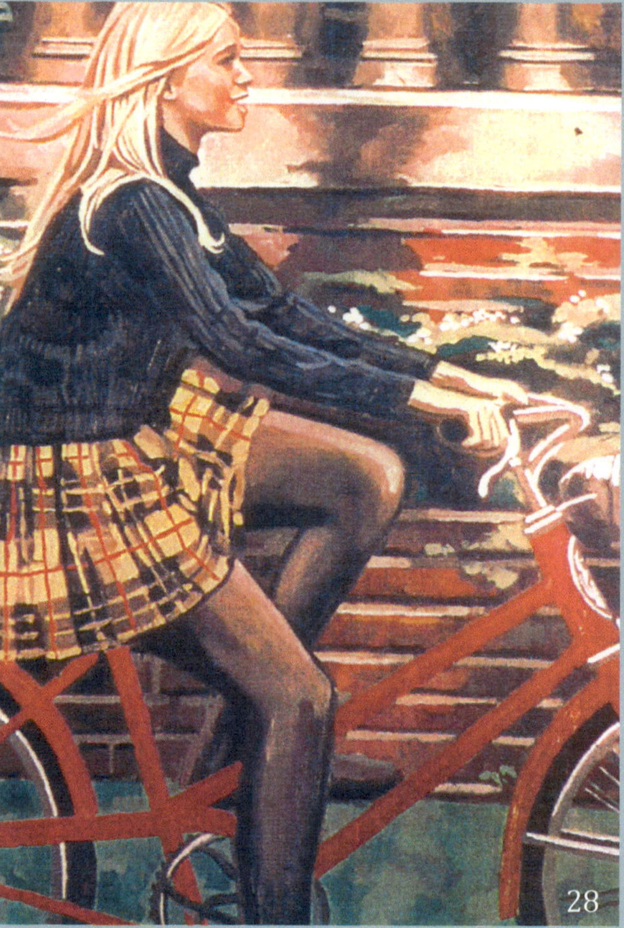
28

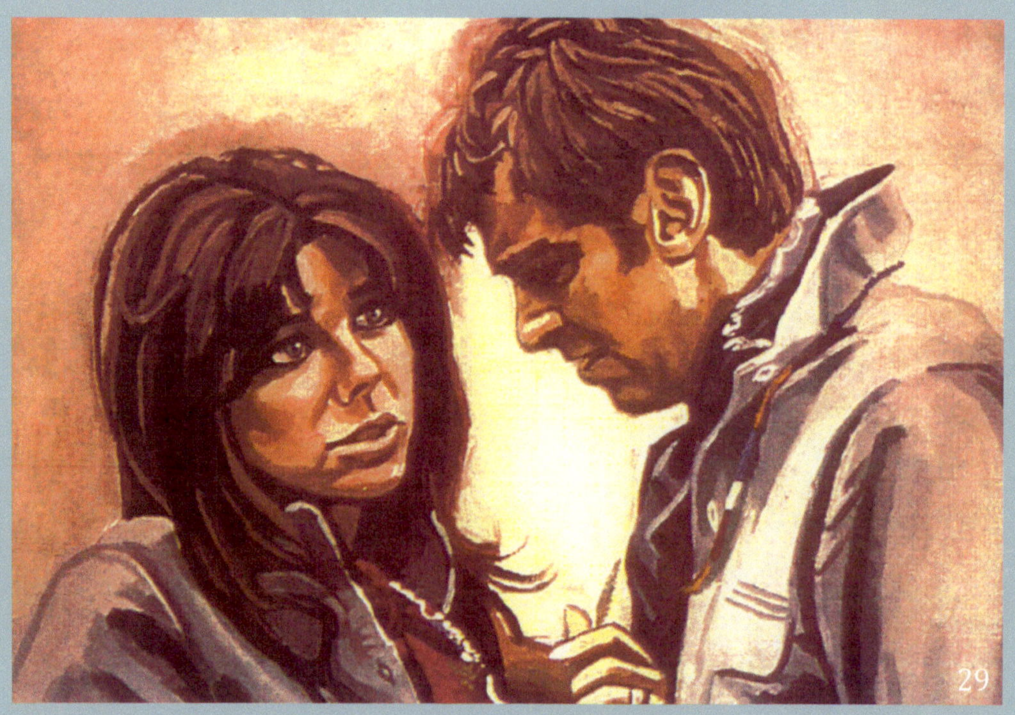
29

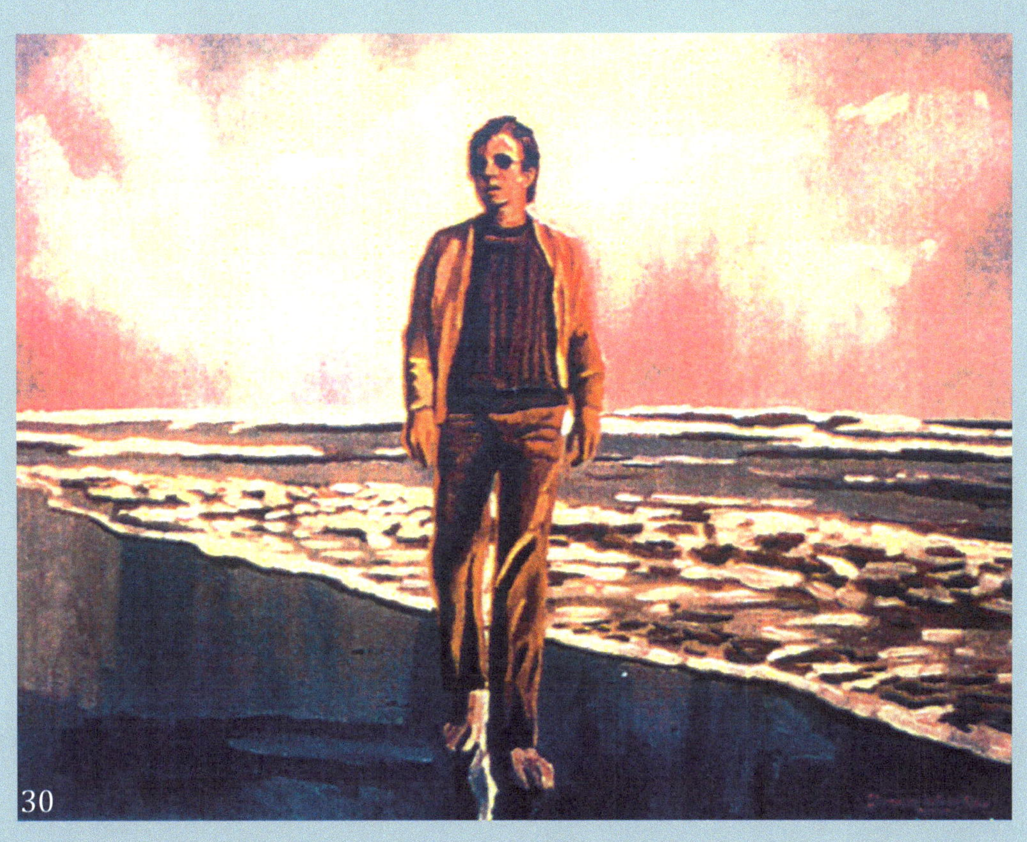
30

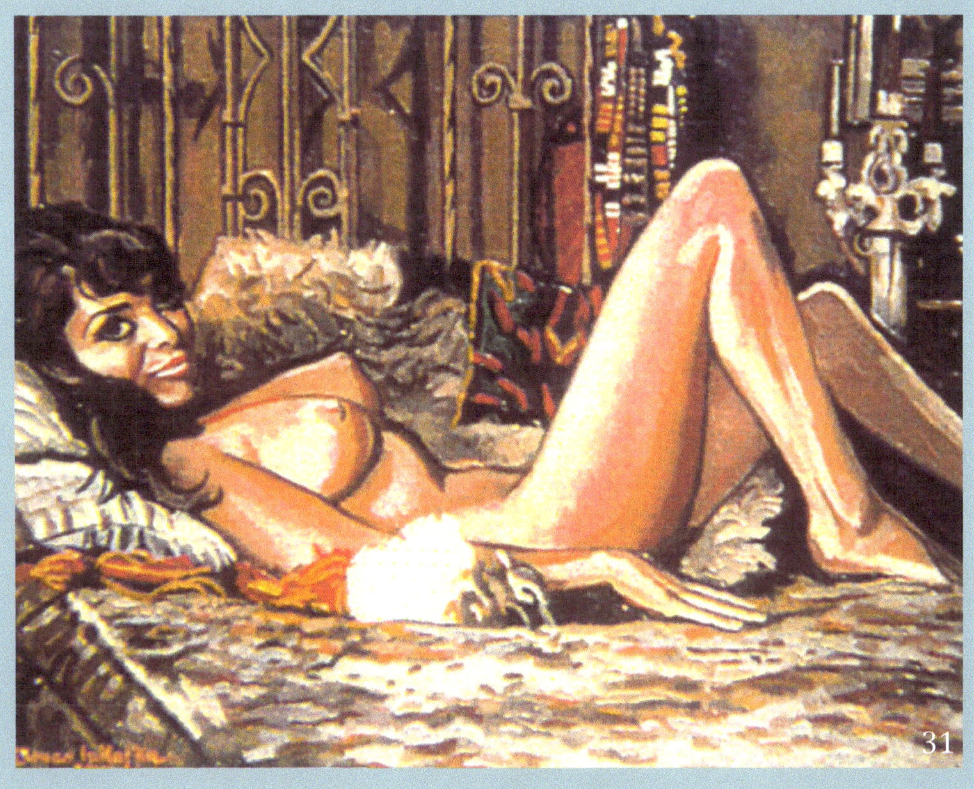
31

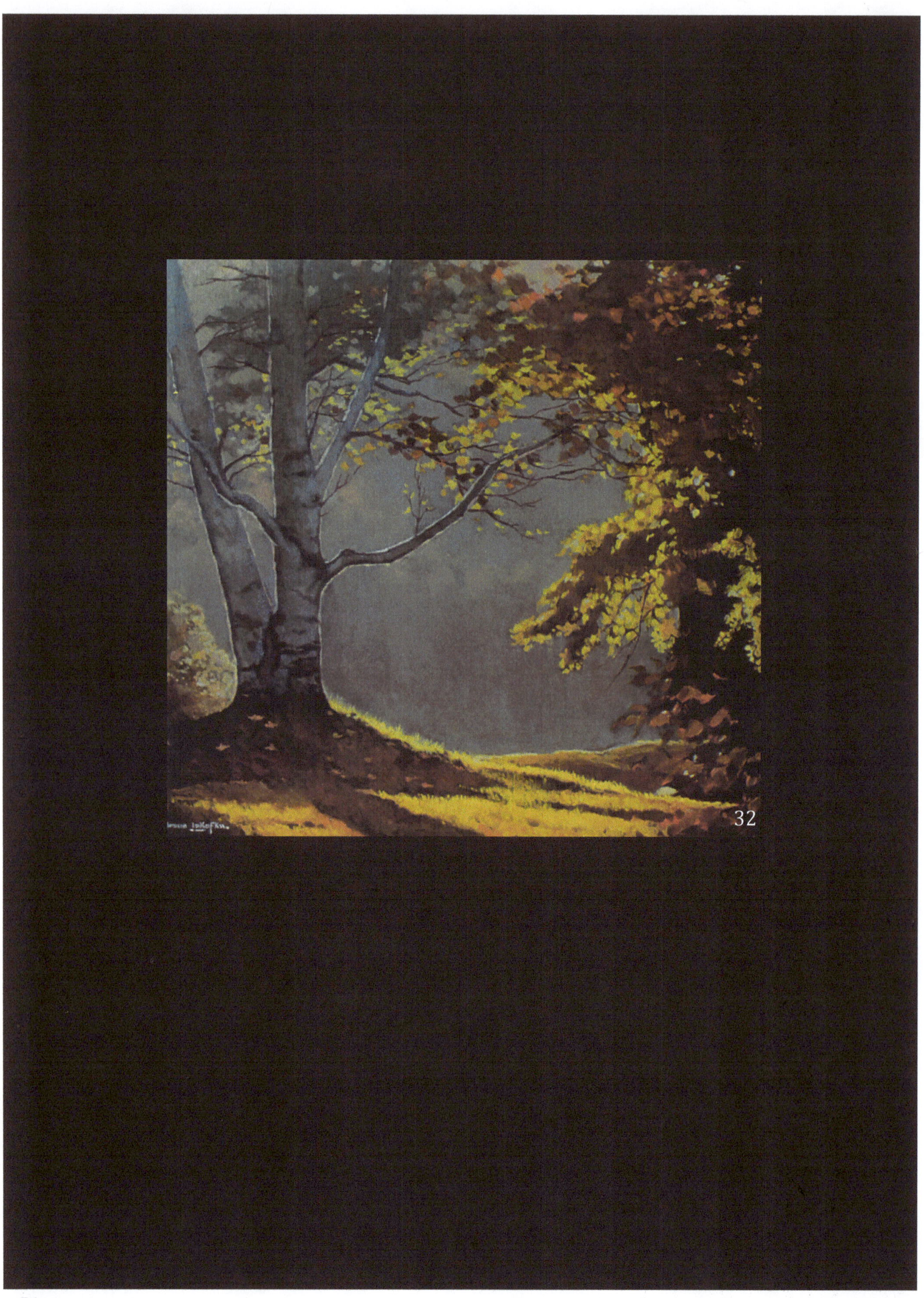
32

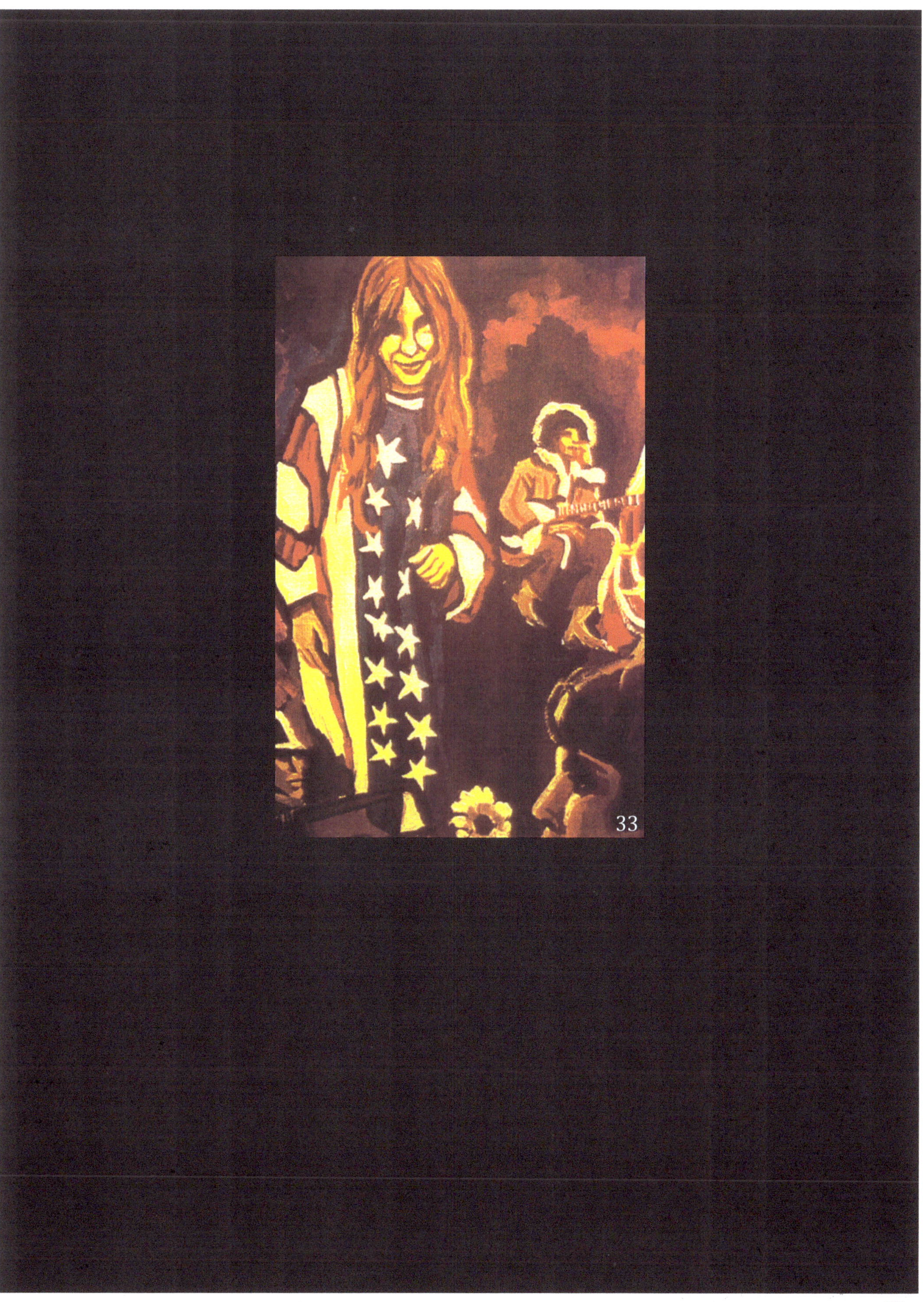
33

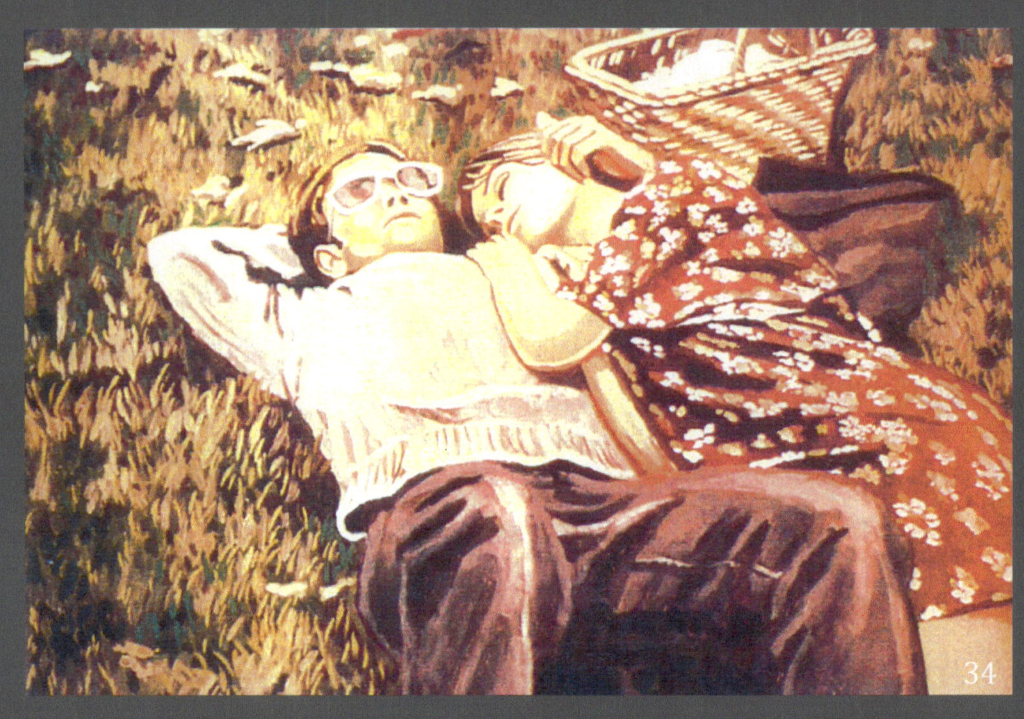

34

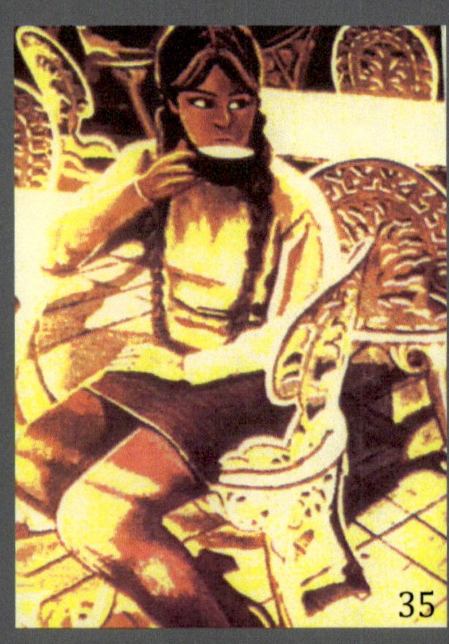

35

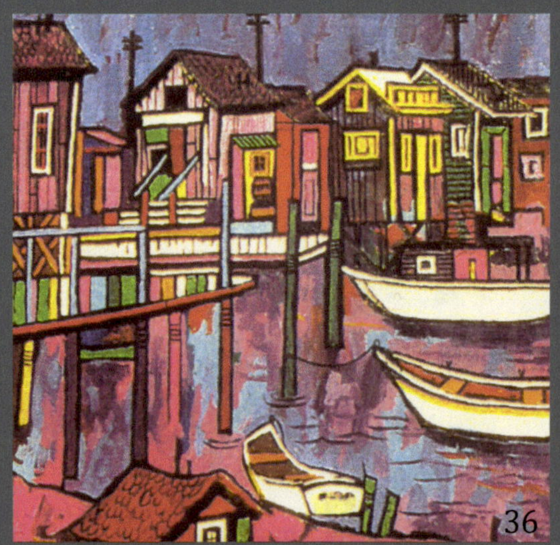

36

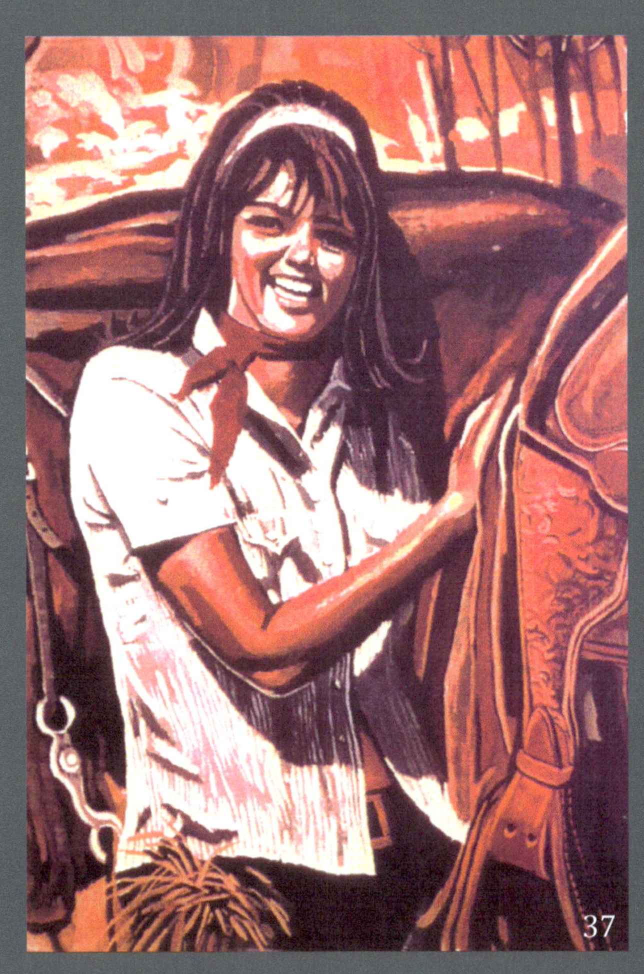

37

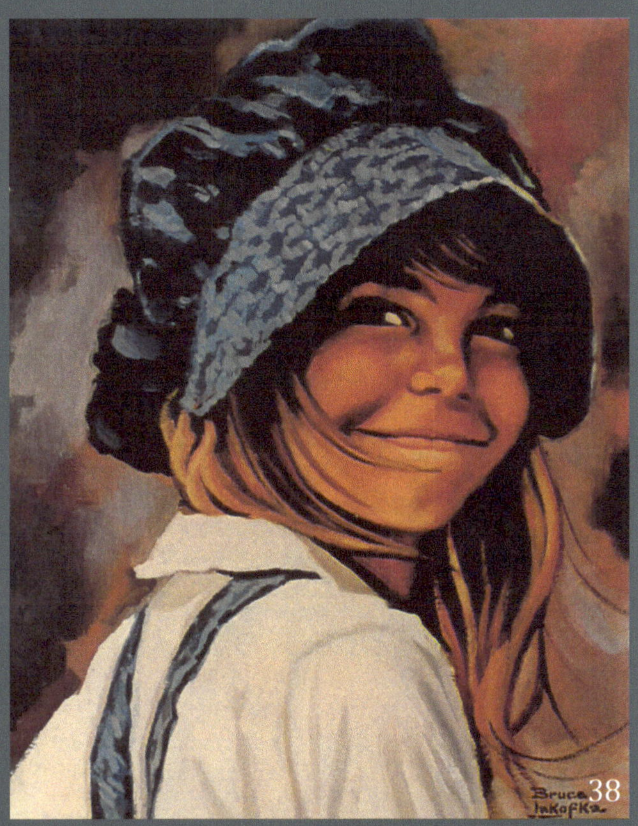

38

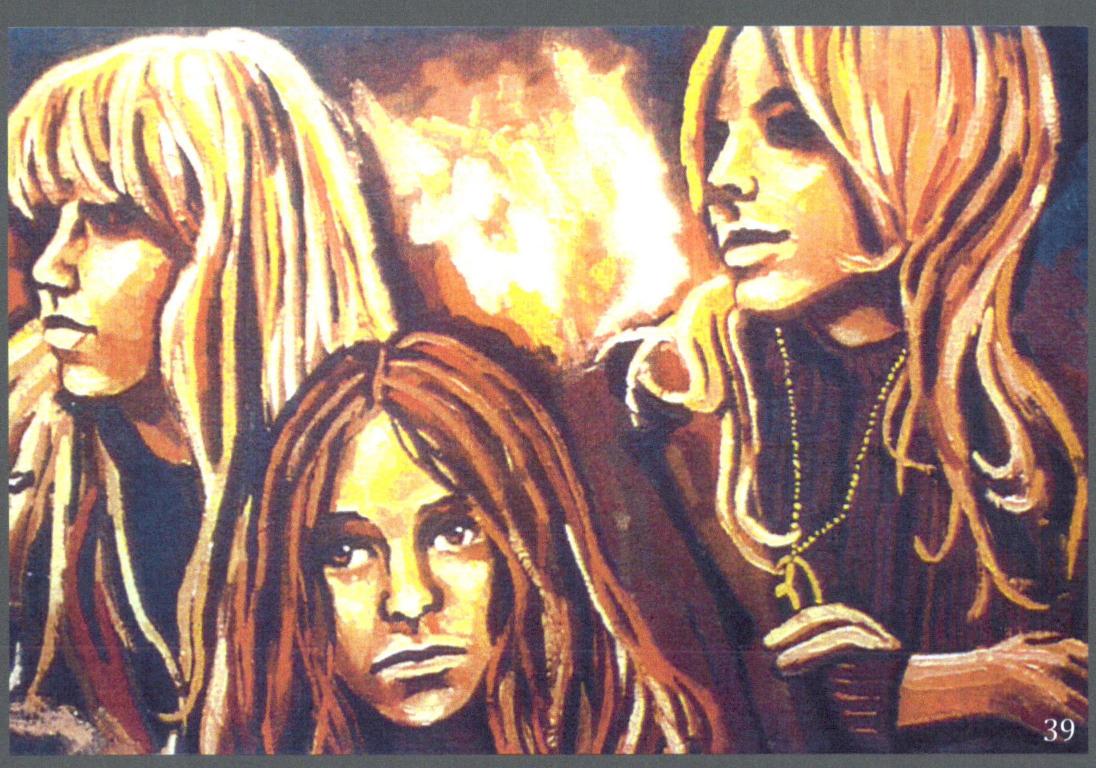

39

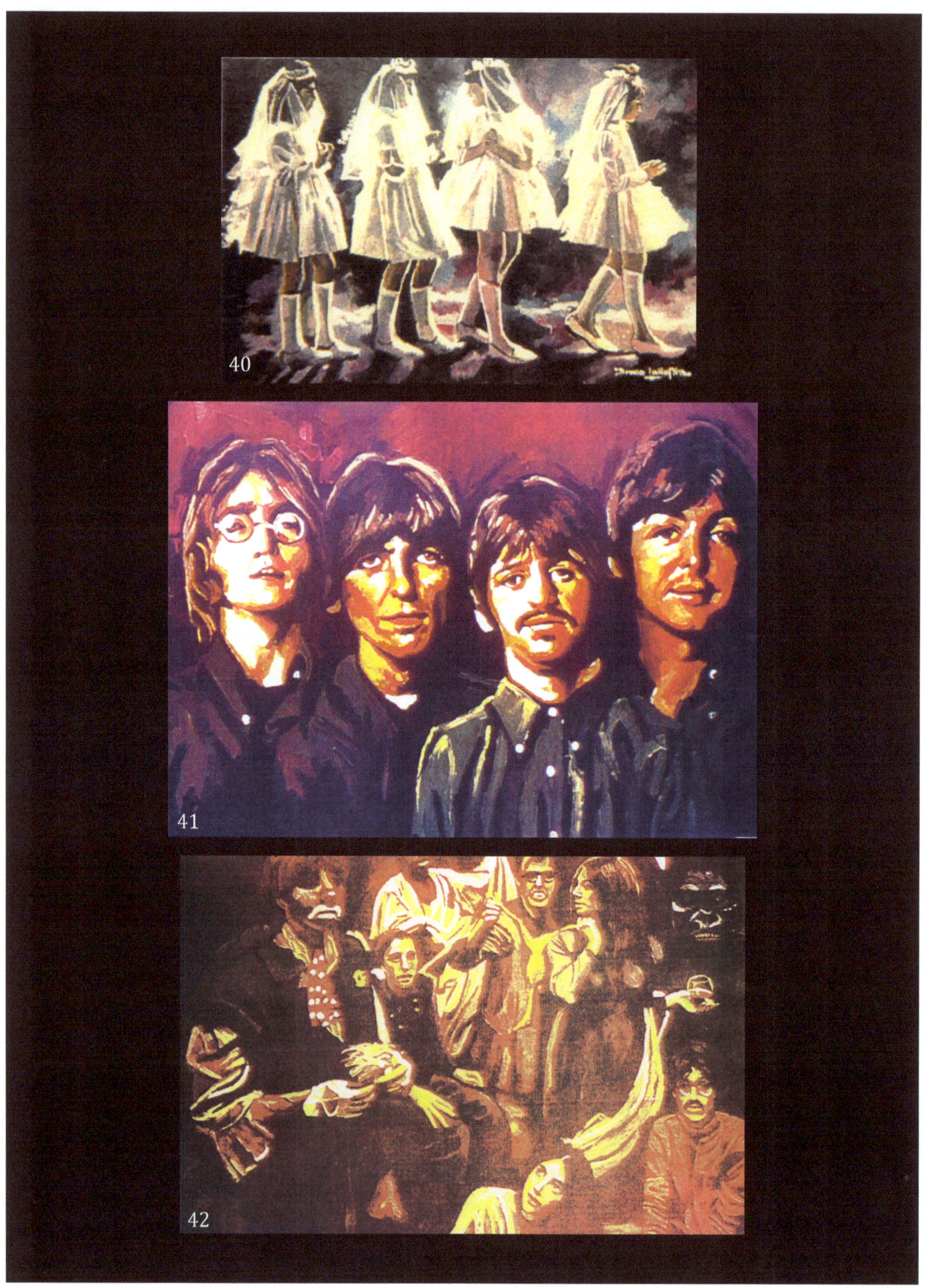
40
41
42

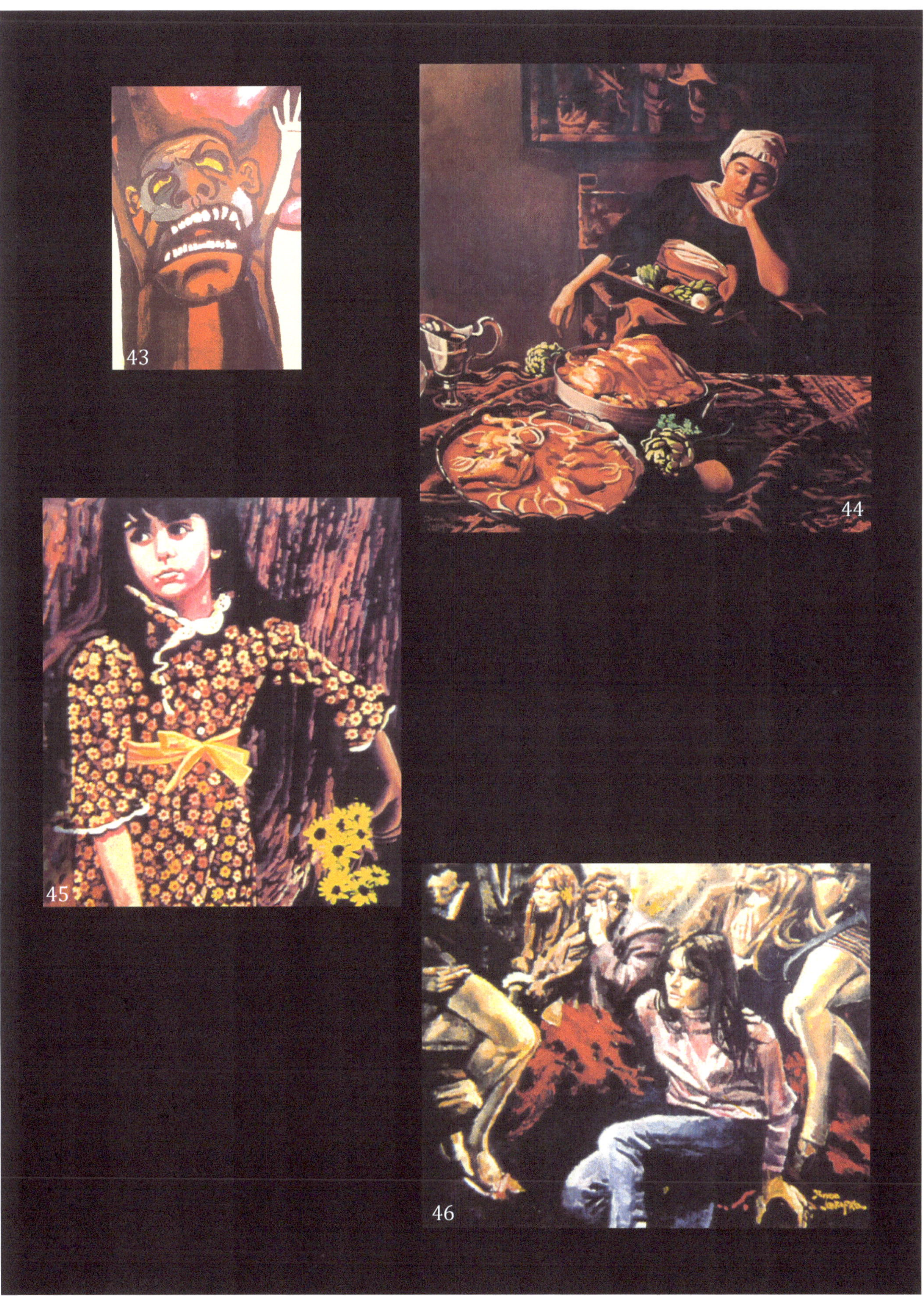
43
44
45
46

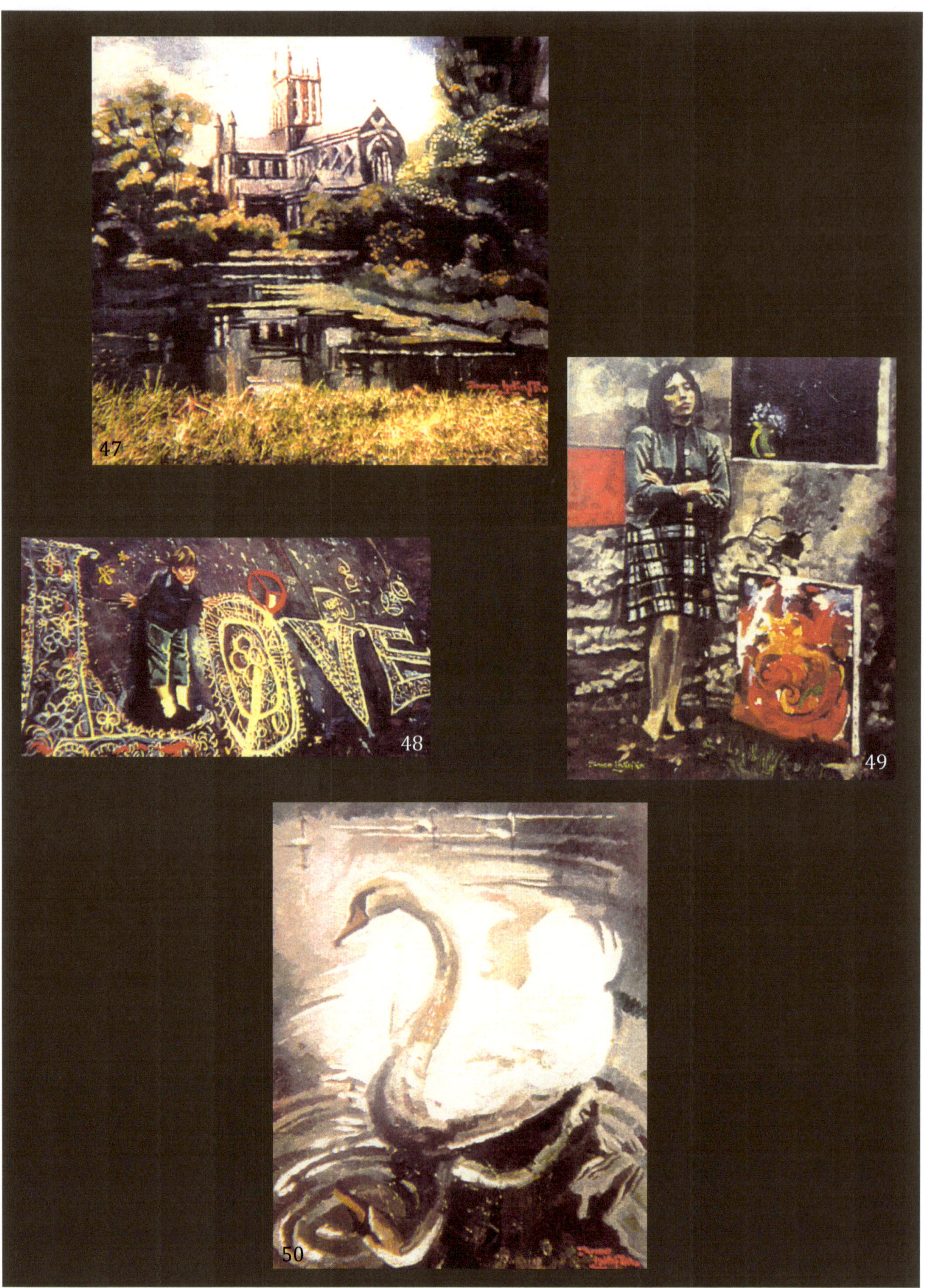

47

48

49

50

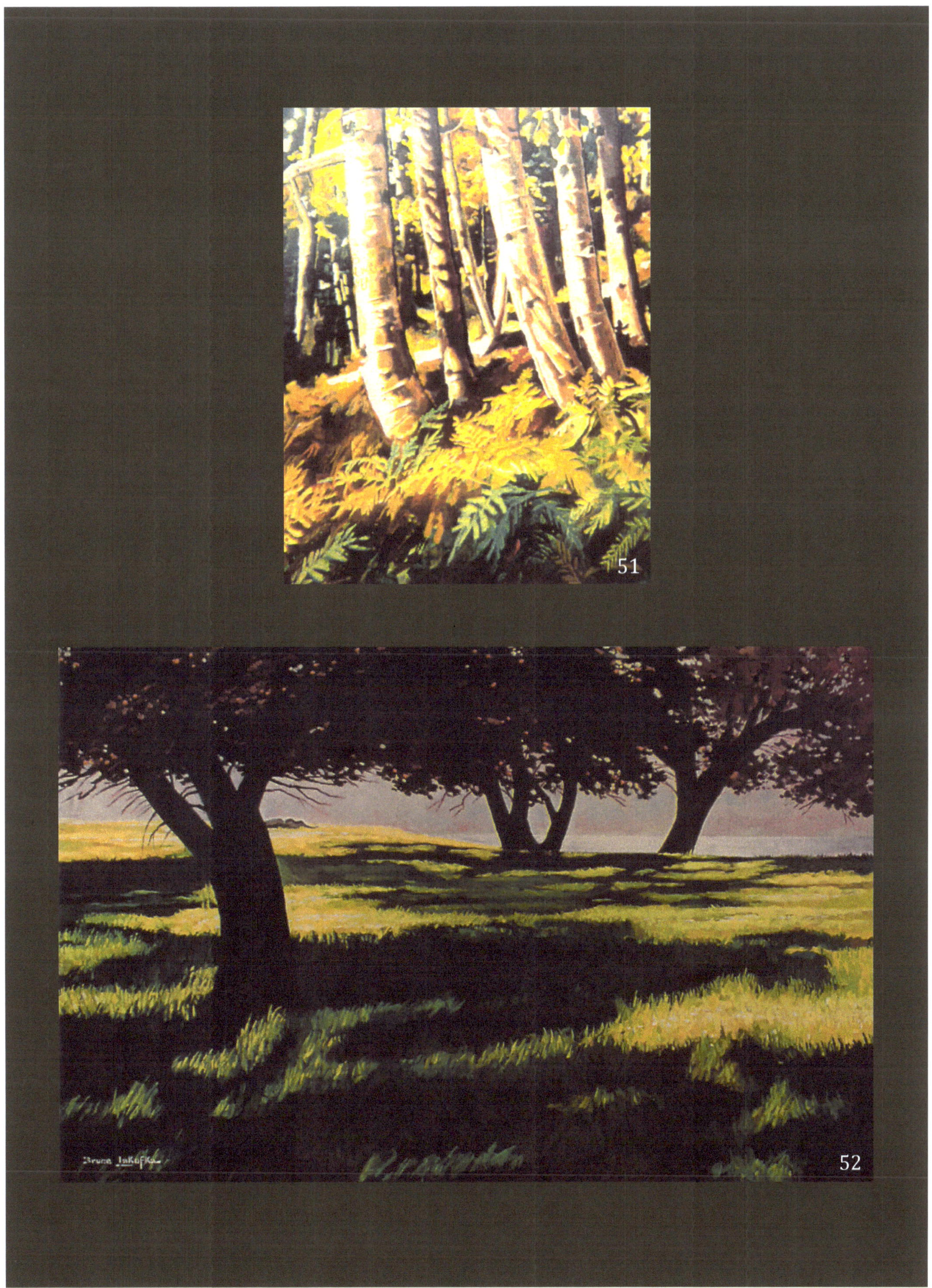

51

52

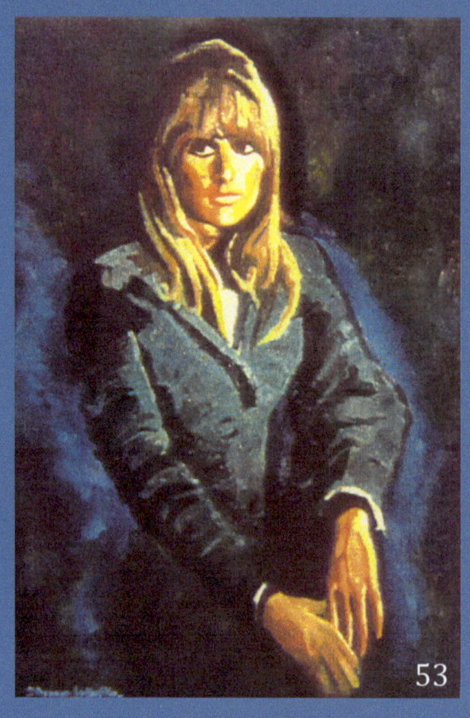
53

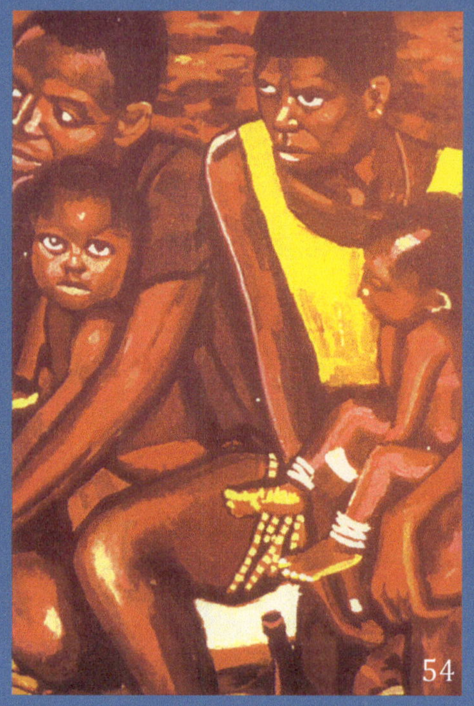
54

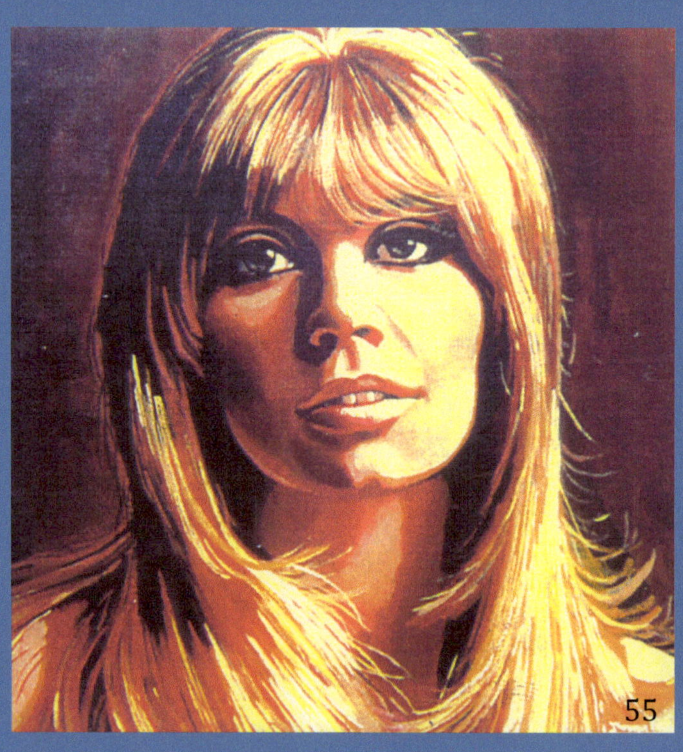
55

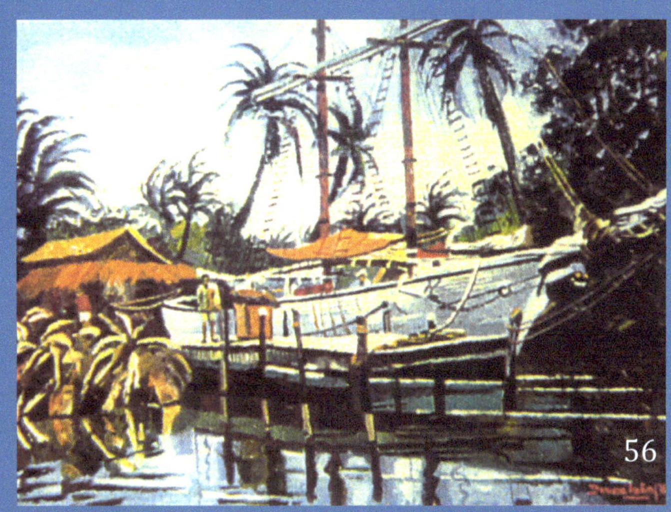
56

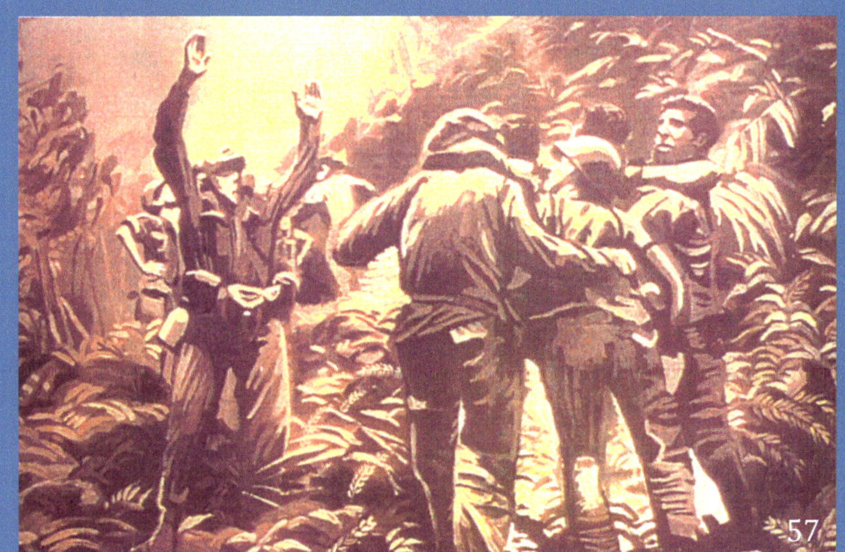
57

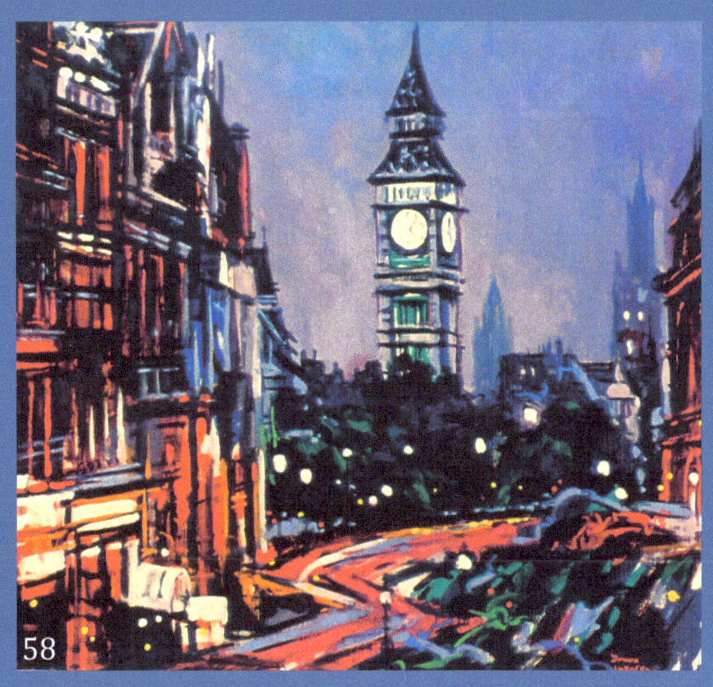
58

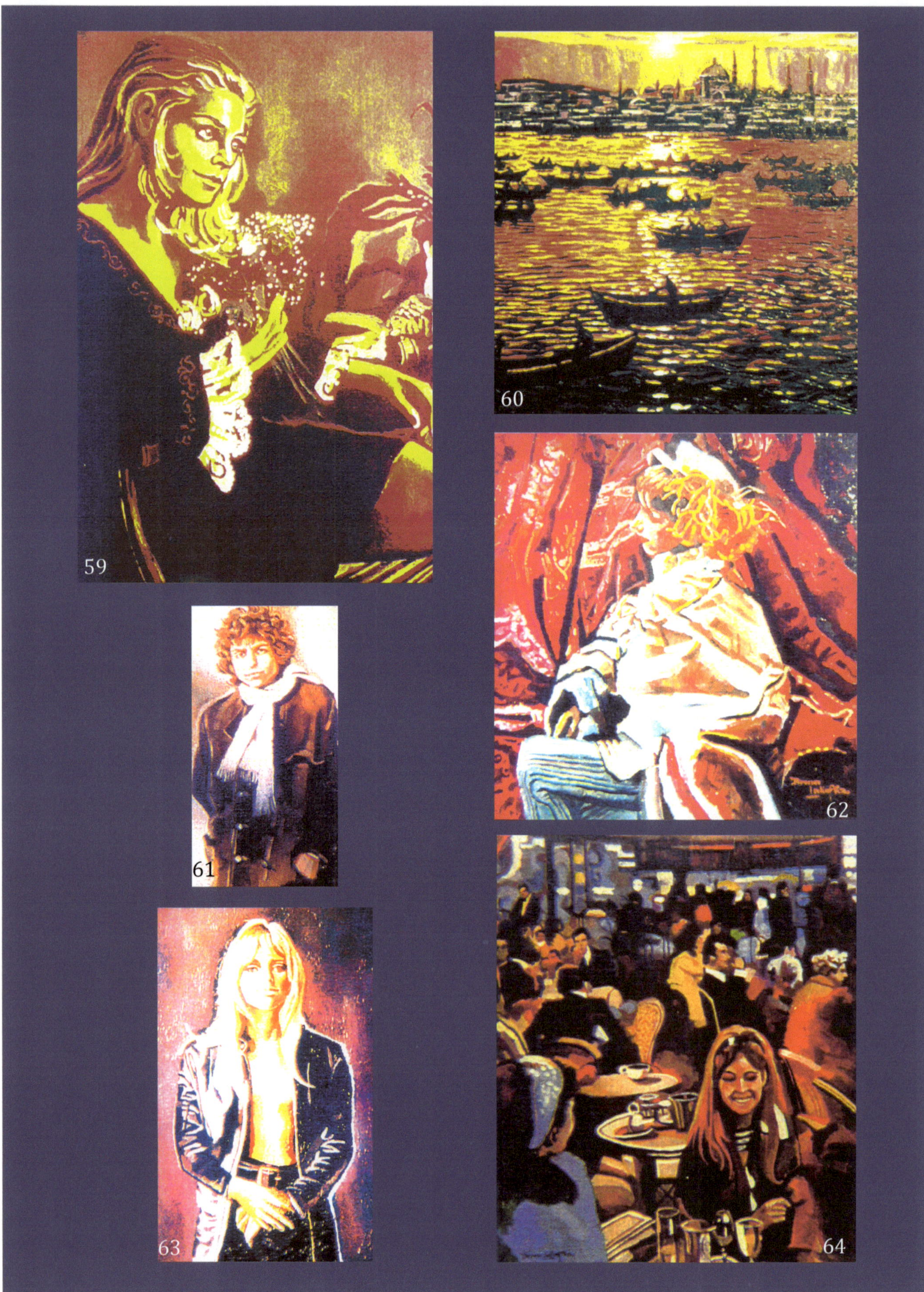
59
60
61
62
63
64

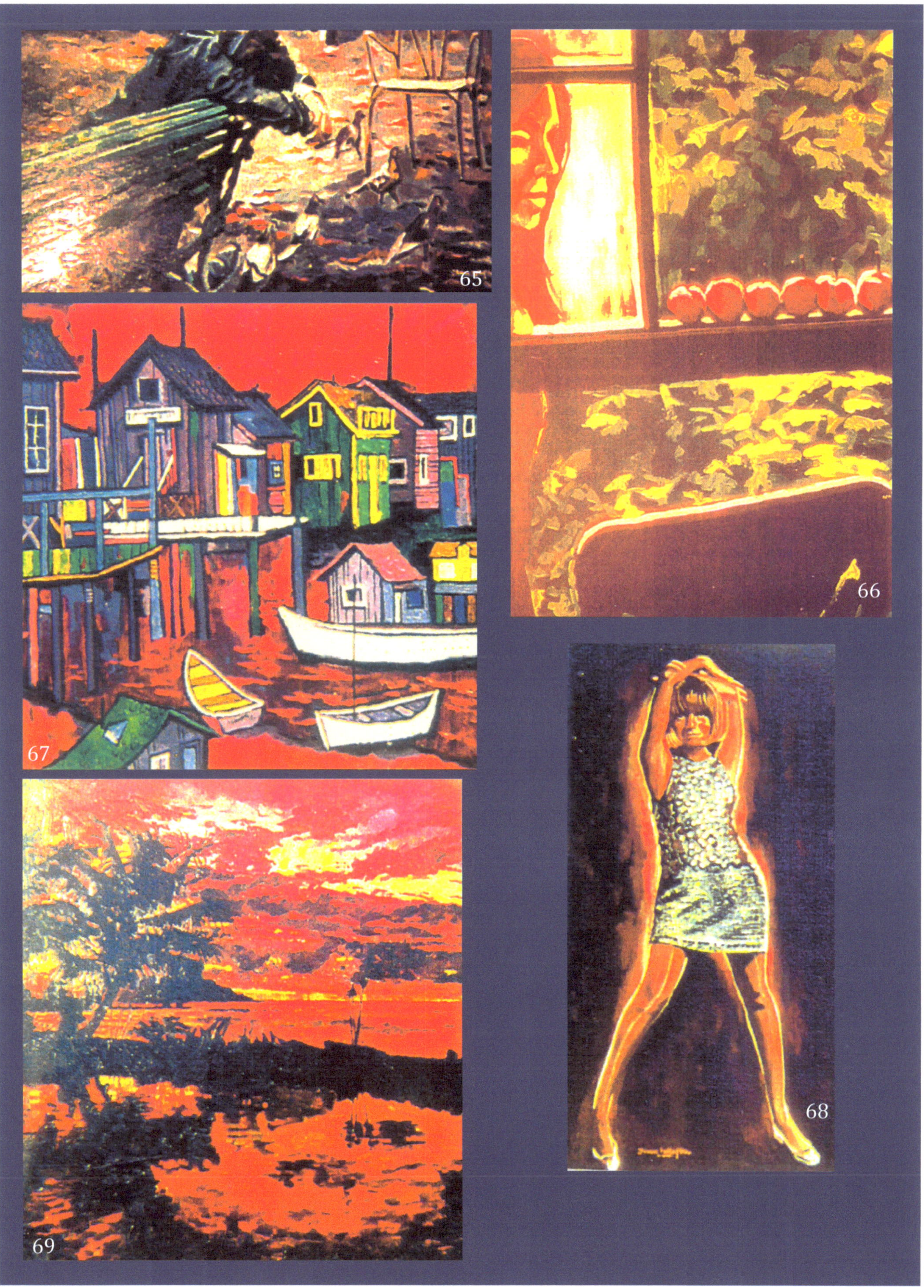
65
66
67
68
69

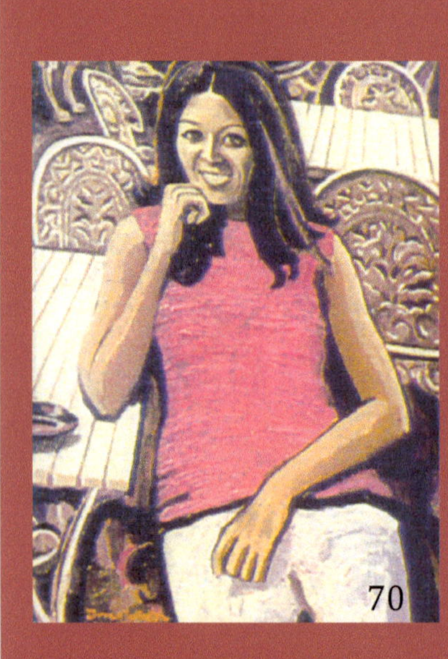
70

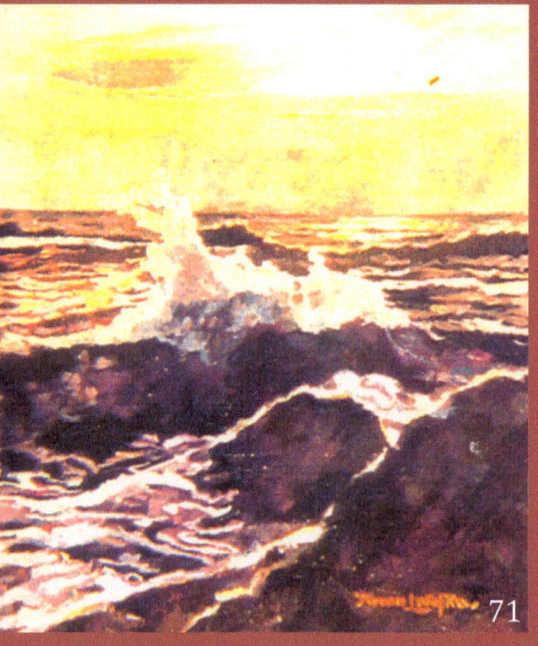
71

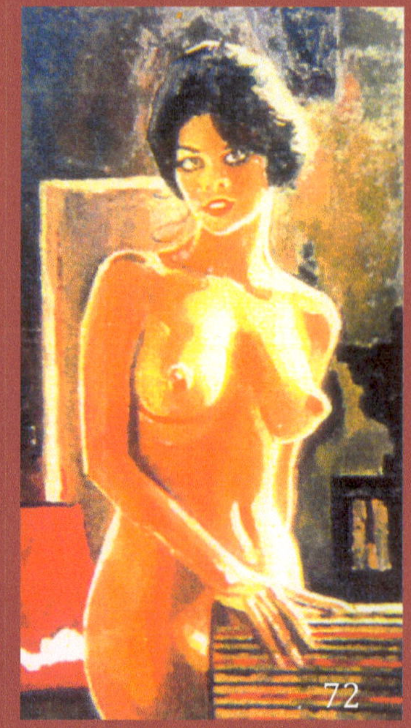
72

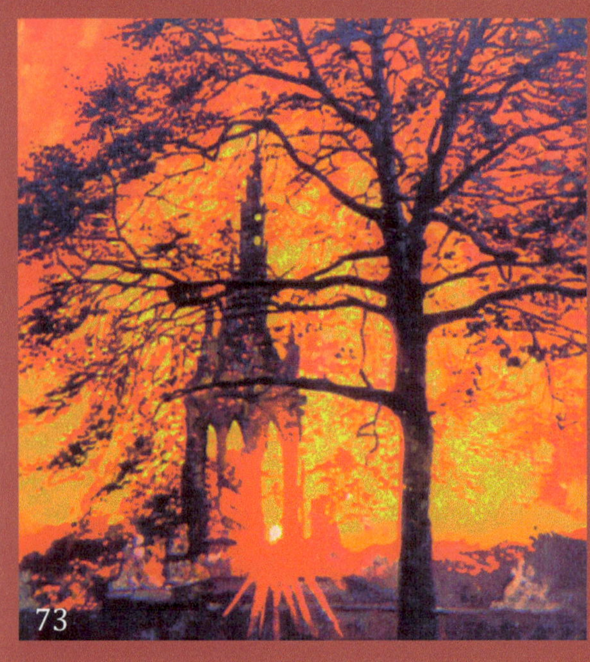
73

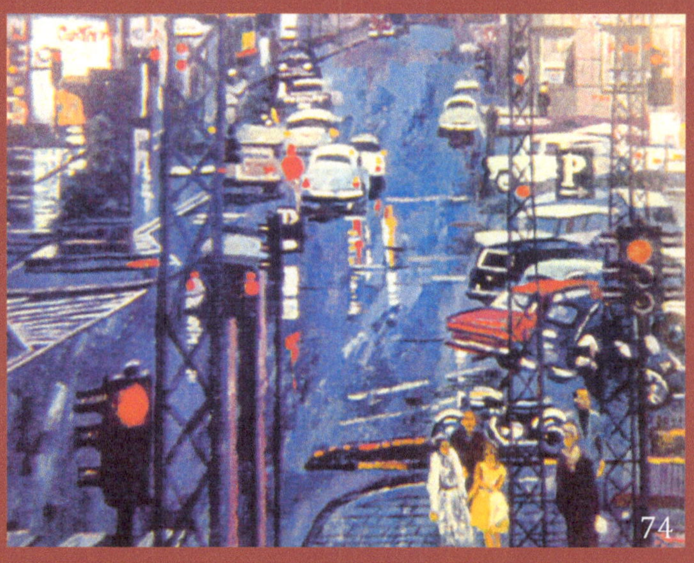
74

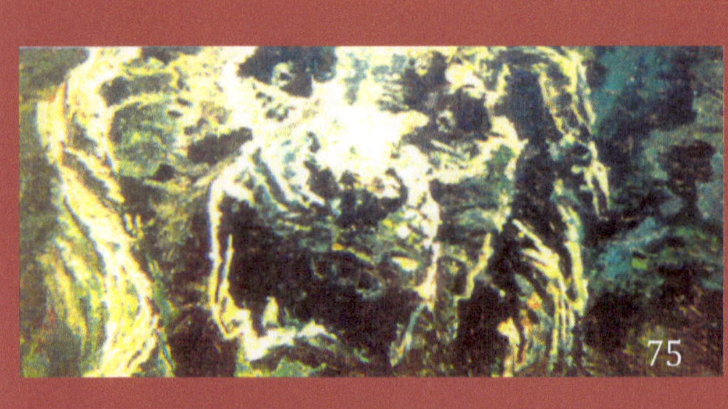
75

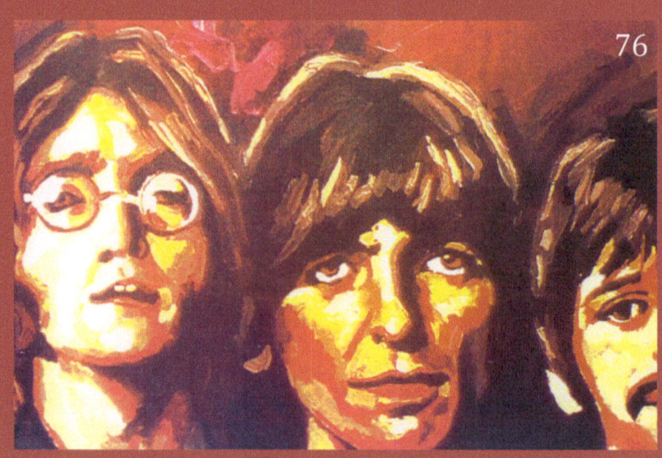
76

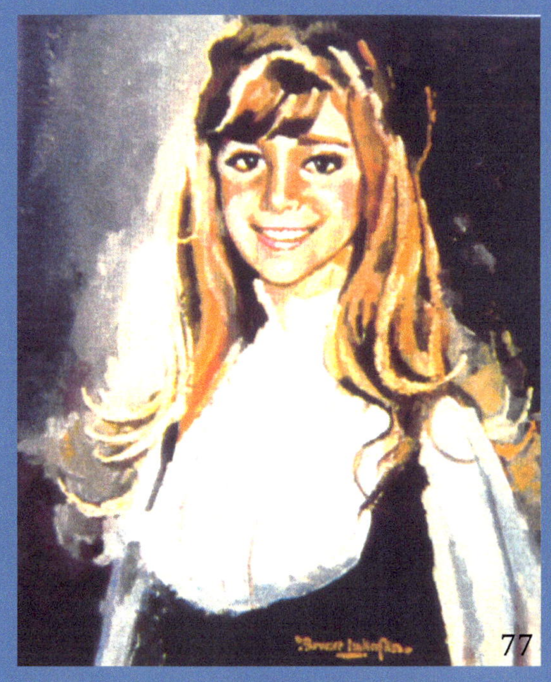

77

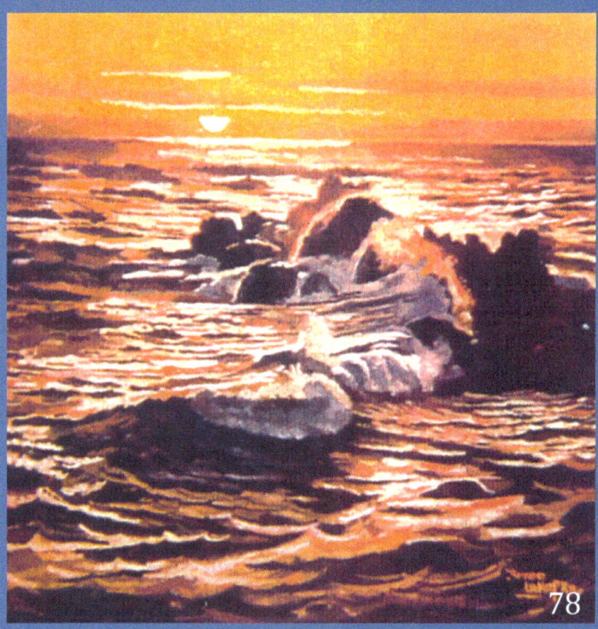

78

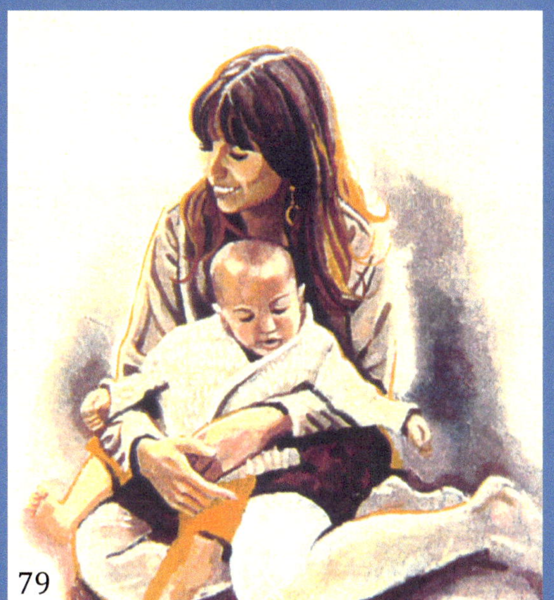

79

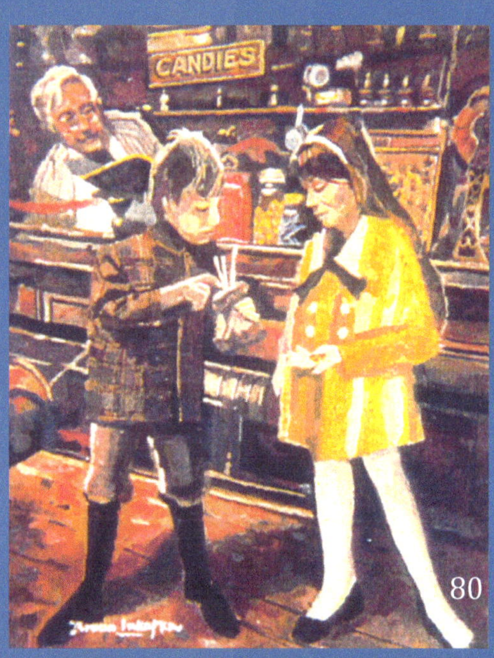

80

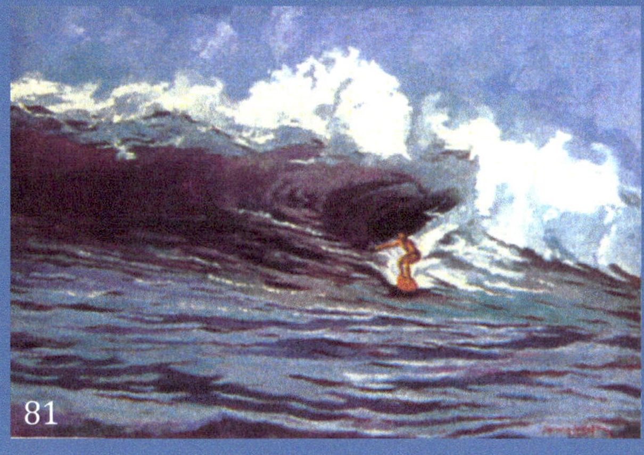

81

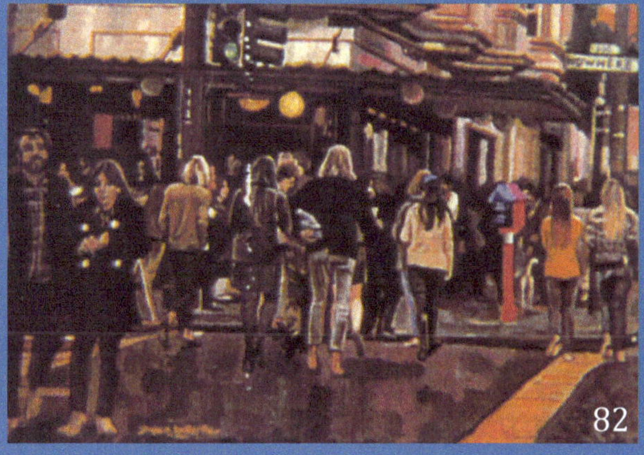

82

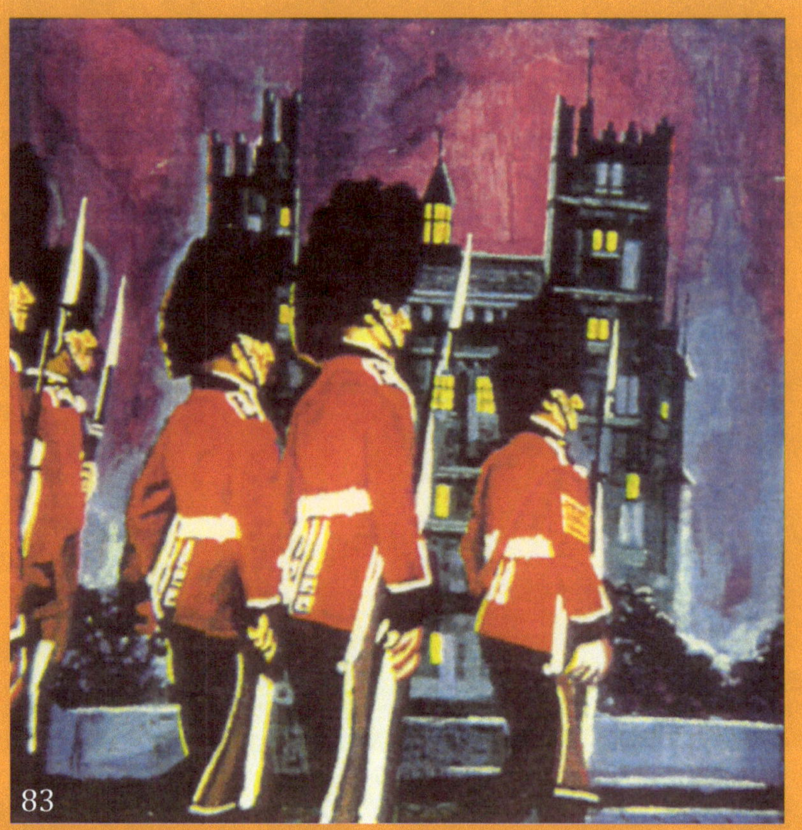
83

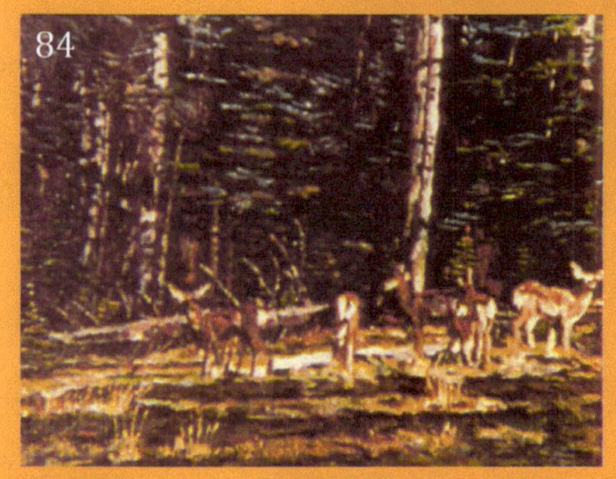
84

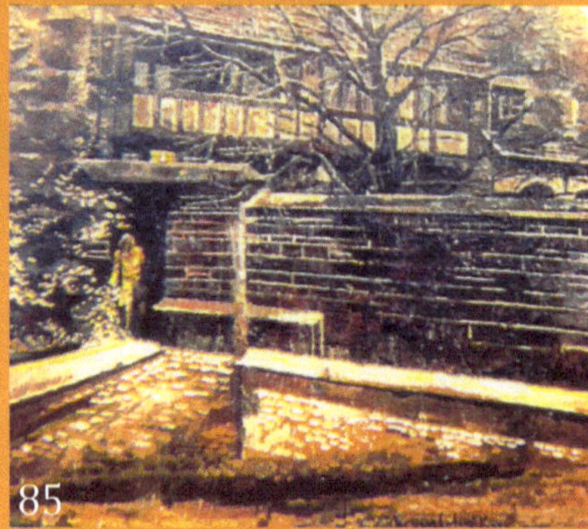
85

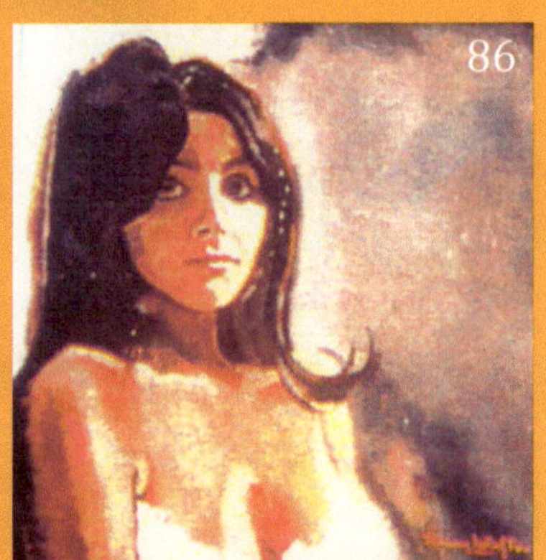
86

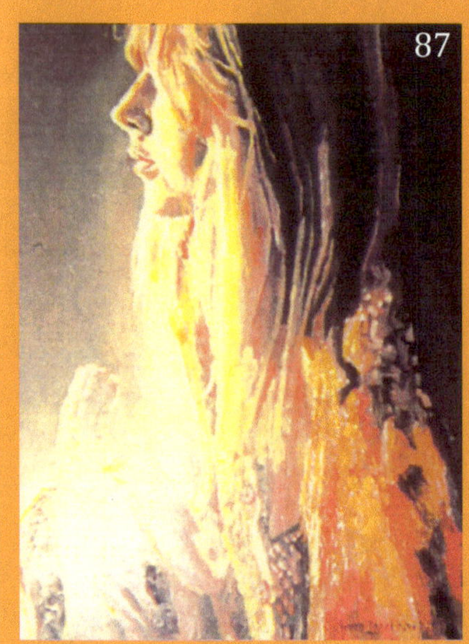
87

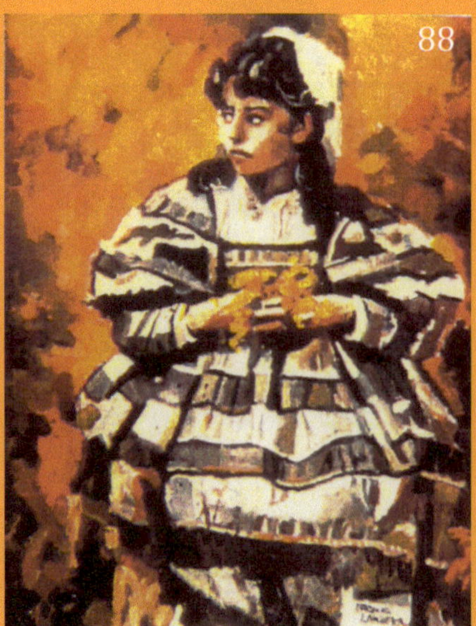
88

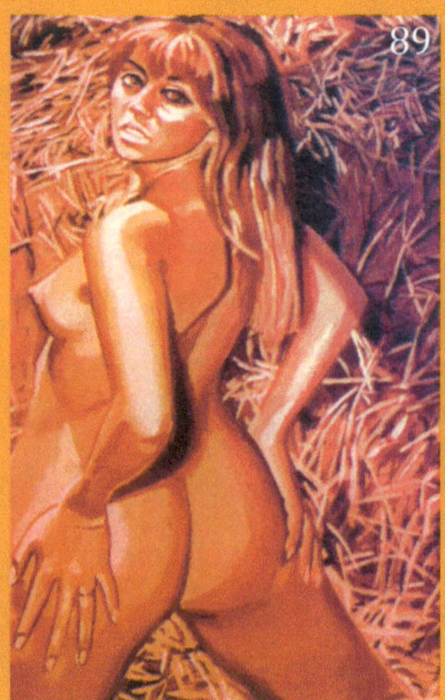
89

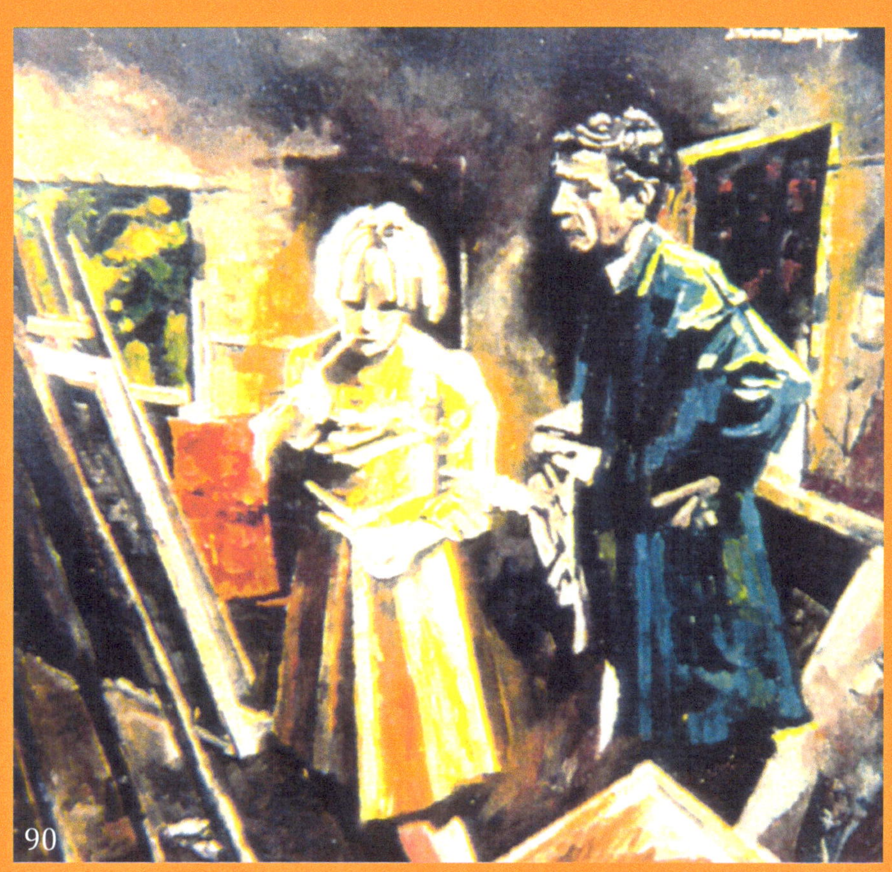
90

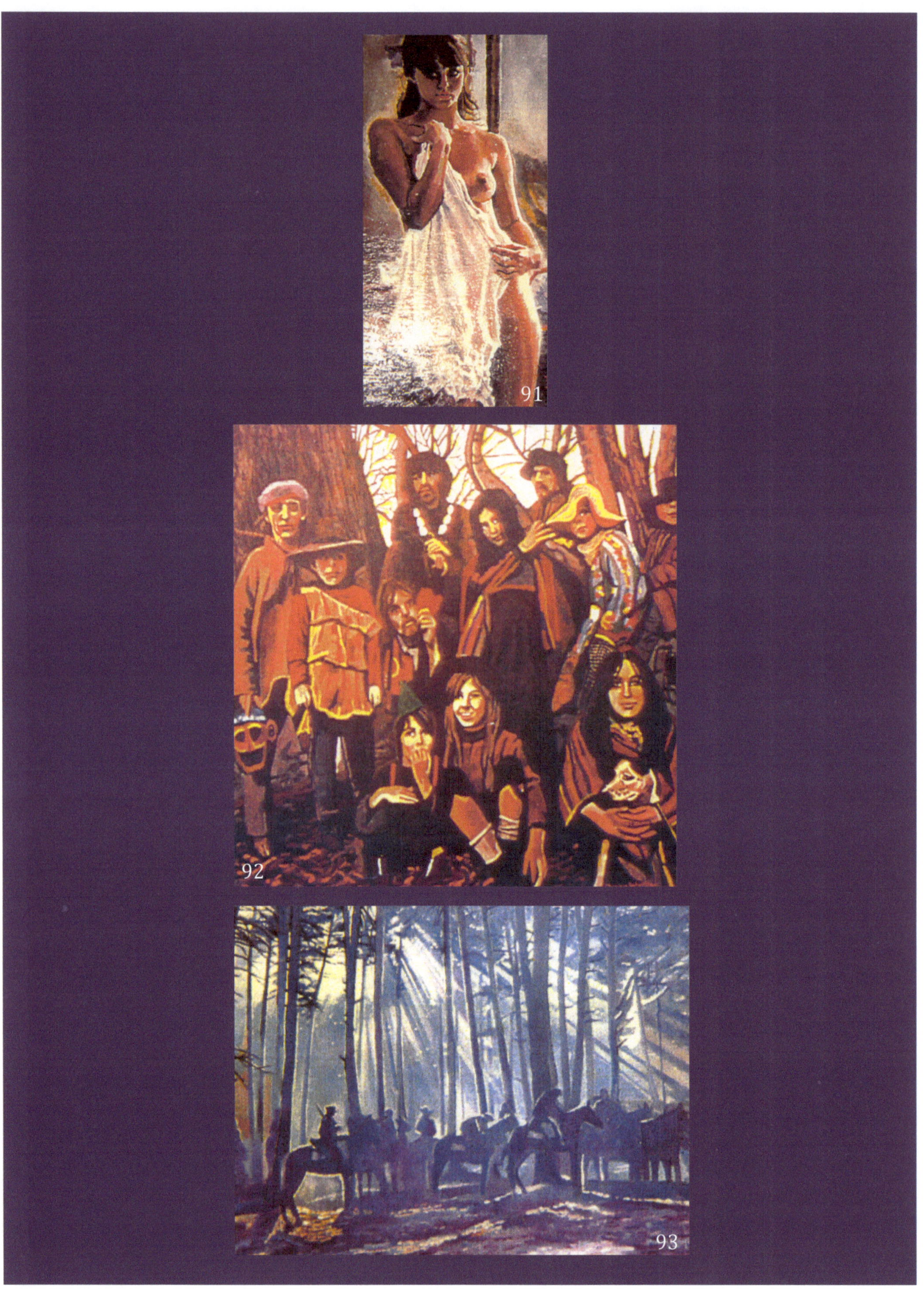
91
92
93

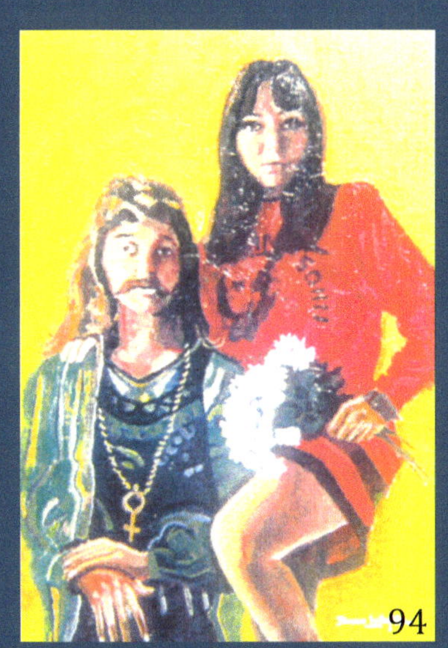
94

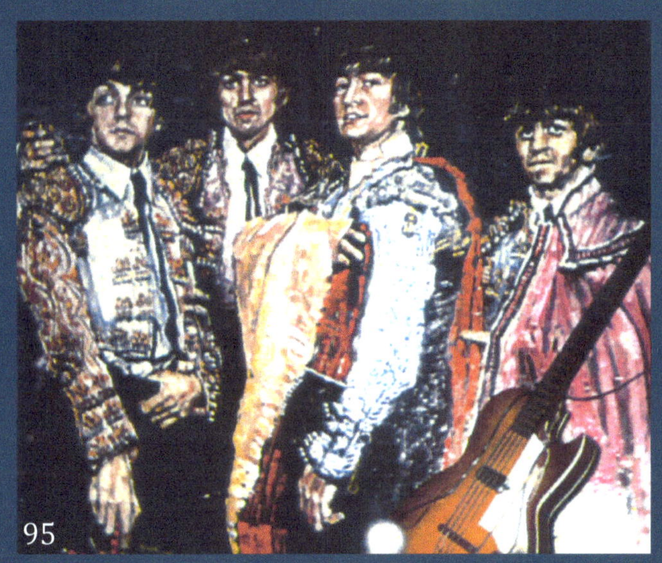
95

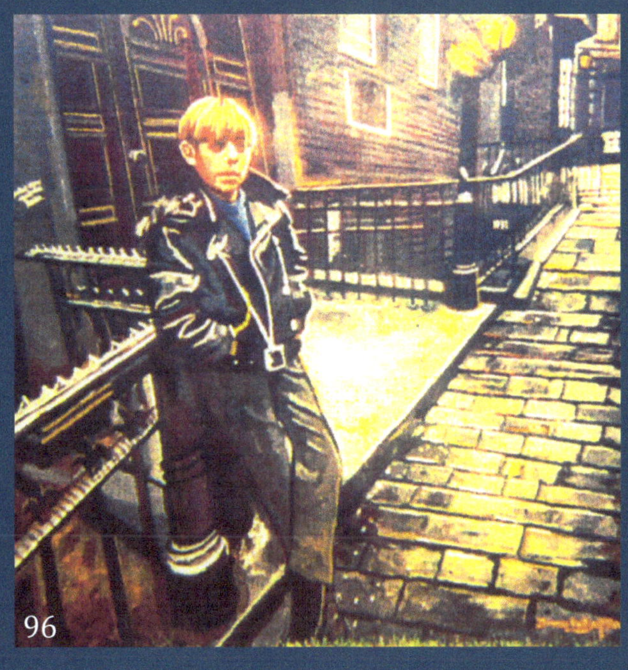
96

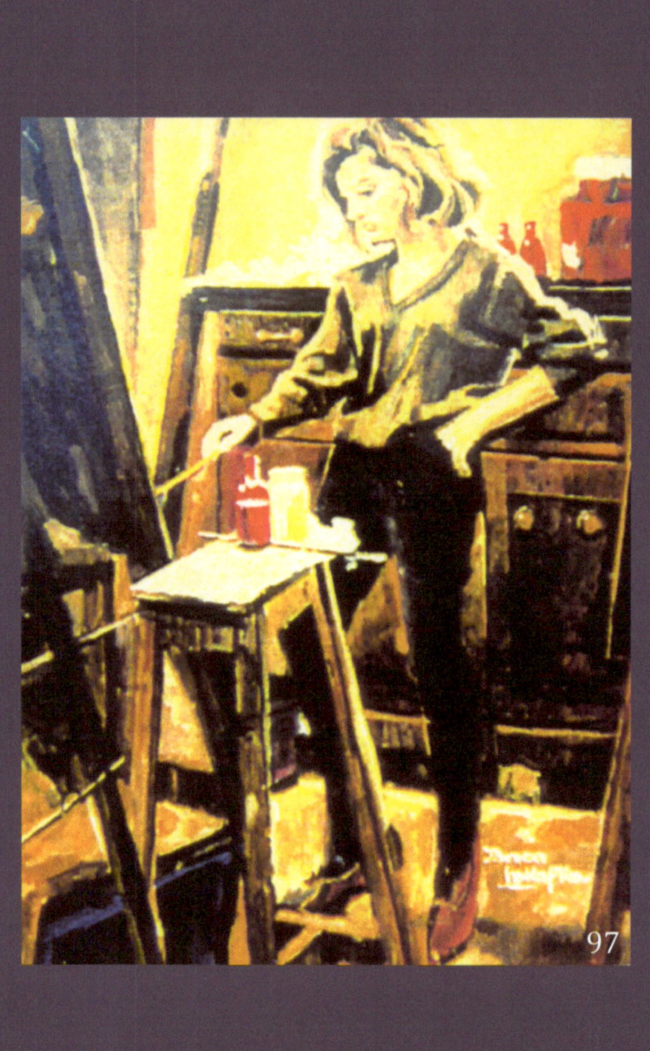

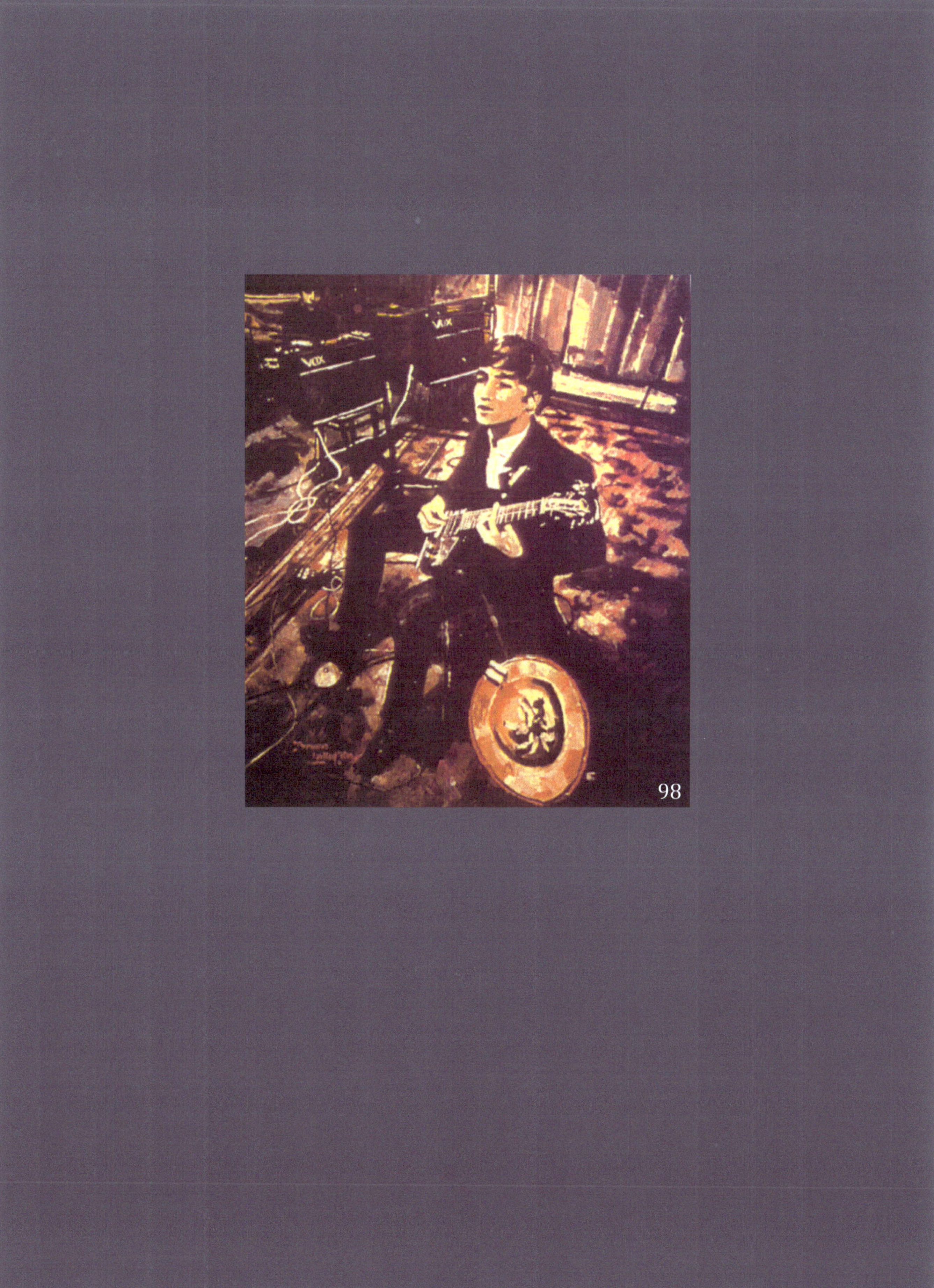

98

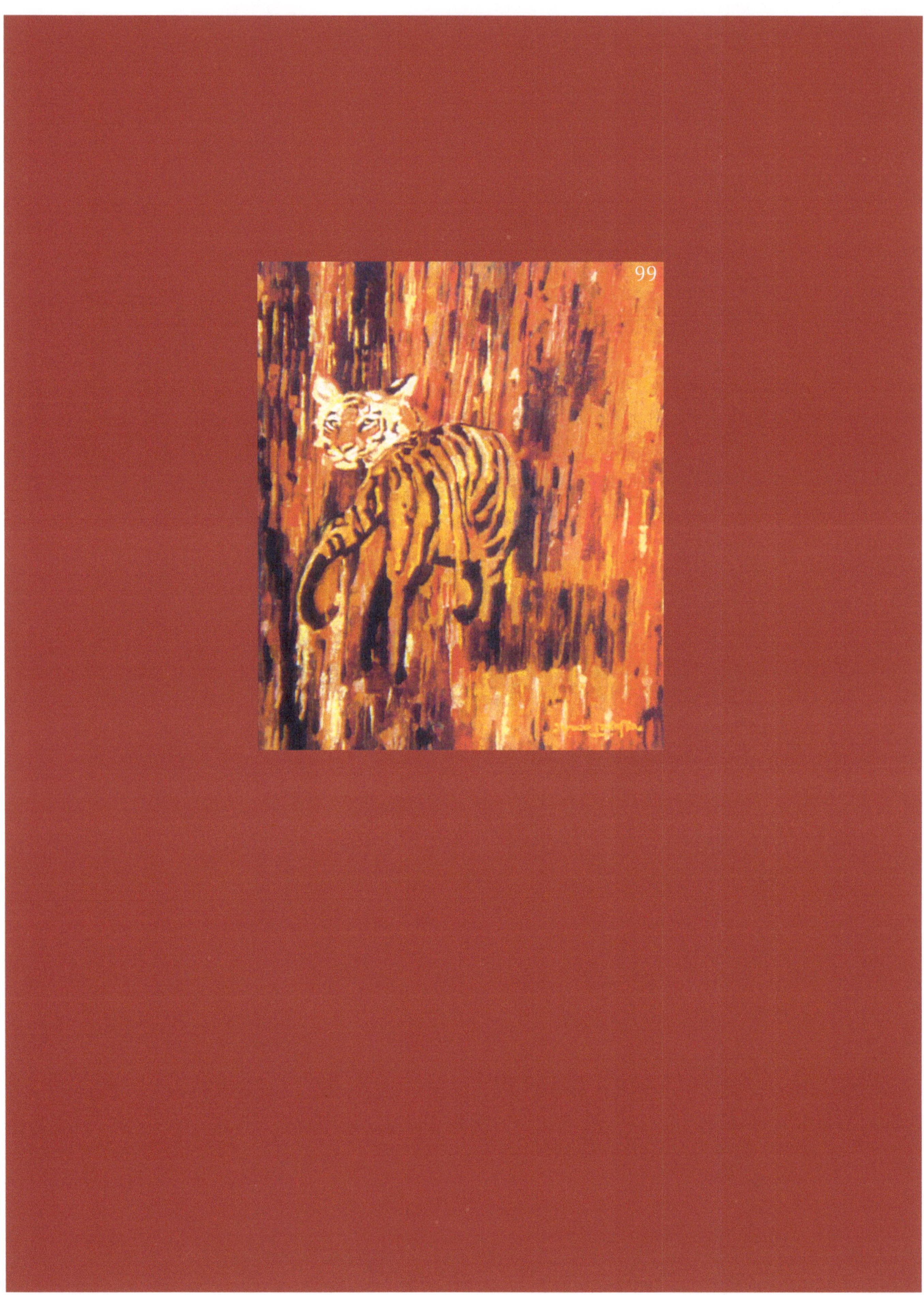
99

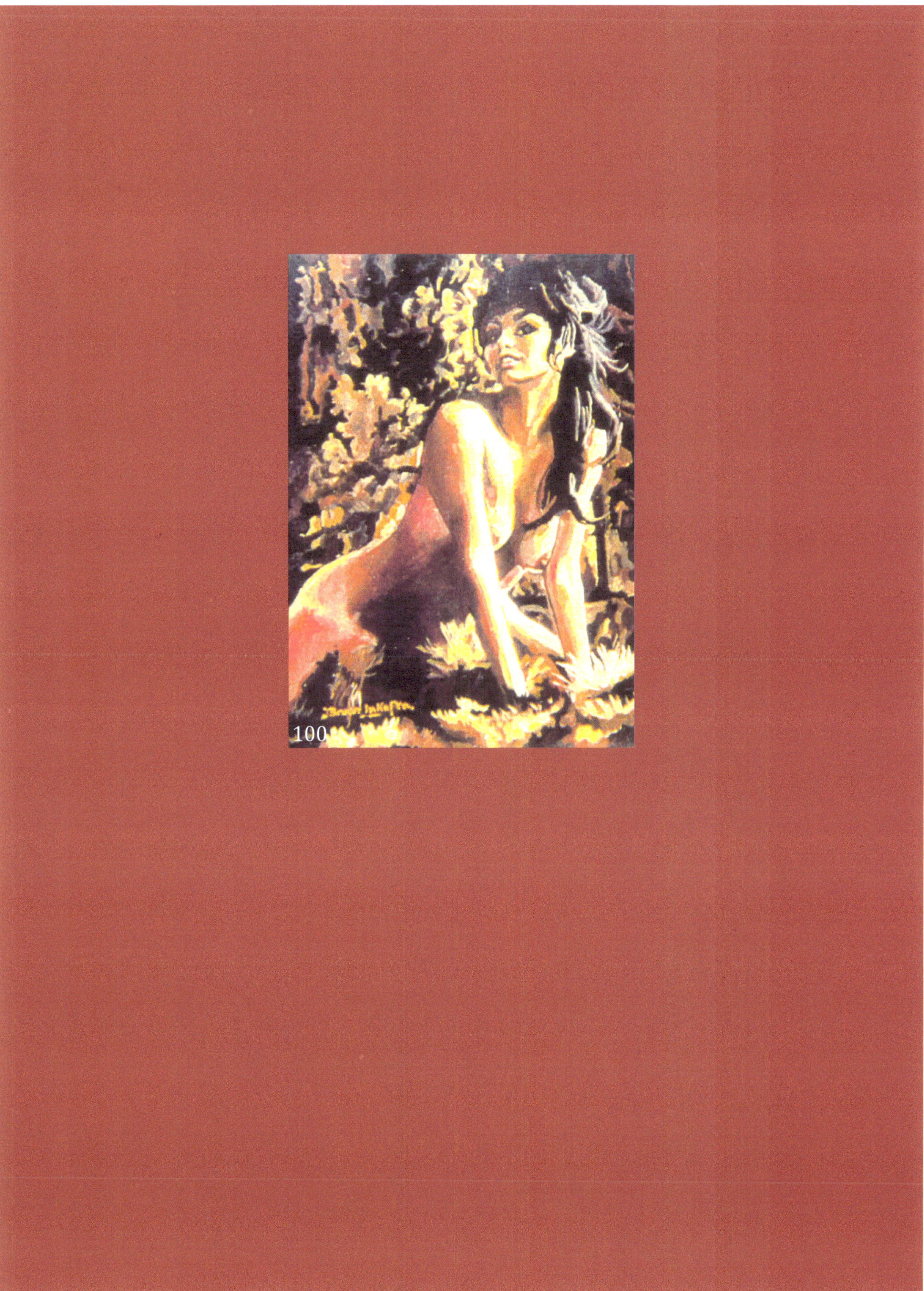
100

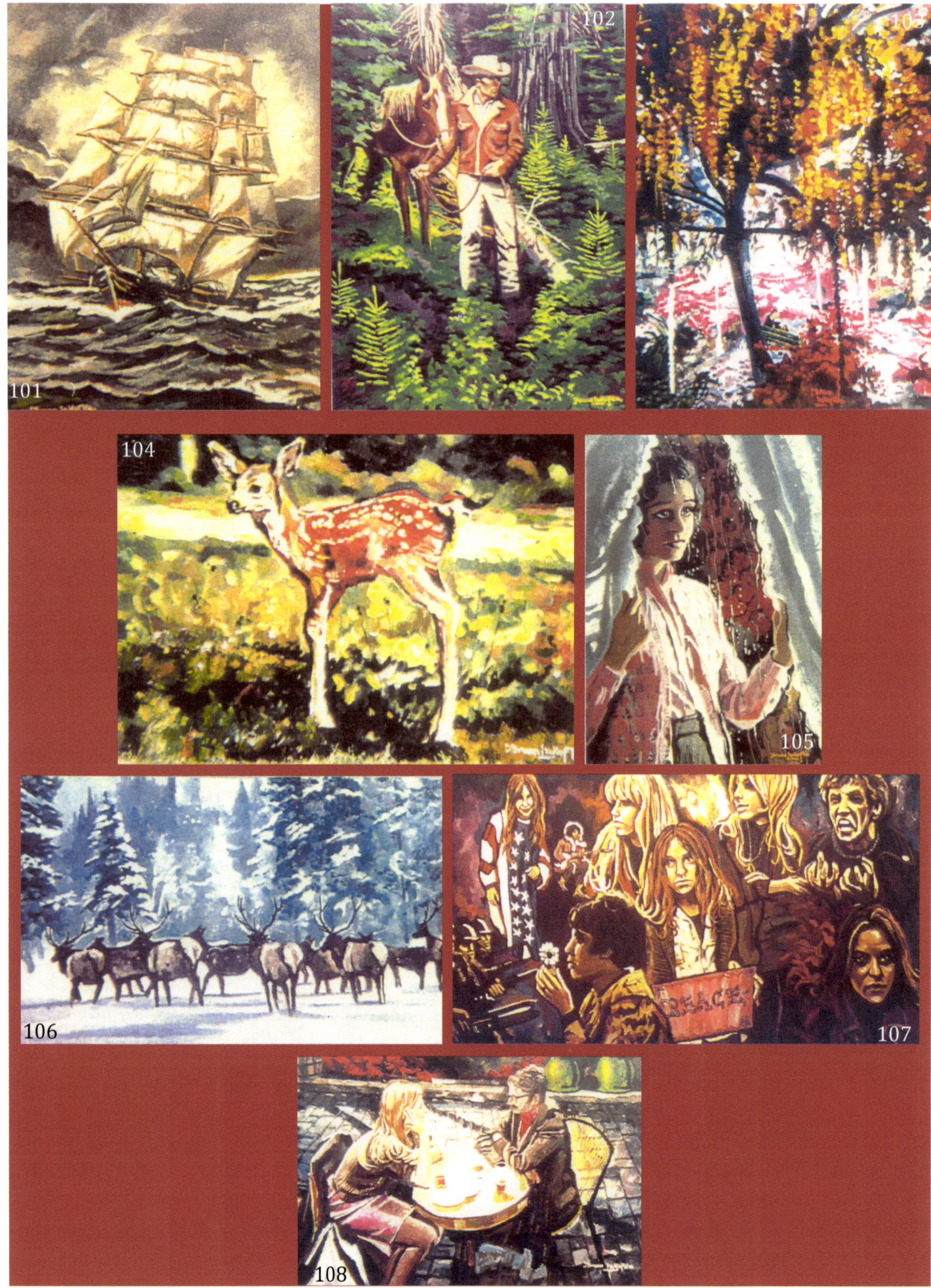
101
102
104
105
106
107
108

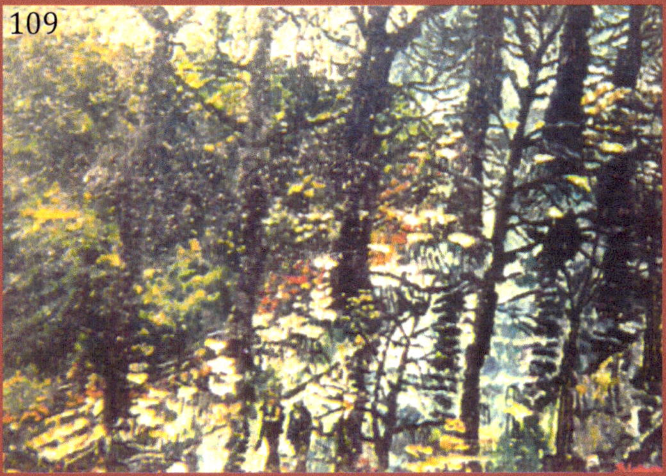

109

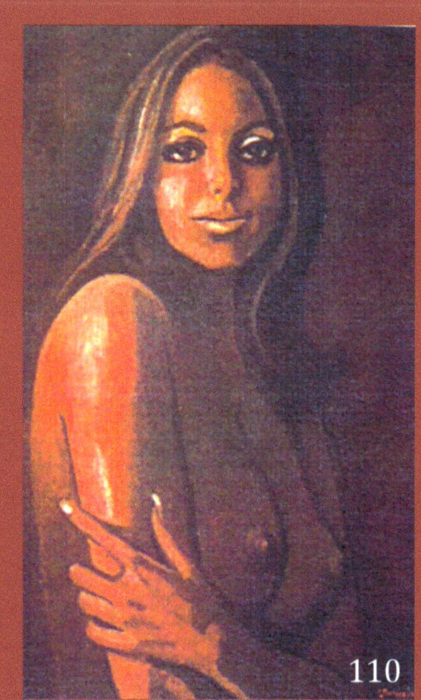
110

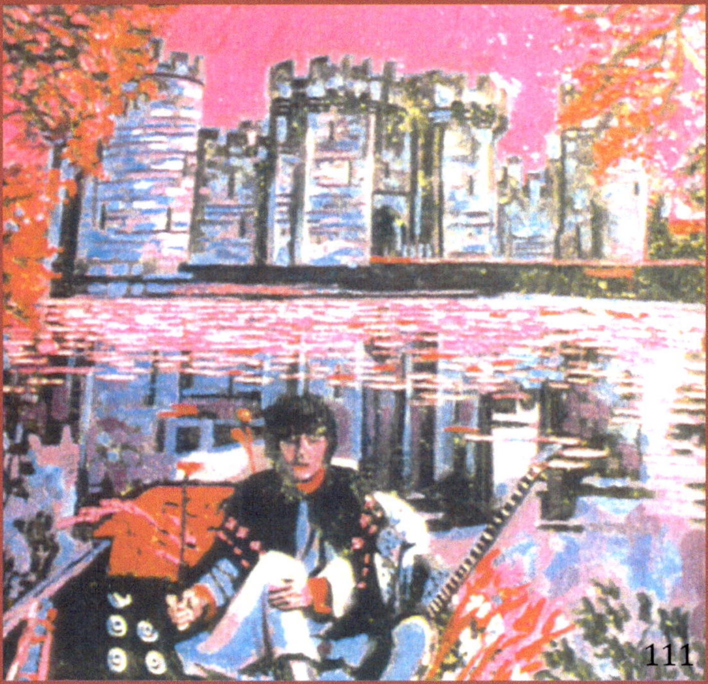

111

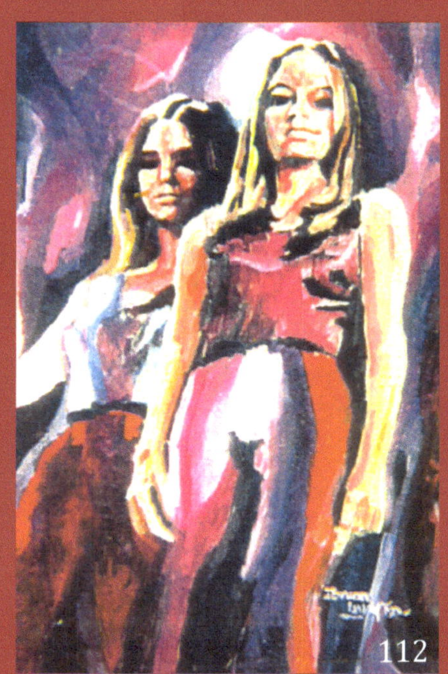
112

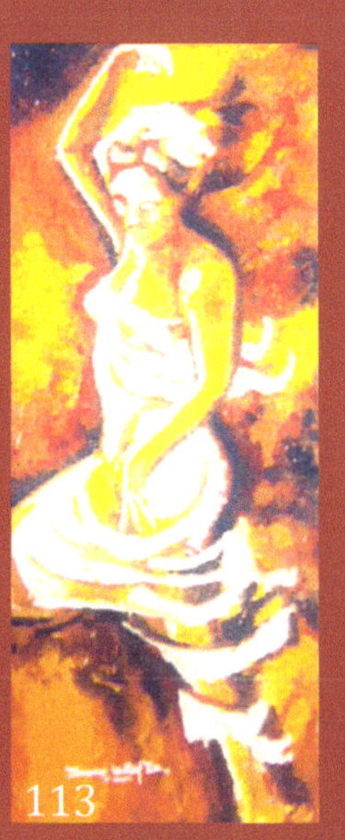
113

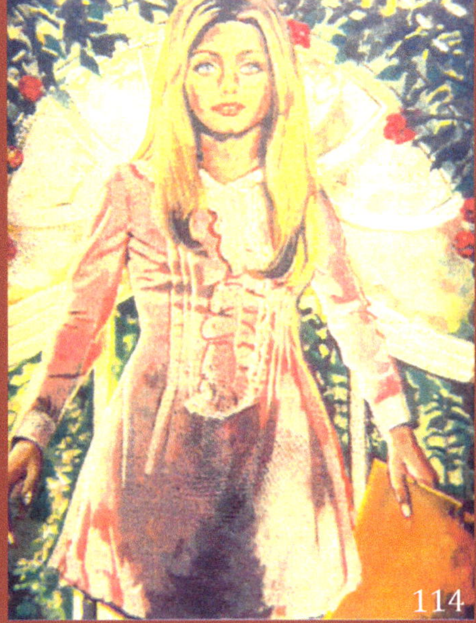
114

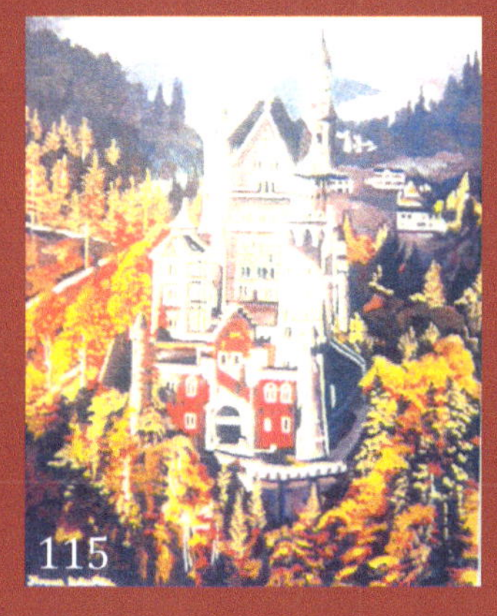
115

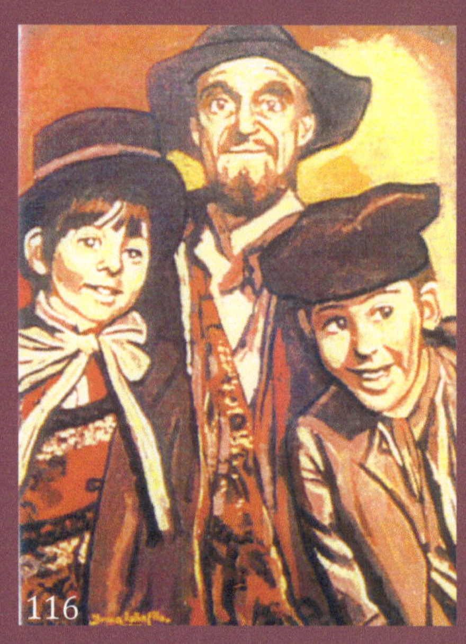
116

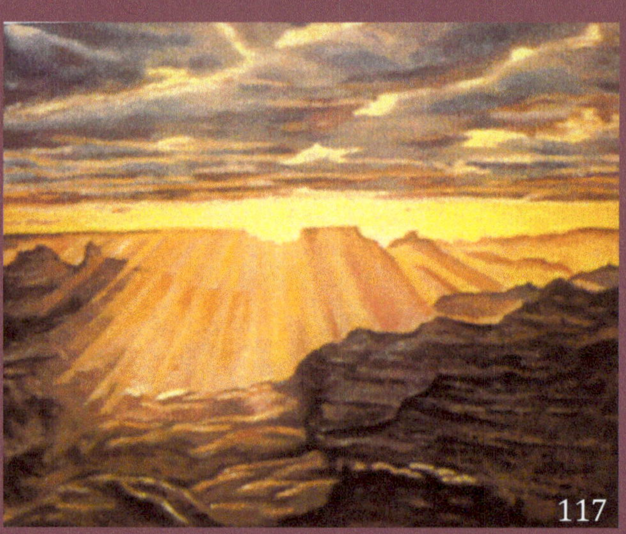
117

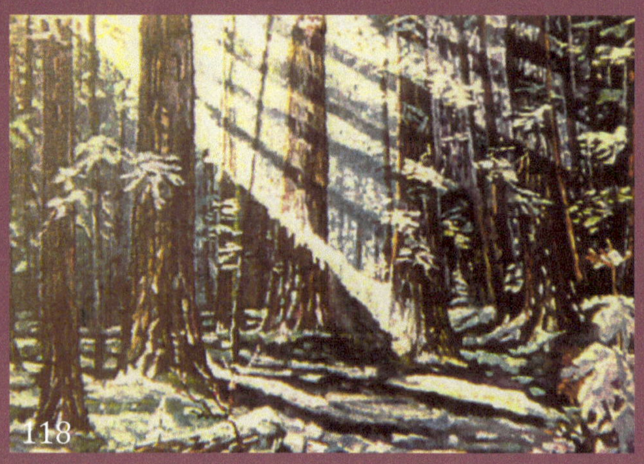
118

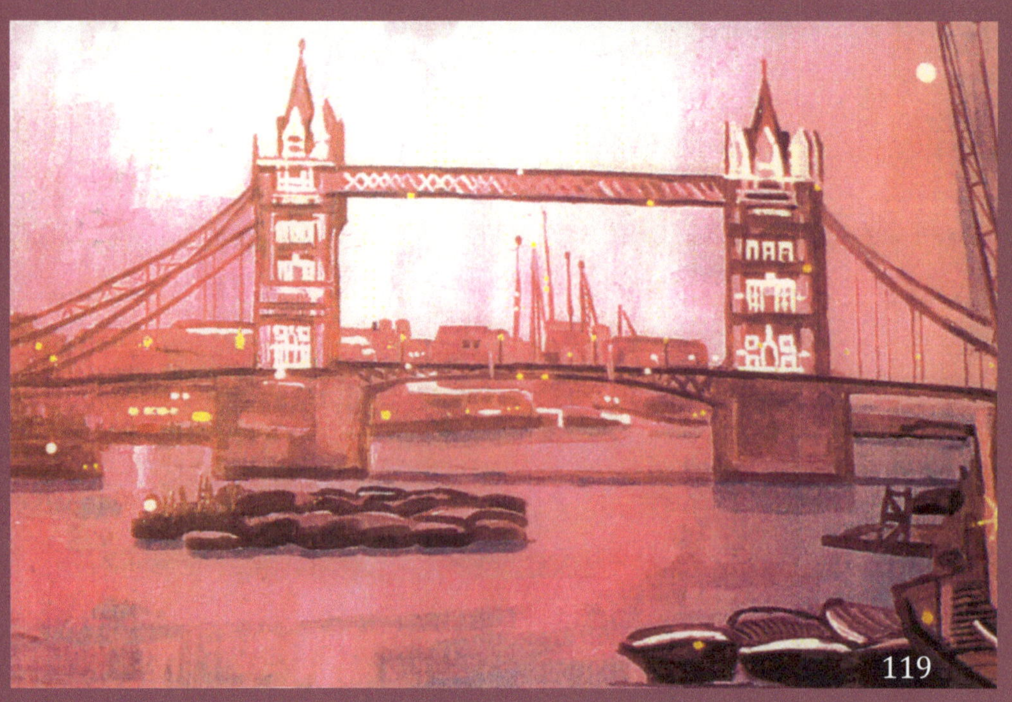
119

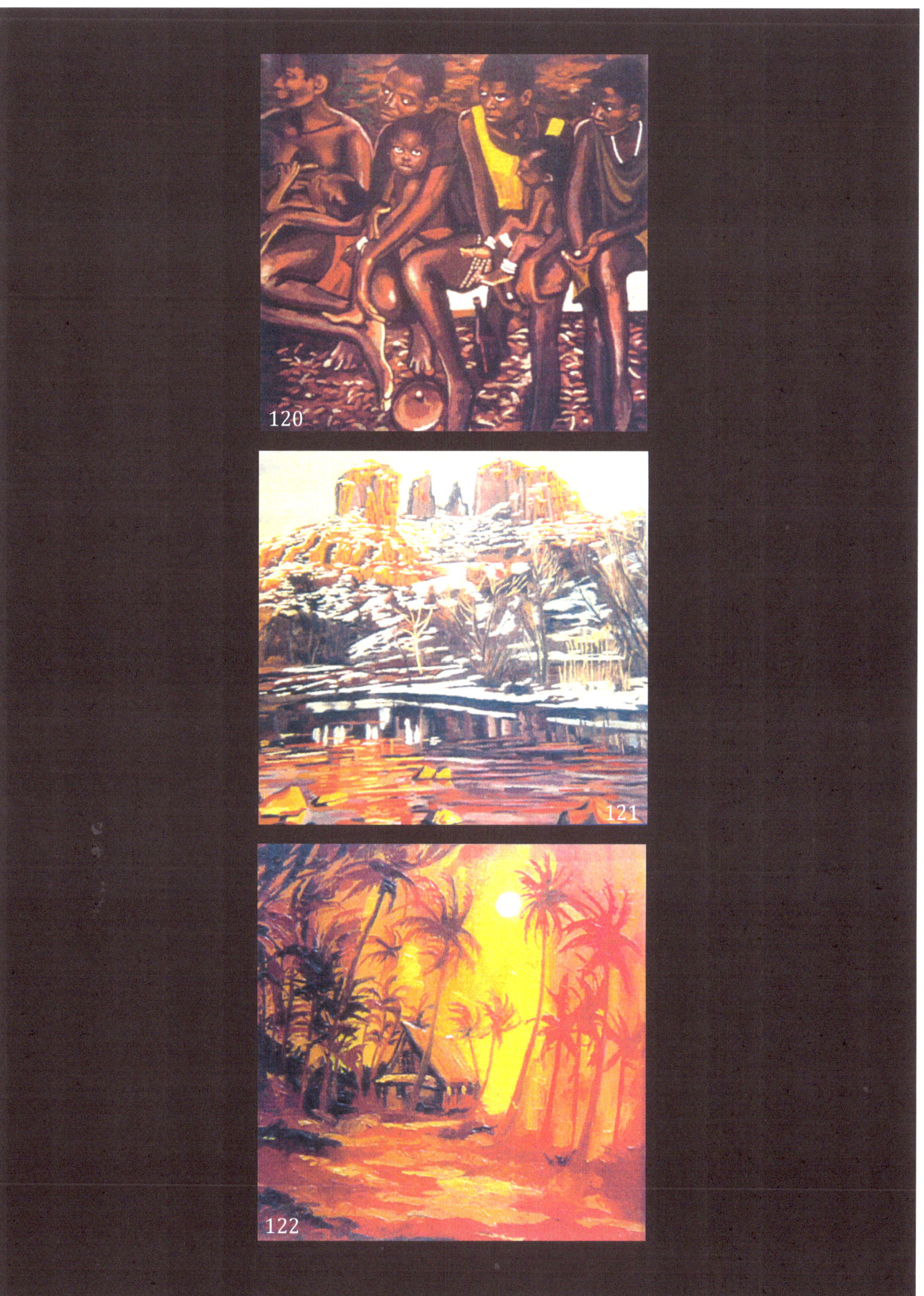
120
121
122

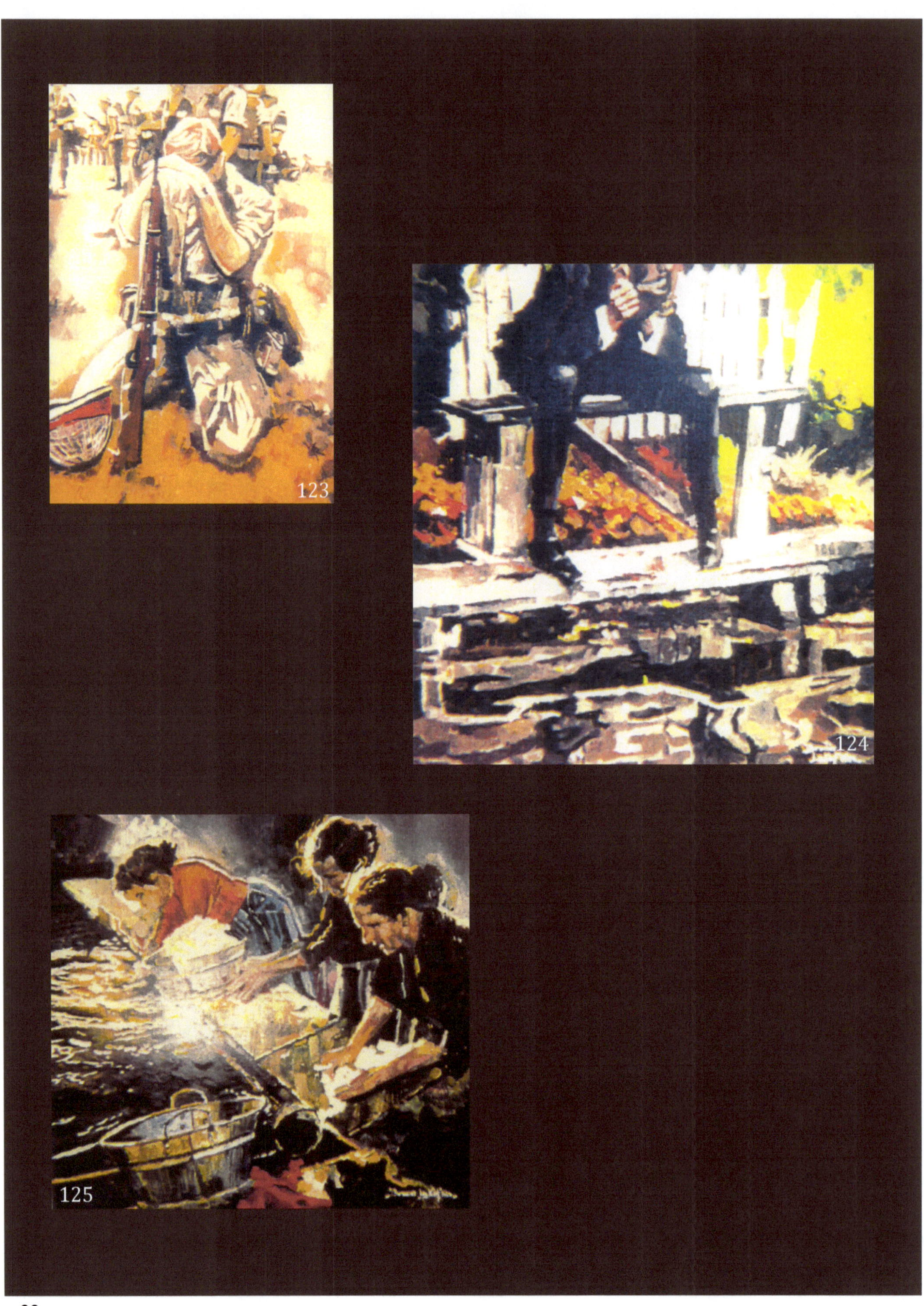
123
124
125

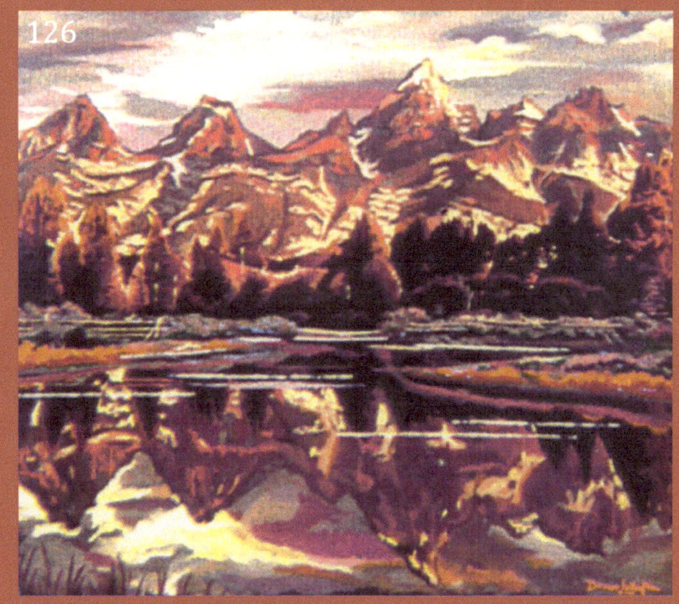

126

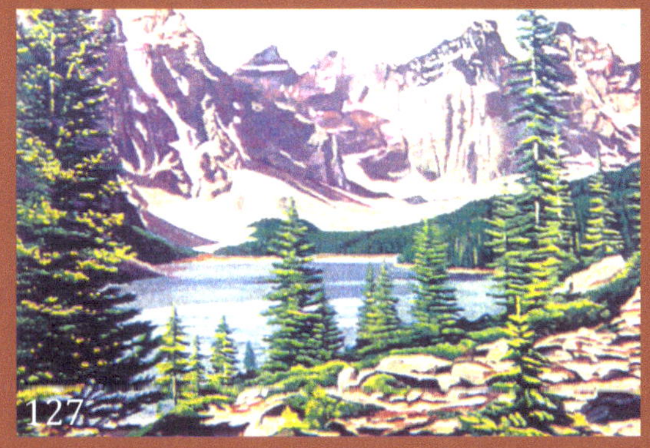

127

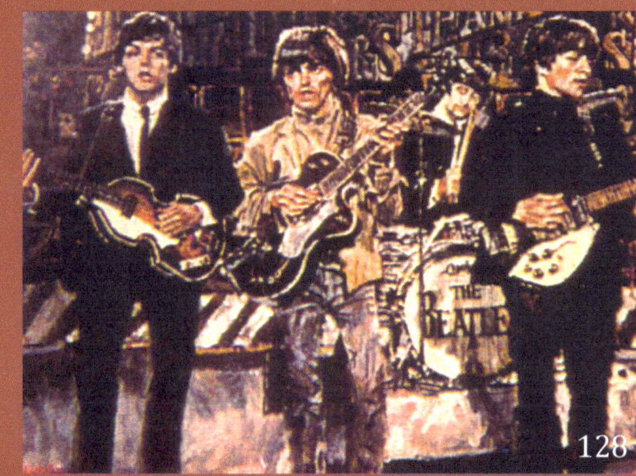

128

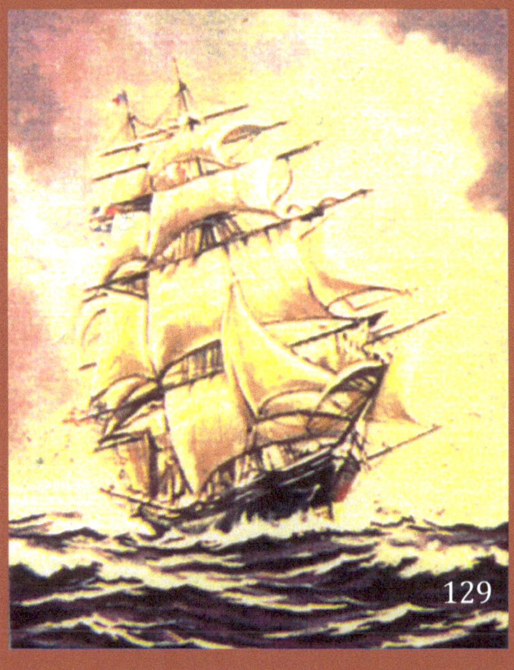

129

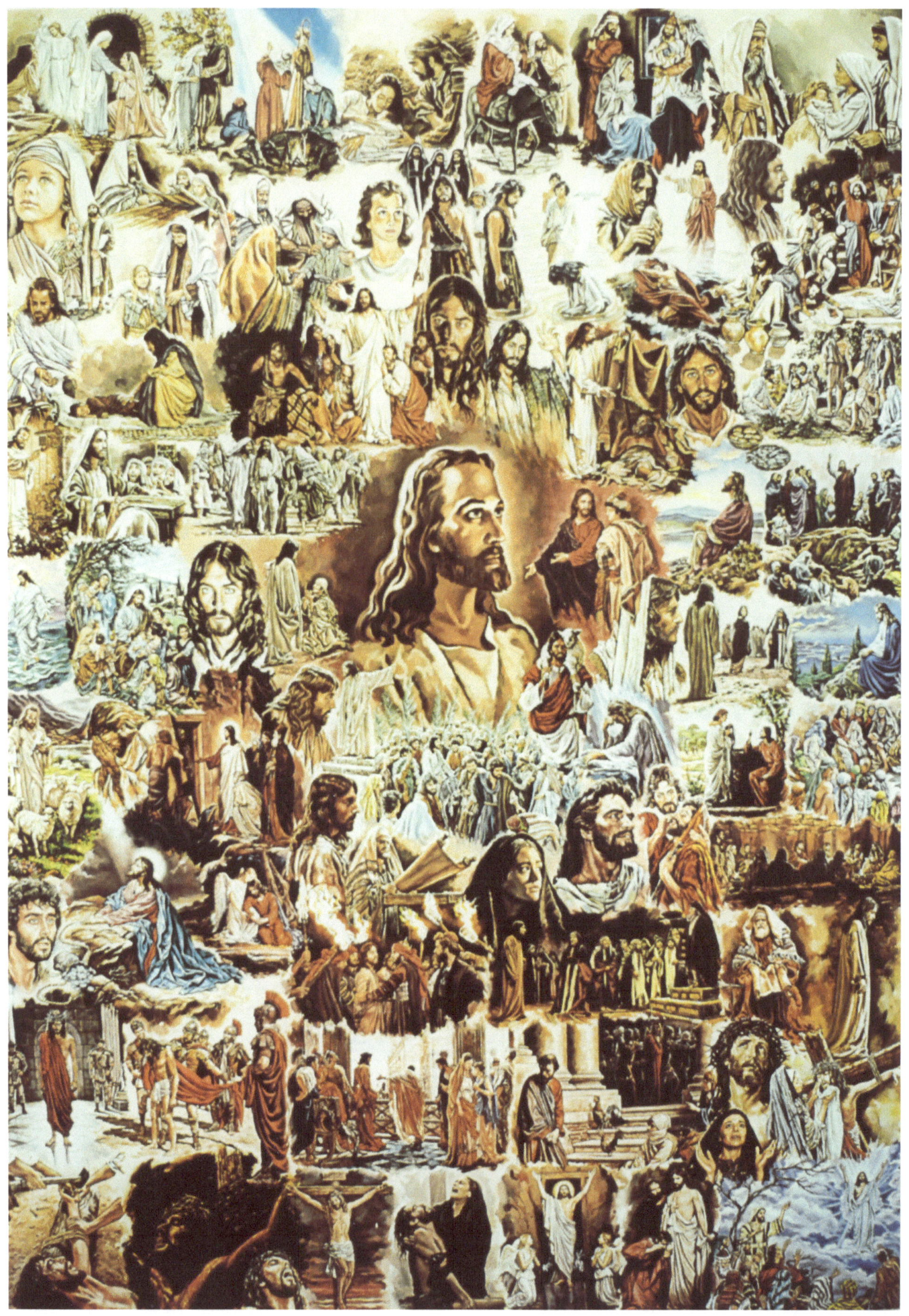

The Life of Christ 74" x 53" Took 2 ½ years to paint. Completed 8/2/82

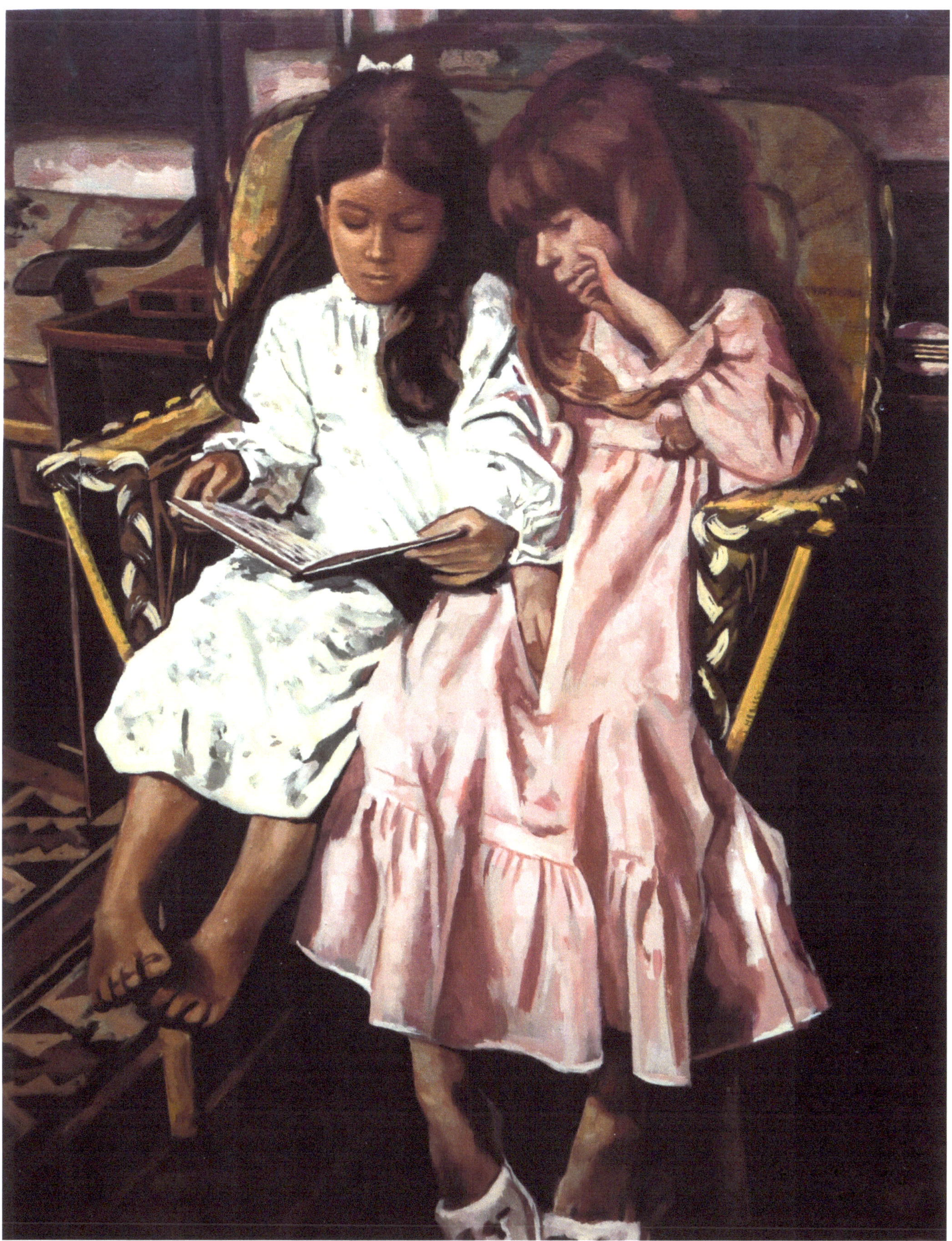

Two Sisters in a Rocker

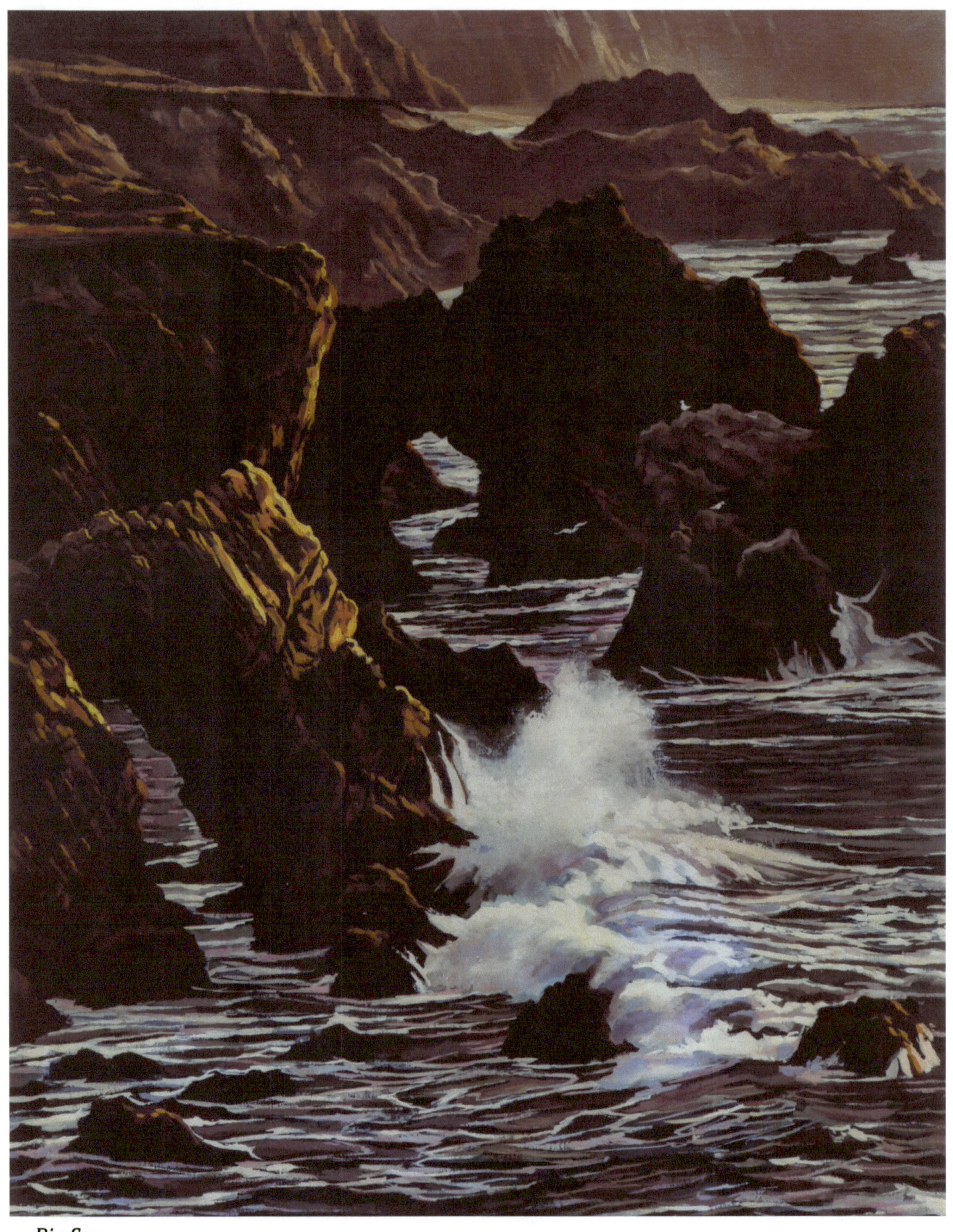

Big Sur

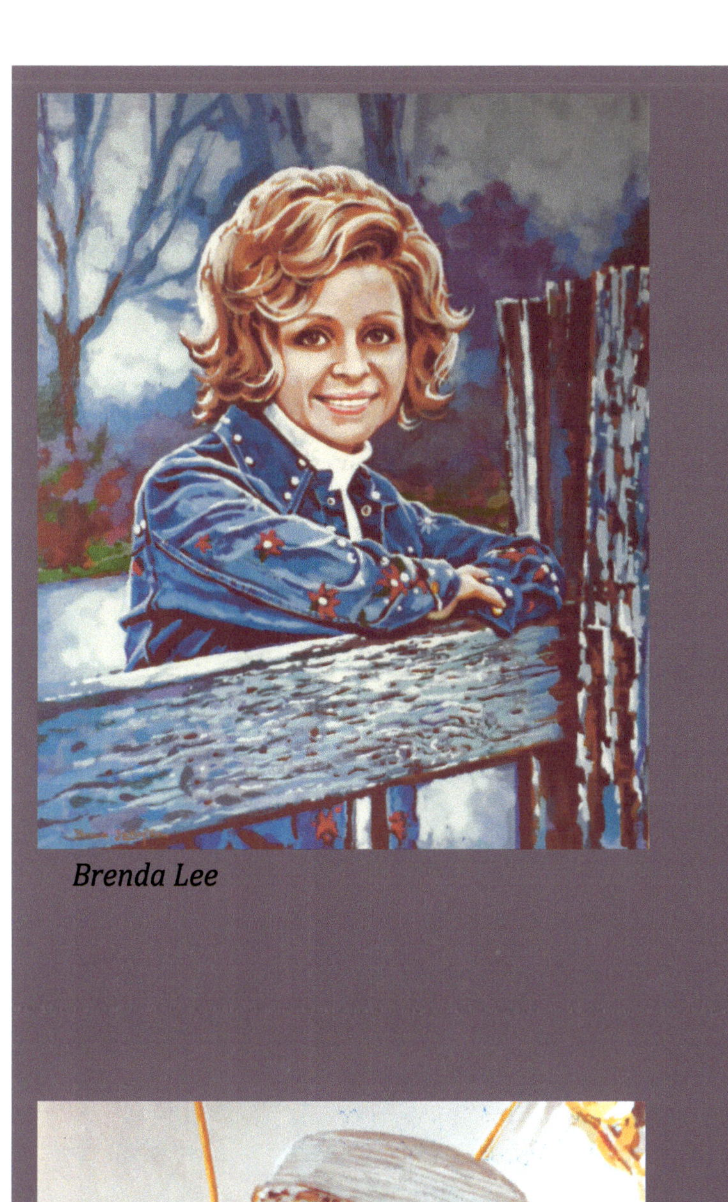
Brenda Lee

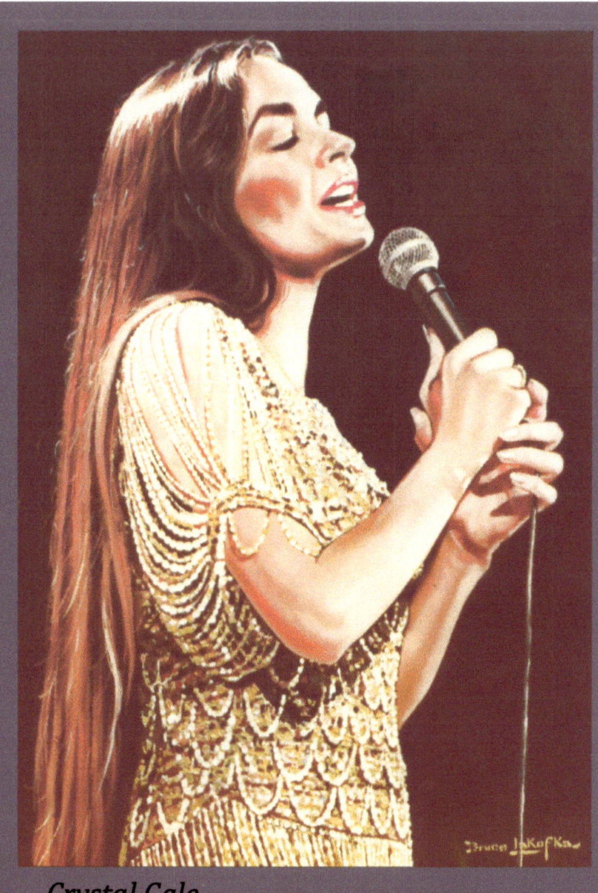
Crystal Gale

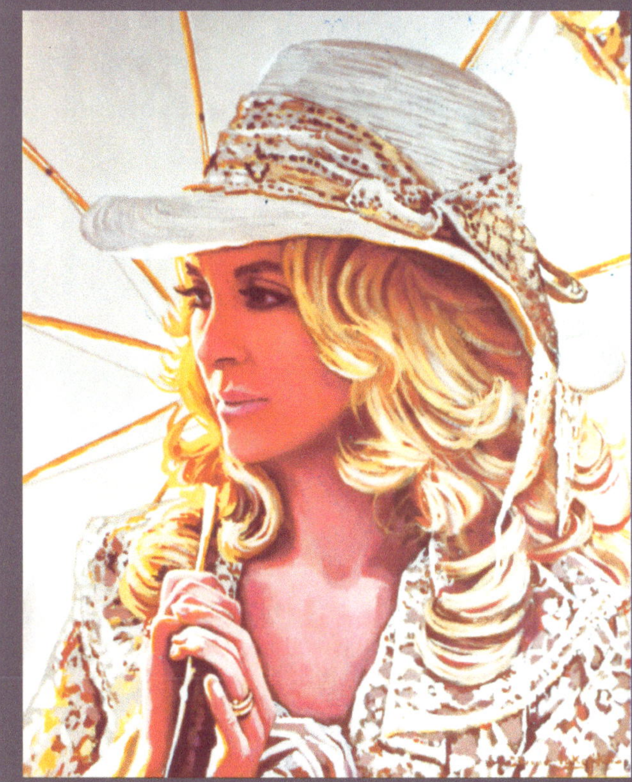
Tammy Wynette

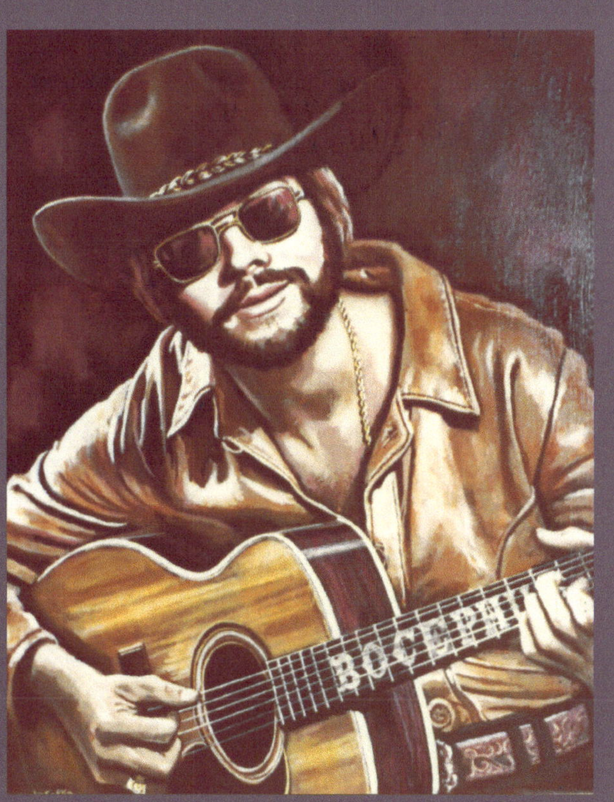
Hank Williams, Jr.

Gifts From

THE COUNTRY MUSIC HALL OF FAME & MUSEUM

Nashville, Tennessee

"THE KING LIVES ON"
Bruce Lakofka brings to life the days of Elvis Presley: the boy, the man, the King of Rock and Roll! A true reproduction of an original painting. 24" × 27".
(S9-244) $5.98 (1.00)

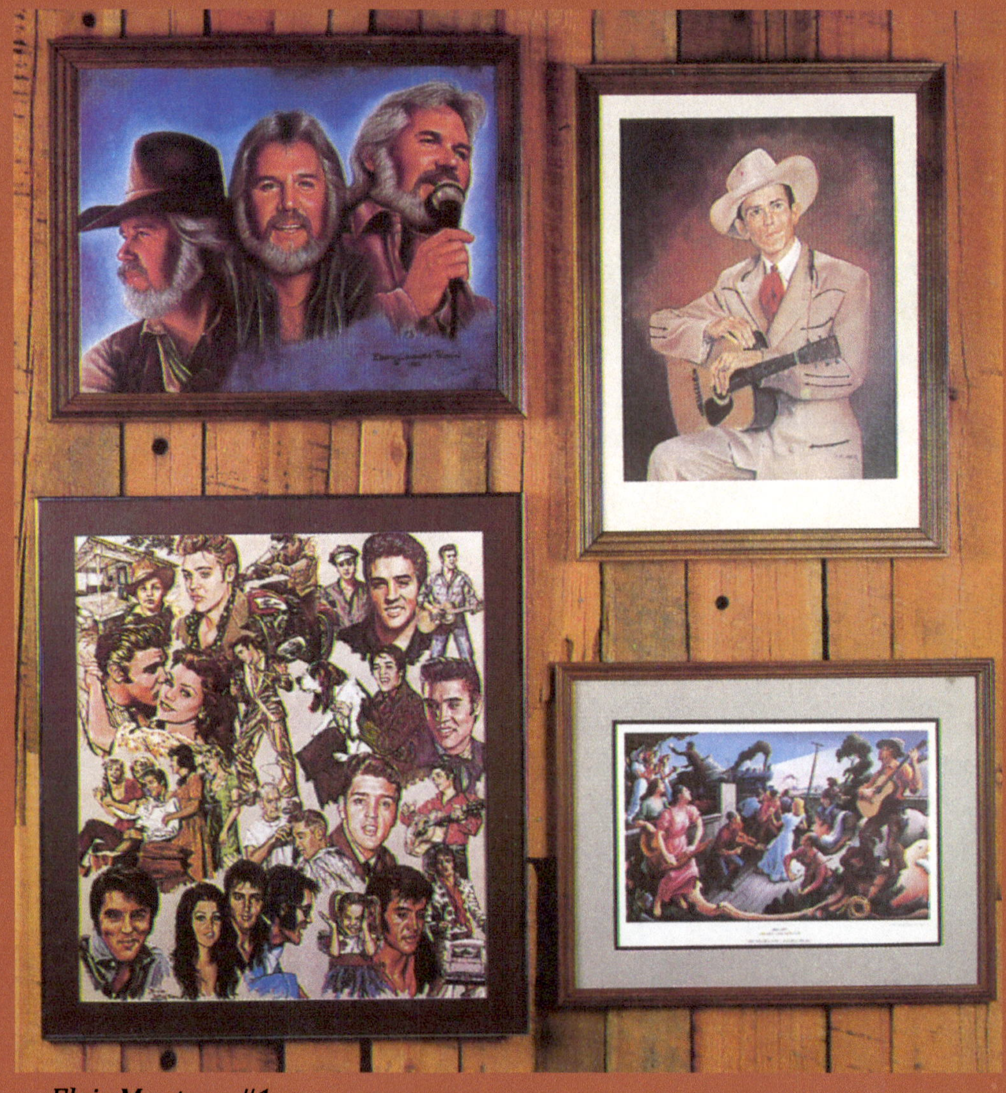

Elvis Montage #1

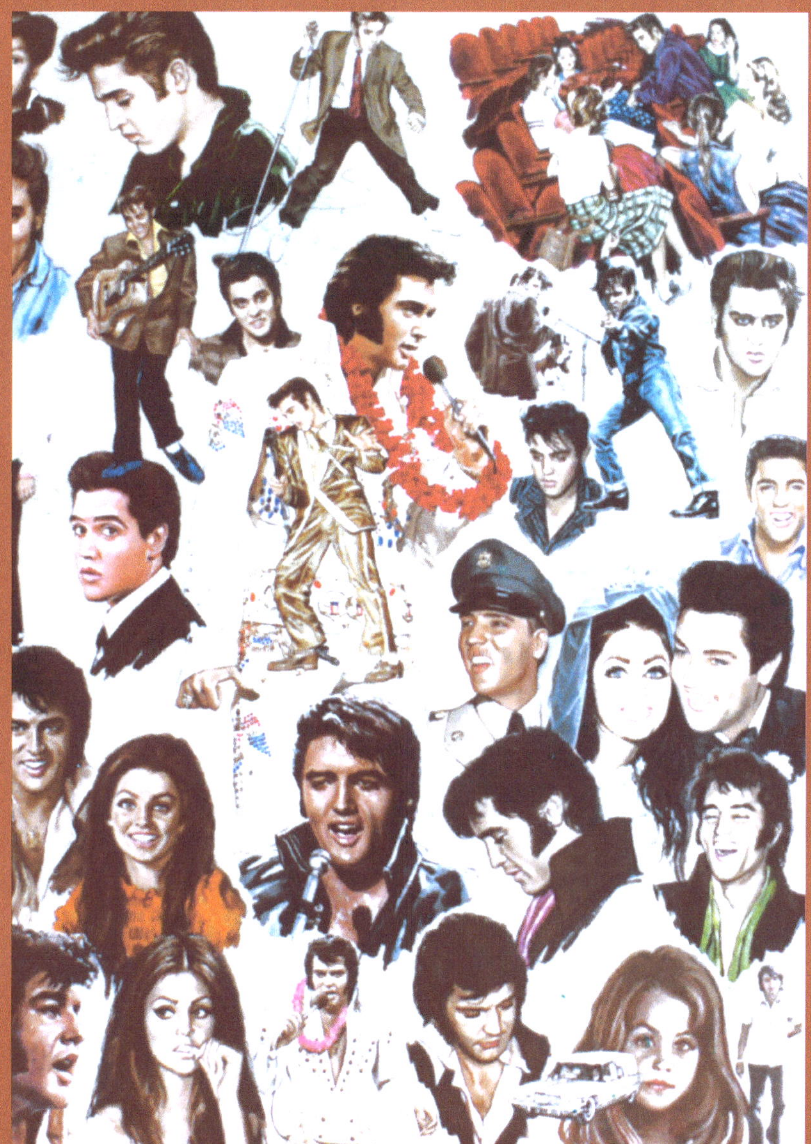

Elvis Montage #2

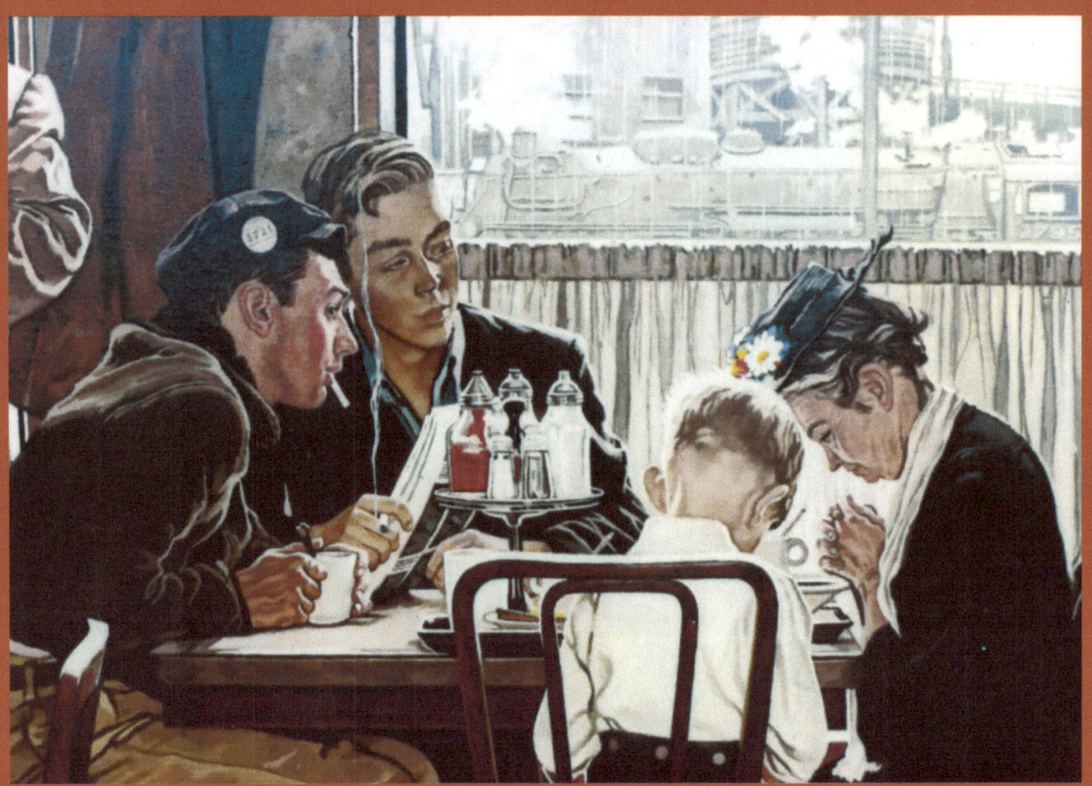

Copy of Rockwell's "Saying Grace"

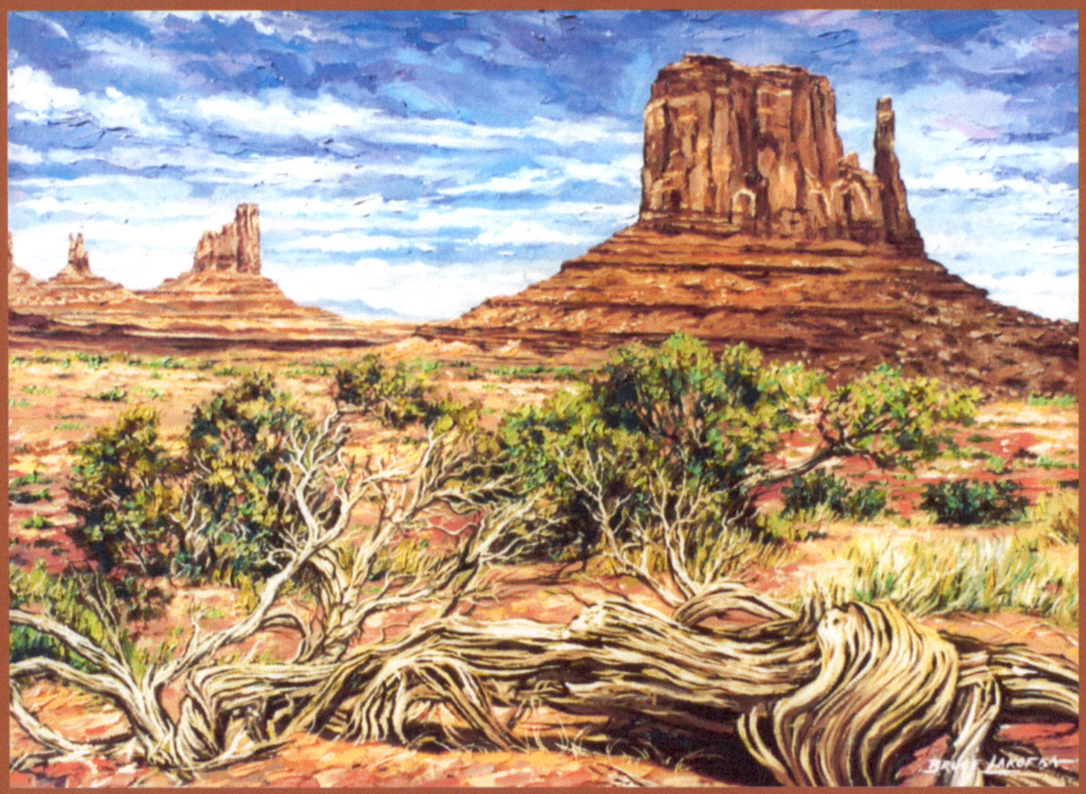

Monument Valley

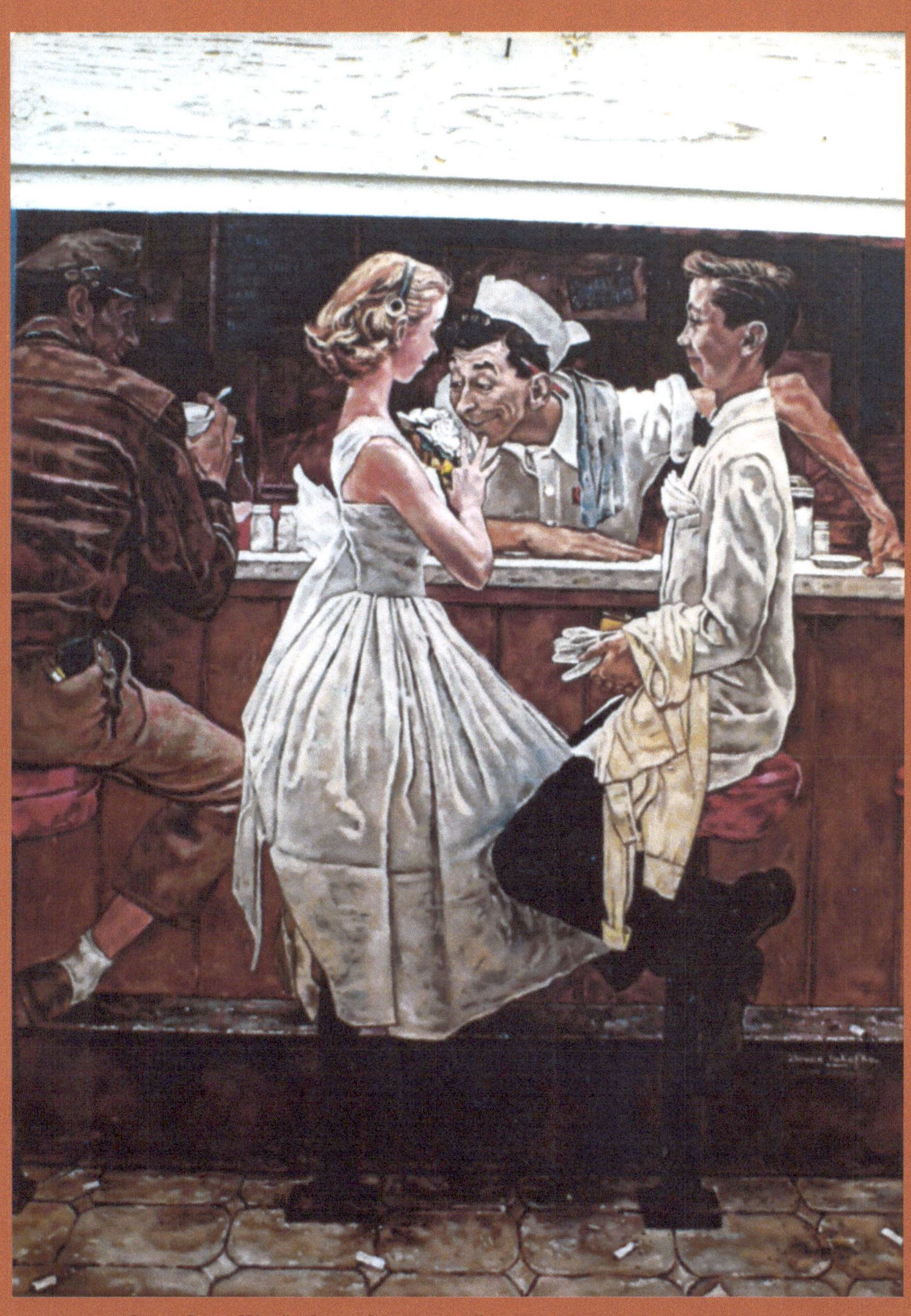

Copy of Rockwell's "After the Prom"

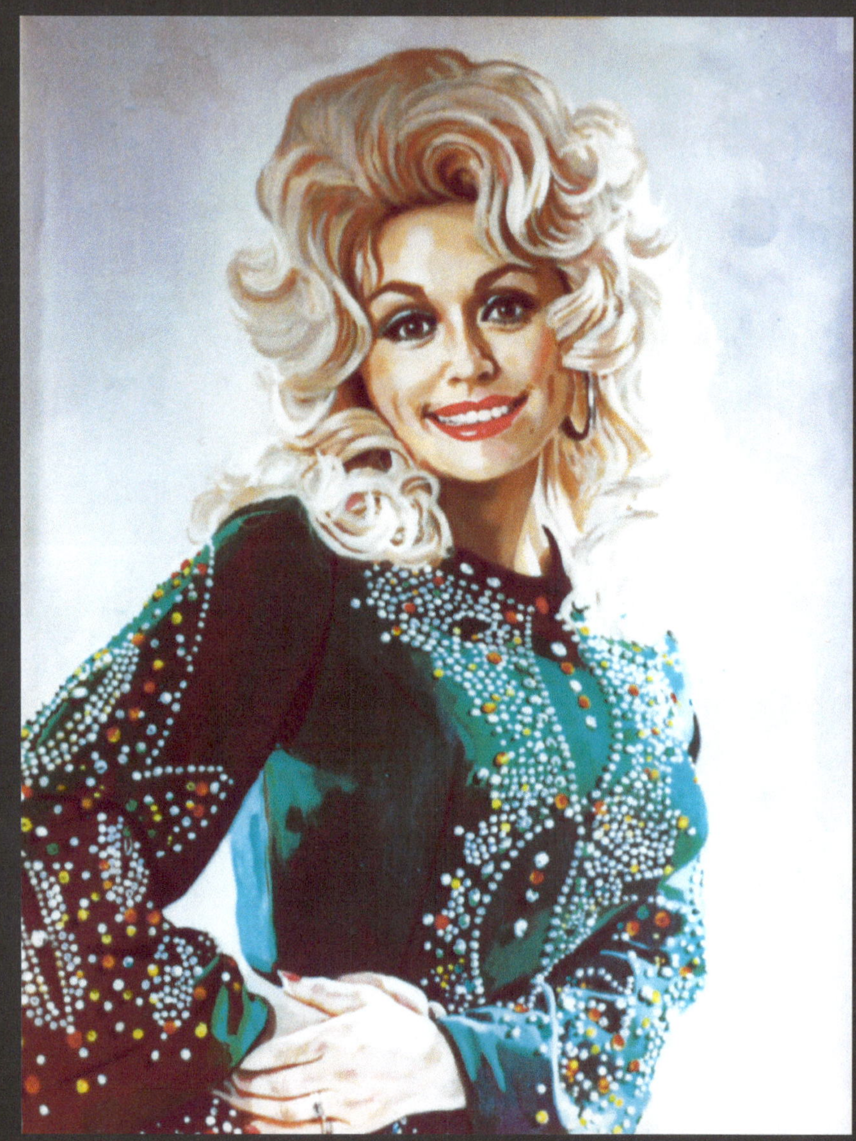

Dolly Parton

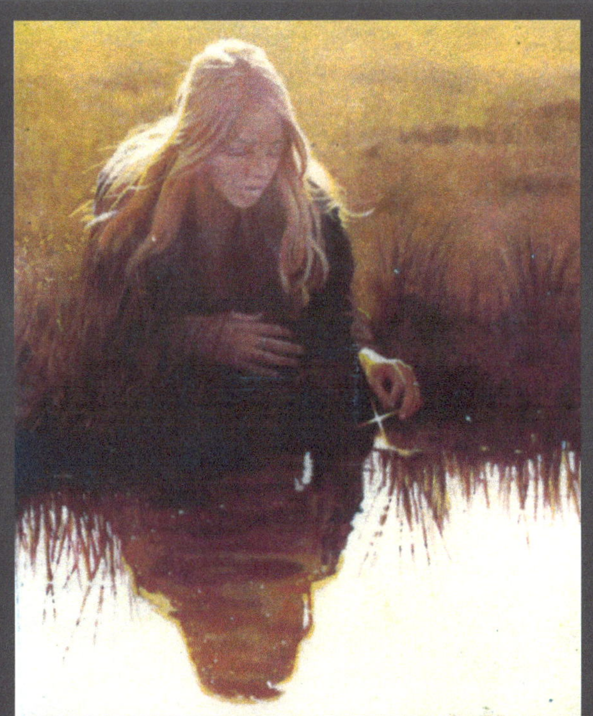

Sailing the Pond

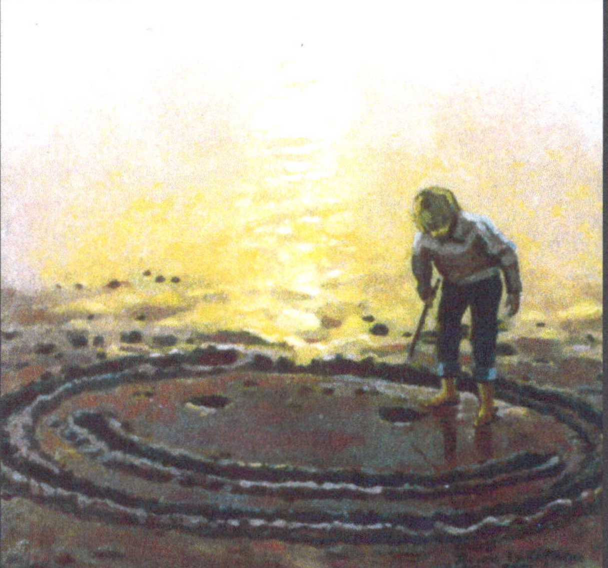

Face in the Sand

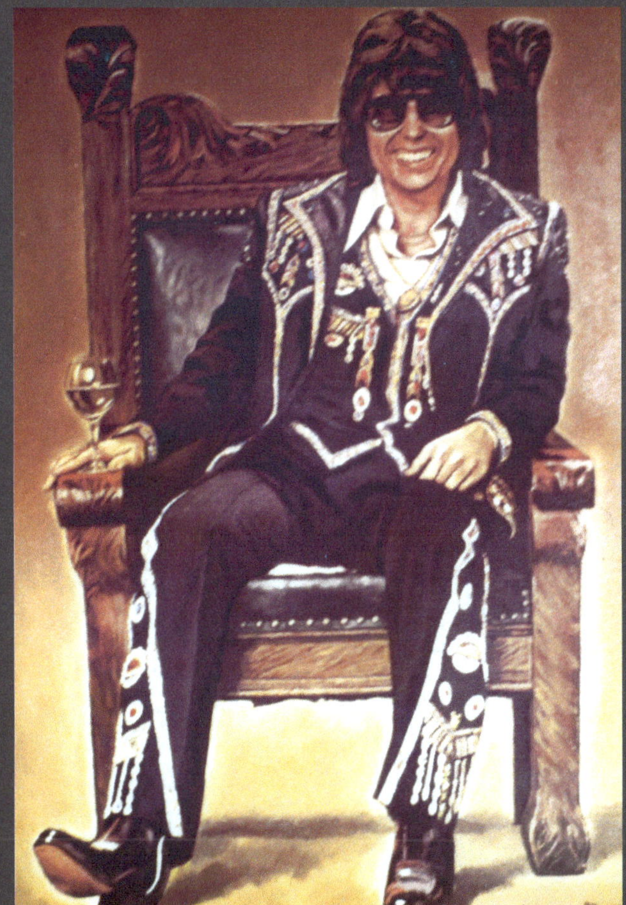

Ronnie Milsap

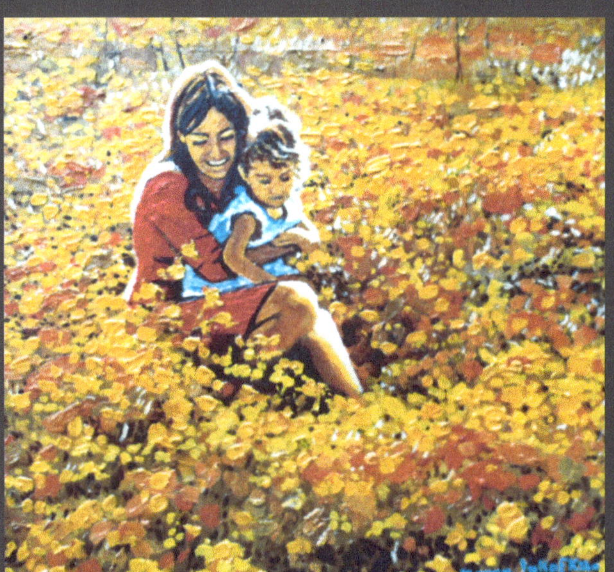

Mom and Kid in Flowers

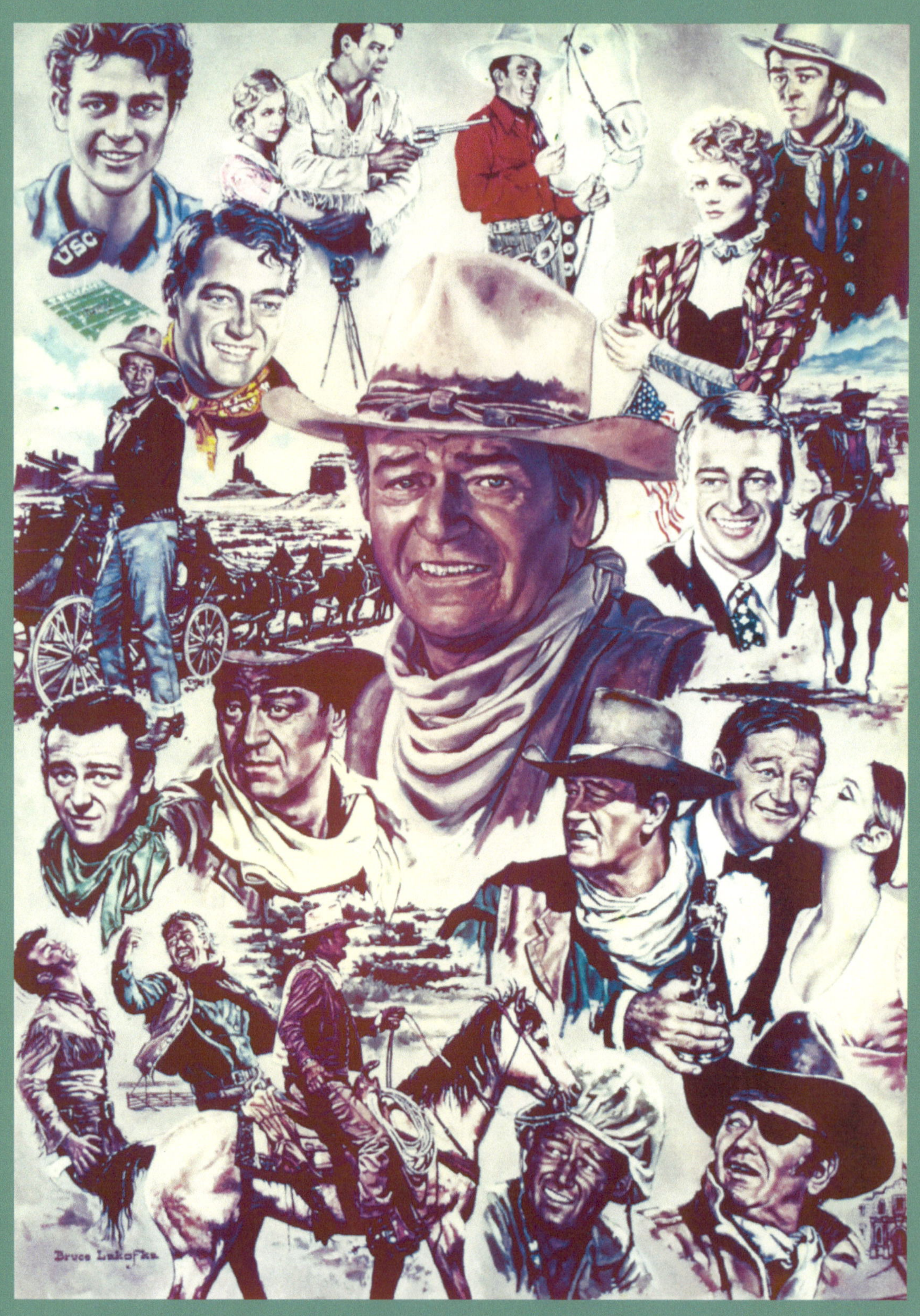

John Wayne Montage

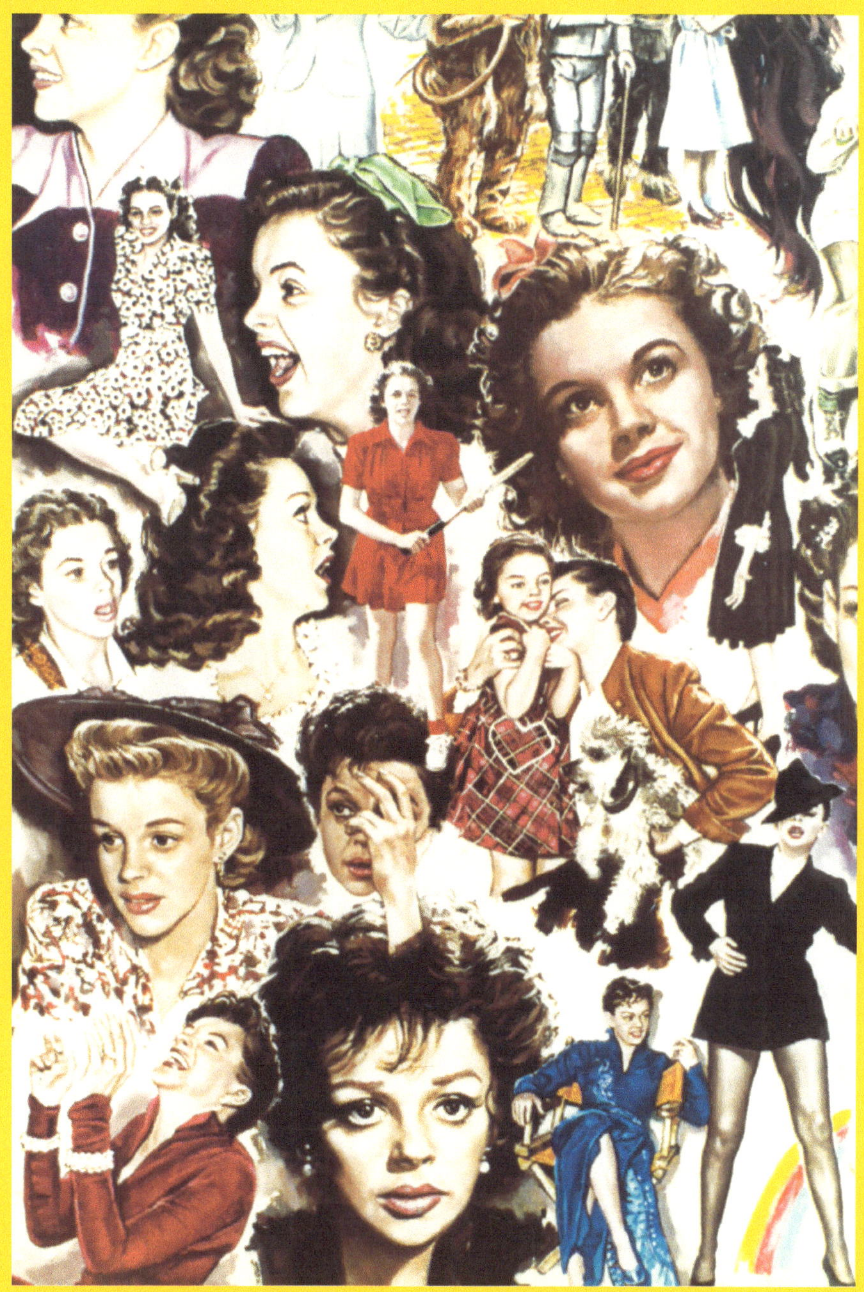

Judy Garland Montage

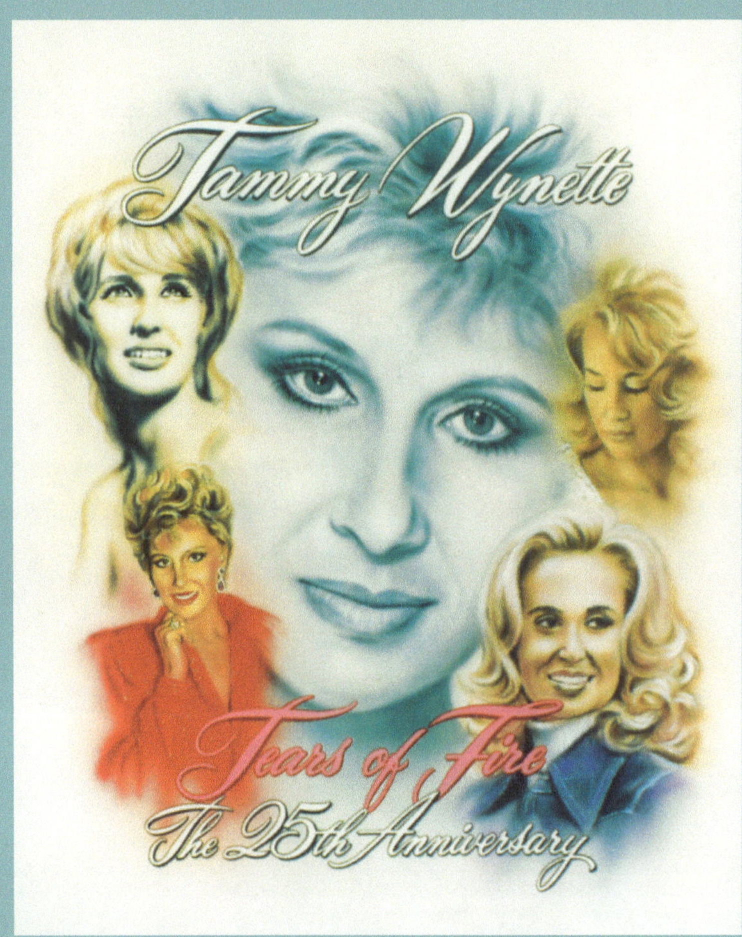

Tammy Wynette, Tears of Fire, 25th Album Cover

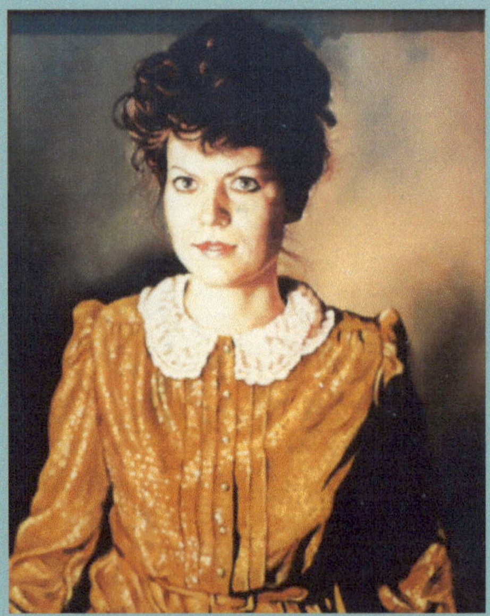

Portrait of Brenda

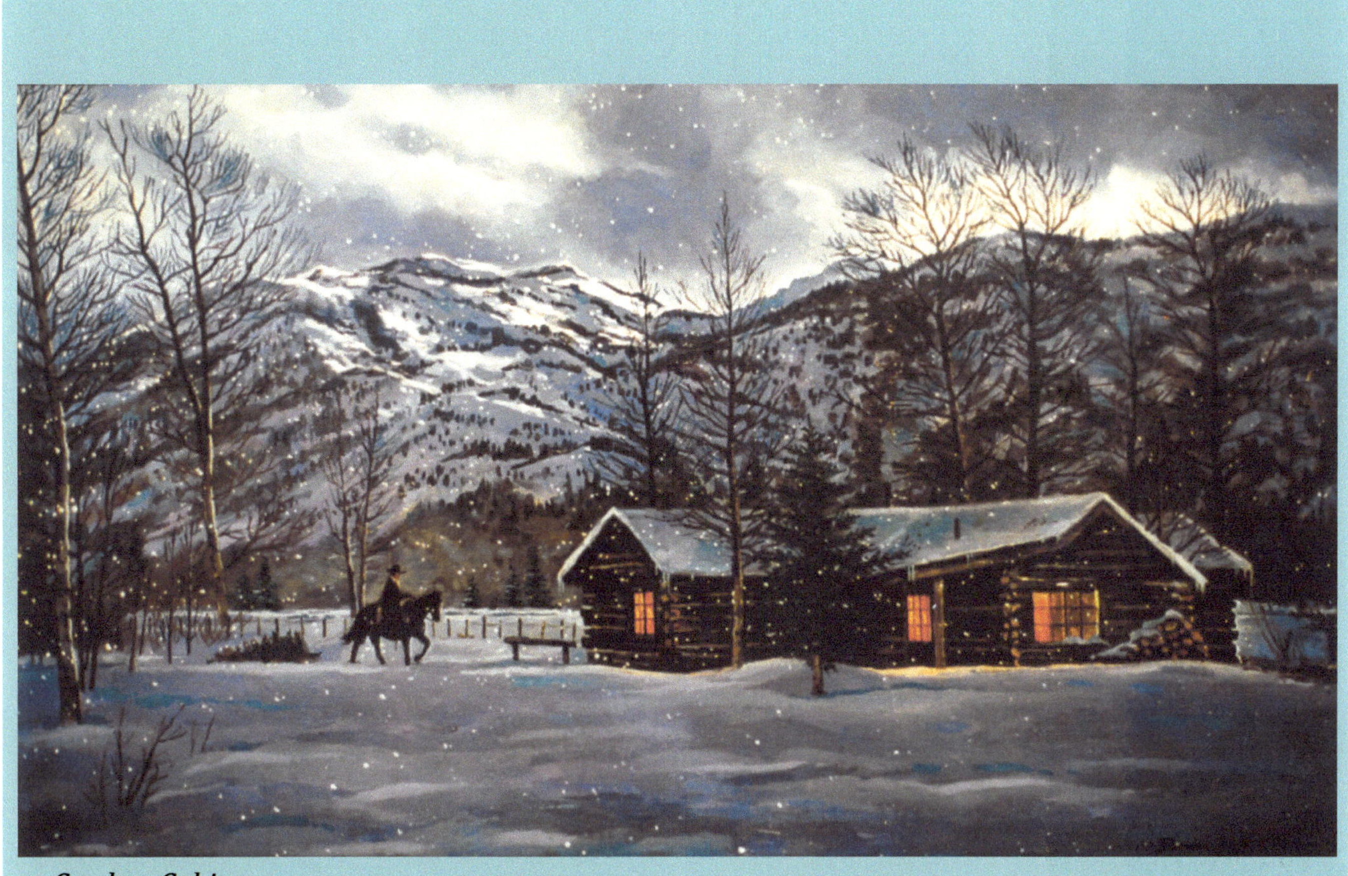

Cowboy Cabin

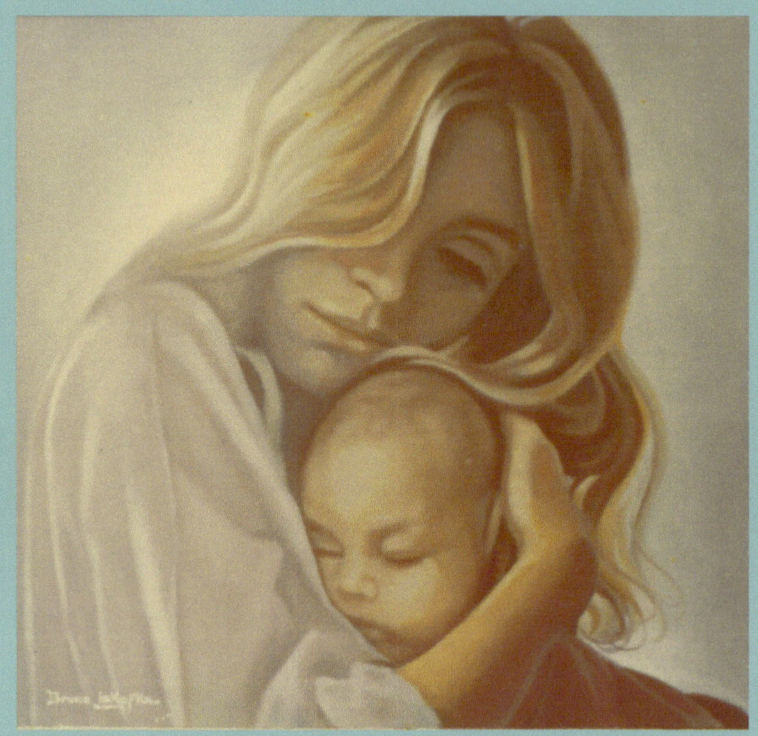

Mother Love

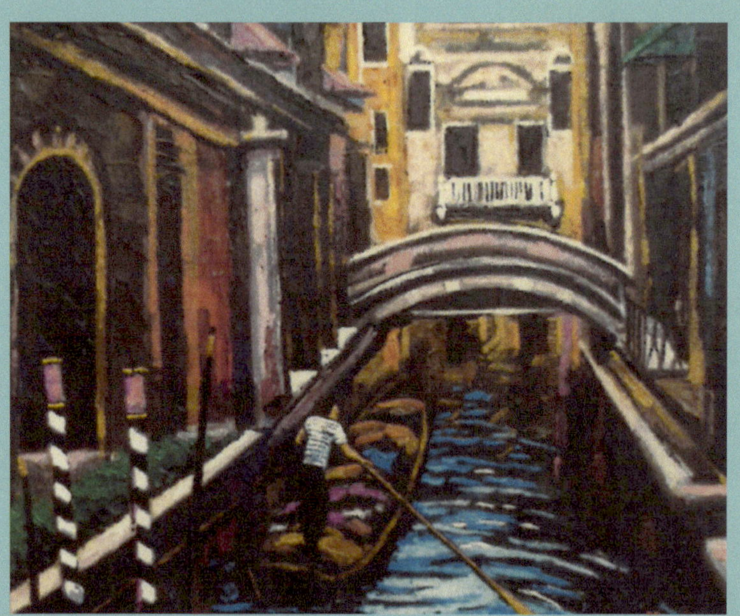

Gondolieri

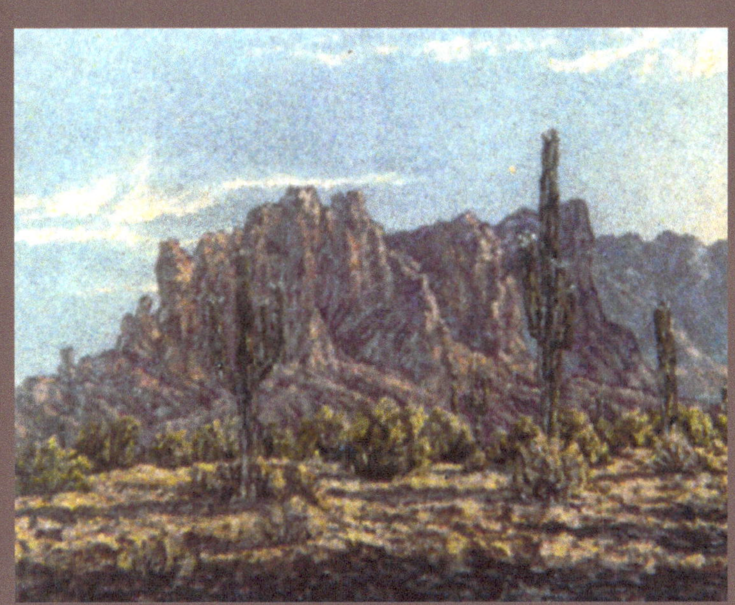

Saguaros

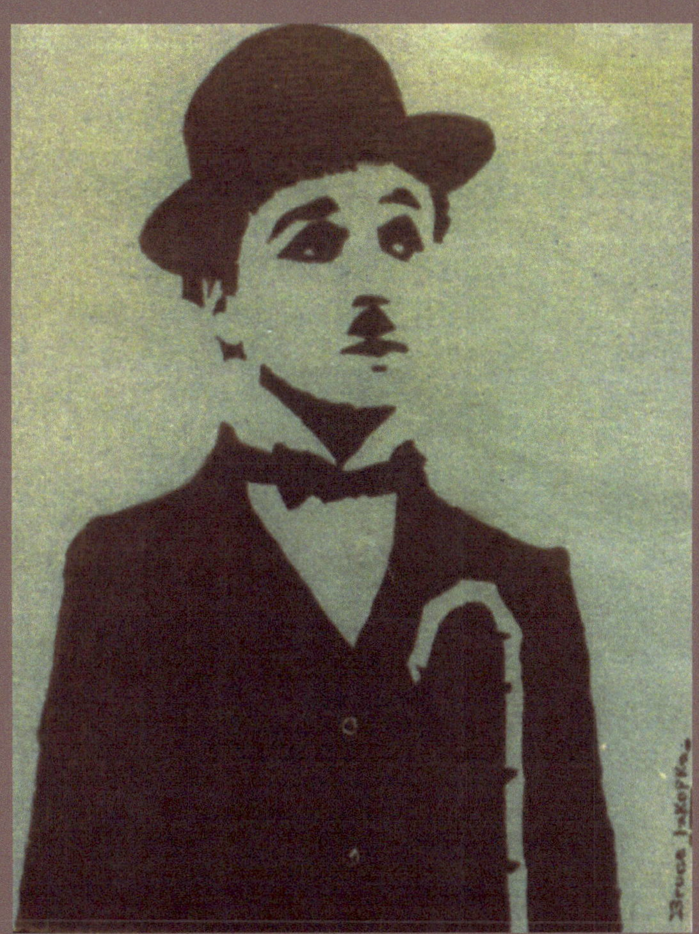

Chaplin

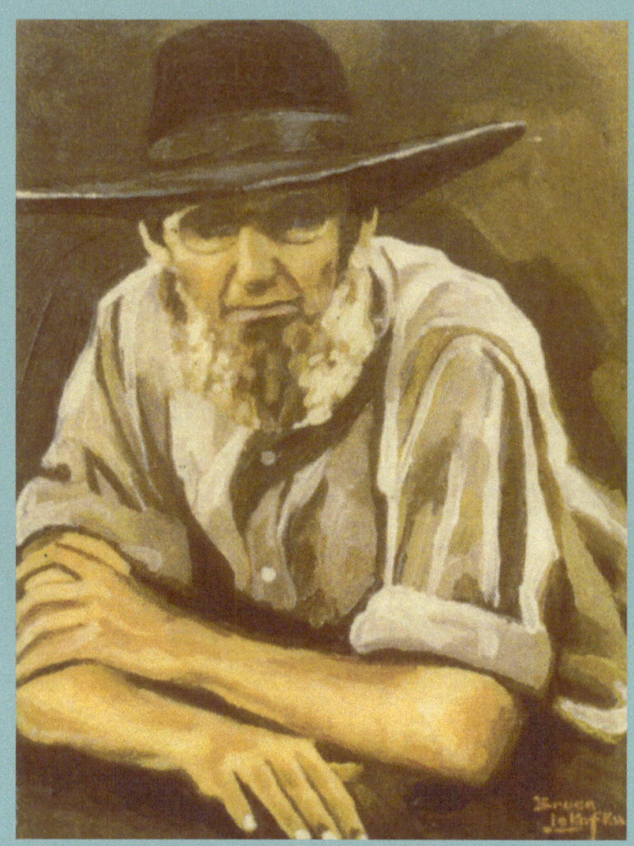

Amish Man

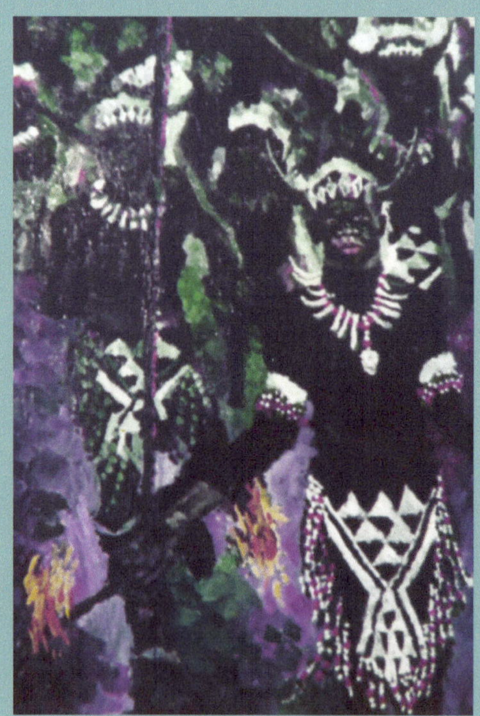

Voodoo Man

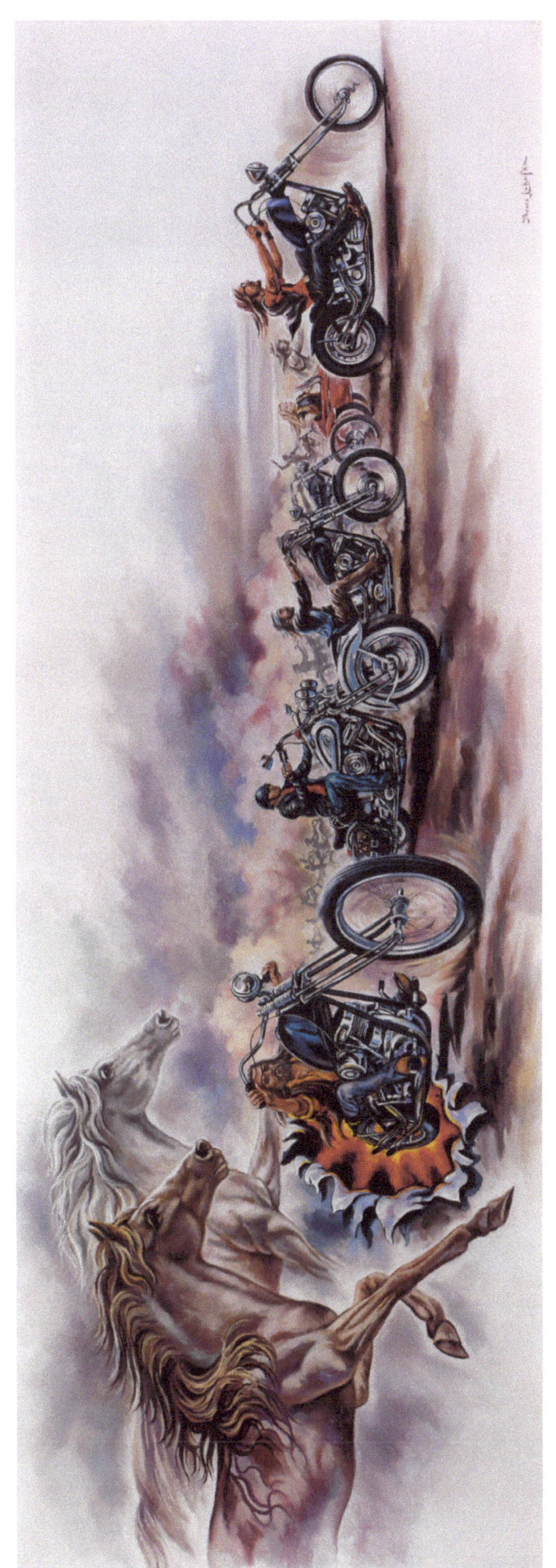

Horsepower

~ 3 ~

Bruce's 38 "Best" Oil Paintings with Commentary

What's to be said about these thirty-eight paintings in the aggregate? If life were fair, all of them should now reside in an art museum, or high-end art gallery, church or synagogue, Indian museum, sports or corporate office, art gallery of an art school, or in the home of well-to-do art lovers. Alas, I suspect most of them are still orphans, but that is not my focus here. Enough to say that this is art of the finest caliber. Let this book be your personal art museum where the best of Bruce is reproduced for your permanent enjoyment.

Las Vegas: The Rat Pack Years: This is a tremendous conceptualization of Las Vegas, the place and the legend; and the movie and entertainment figures who defined that period in history. Bravissimo.

Be a Clown: Another spectacular montage painting. Is there a clown school somewhere? If there is, this should be hanging in their lobby as a primer of how to make a clown face.

Sweet Dreams: What does a little girl dream of? Fairies and angels, horses, polar bears, benign lions, castles, comets and rainbows. And lots more. A great and beautiful, joyful concoction.

Wild Earth: For those that love the wild, this is a potpourri of lovely images. Our neighbors on planet earth, at least for now.

Meow: The Cat Family: For those who love cats, especially those of the wild, this is a visual treat. And a test of your natural history knowledge. Bruce did a lot of research here before he started painting.

Iloni: The painting is sort of a road map to that secret part of the Congo you won't find on any current day map. It portrays the unbelievable events and strange people of all species, who all came together there for an intergalactic event that should have put Iloni on the map, if it had wished it.

The Prayer: She is praying with great earnestness to the Great Spirit. This painting and the others in this section show Bruce accorded Native Americans' religious beliefs the same seriousness as Judaism and Christianity.

Israel: This is a spectacular and respectful montage showing both the old Israel of the Old Testament and the new. There is Moses and the children of Israel and the Burning Bush and many other images from Jewish religious history. An astounding biblical painting, whether you are Jewish, Christian or something else.

Tradition: Bruce's reverence for Jewish religious tradition and history shows in this intelligent, tasteful, thoughtful, and beautiful painting.

Fallen Comrade: Bruce painted this picture before-during the Vietnam War. This "update" (because our soldiers still die in far-flung places) he has imbued with a powerful Christian solace. Even if you are not Christian or a soldier, this man's pain touches you. That's what a master painter does.

A Mother's Prayer: Stunning, reverent, beautiful. What more needs to be said about this respectful image?

Shenandoah: The background for this lovely Indian maiden is unusual. Originally, Bruce conceived this as a portrait of Sacagawea, who guided the Lewis and Clark Expedition. Instead, he titled it after the Virginia Valley whose name is synonymous with beauty and bountifulness. I think he did right in changing the title. Bruce told me paintings often "evolved" as he was painting them. What has also evolved is the function of painters in our society. C. M. Russell painted Sacagawea using sign language to communicate with the Chinooks in a rustic tableau. Painters often painted famous historical events or battles and were considered adjuncts to historians, a function now taken by photographers and correspondents.

Morning Light: This is Bruce's "Mona Lisa." It is just as good as the original, maybe better. I have seen the original up close in the days before they put it behind bulletproof glass and high security. Famous paintings are not necessarily spectacular, they are just famous. The 20th century deserves its own "Mona Lisa" and this is it. With its studio wrap it looks striking on a white wall. Look at the eyes and the smile.

Fourth Down and Inches: This is the best painting I have ever seen portraying the spirit of football, our national pastime and madness. Simple but brilliant.

Moon-jumping: This is a celebration of skateboarders, their daring, skill and craziness. A cosmic sports painting. Chuck Yeager would understand it.

Soccer Ballet: A photographer might get lucky and snap this image in a lucky split second but to paint four bodies (and a ball and their shadows) in motion takes great skill.

Dance of Tradition: The authenticity of the costumes may be in doubt here but the earnestness and reverence of the dancers is not. Like Rockwell, Bruce made them more spectacular than they really are. Enjoy.

The Last Reservation: Although not as well-known as "Spirit" this painting has been referred to in the text for its ecological and cultural foresight. Bruce had a deep understanding of how Indians depended on Mother Earth (and its buffalo) for their physical livelihood and spiritual health. They adapted to the reservation system to save some vestige of their culture. Maybe he was saying our society has worked us onto our own sad "last reservation" if we find life is native to only this planet and we have killed off most of it making earth a tame, overcrowded human park where man rules and Mother Nature weeps. This is a deep and haunting painting.

One with the Sky: In this painting, Bruce celebrates how Indians lived (more closely than we do) under the big sky, day as well as night. Using circle of life motifs, spectacular planetary and astronomical depictions, thunderbird motifs, and geometric designs, he created a cosmic painting of great beauty.

Spirit of the Full Moon: A full moon, an Indian teepee encampment, and Indian chief in the foreground. Swirls of color and Indian symbols and designs. This combination made an unforgettable image and one which people the world over related to on an aesthetic and reverential basis.

Thanks for the Memories (Bob Hope): This is a lovely testament to the many faces and talents of a much-loved American comic and personality. A tour-de-force.

Bouquet of Kittens: Kittens and roses, what a combination. Note the kitten that's spotted the butterfly. Enchanting and delightful.

The Rival: This painting, unlike the two early Rockwell copies that Bruce did (discussed in Chapter 2), is inspired by Rockwell but is Bruce's own creation. The painting tells a cute little tale. Read it.

The Dance: Every good painter tries to do a ballet picture. It is sort of like a test of skills and coming of age. This painting is as good as any of the ballet pictures I saw in the galleries of Europe.

Doll Friends: This painting is a doll-collector's dream. A spectacular rendering with a subtle twist of humor. Some of their expressions seem so alive.

Southern Cross: This painting was discussed in some detail in the text of Chapter 1. It was commissioned by a couple whose daughter married into a family descended from the Lees of Virginia. Usually commissions go to famous painters. How did Bruce get it? The father of the young lady went to high school with Bruce and his brother, Bob. They often came over to watch Bruce paint in his mother's garage in Pomona in the 60s. When the painting was needed in 2006, the father tracked Bruce down to give him the commission. This is a powerful painting but simple, the work of a modern day master.

The Smell of Summer Flowers: Another example of a painting simple in concept (lavishly embellished). Children and flowers. And that trademark innocence.

Wish Upon a Star: Another example of a painting so simple in concept but so effective. Who among us never looked out at the stars and made a wish?

Rain, Rain, Go Away: As pointed out in the text, this is a "revisiting" of an earlier image (#105) in the old paintings. Despite their similarities, each is different. Look at that wistful child and notice how Bruce worked a lot of color into this rainy day tableau.

The Tire Swing: So simple in concept, yet so effective. A classic painting of childhood joy and innocence.

Children of the Great Spirit: There is so much joy and beauty in this painting that it radiates happiness. The images are authentic, lovely, and diverse. A great trip.

Wreath of Joy: Santa is a lover of all children of all races and color. Look at those faces. What detail. What joy.

World of Imagination: This is a celebration of childhood and the fairy tales and other adventure bedtime stories that fuel the dreams of youth. A truly lovely conceptualization. The children here used as models are the artist's own.

Back in the Fifties: This is a beautiful evocation of that period, for those of us who were there and remember. Sure, it is a bit idealized and the teenagers look so innocent, but so what? Maybe we need painters to remind us that teenagers are still children and not small adults; they need to hold onto sixteen as long as they can.

The Competitor: This is the flip side (speaking gender-wise) of "The Rival" (#23) with the same little tale to tell. Bruce believed in a lady's right to ride the horse too.

Moonbeams: This is a crazy painting. It reminds me of Hieronymus Bosch but on the glad side, not the sad, dark side of reality. What are the secrets of a young girl's heart? Why shouldn't she dream of girl angels? Enough with those boy angel/cherubs. Pixies and fairy dust: those are girl things.

Christ and the Children: When Bruce first told me he was working on a painting about the biblical passage, "Suffer the children to come unto me," I thought, "Wow, that would be a daunting task." Having read most of the Bible, I knew that passage. When I saw the painting eleven years later, I thought immediately that he got it all right; the title, a sunny Jesus, and truly happy children. This is not the Jesus of the Pieta and the flagellants, but the other Jesus. Such radiant smiles—what a painting.

Lions, Tigers and Bears...OH MY!: My first impression of this startling painting was that Bruce had crammed too much into it. Then I realized that was the point of the painting, as it was the point of the actors' lines from the *Wizard of Oz* movie. As mentioned in the text, Bruce looked everywhere for effective painting titles, even popular American culture. This was a winner.

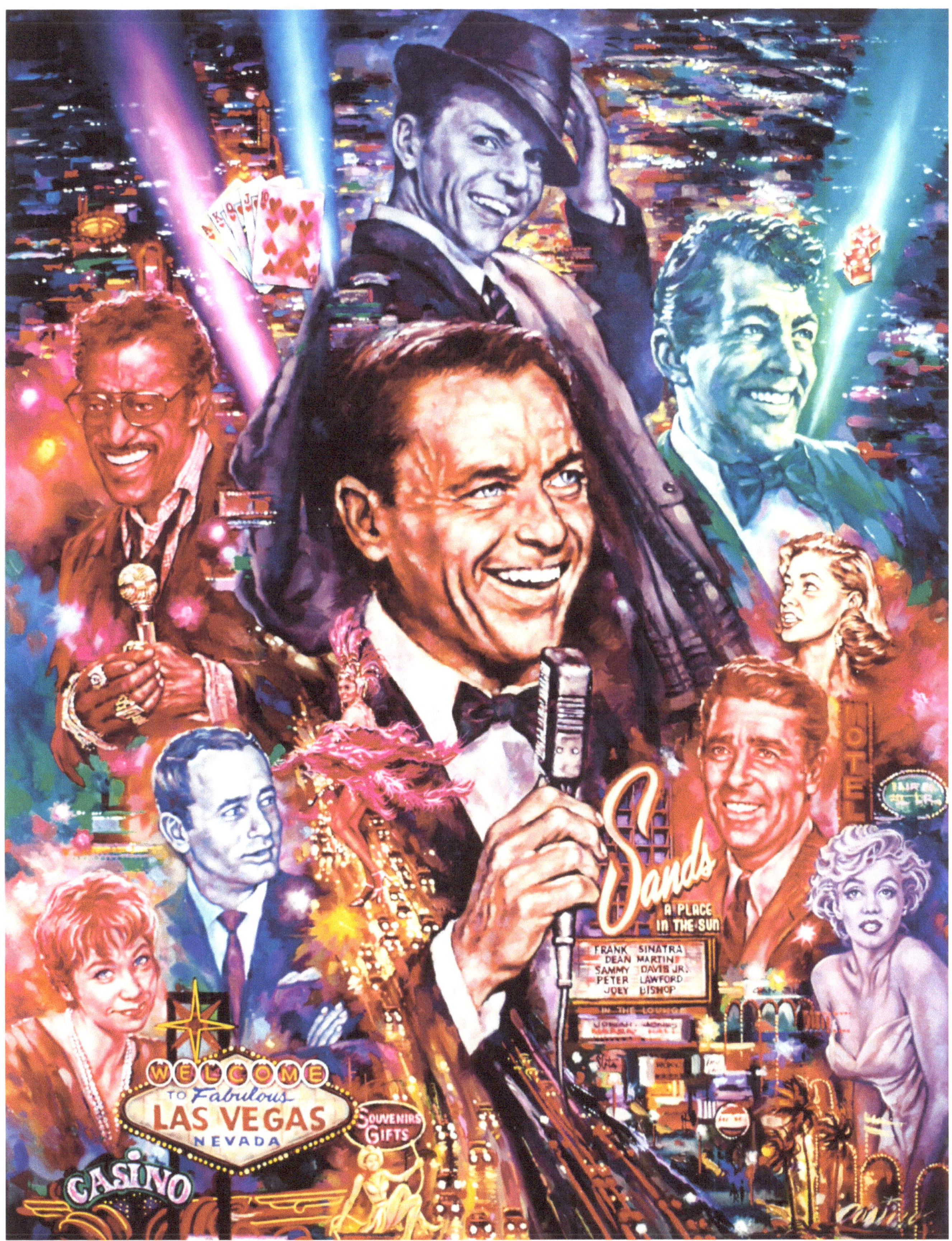

Las Vegas: The Rat Pack Years

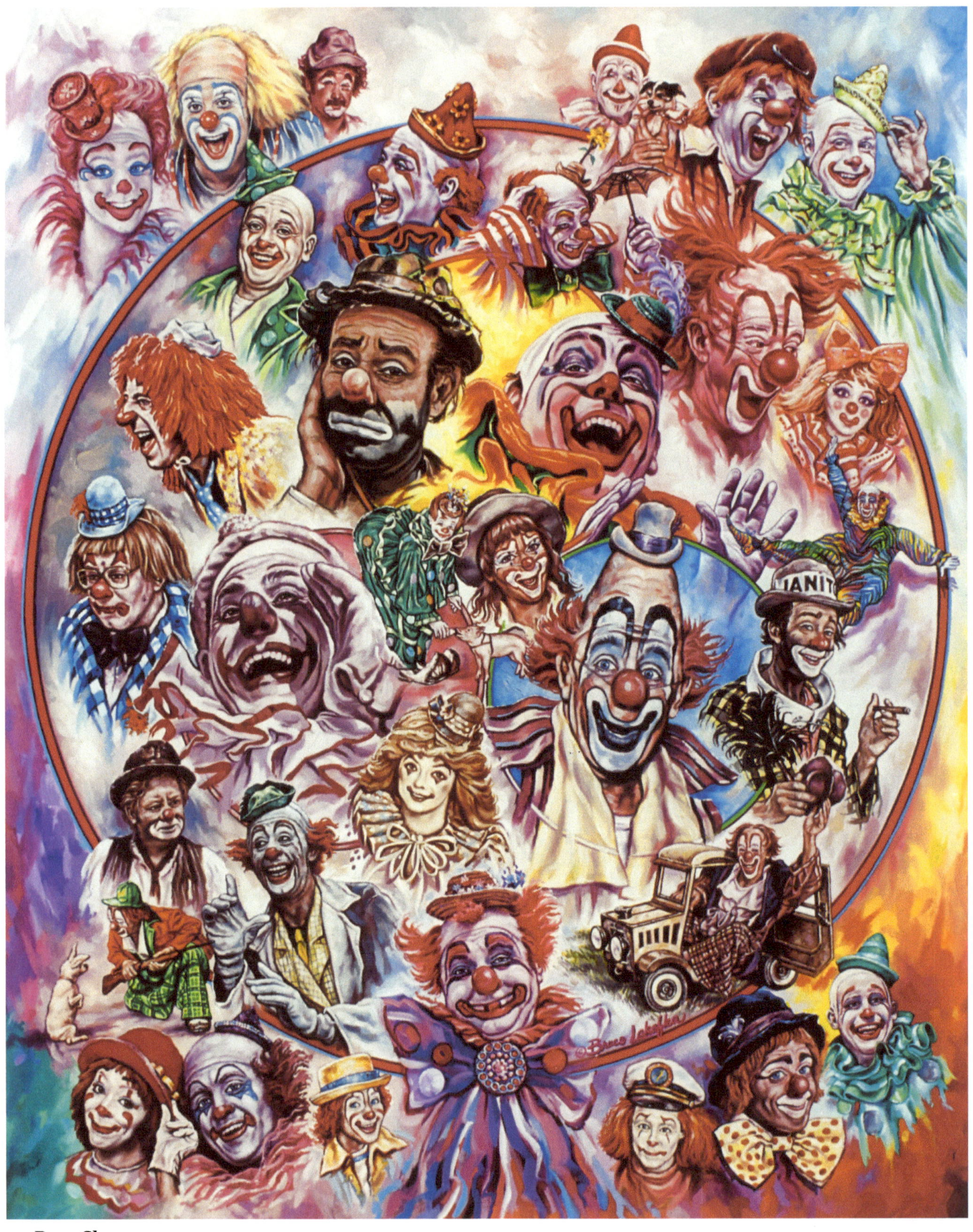

Be a Clown

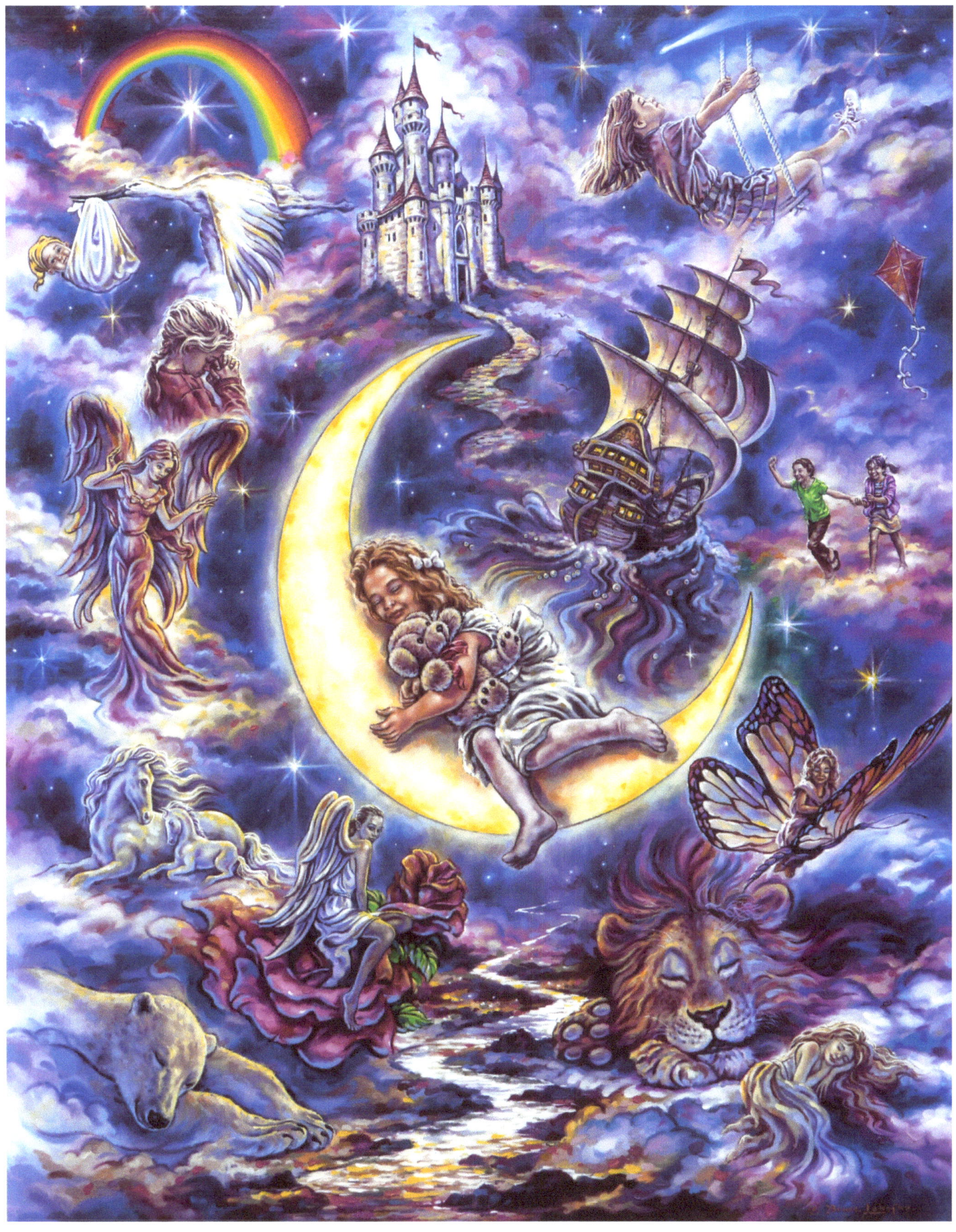

Sweet Dreams

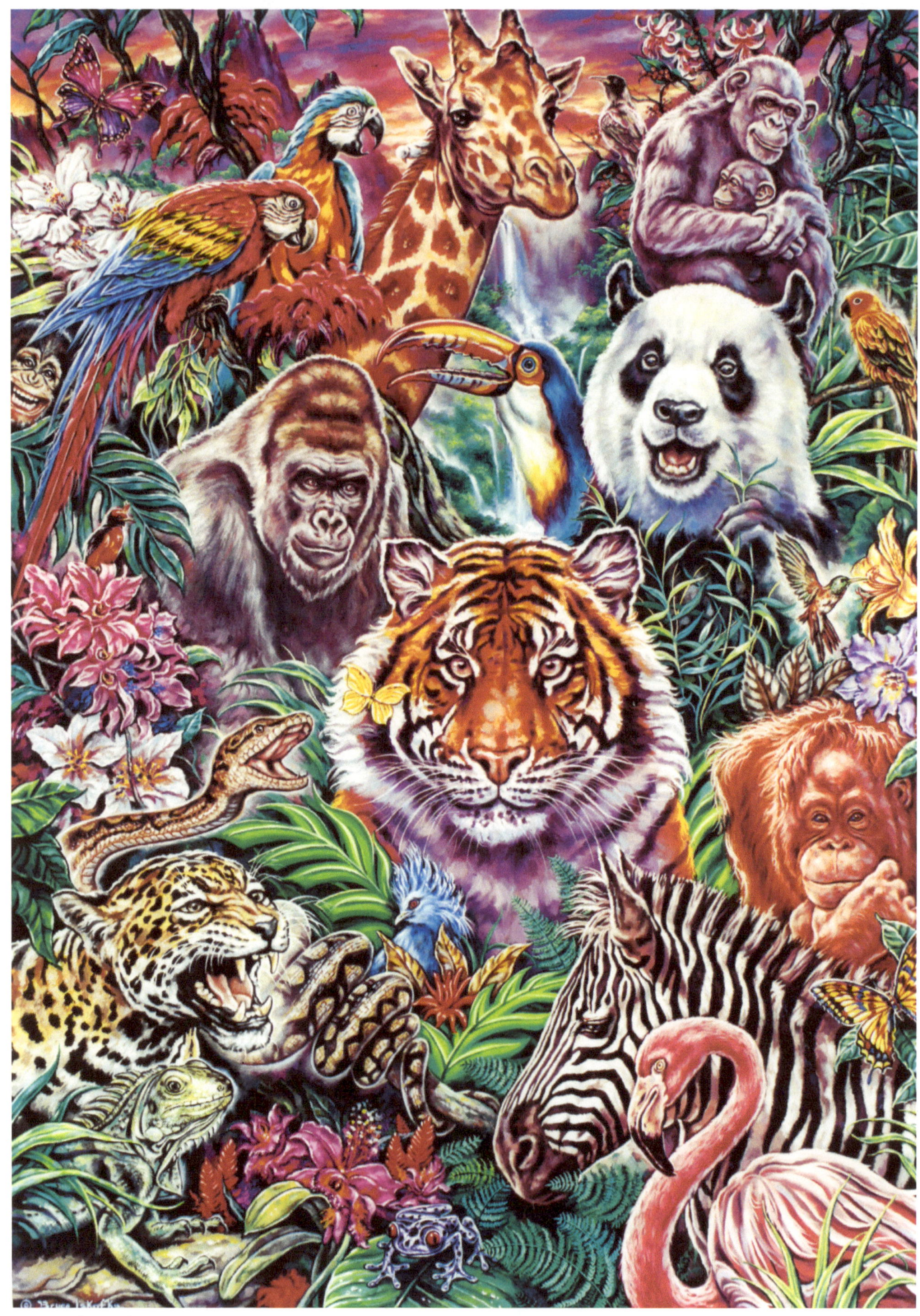

Wild Earth

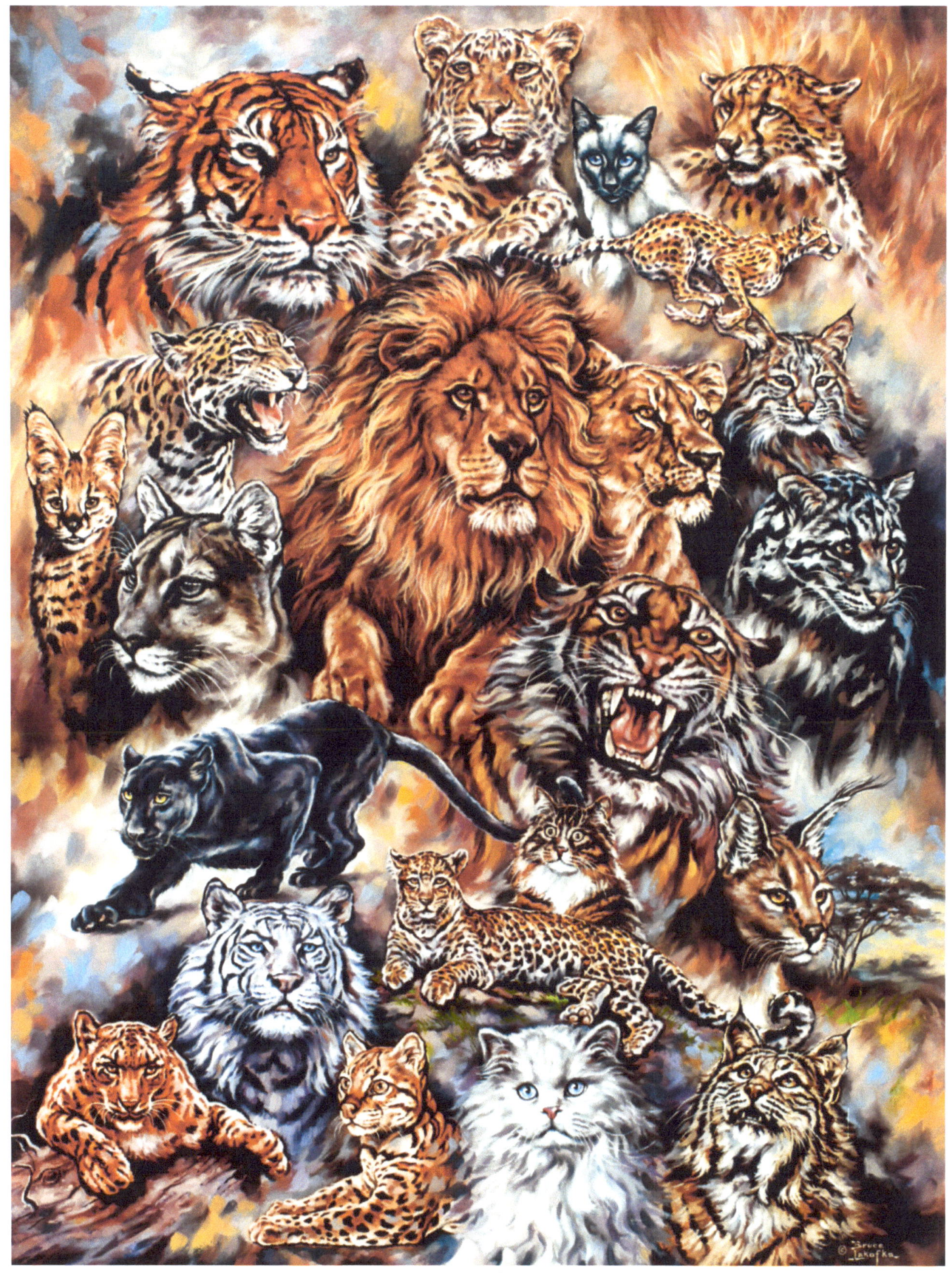

Meow: The Cat Family

ILONI
CONGO
TO KISANGANI (very far)
Makoto
RT. 61
Kipulo
X Primatologist Camp
ILONI
LAKE VICTORIA
(White Nile)
River
BARKERVILLE
China Grill
Illidongo
RWANDA
CONGO RIVER
ROUTE 61
KINSHASA

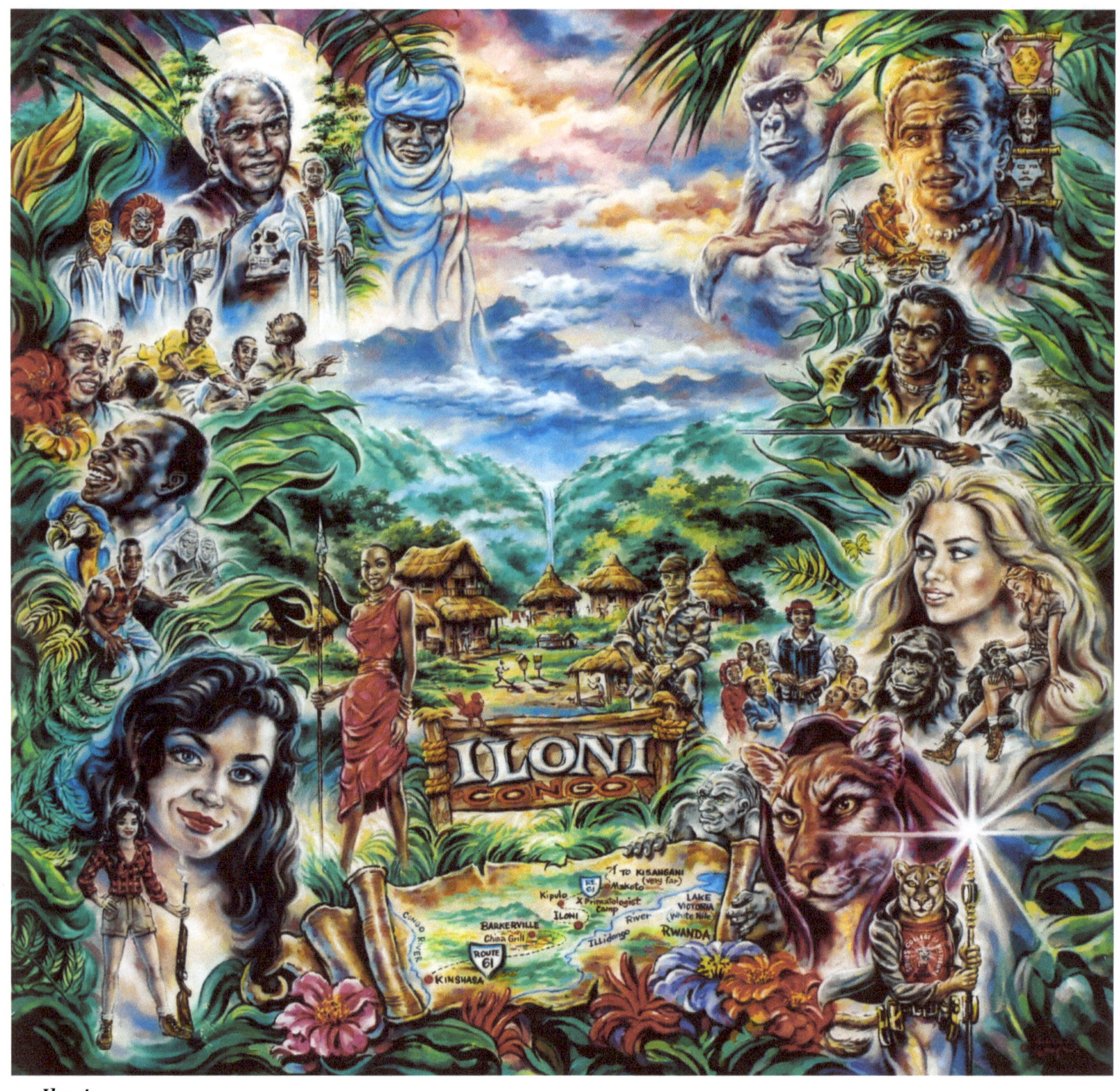

Iloni

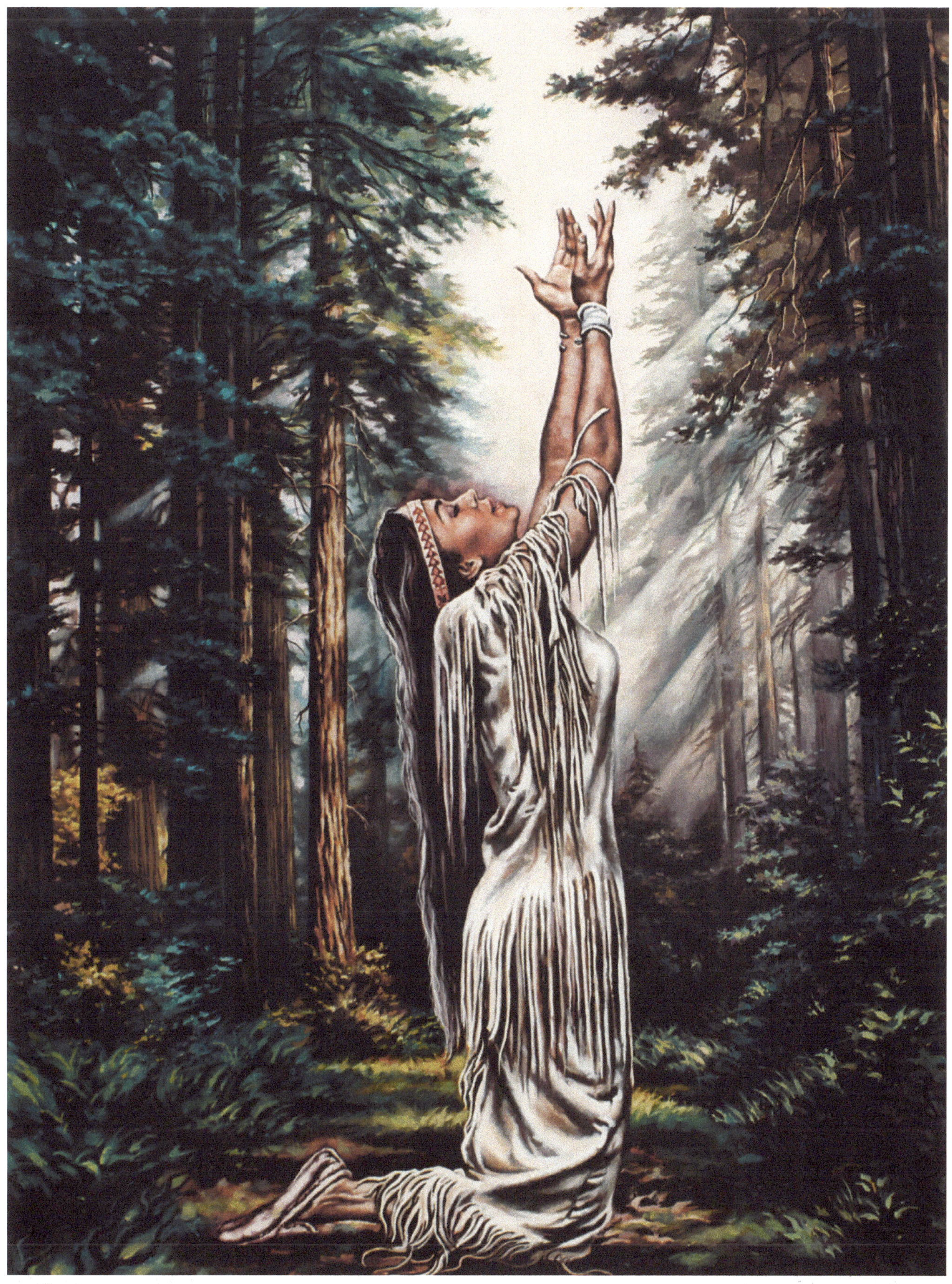

The Prayer

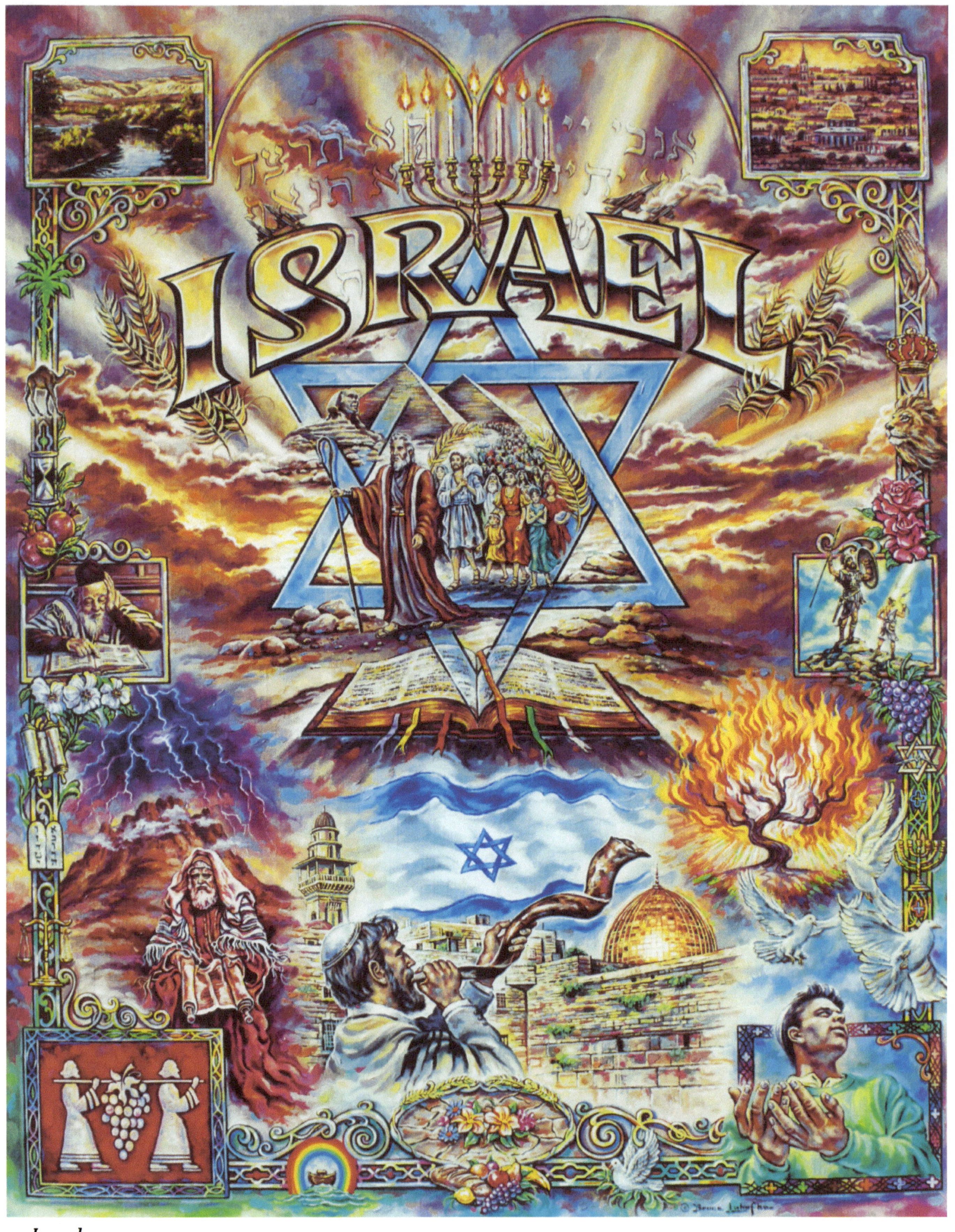

Israel

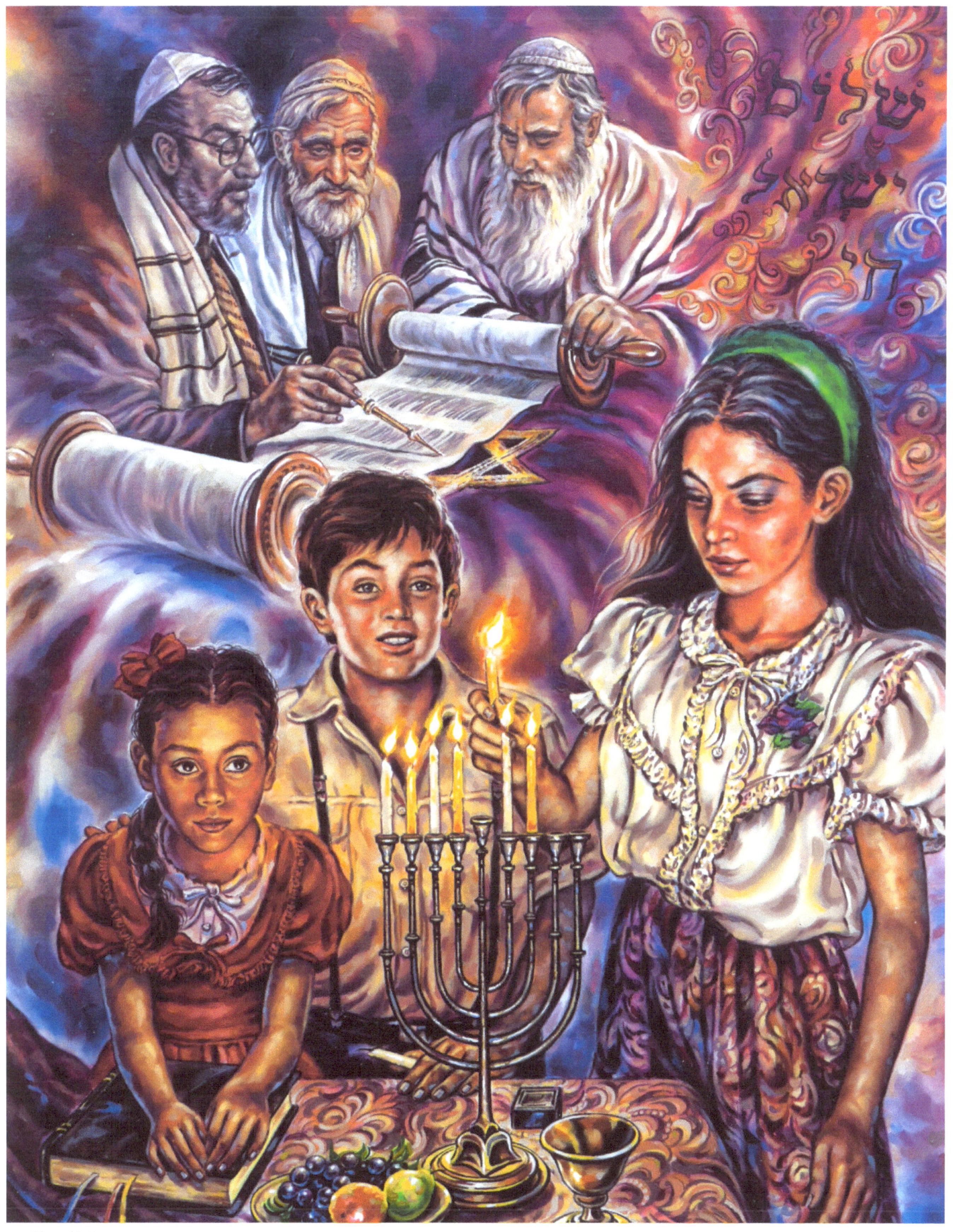

Tradition

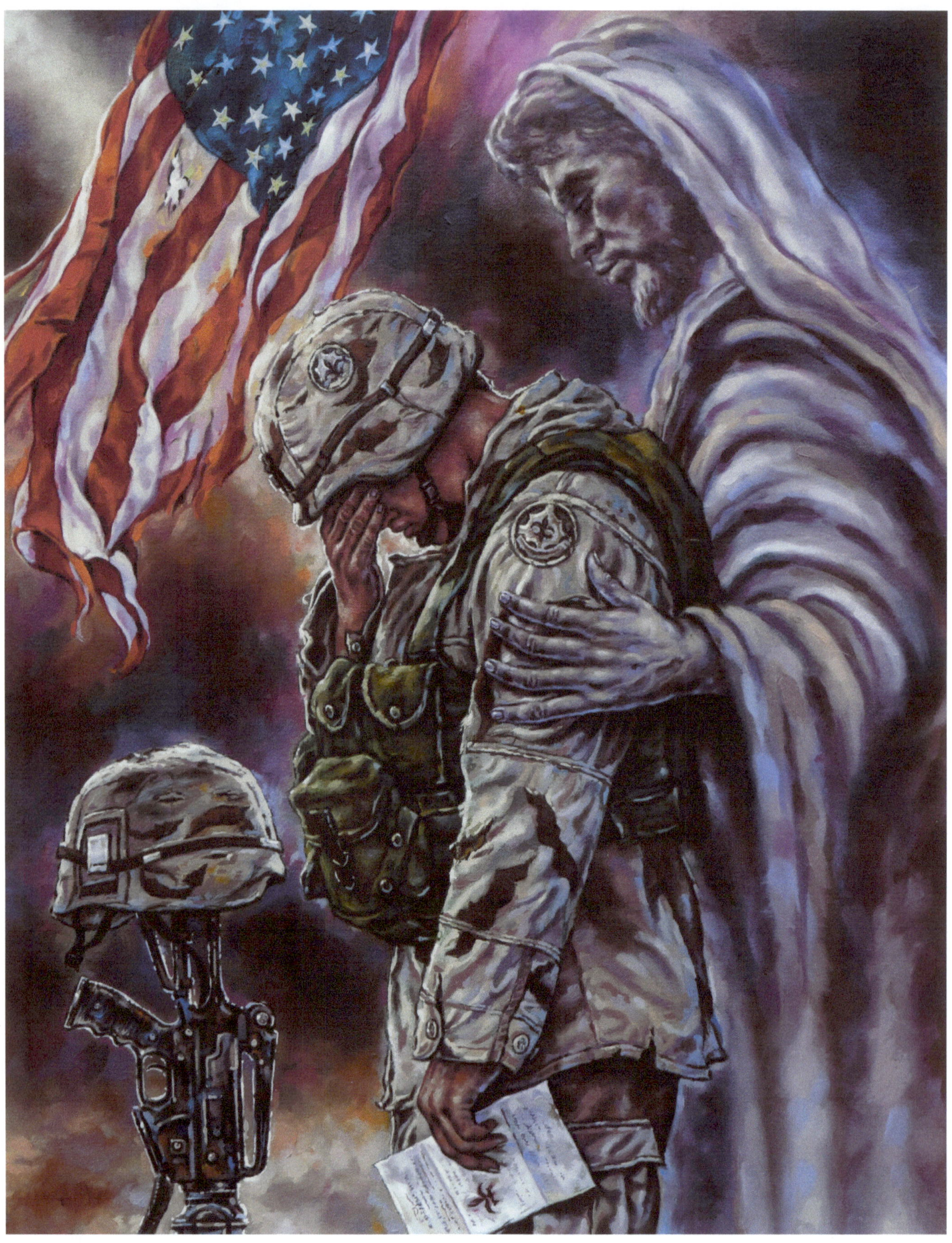

Fallen Comrade

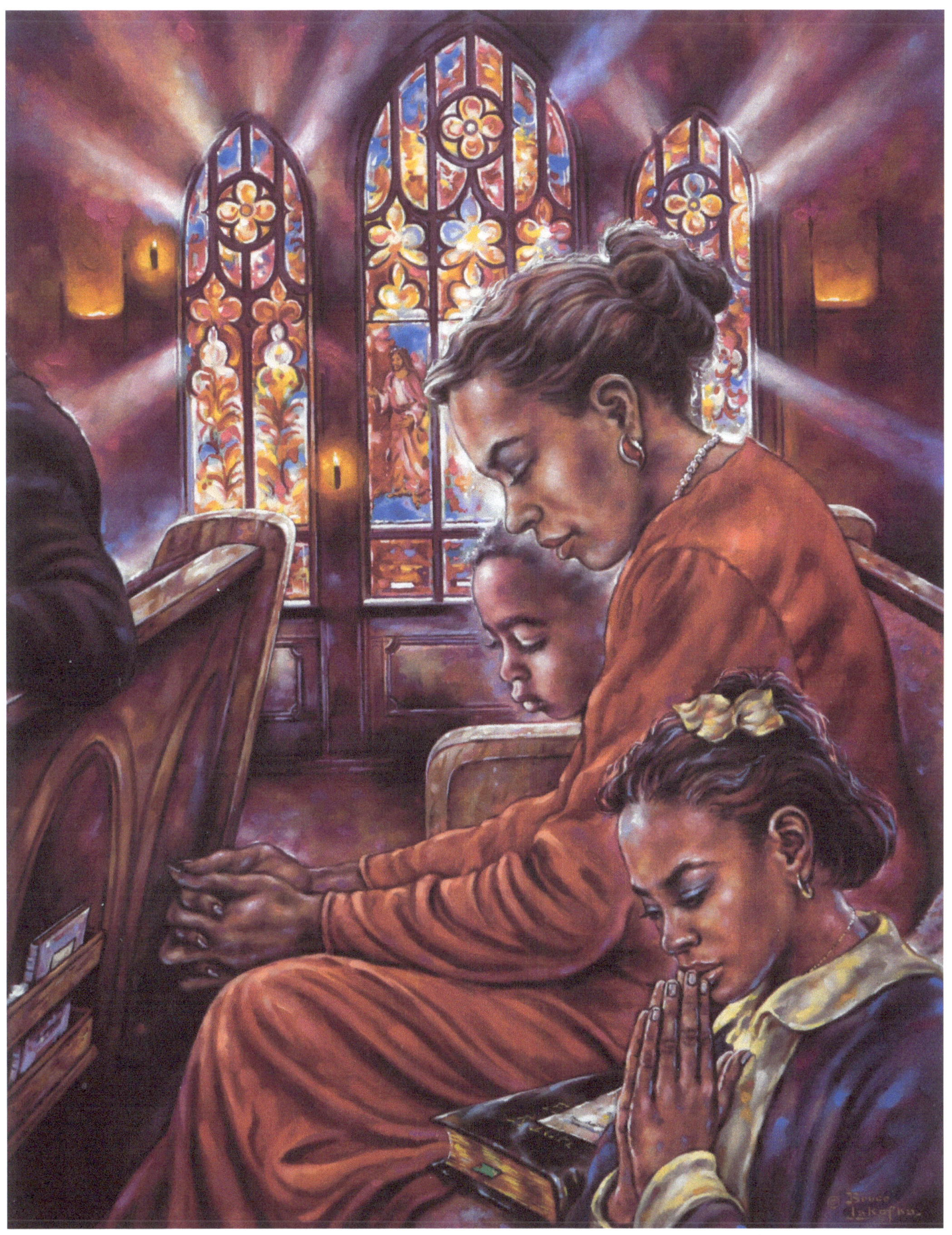

A Mother's Prayer

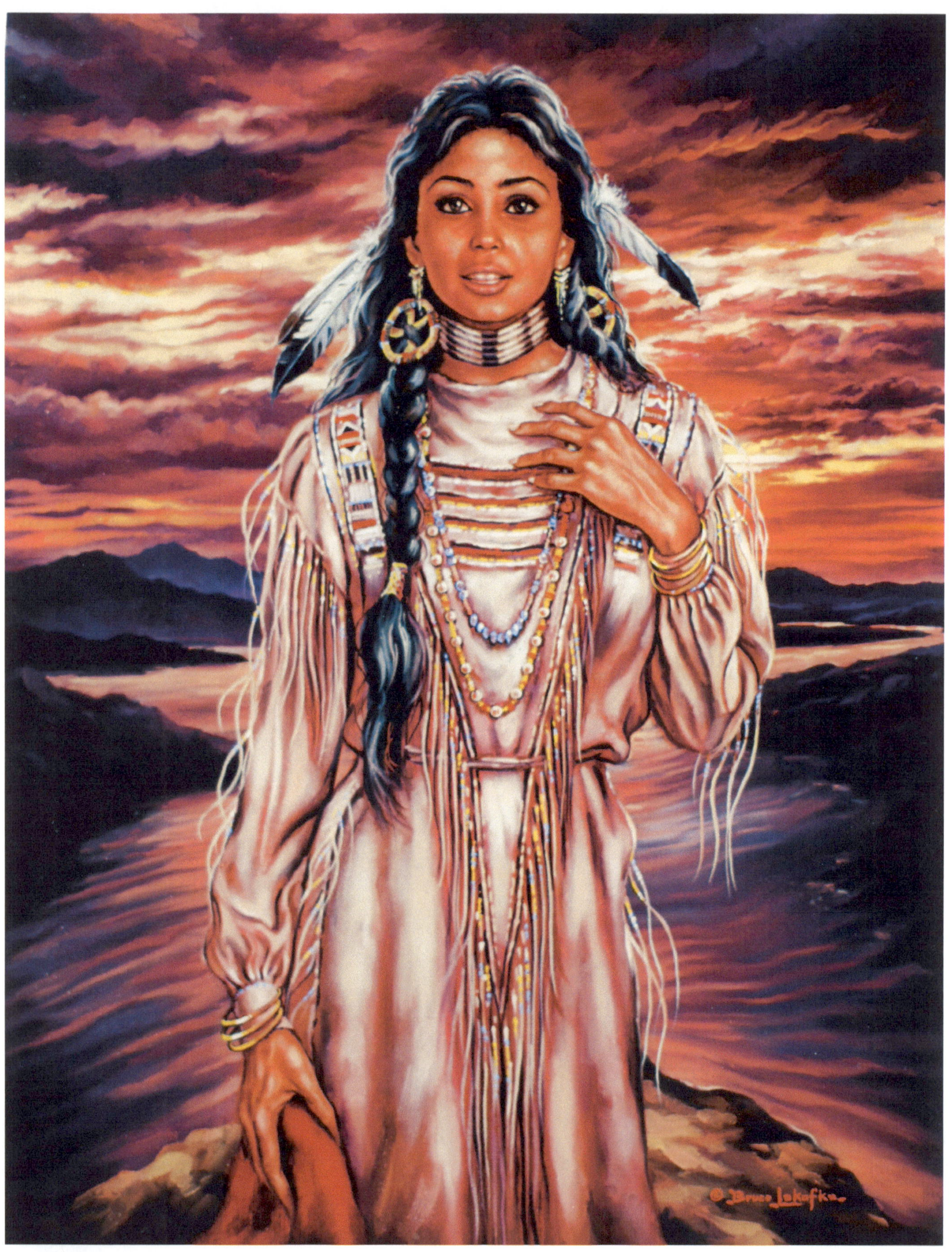

Shenandoah

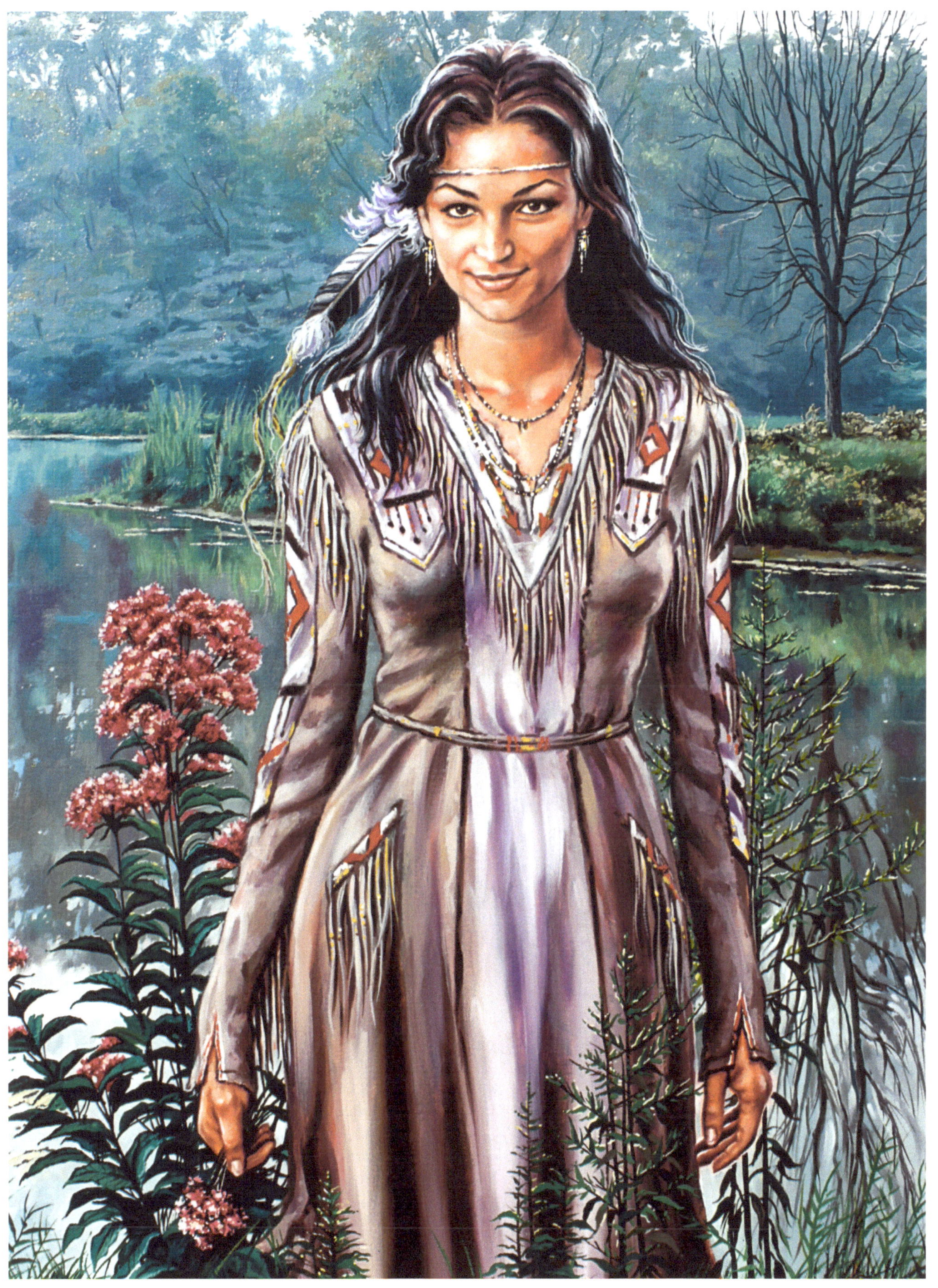

Morning Light

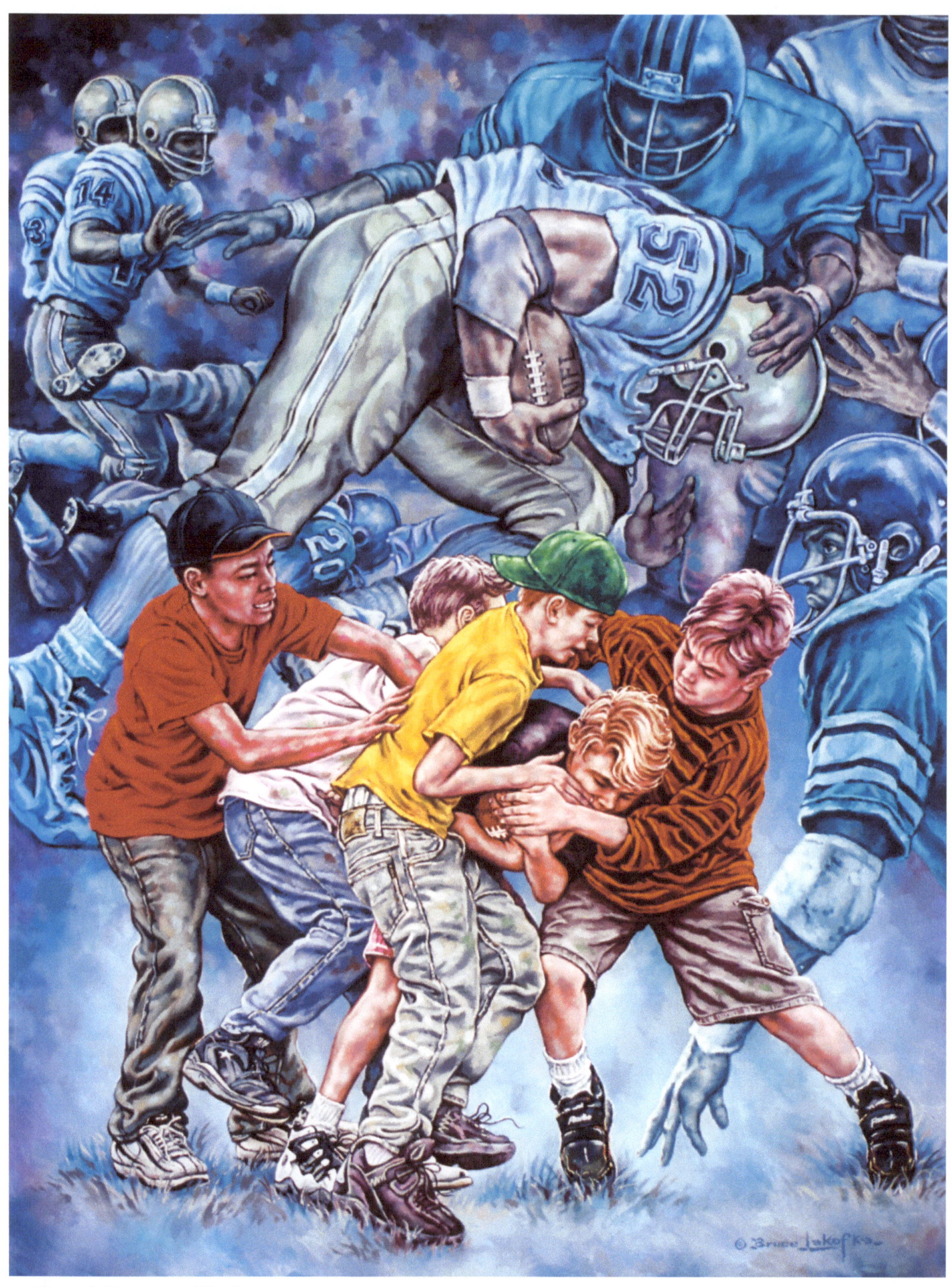

Fourth Down and Inches

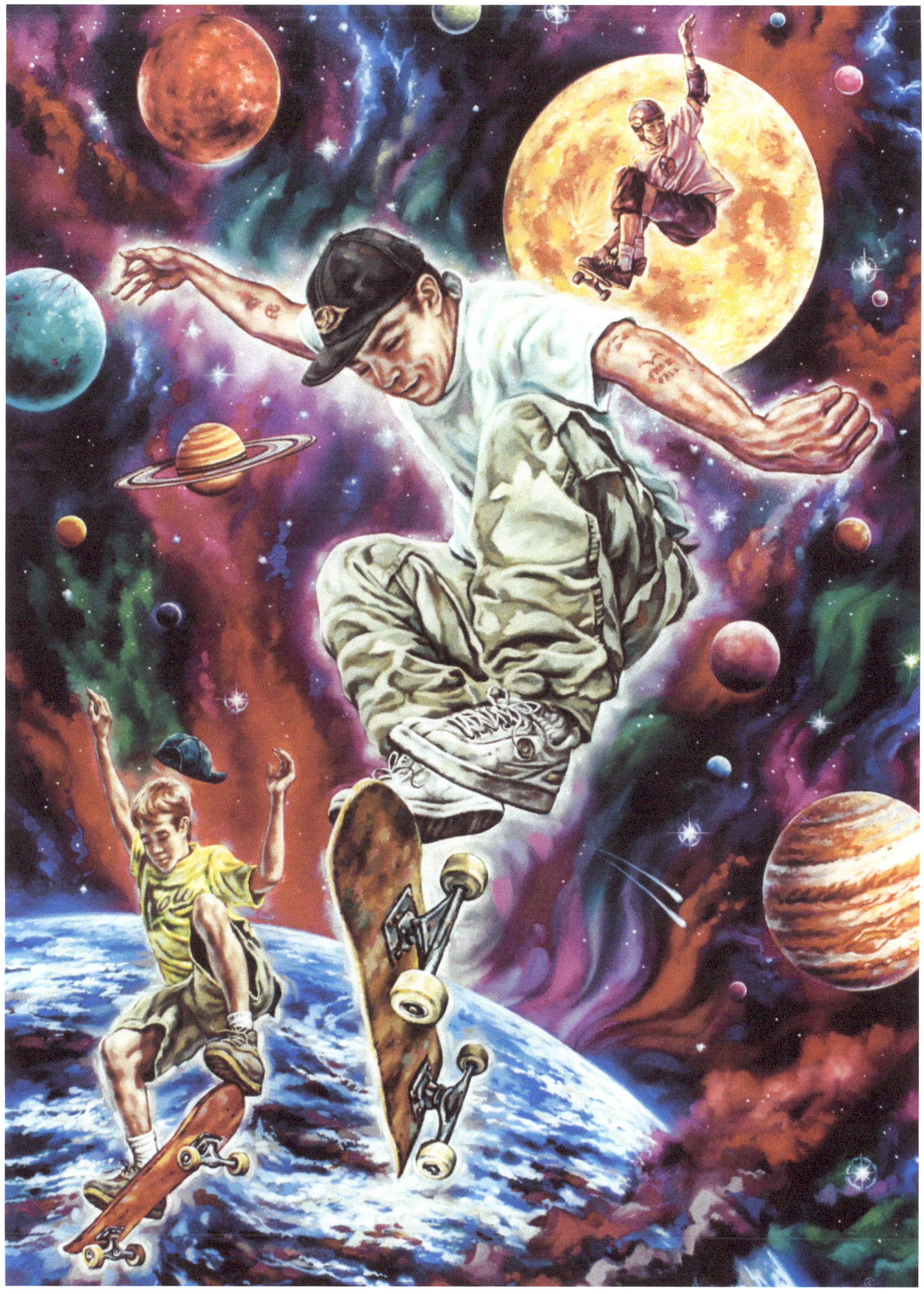

Moonjumping

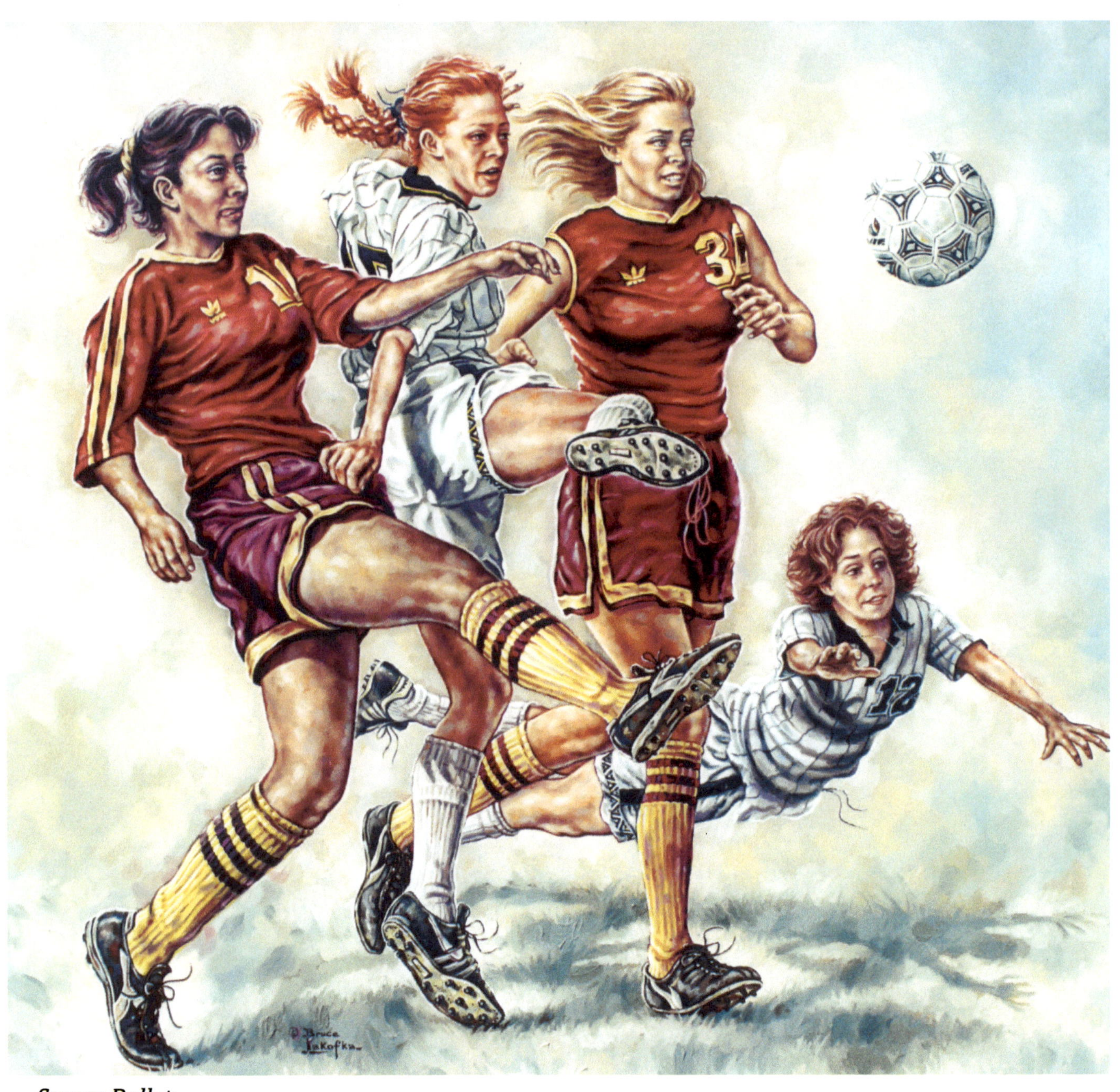

Soccer Ballet

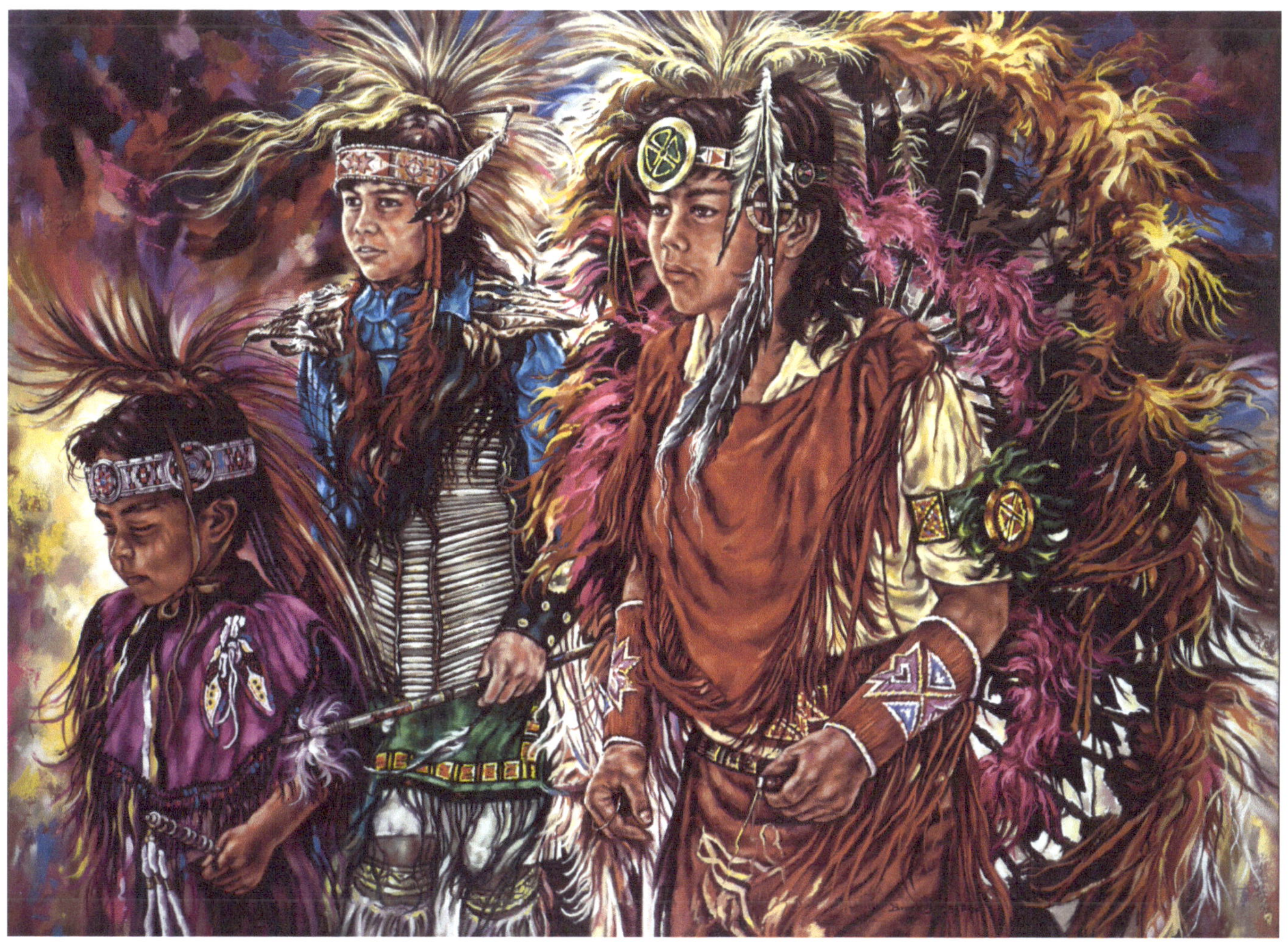

Dance of Tradition

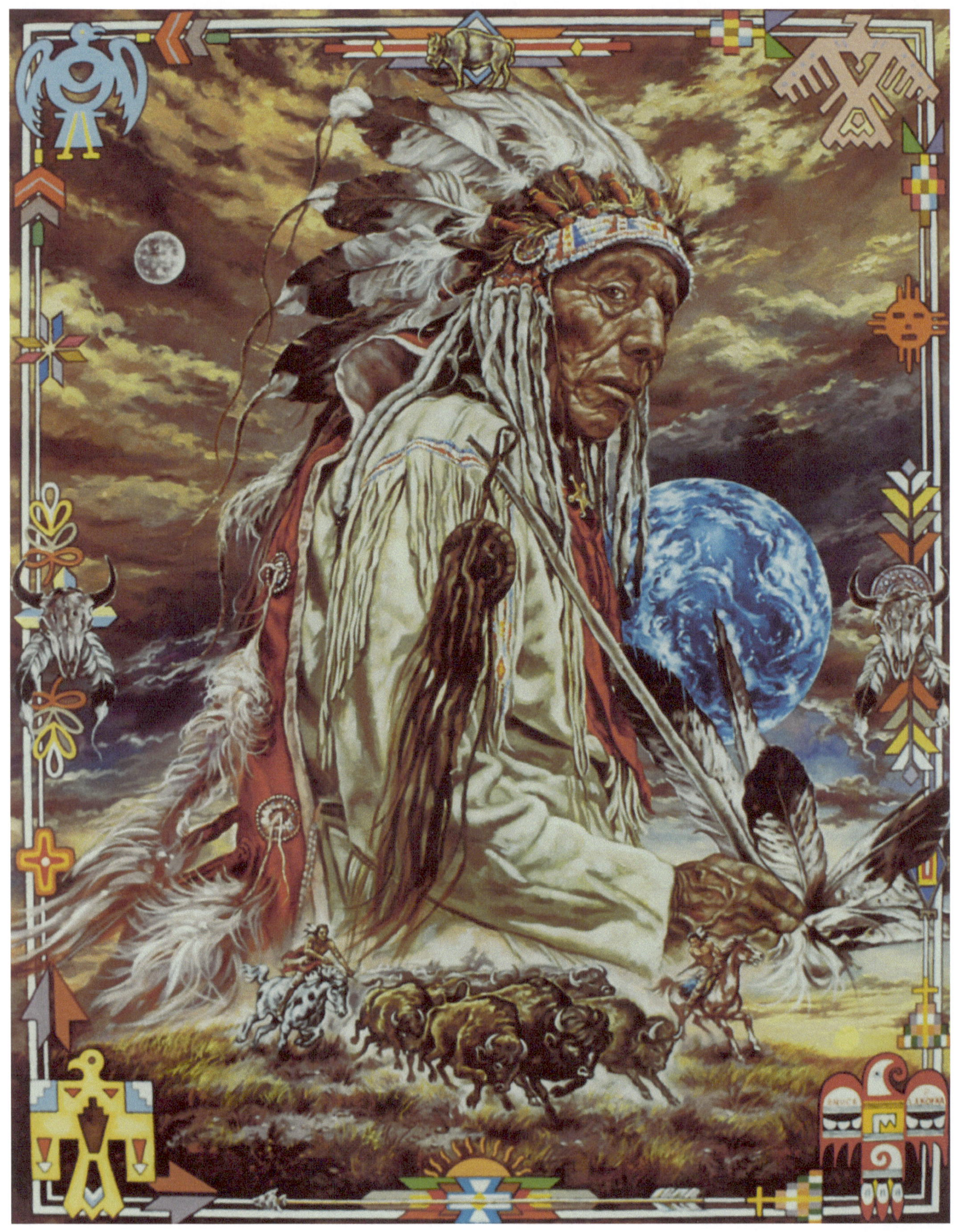

The Last Reservation

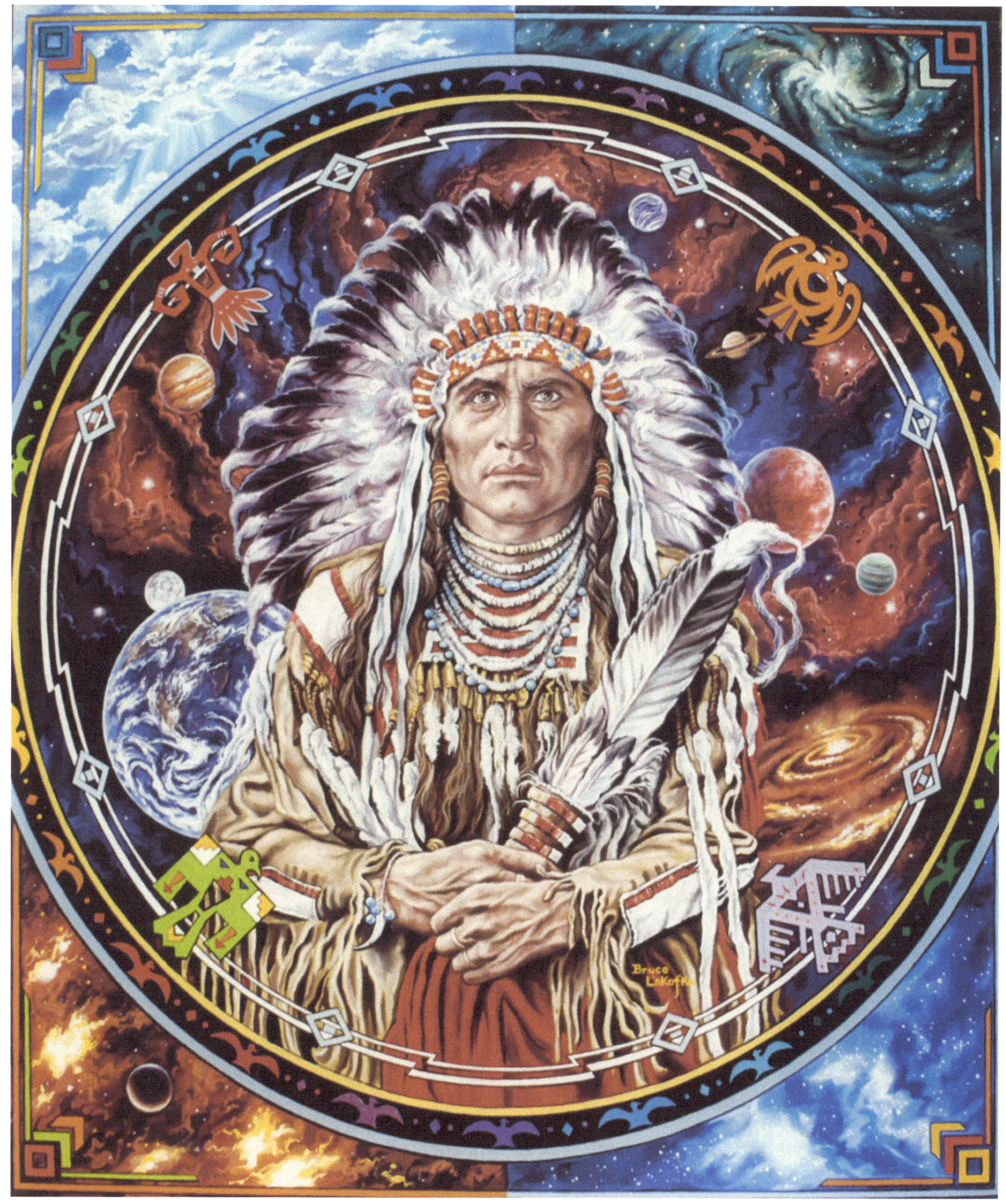

One With the Sky

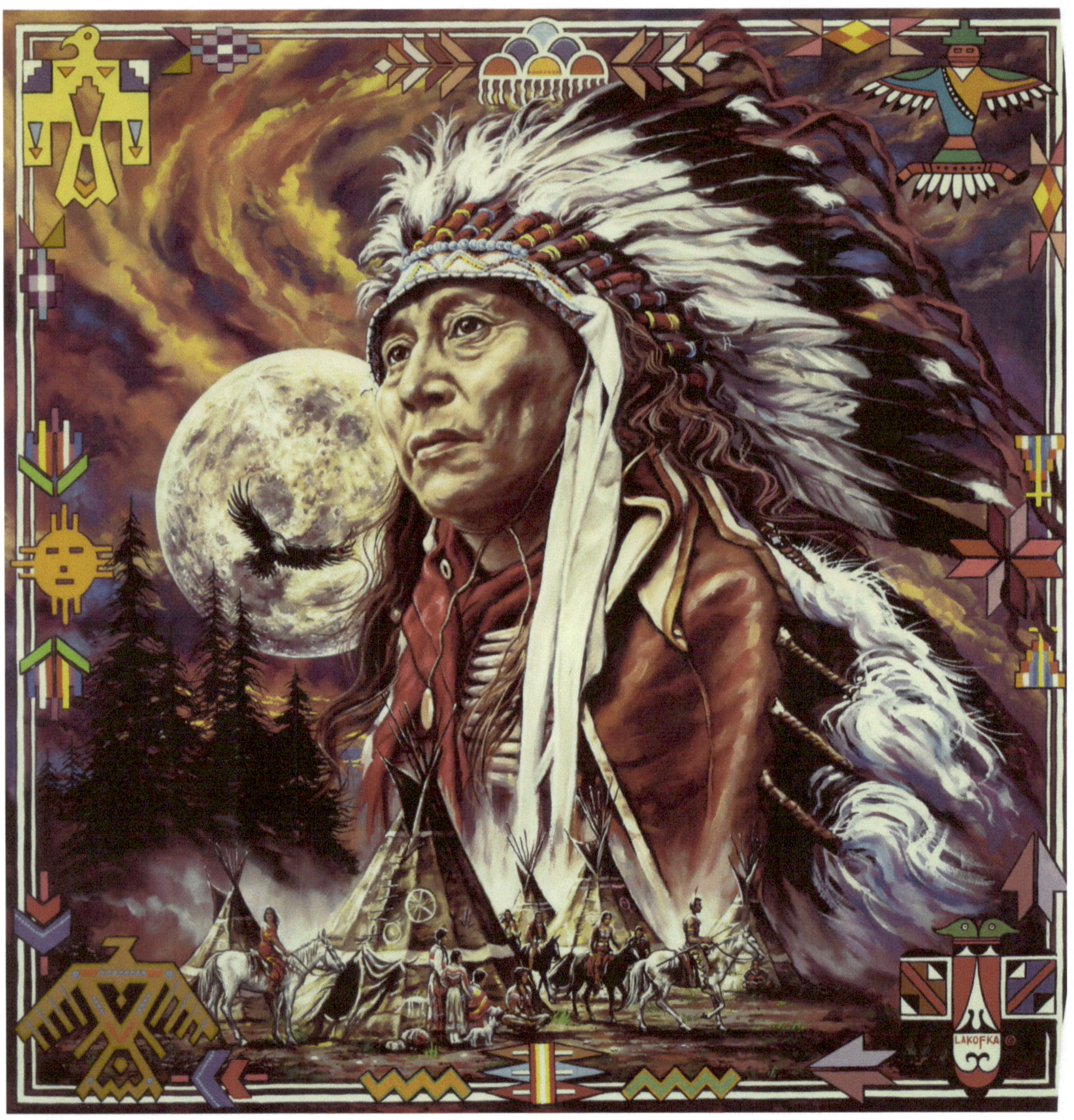

Spirit of the Full Moon

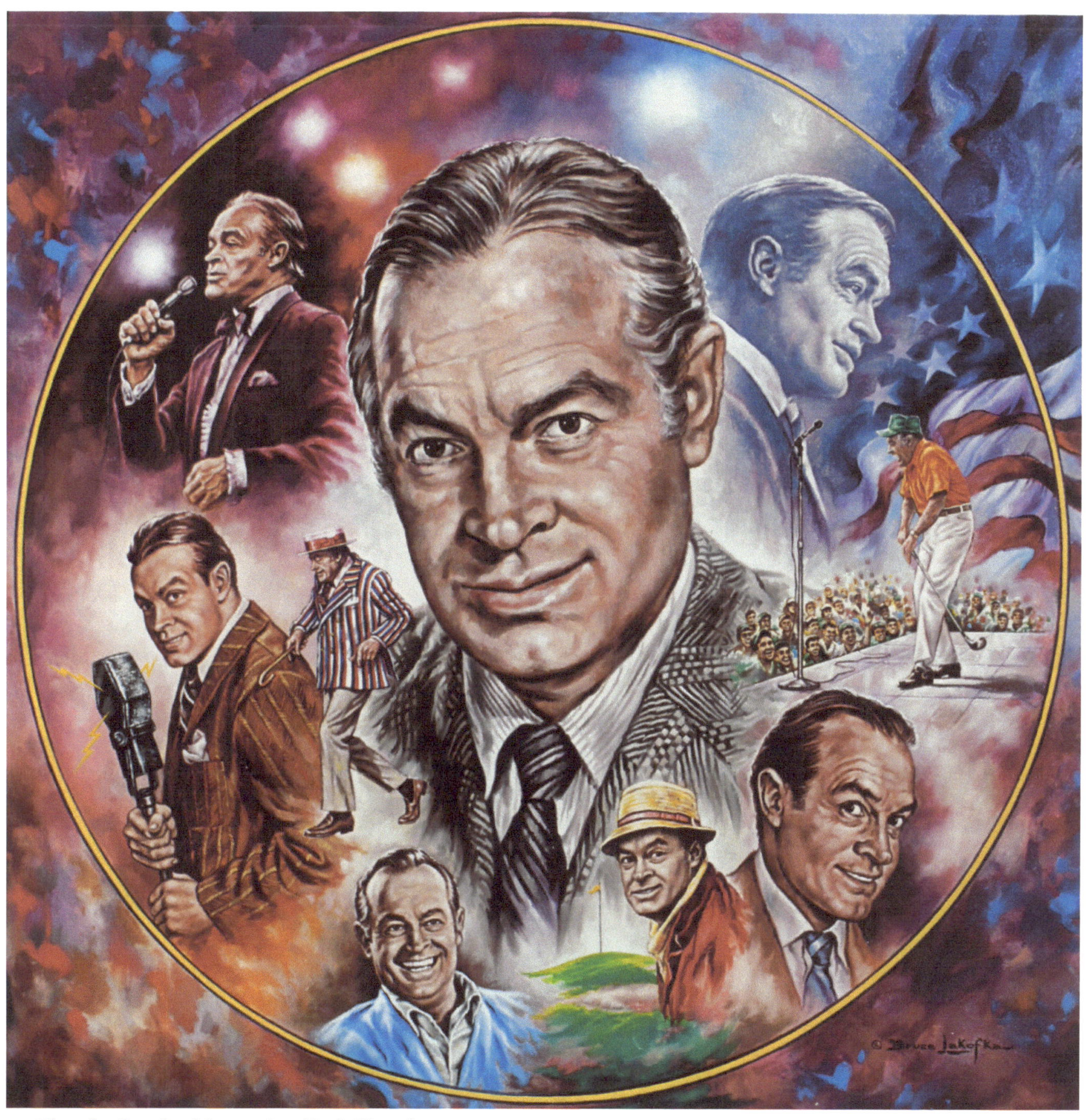

Thanks for the Memories (Bob Hope)

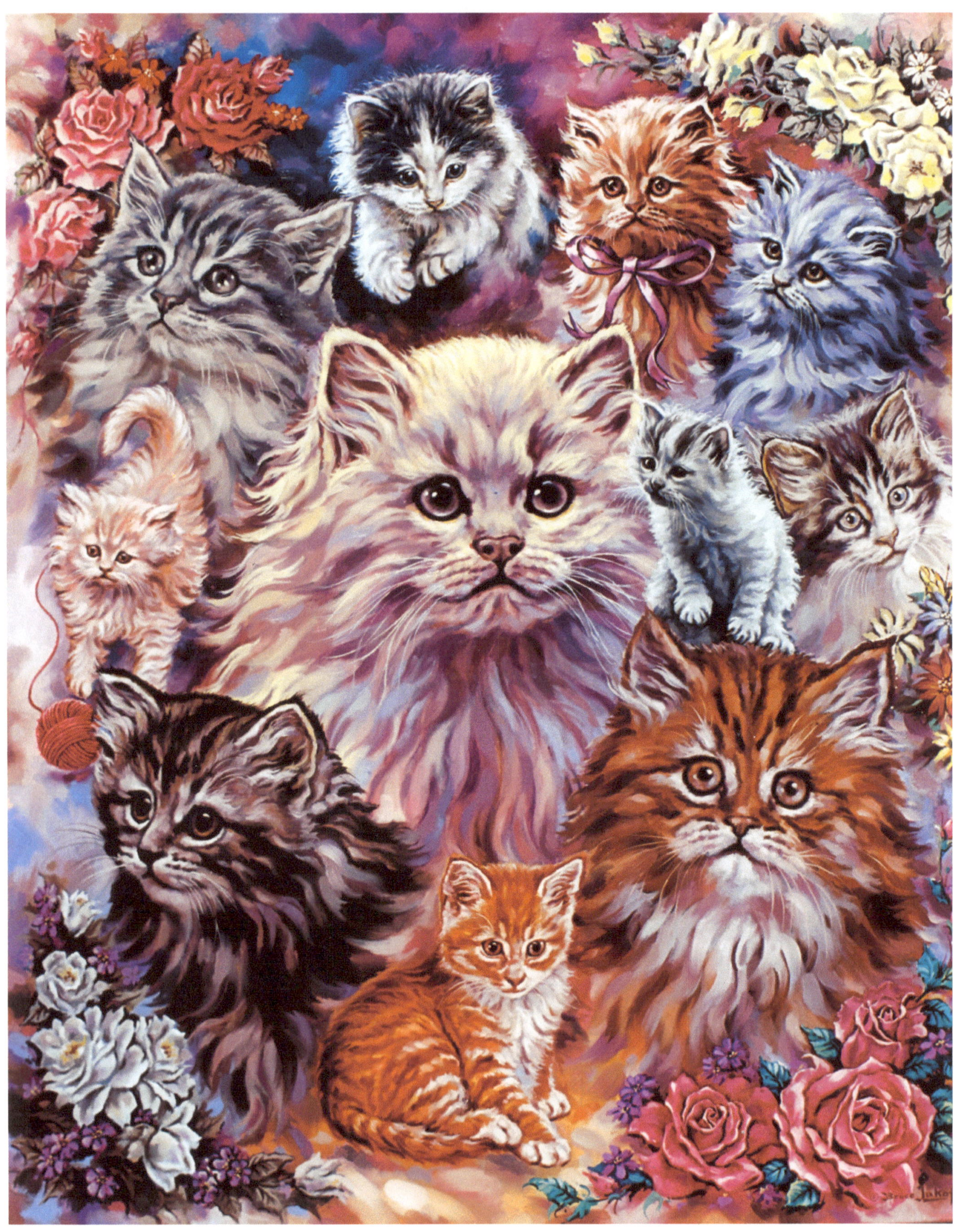

Bouquet of Kittens

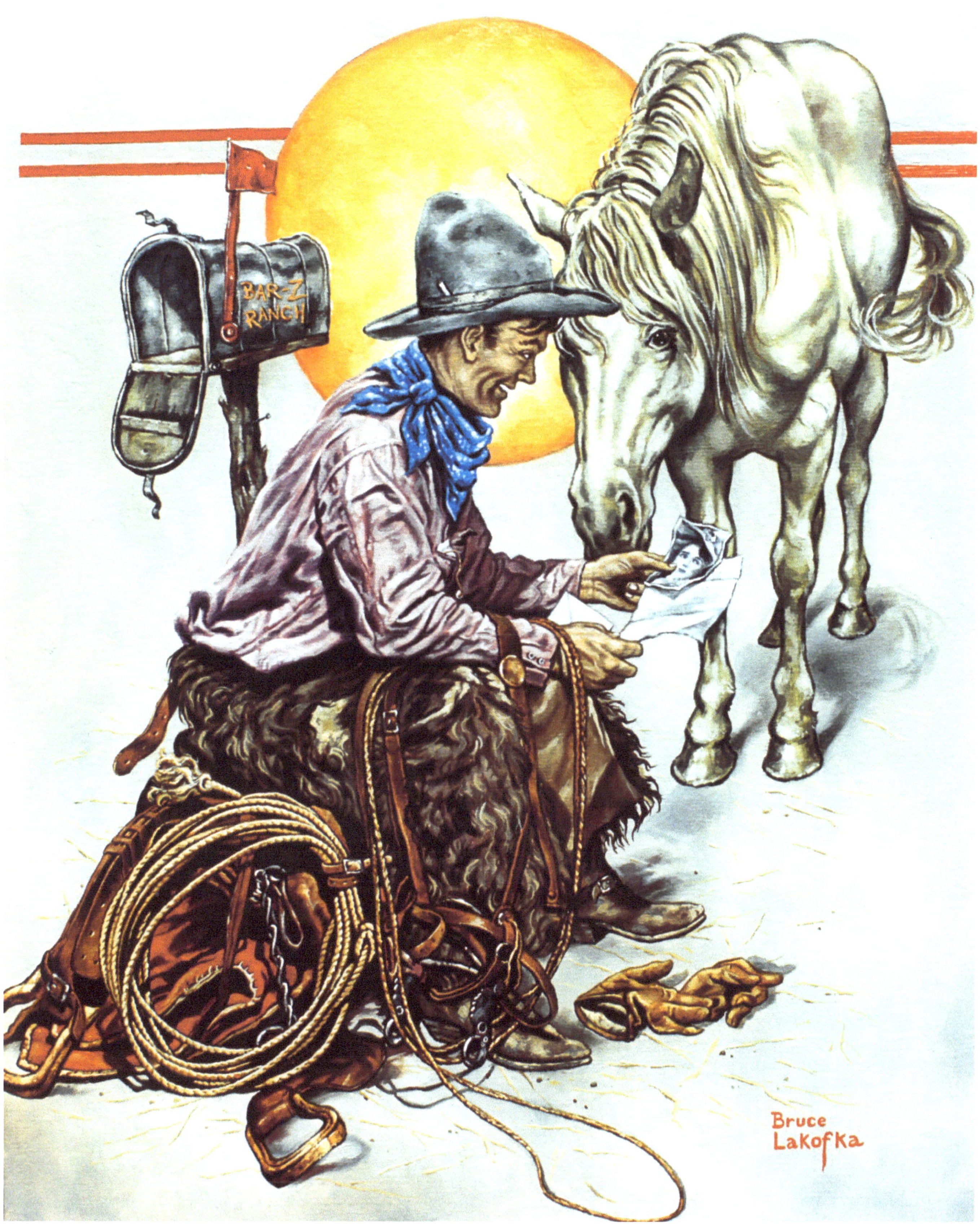

The Rival

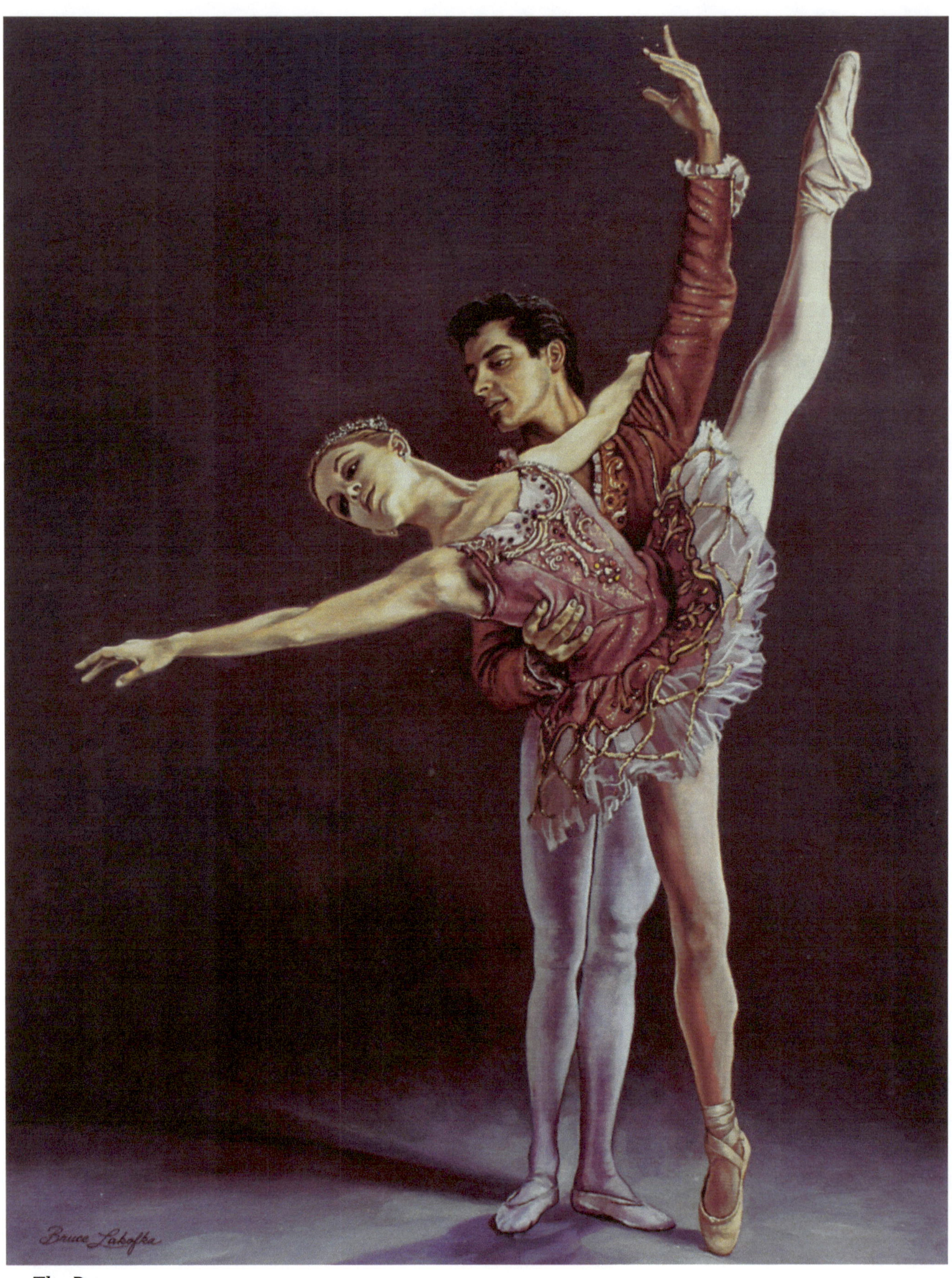

The Dance

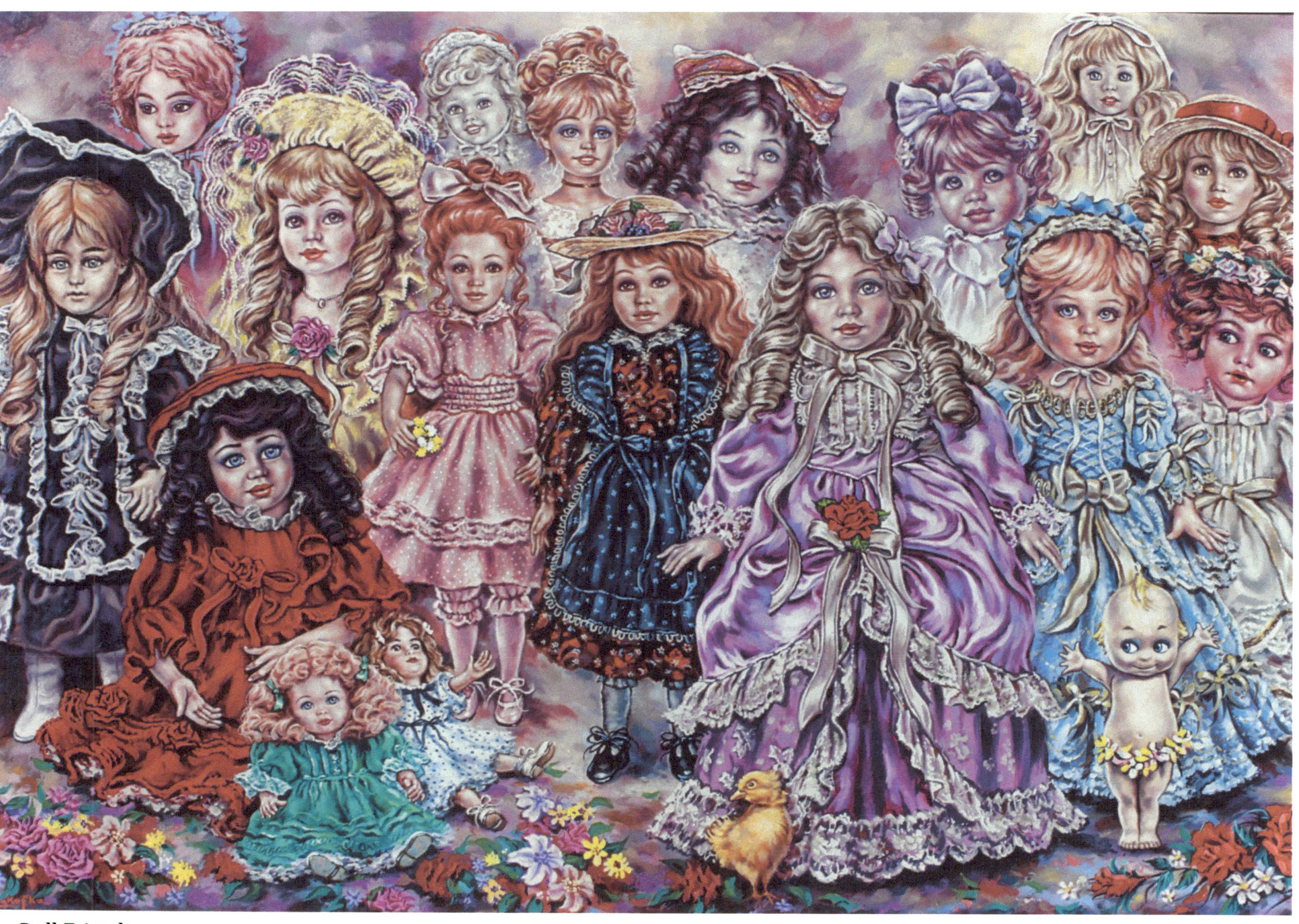

Doll Friends

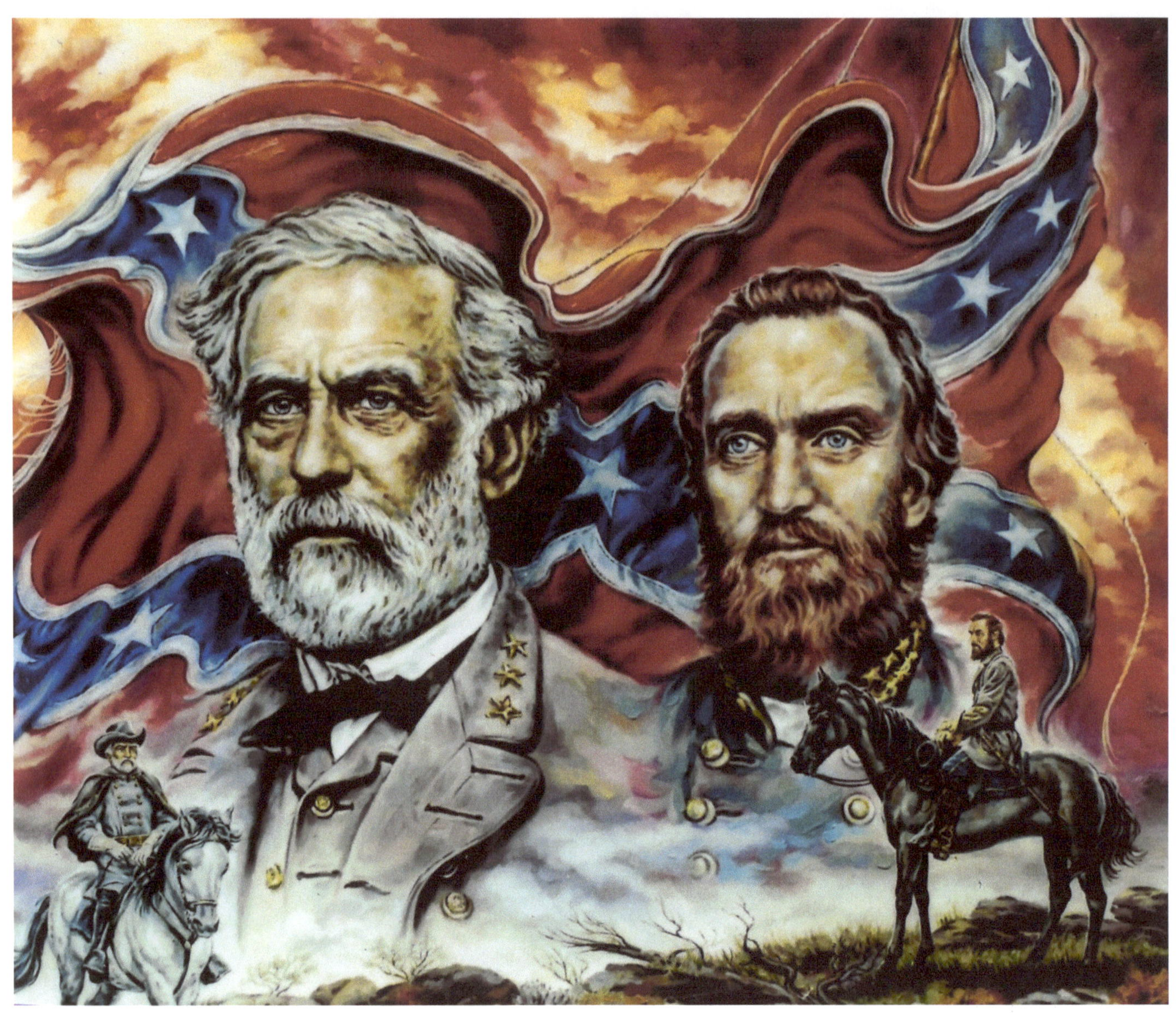

Southern Cross

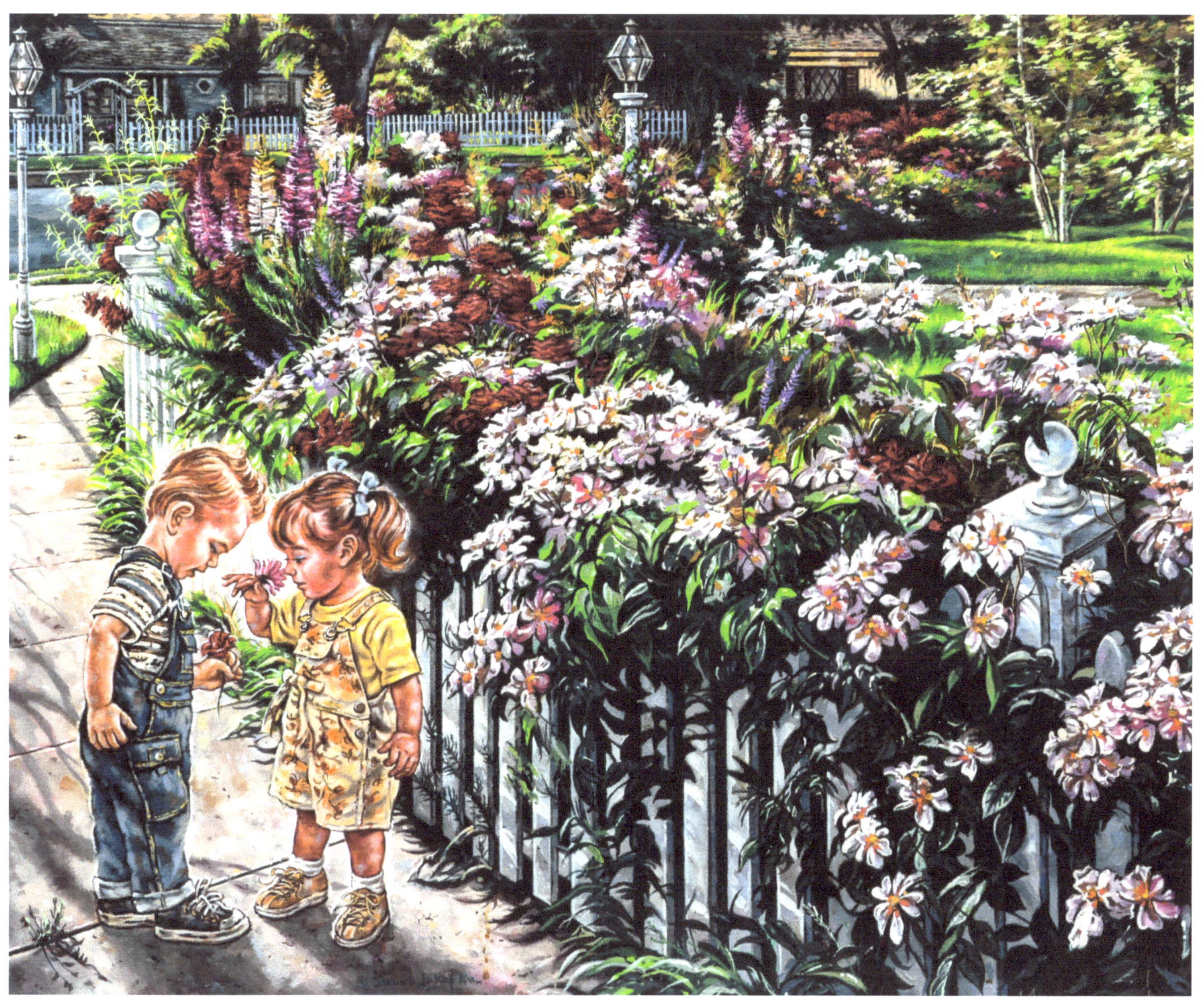

The Smell of Summer Flowers

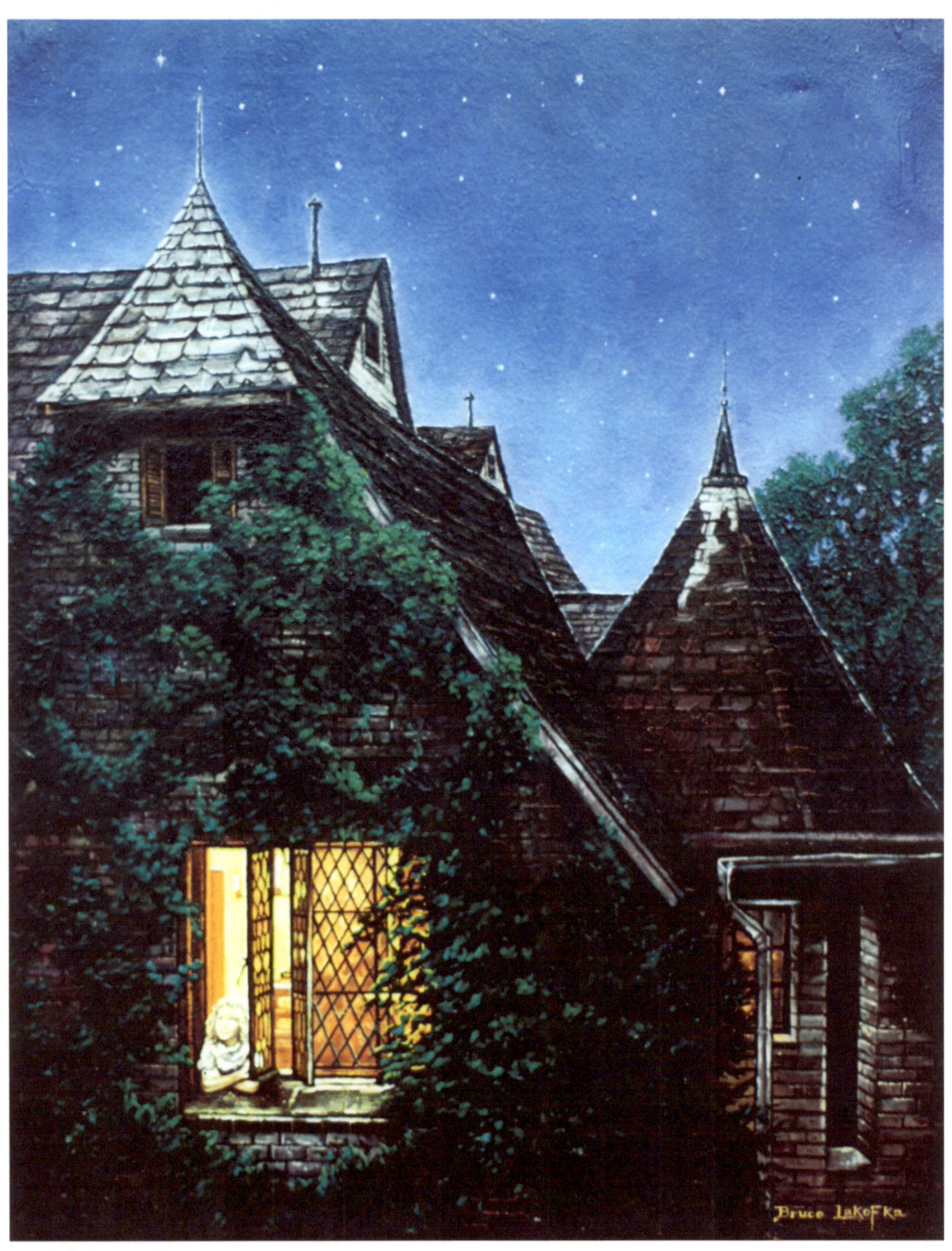

Wish Upon a Star

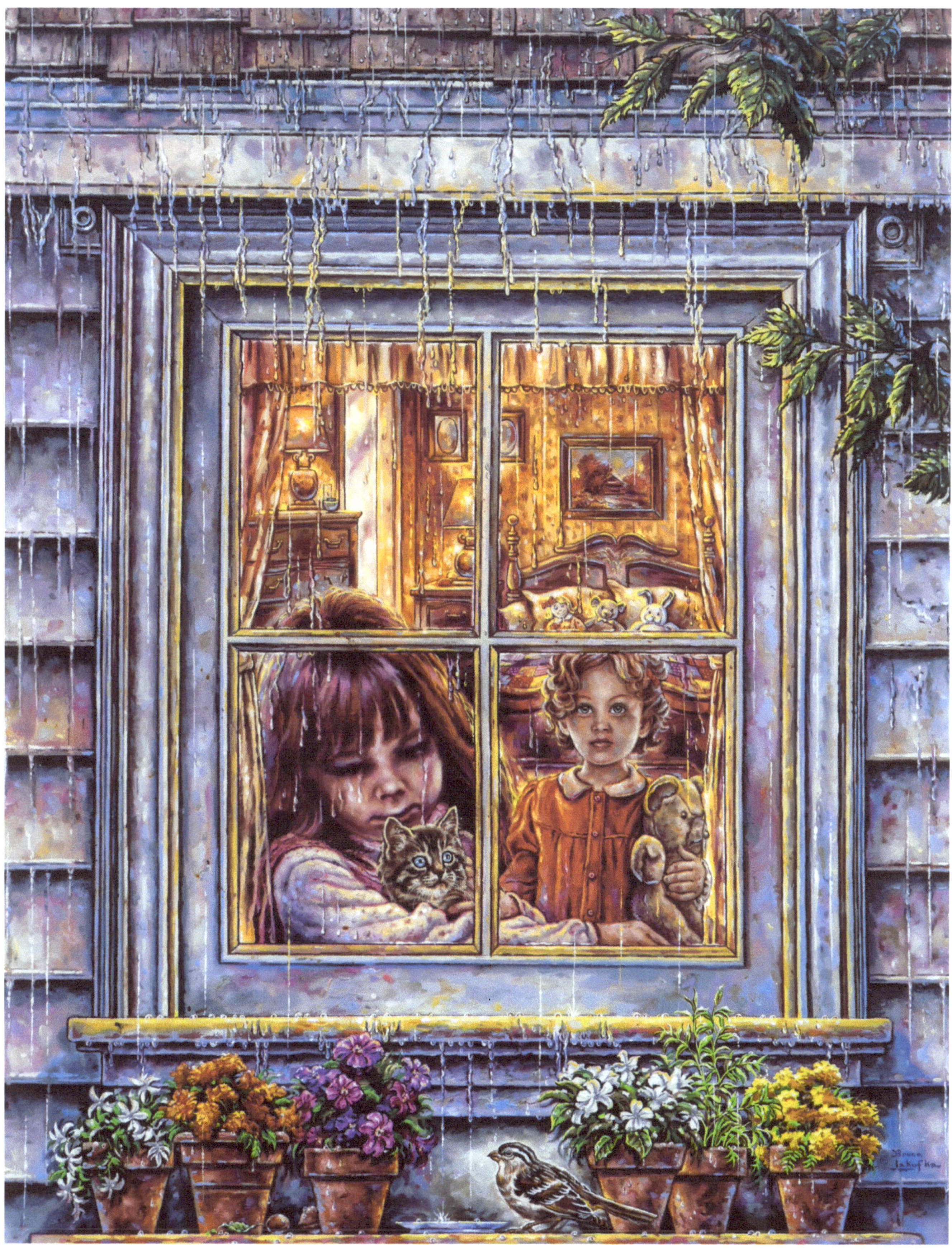

Rain, Rain Go Away

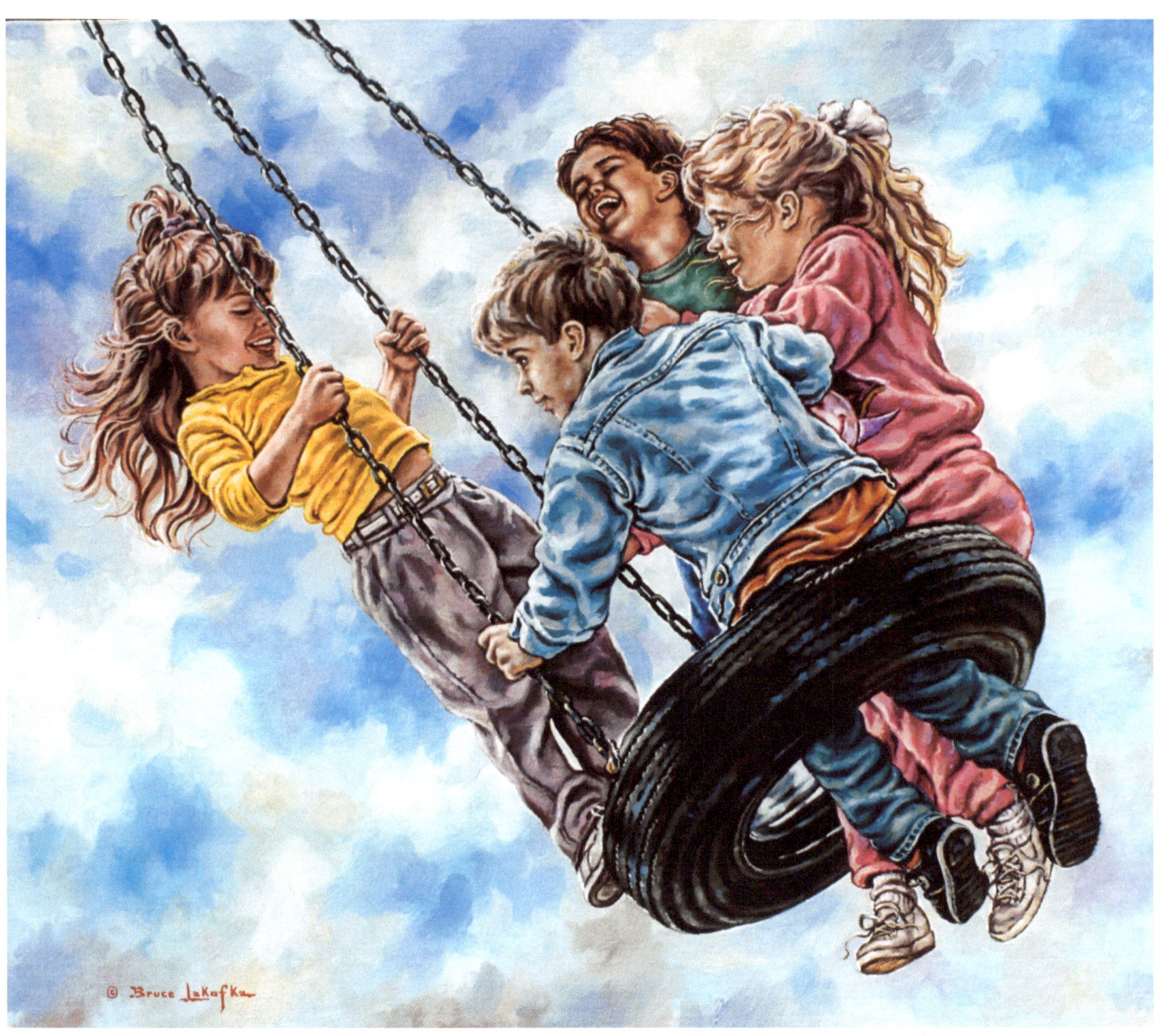

The Tire Swing

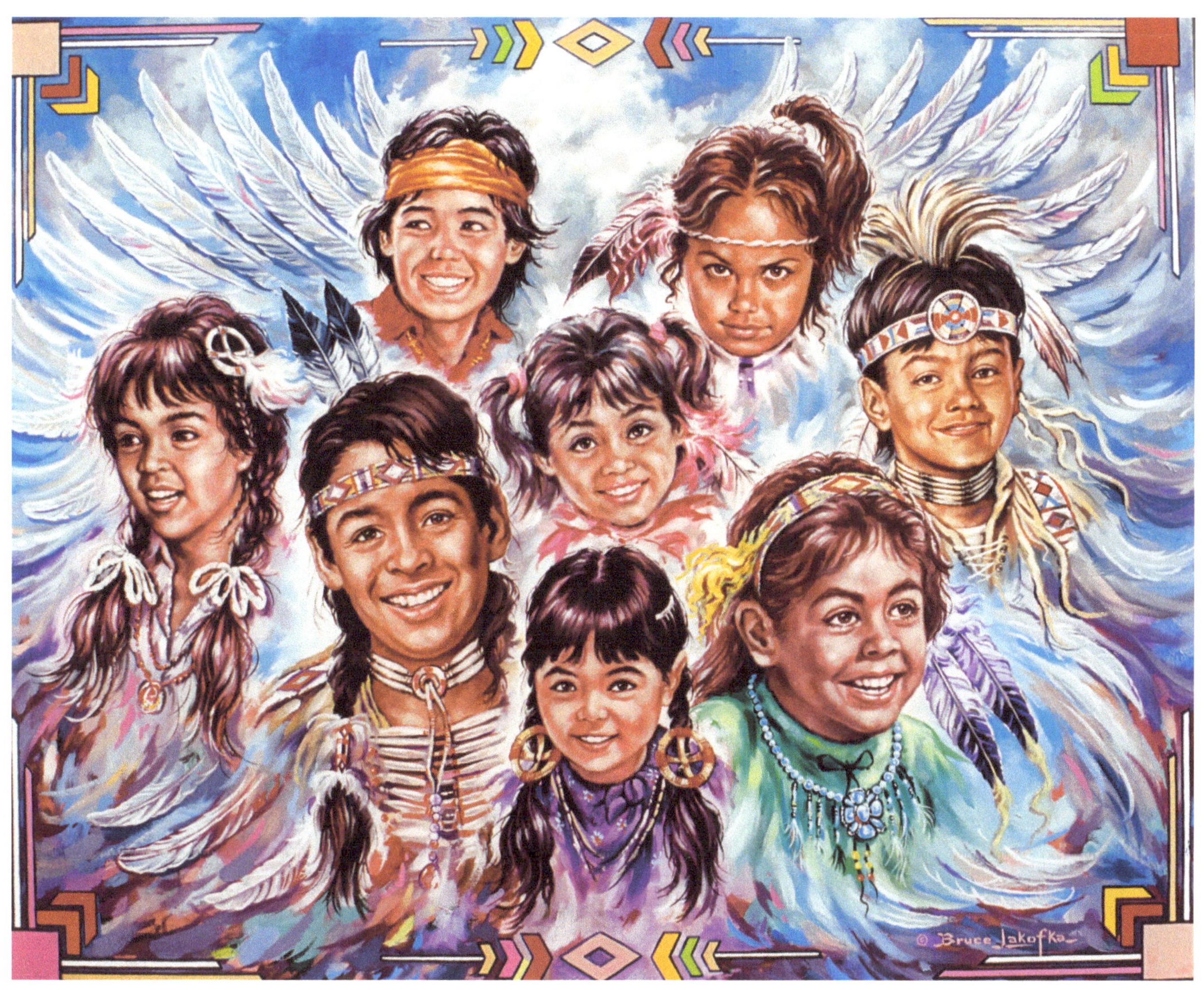

Children of the Great Spirit

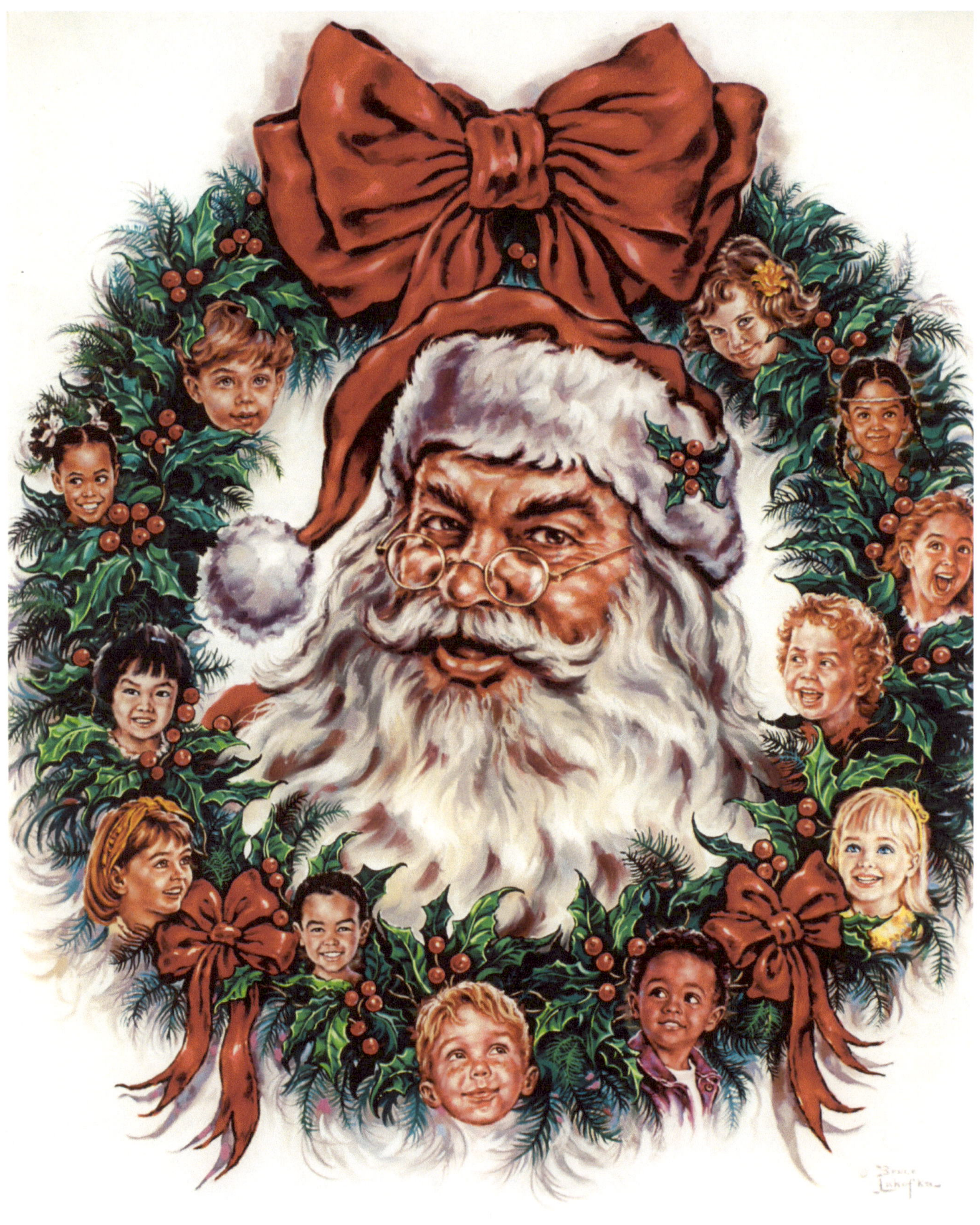

Wreath of Joy

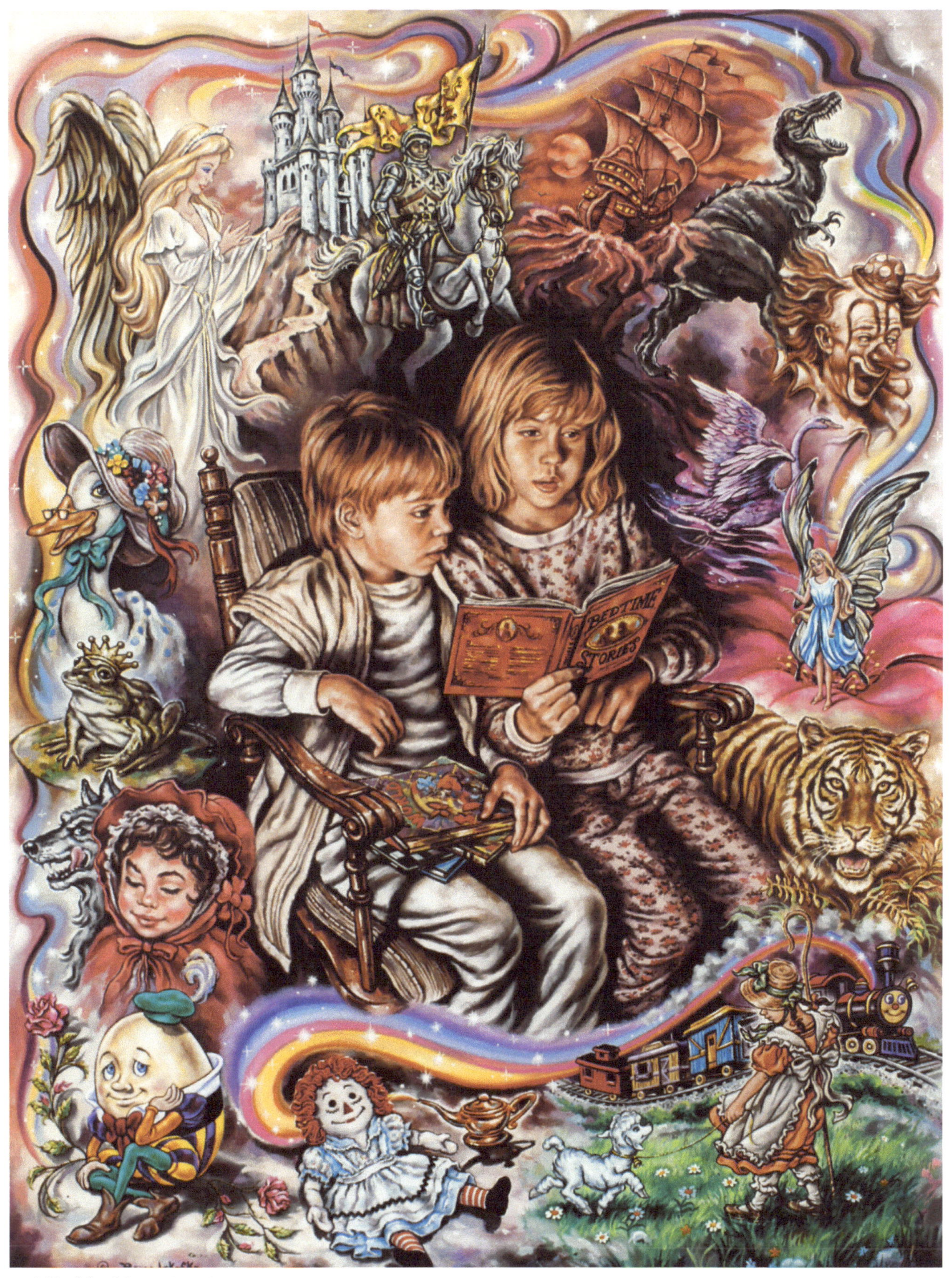

World of Imagination

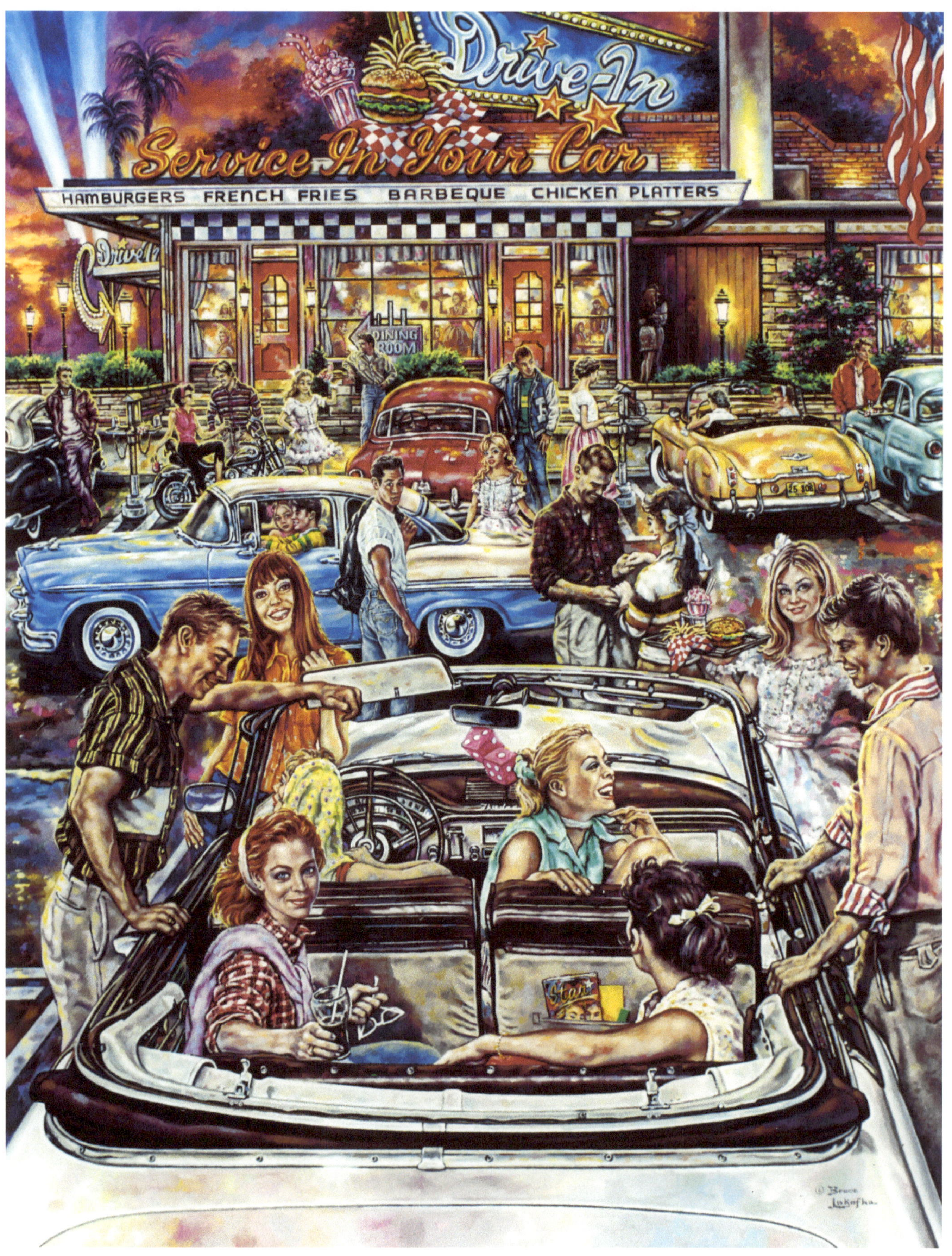

Back in the Fifties

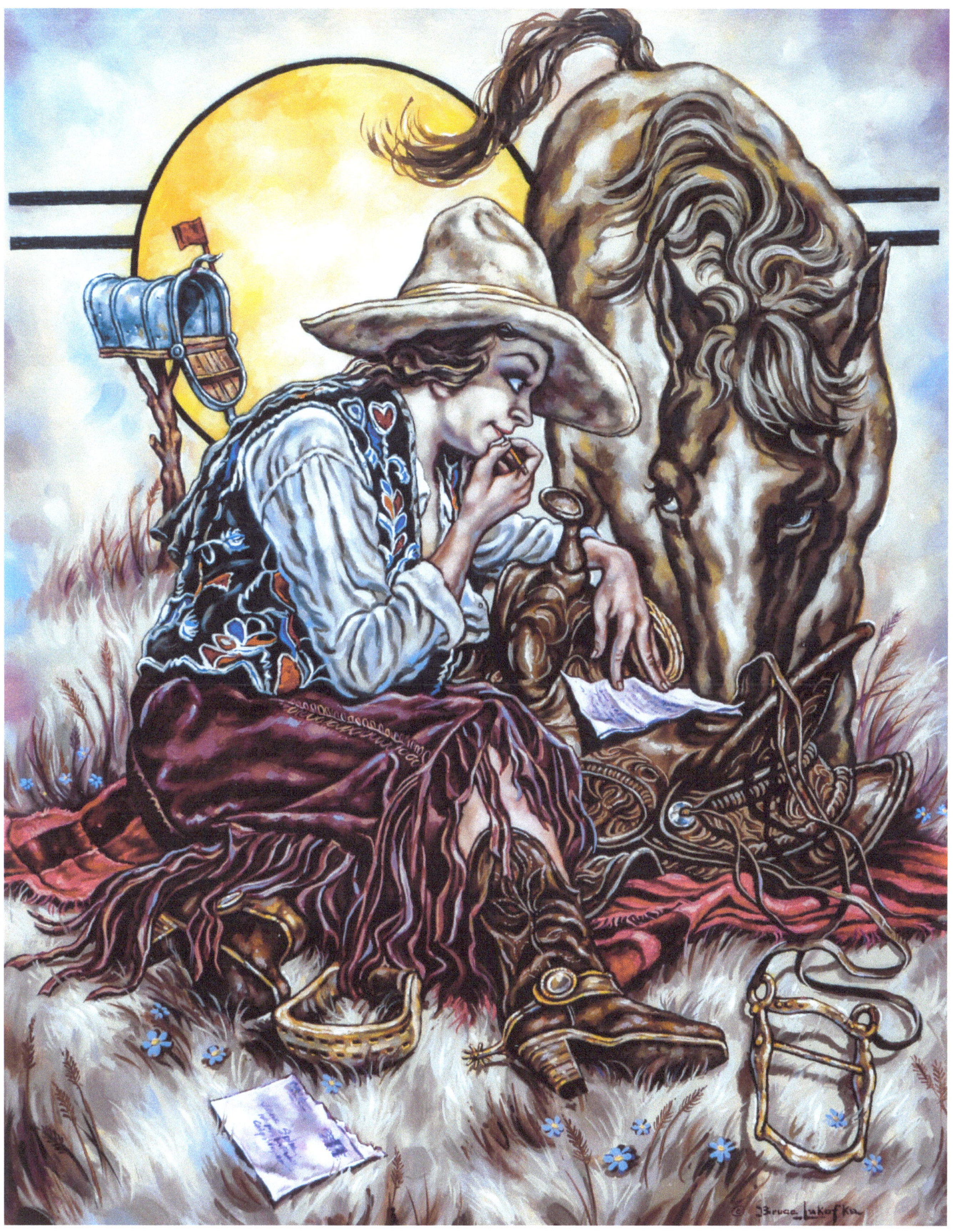

The Competitor

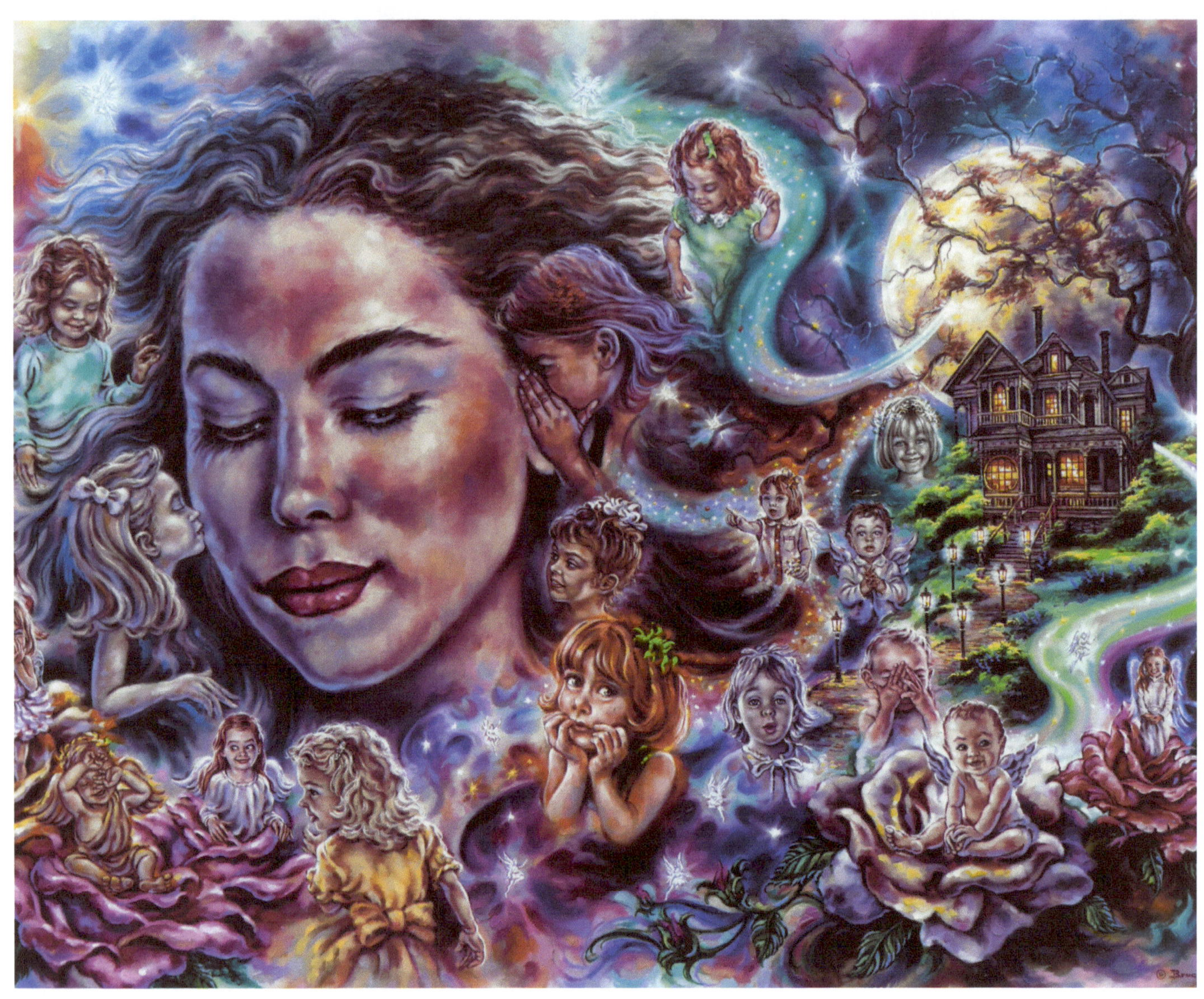

Moonbeams

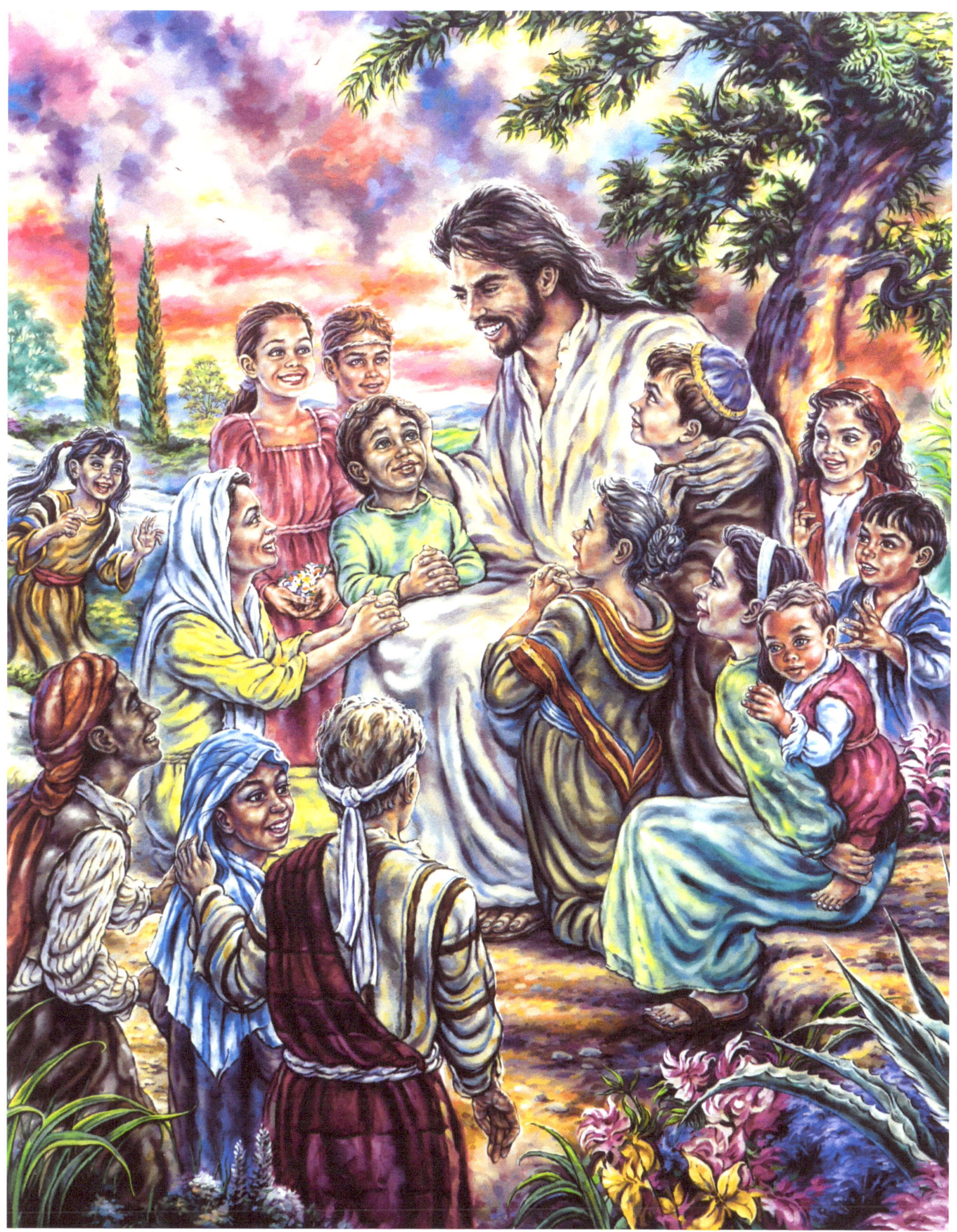

Christ and the Children

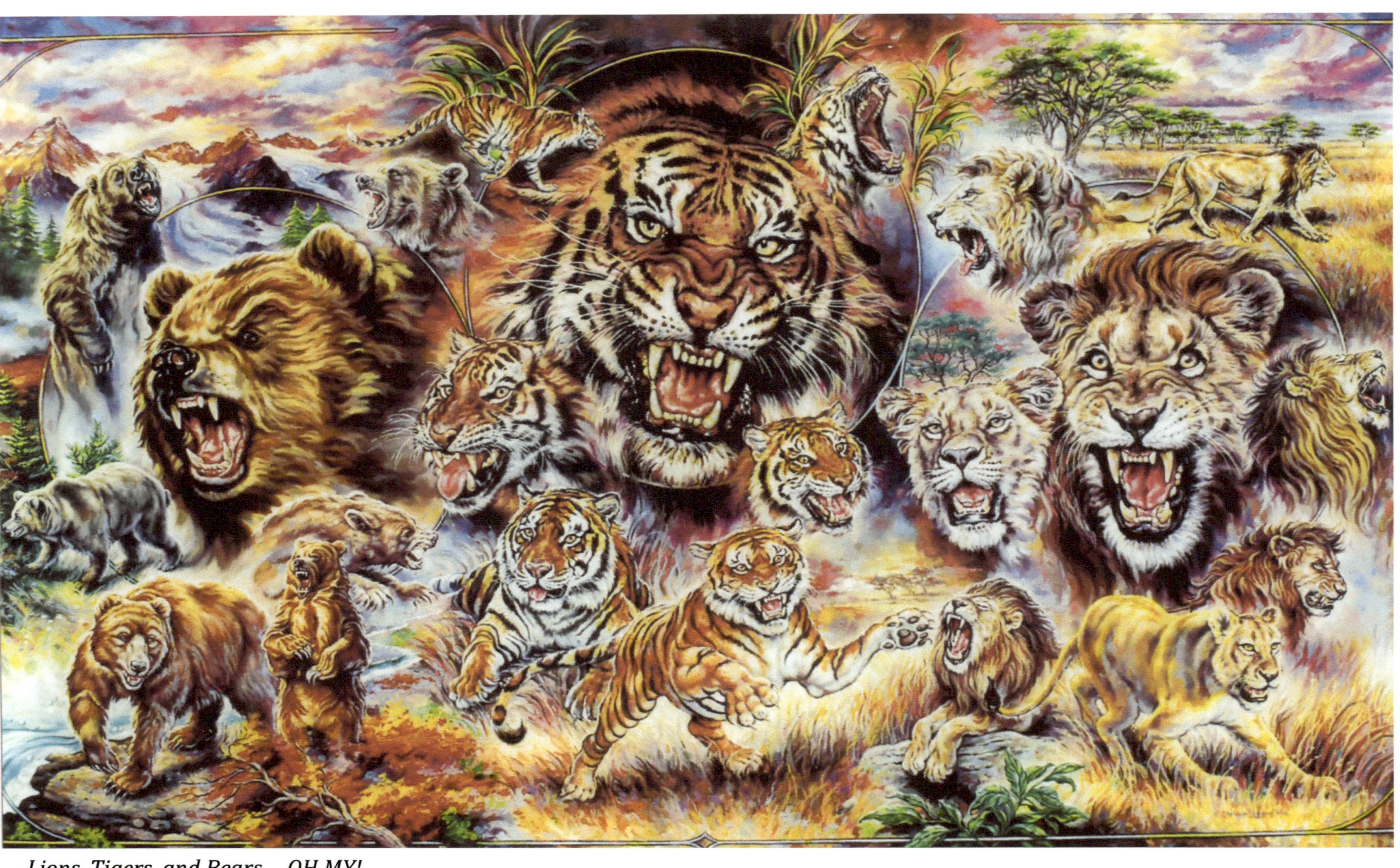

Lions, Tigers, and Bears ... OH MY!

~ 4 ~

Miscellaneous Recent Oil Paintings

What's to be said about this group of sixty-seven paintings? First, Bruce painted them. His second-string (Americans hate this word, they all want to be varsity) paintings are as good as most painters' best. To most admirers the technical problems in some of these paintings won't even be visible. Some do not have any such problems. Maybe the subject of the painting has been too often done before. Or maybe it does not strike the viewer as interesting.

As an example, I love the concept behind "Night Eyes" (E-22) but the inclusion of the eagle is wrong (eagles can't see at night but owls can). And more importantly, Indians did not wander around or fight at night. They believed unruly spirits were out then.

"Eyes of the Jungle" (H-11) is a forceful painting but a Sahib or Native Indian would know what was wrong. Full grown tigers are totally anti-social and would never walk down a jungle path with another tiger.

Bruce did not finish "The Rainmaker" (E-24) but it had interesting potential. "A Teacher Lady" (H-21) is mentioned in the text as a superb example of a portrait. "Moon Wolves" (H-22) is a design for a check face Bruce did for a bank in Florida.

Slowly peruse these sixty-seven images and you might find some personal gems that are to your liking.

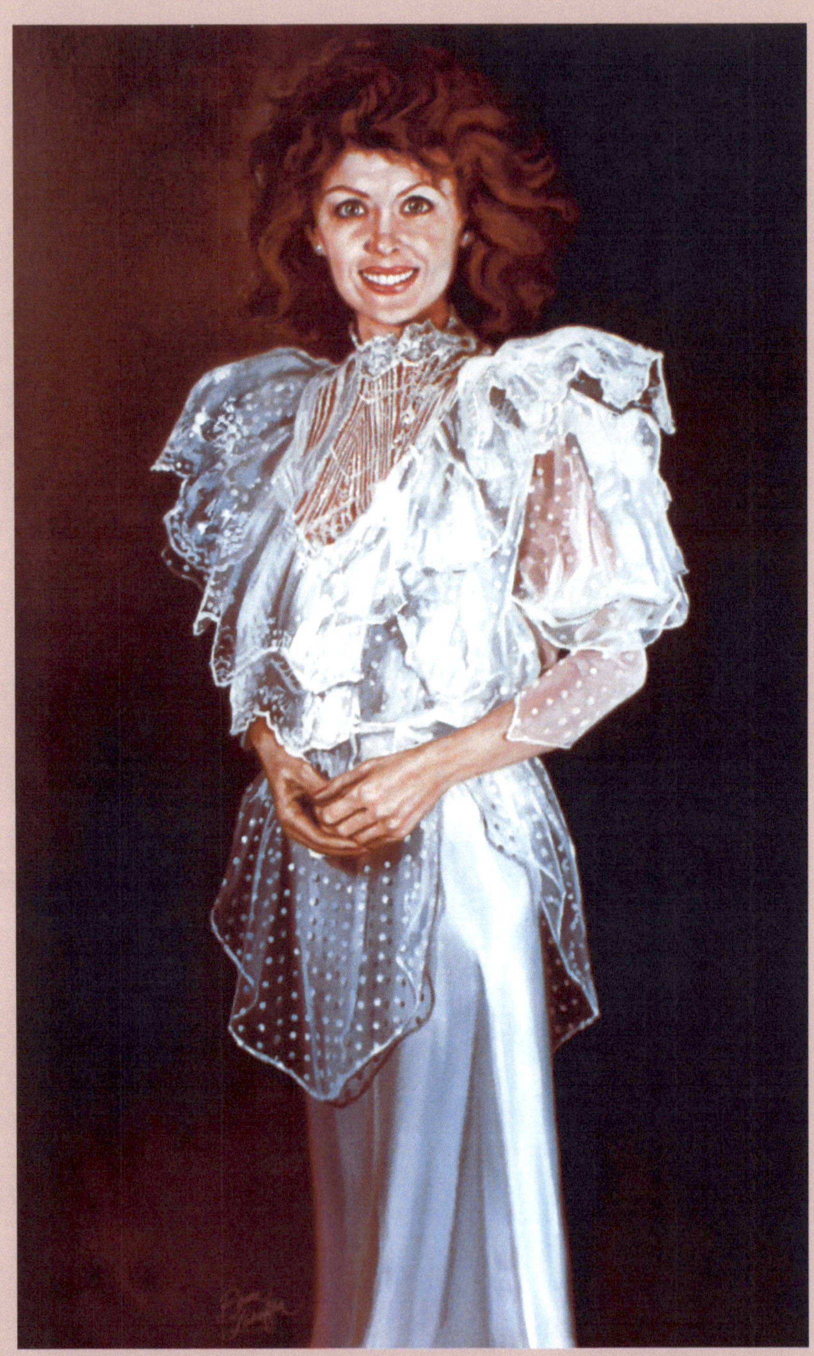

Teacher Lady

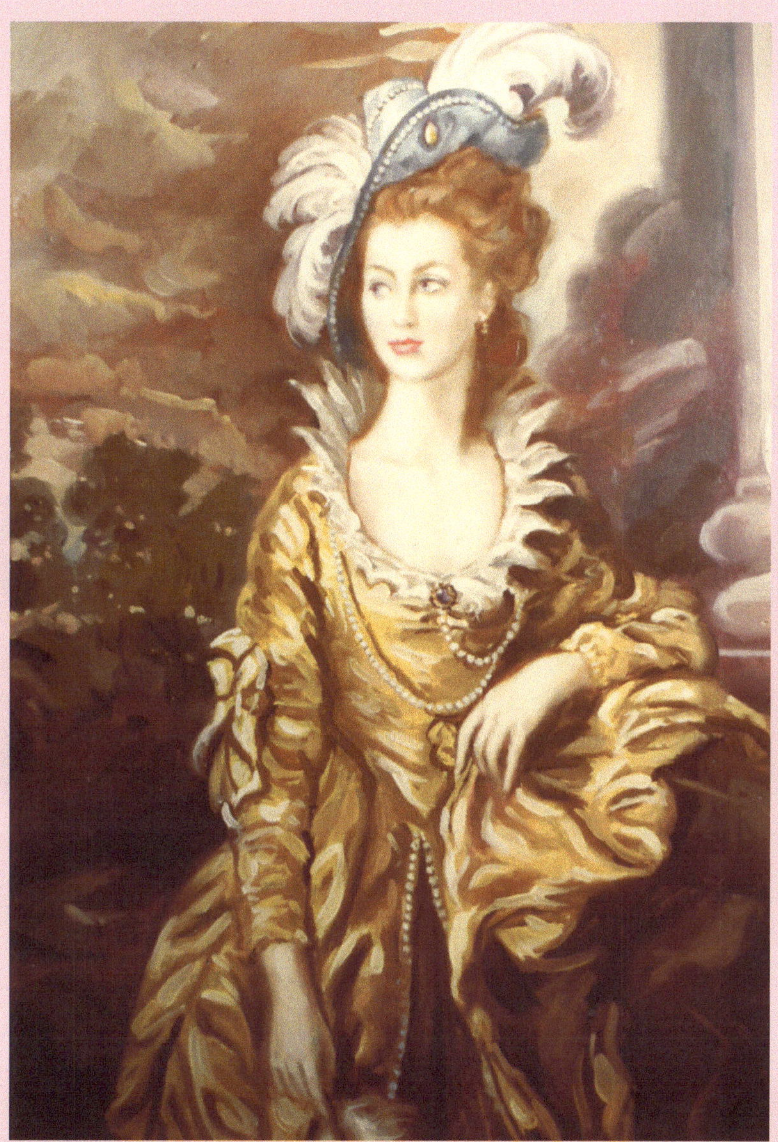

The French Lady

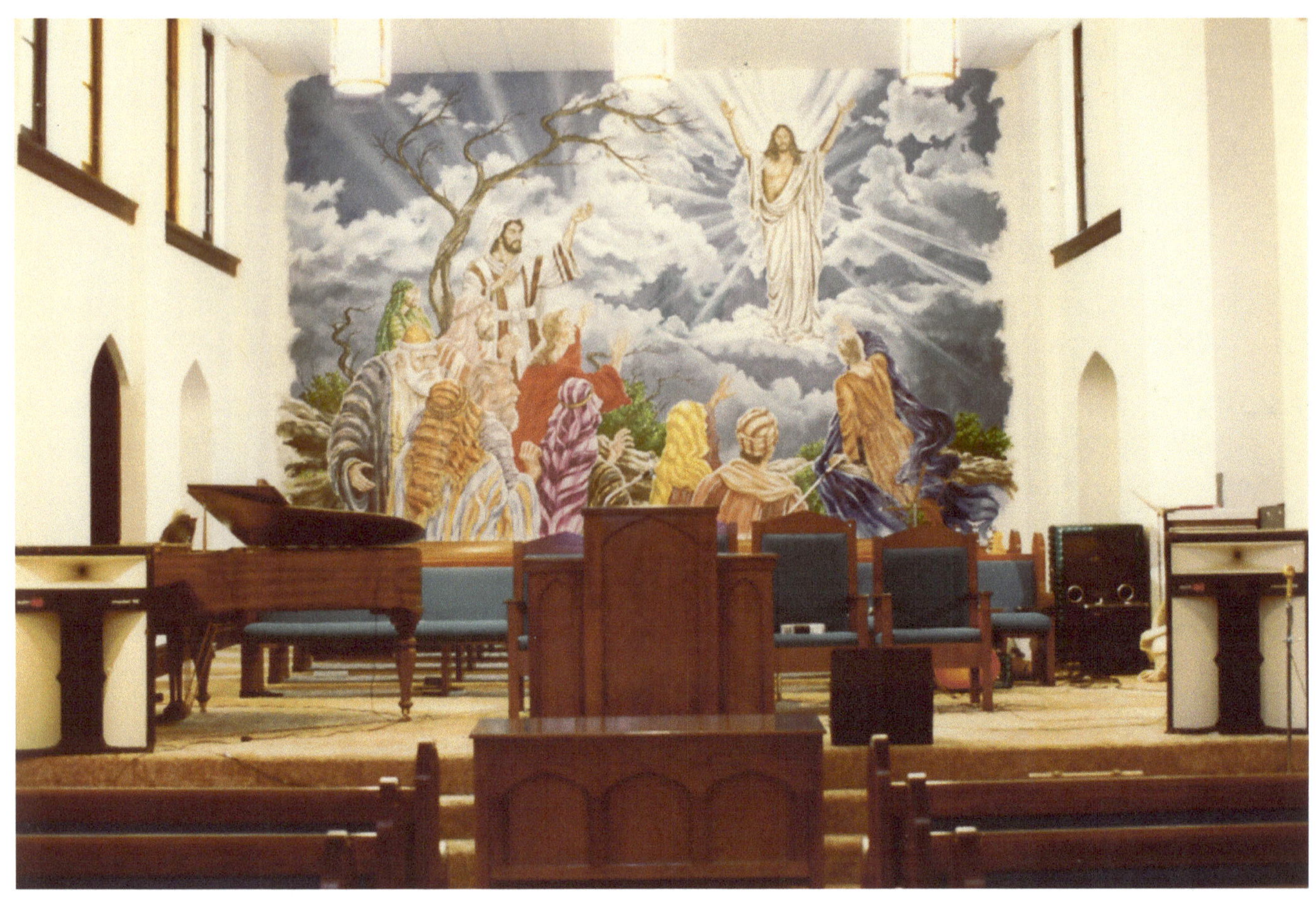

The Ascension, *Music Square Church, Nashville*

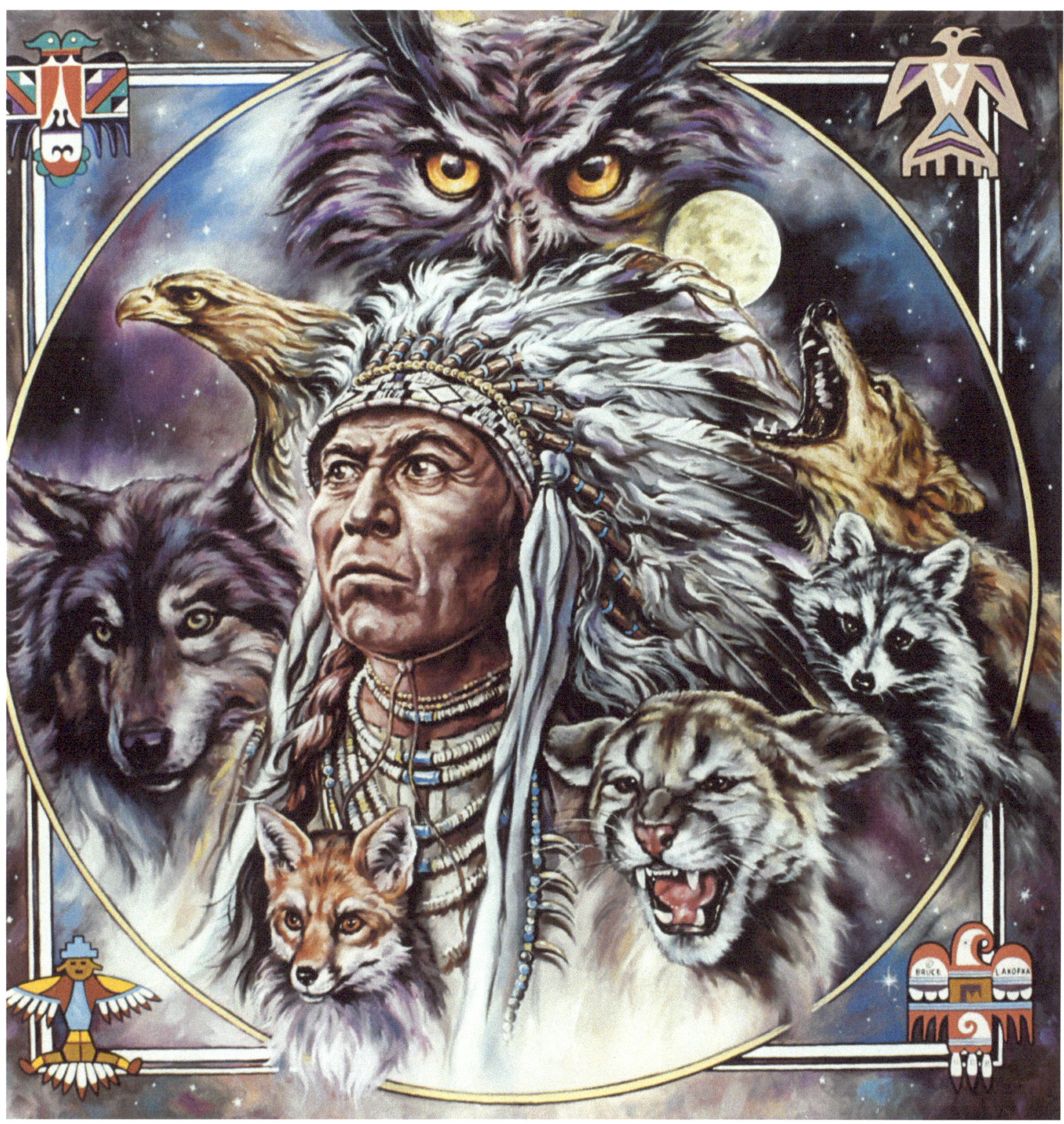

Night Eyes

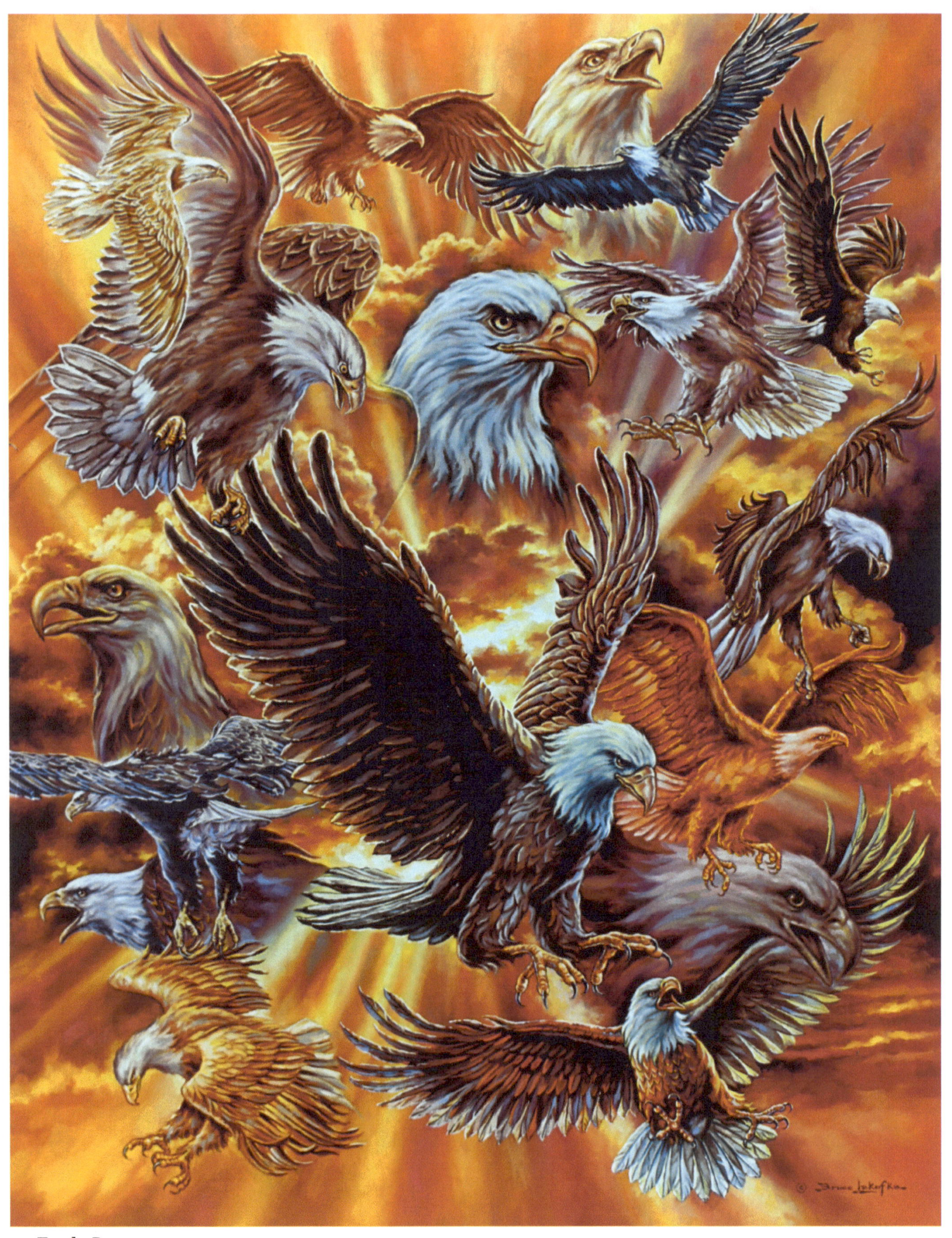

Eagle Dance

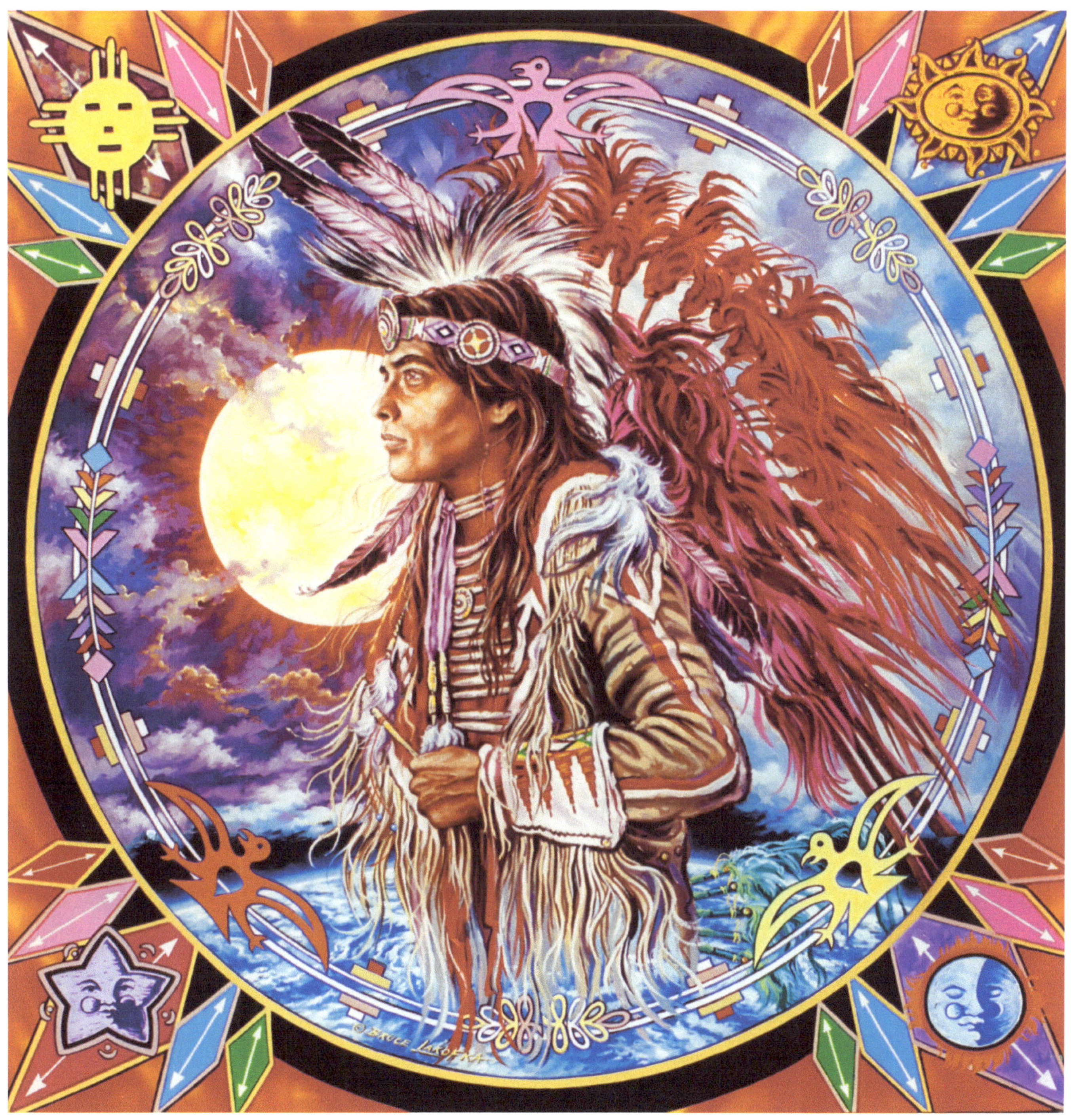

Dance in the Sun

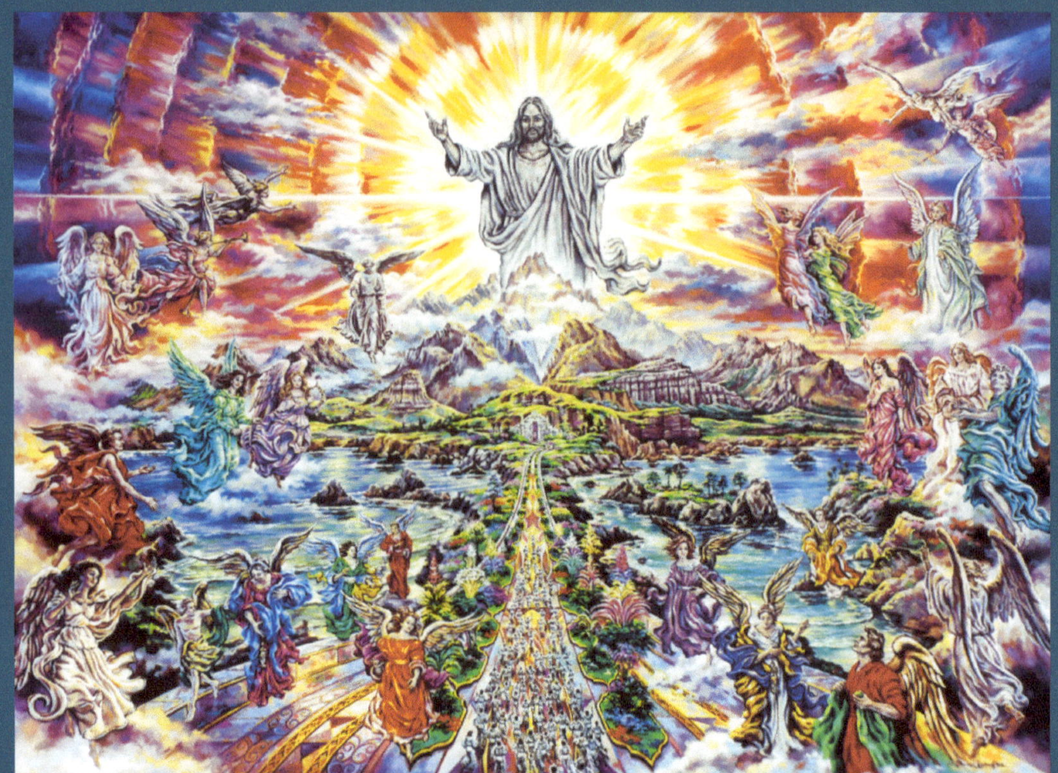

Heavenly Welcome

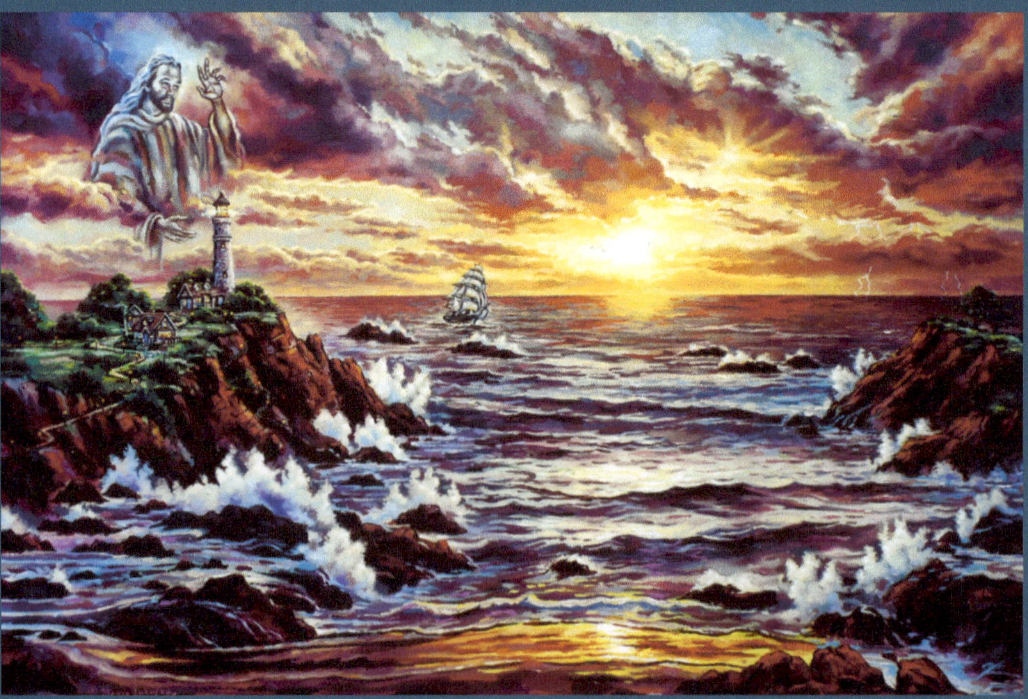

Peace, Be Still

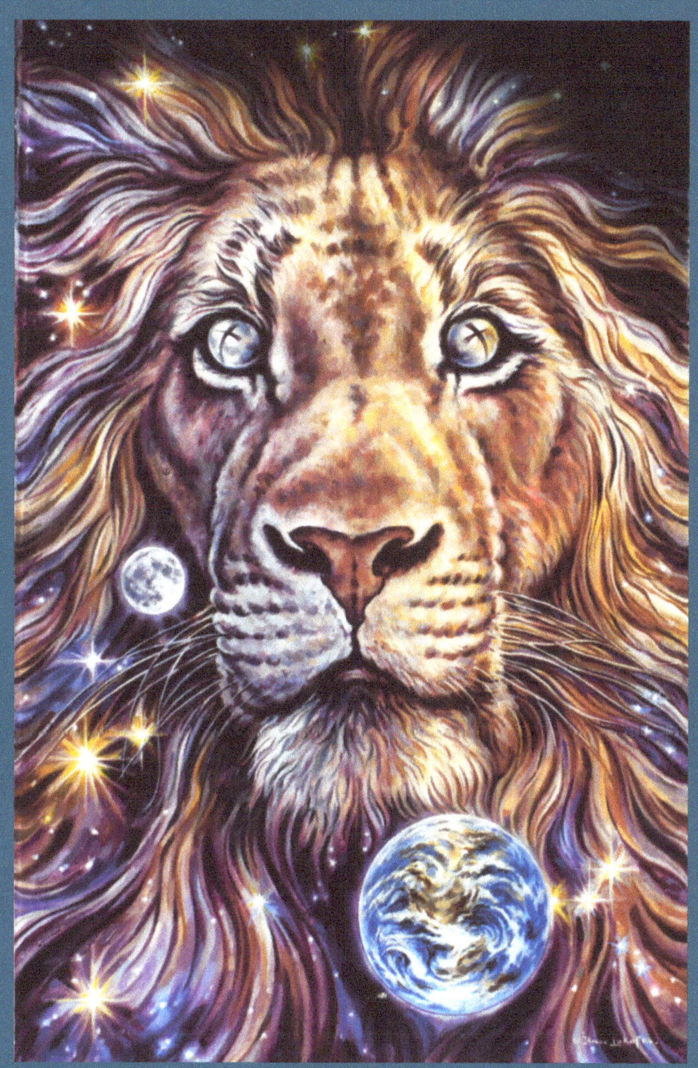

The Lion of the Tribe of Judah

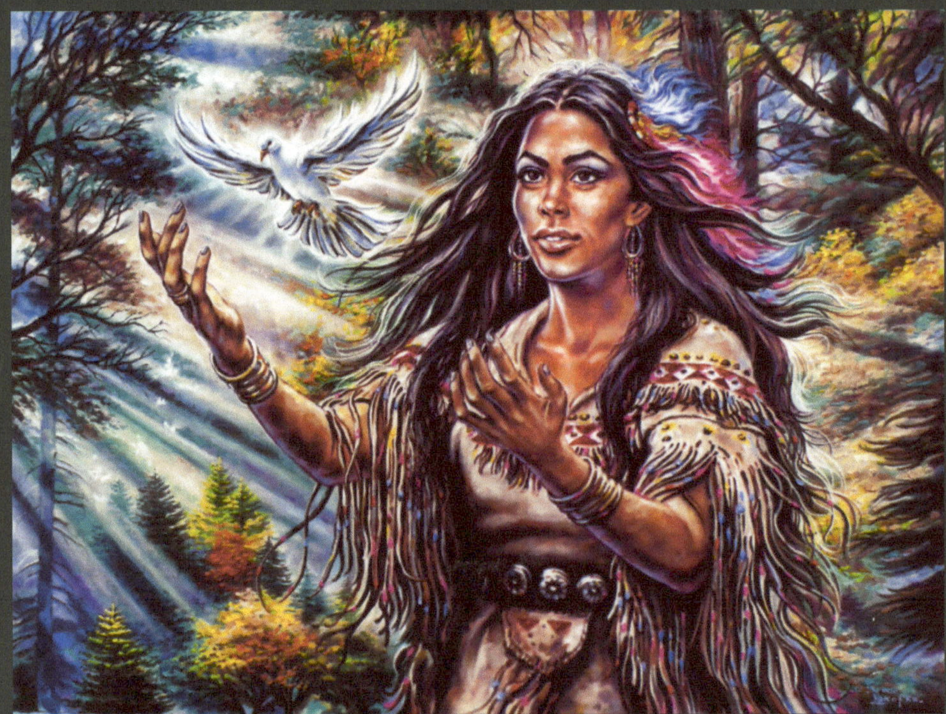

White Dove

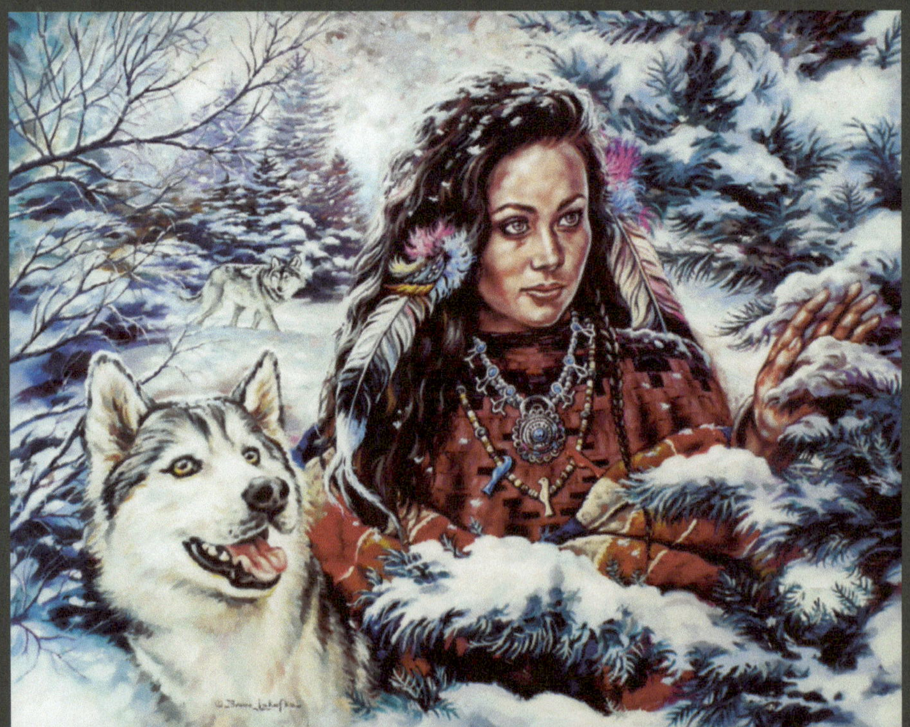

Snowfall

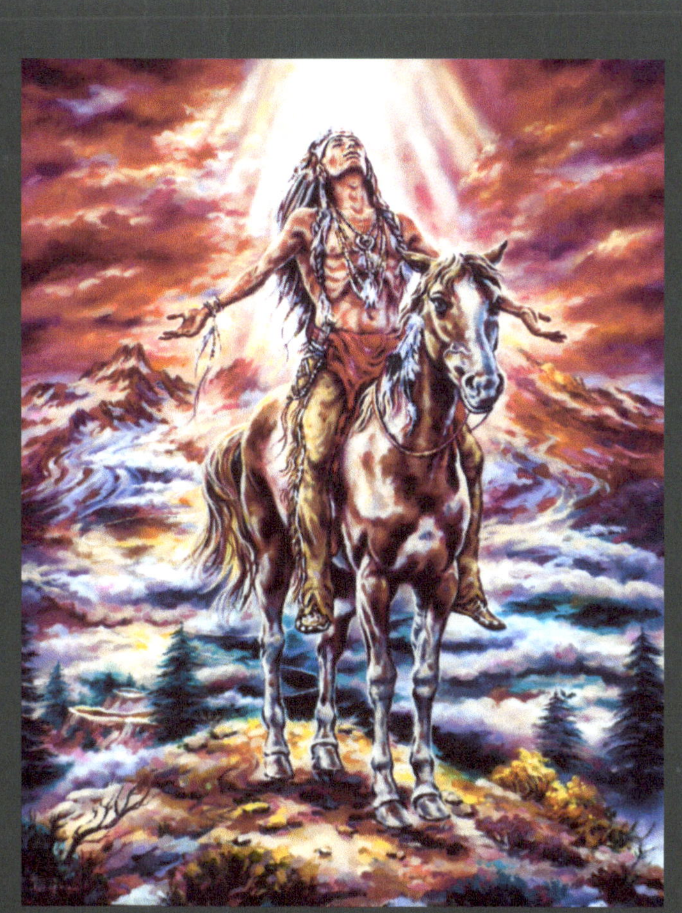

Journey's End

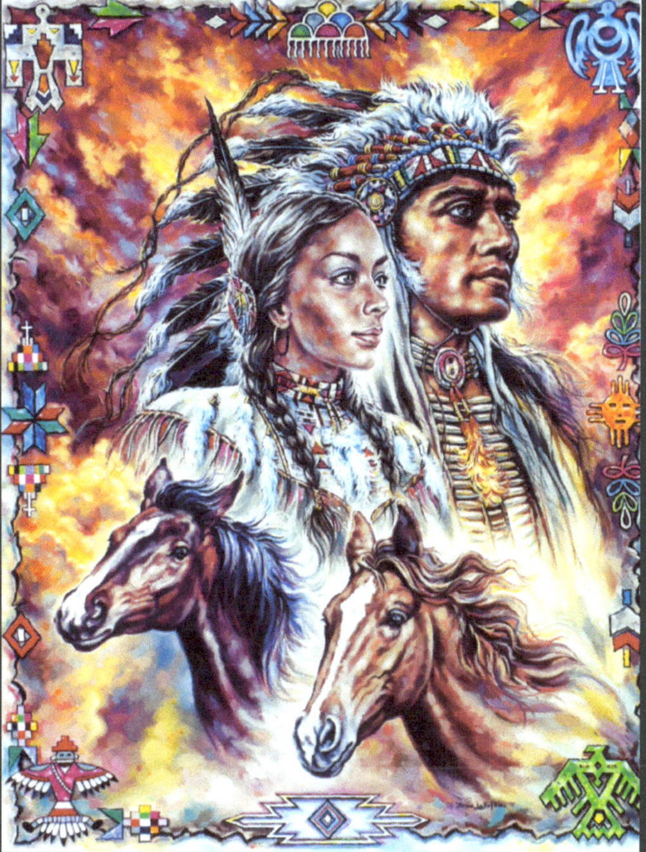

One in Spirit

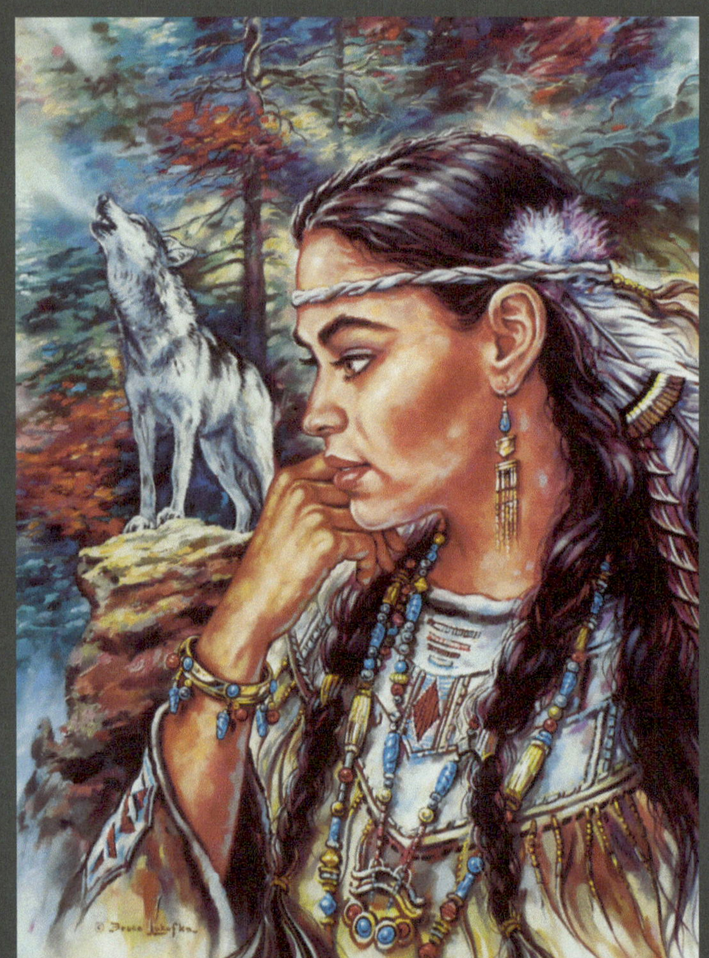

Cry of the Wolf

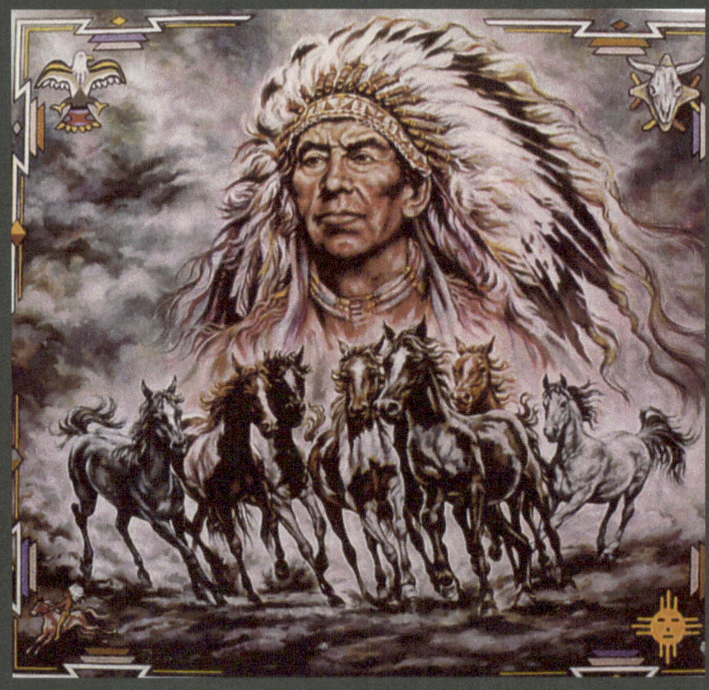

Ride the Wild Wind

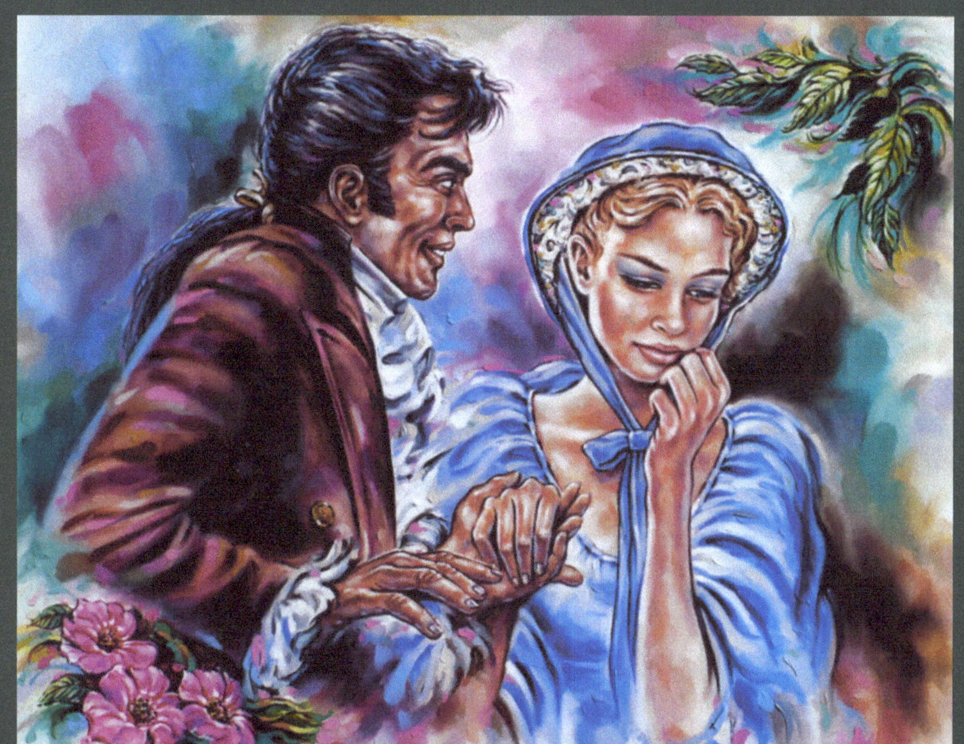

The Proposal

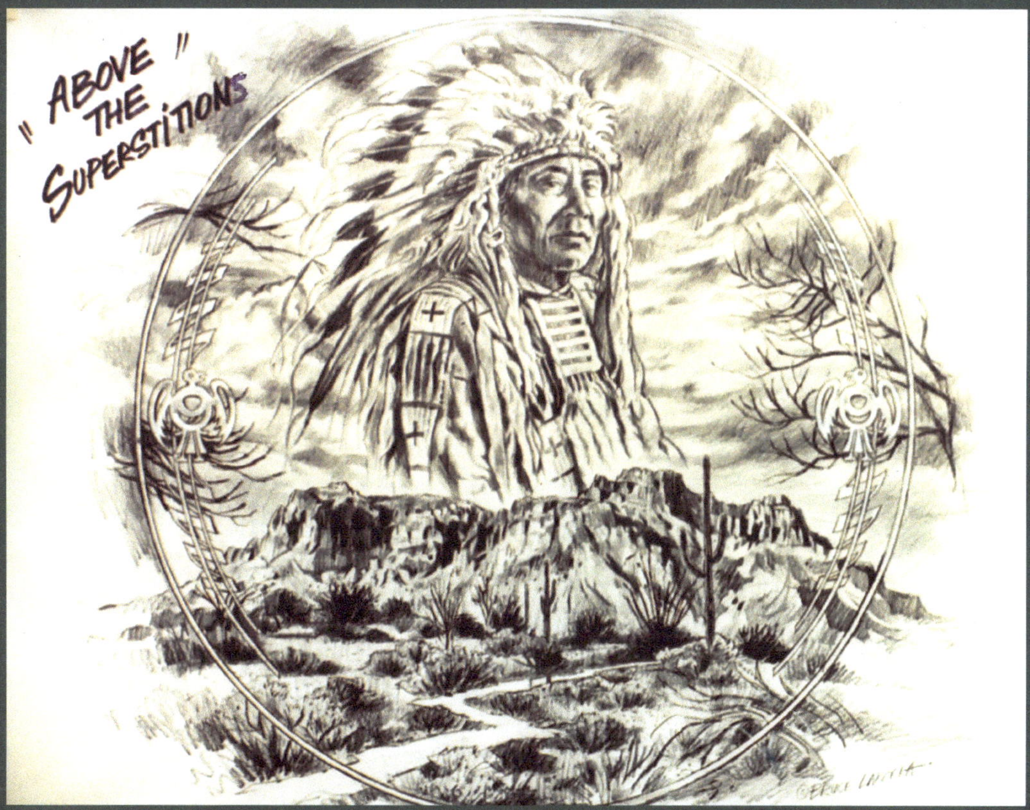

Above the Superstitions

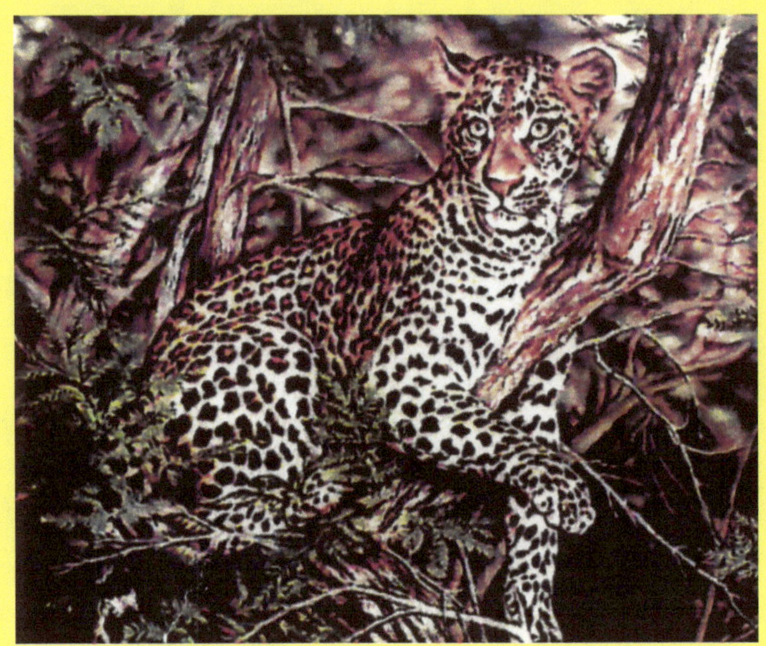

Leopard's Domain

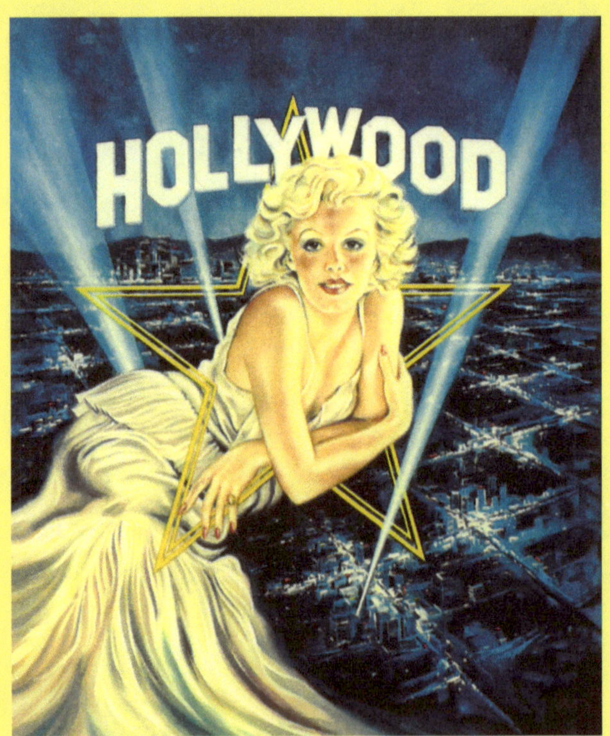

Spirit of Hollywood

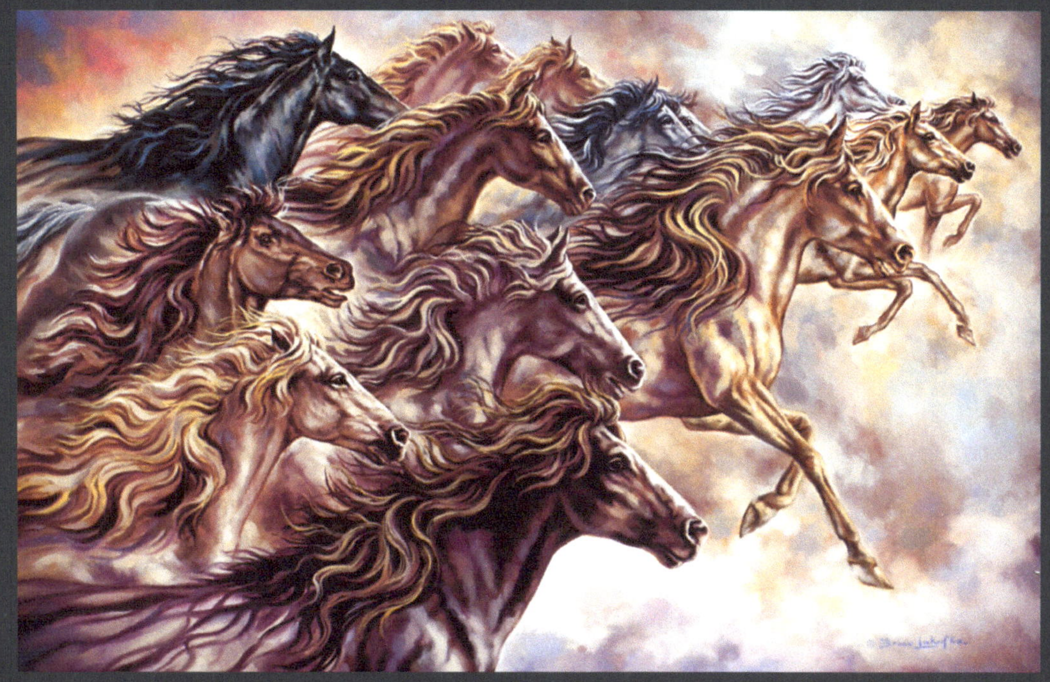

Into the Wind

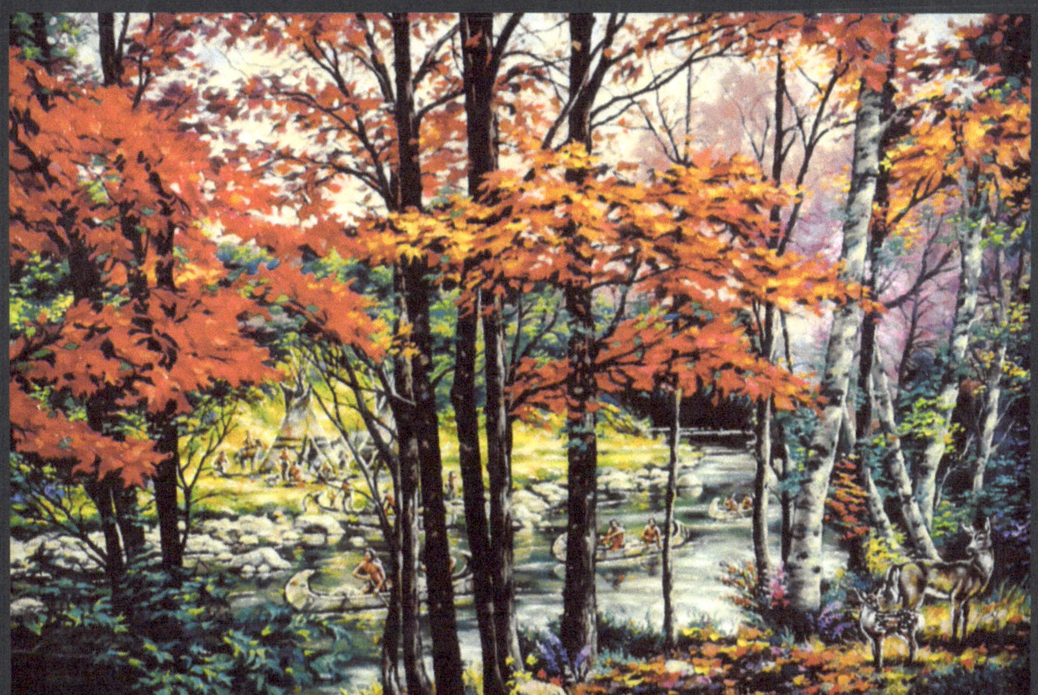

Fall River Camp

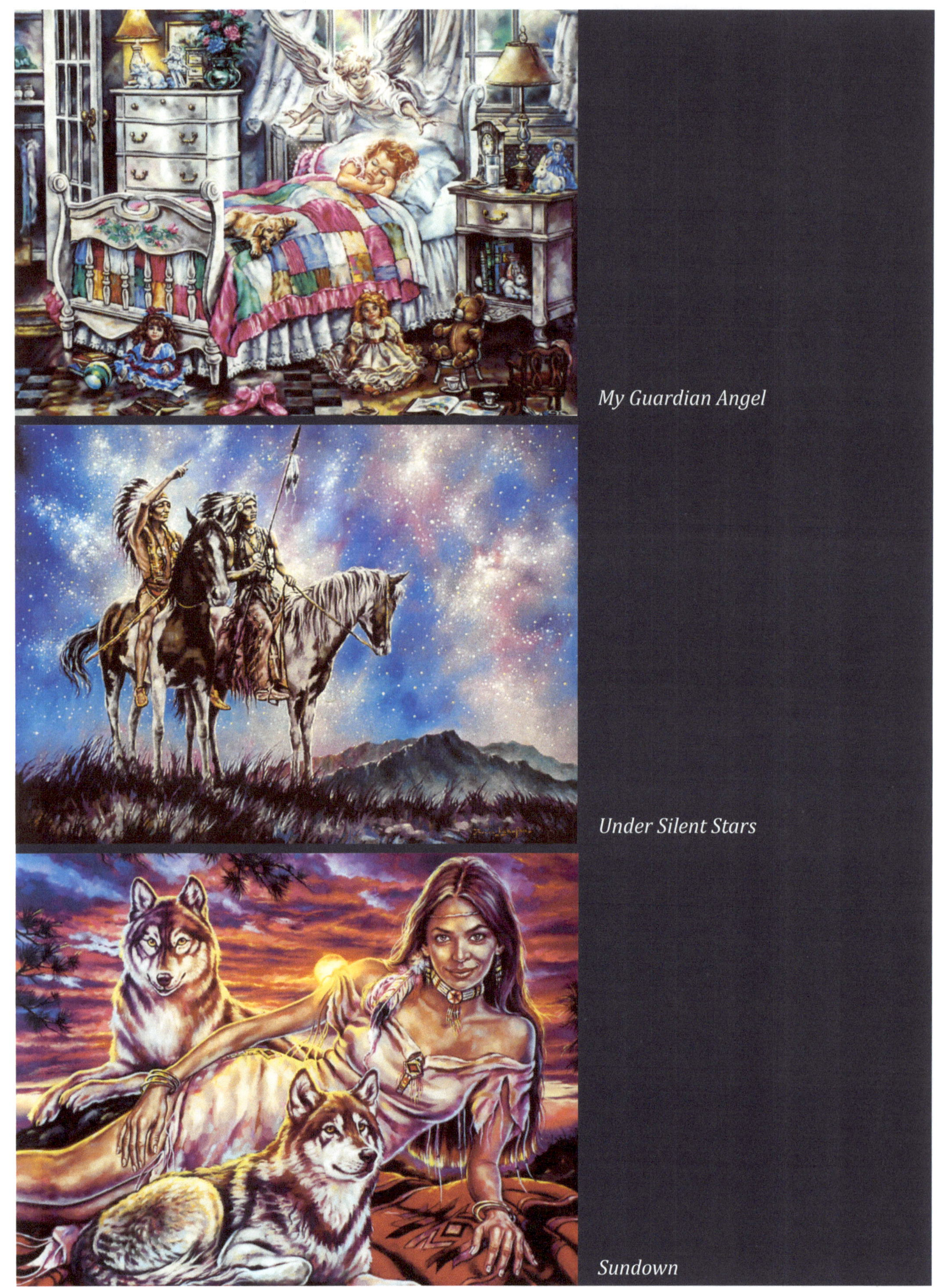

My Guardian Angel

Under Silent Stars

Sundown

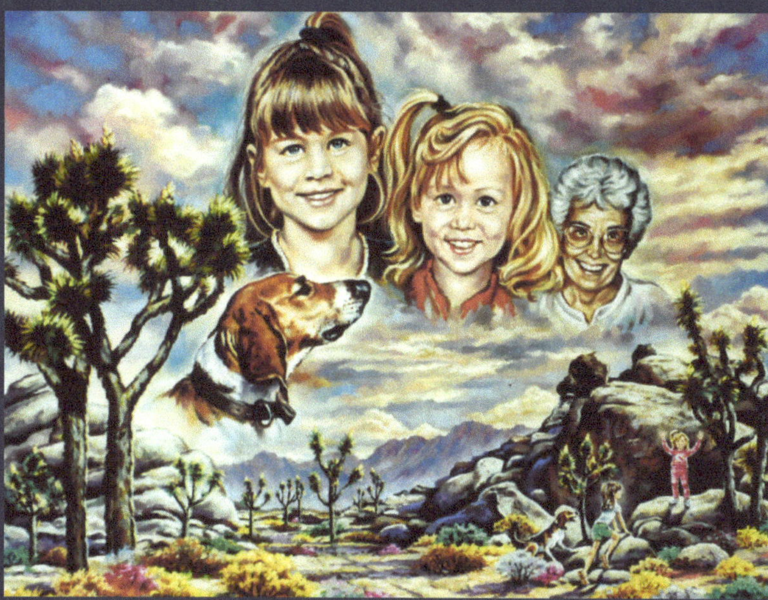

Desert Sunshine

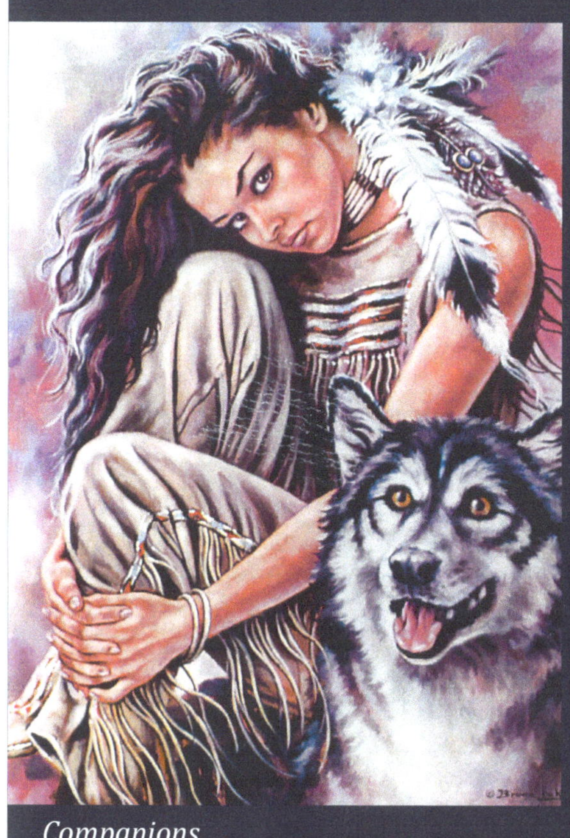

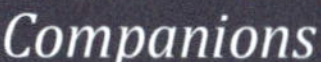

Companions

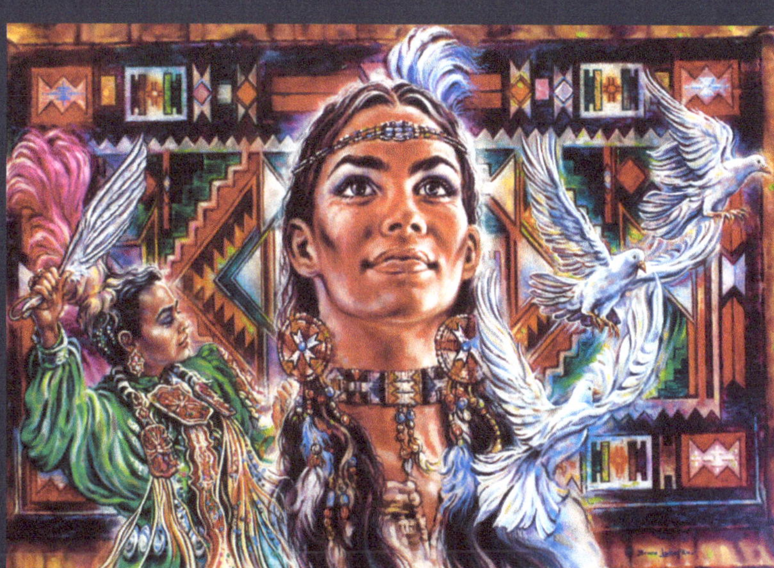

Native Tapestry

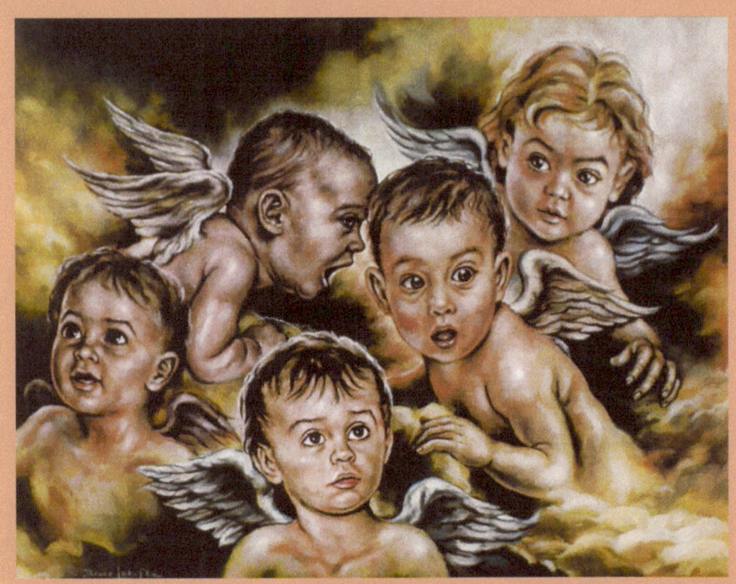

Angel Whispers

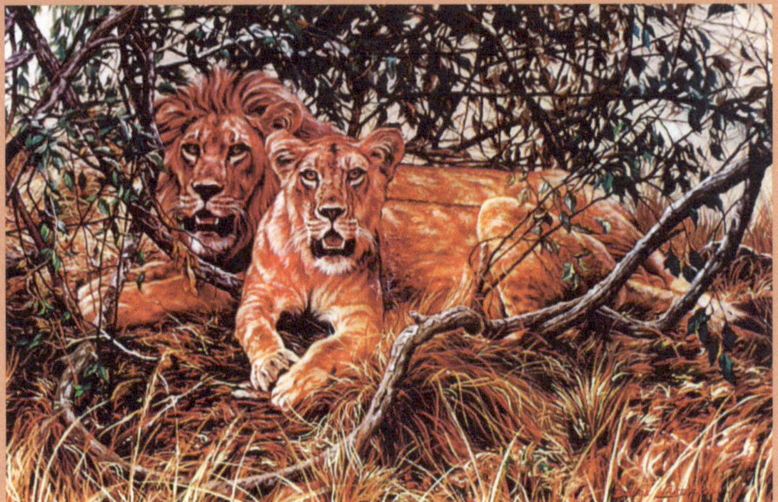

Afternoon Shade

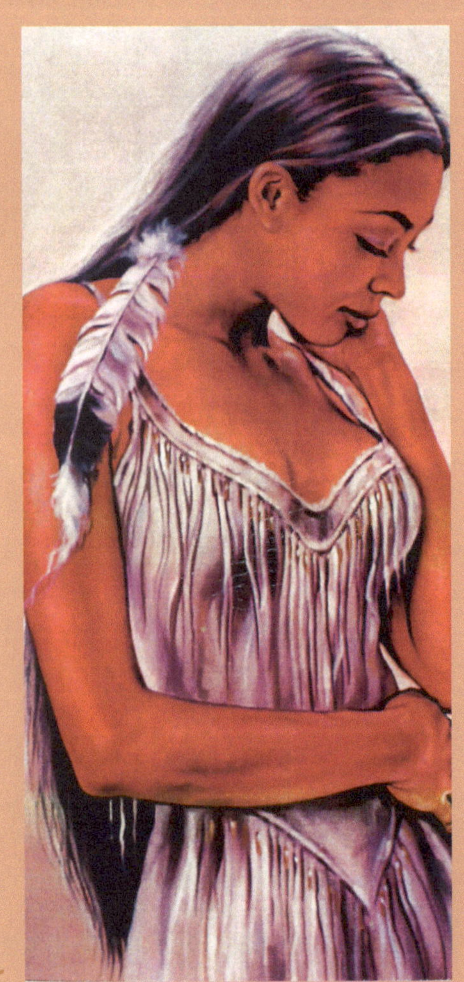

The Touch

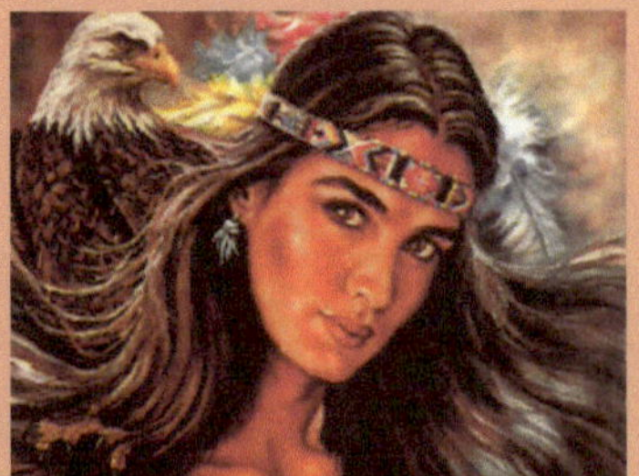

The Guardian

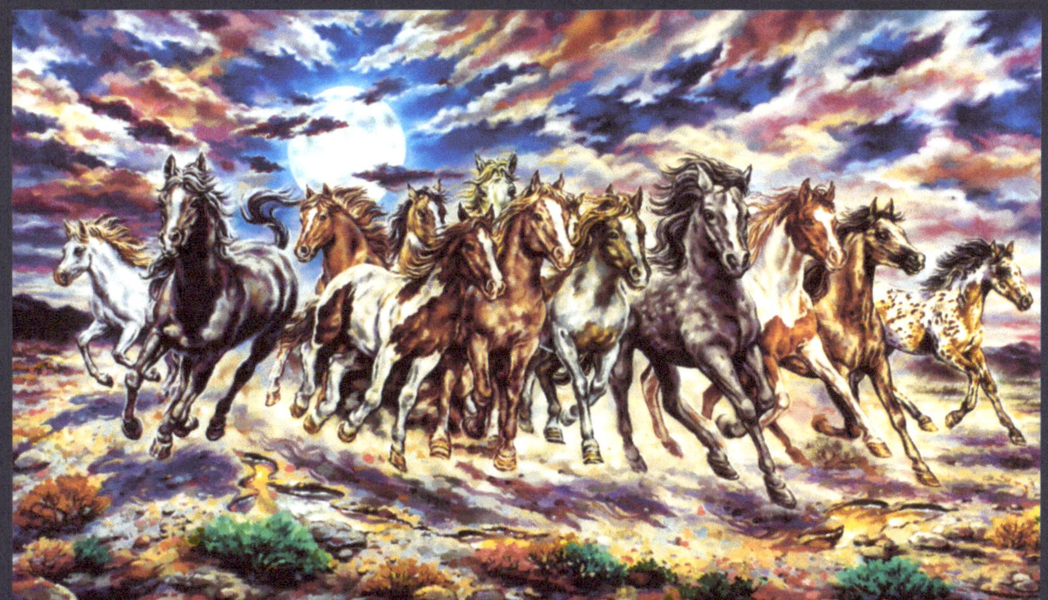

Racing with the Moon

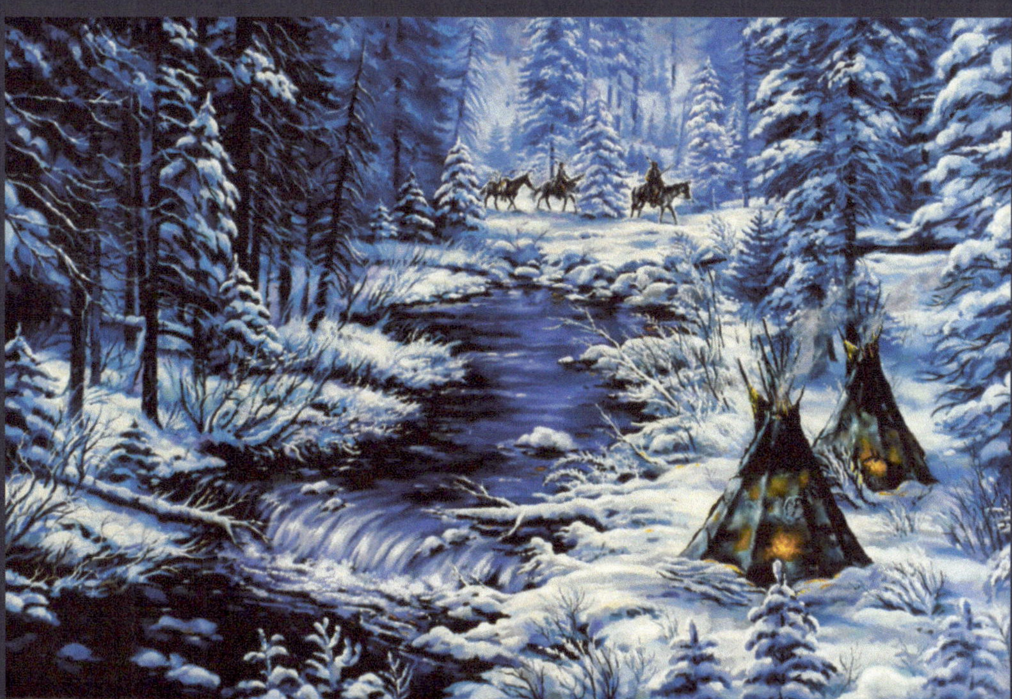

Home from the Winter Hunt

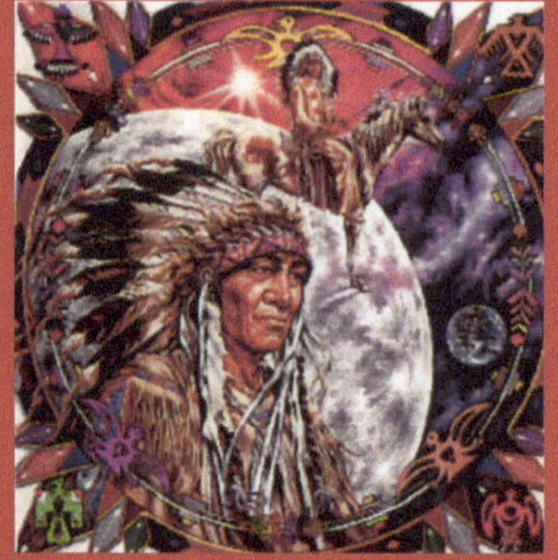

Other Worlds

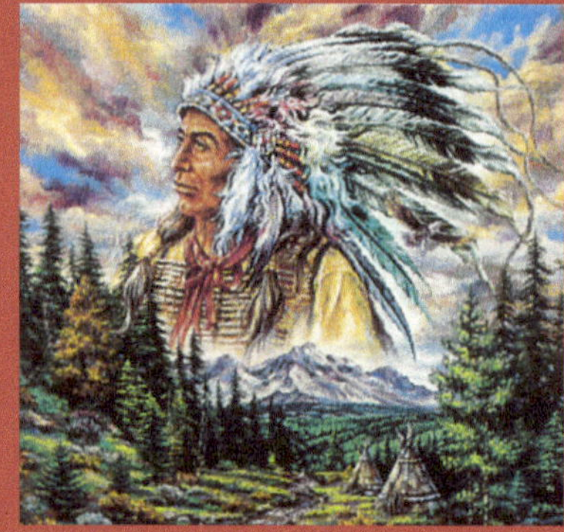

Under the Big Sky

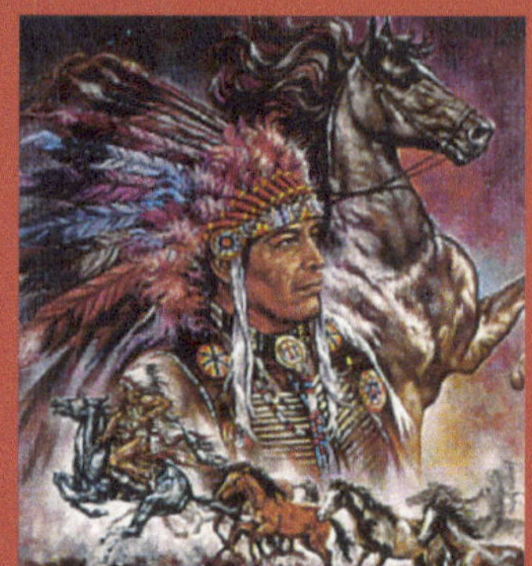

Night Riders

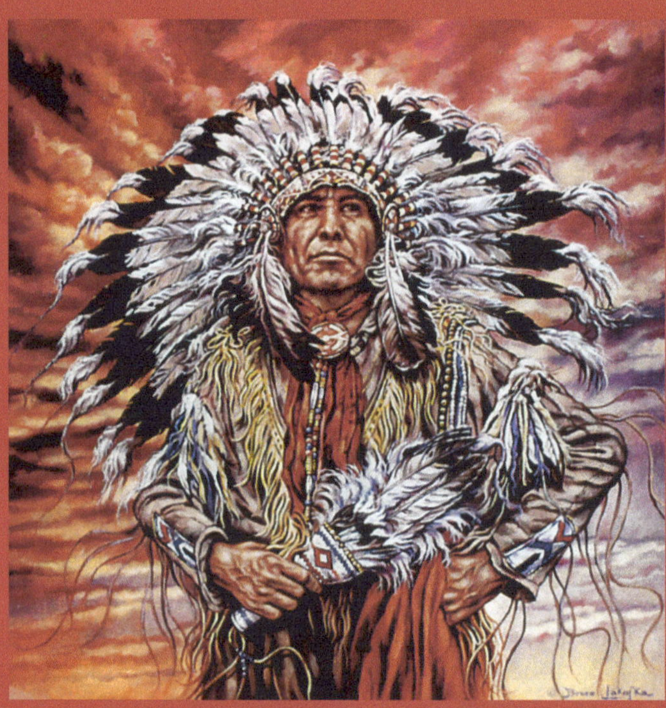

Sunset and Glory

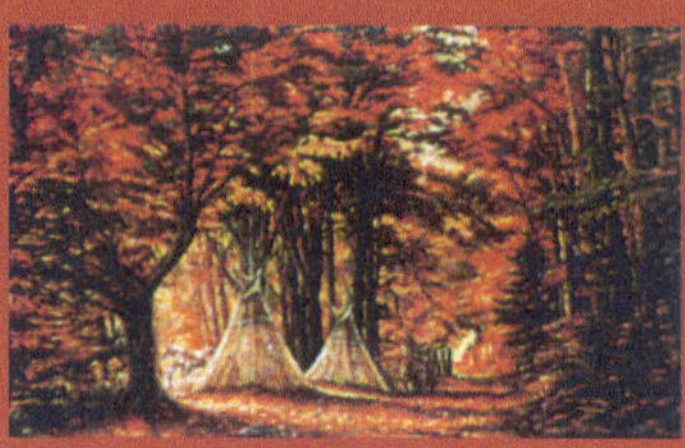

Native Cathedral

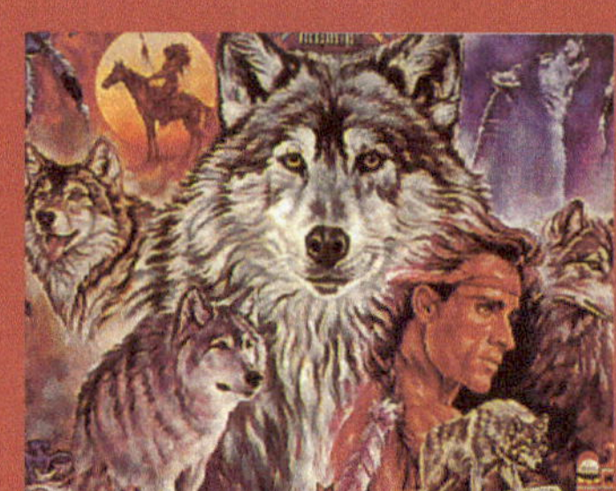

In the Shadow of the Wolf

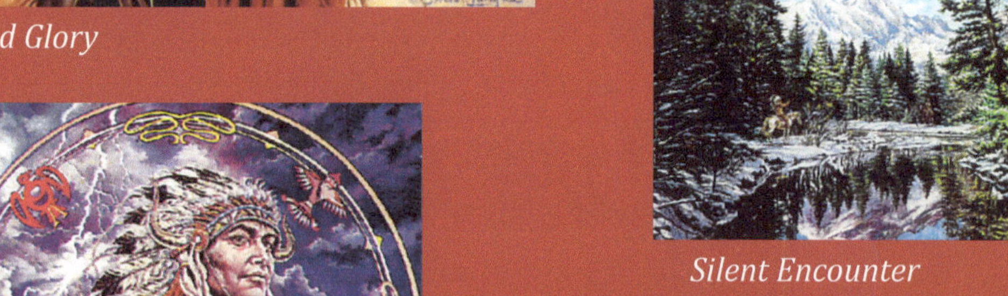

Silent Encounter

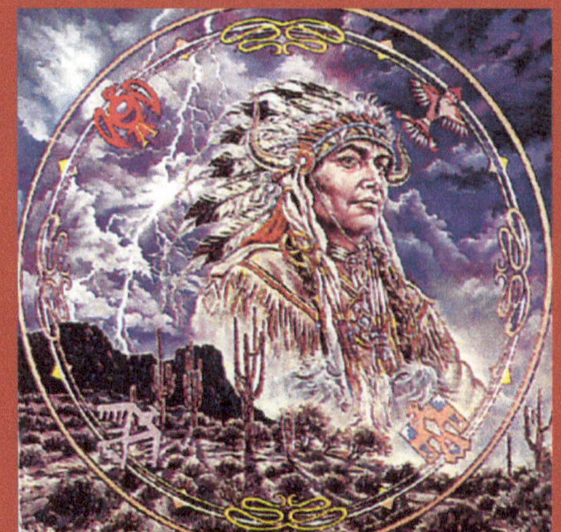

When Lightning Casts Shadows

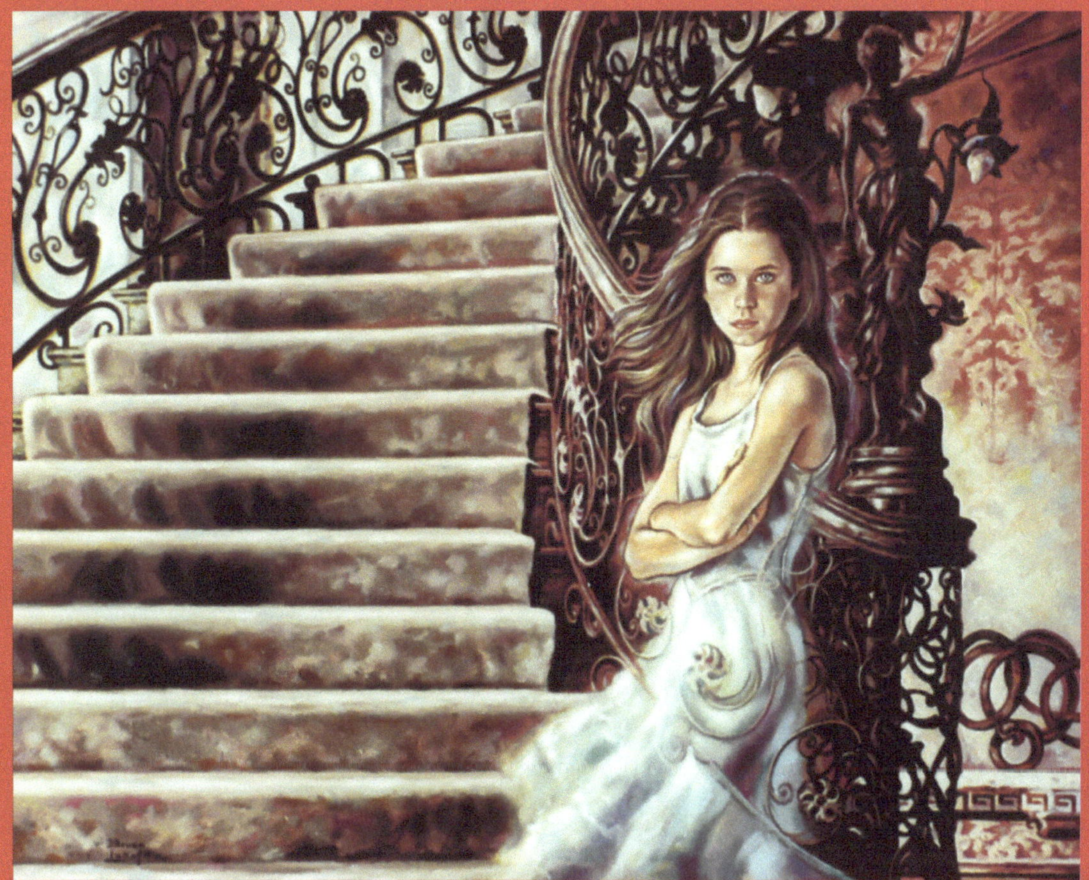

The Girl on the Staircase

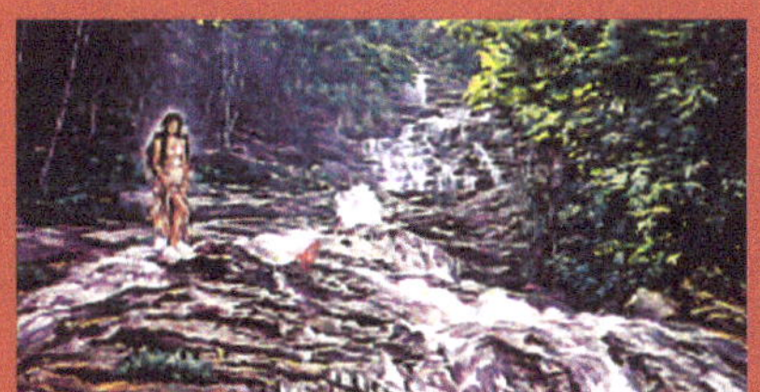

Maiden of the Falls

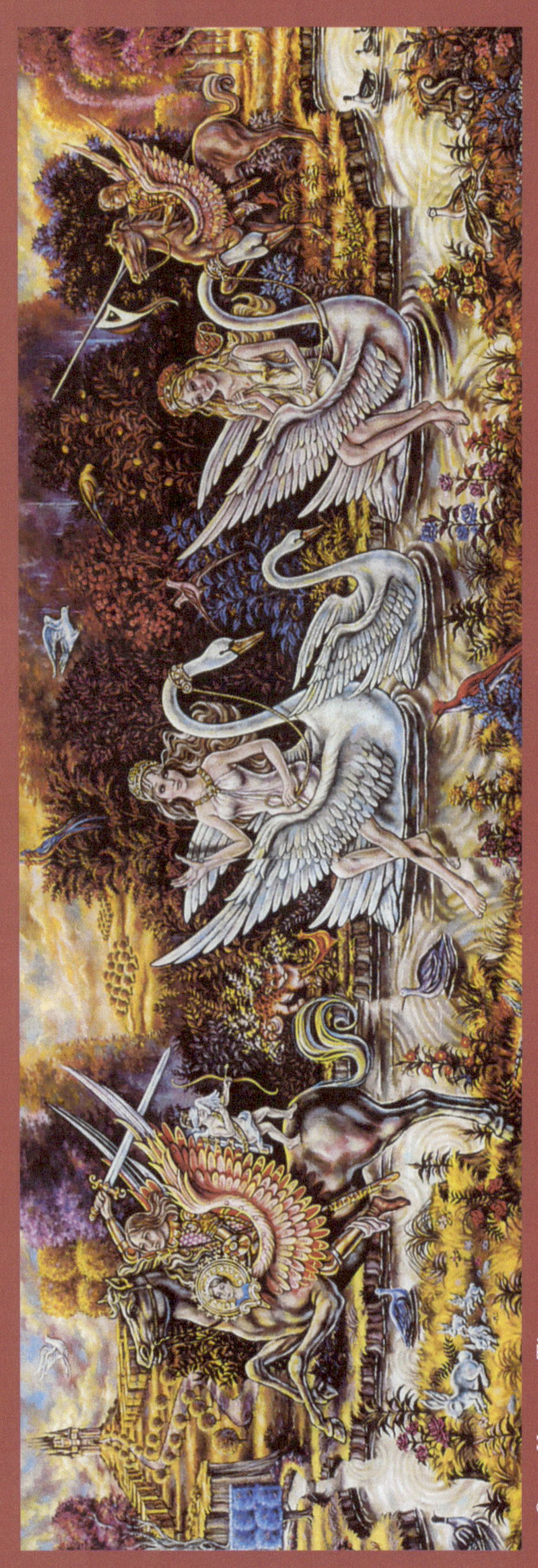

Once Upon a Time

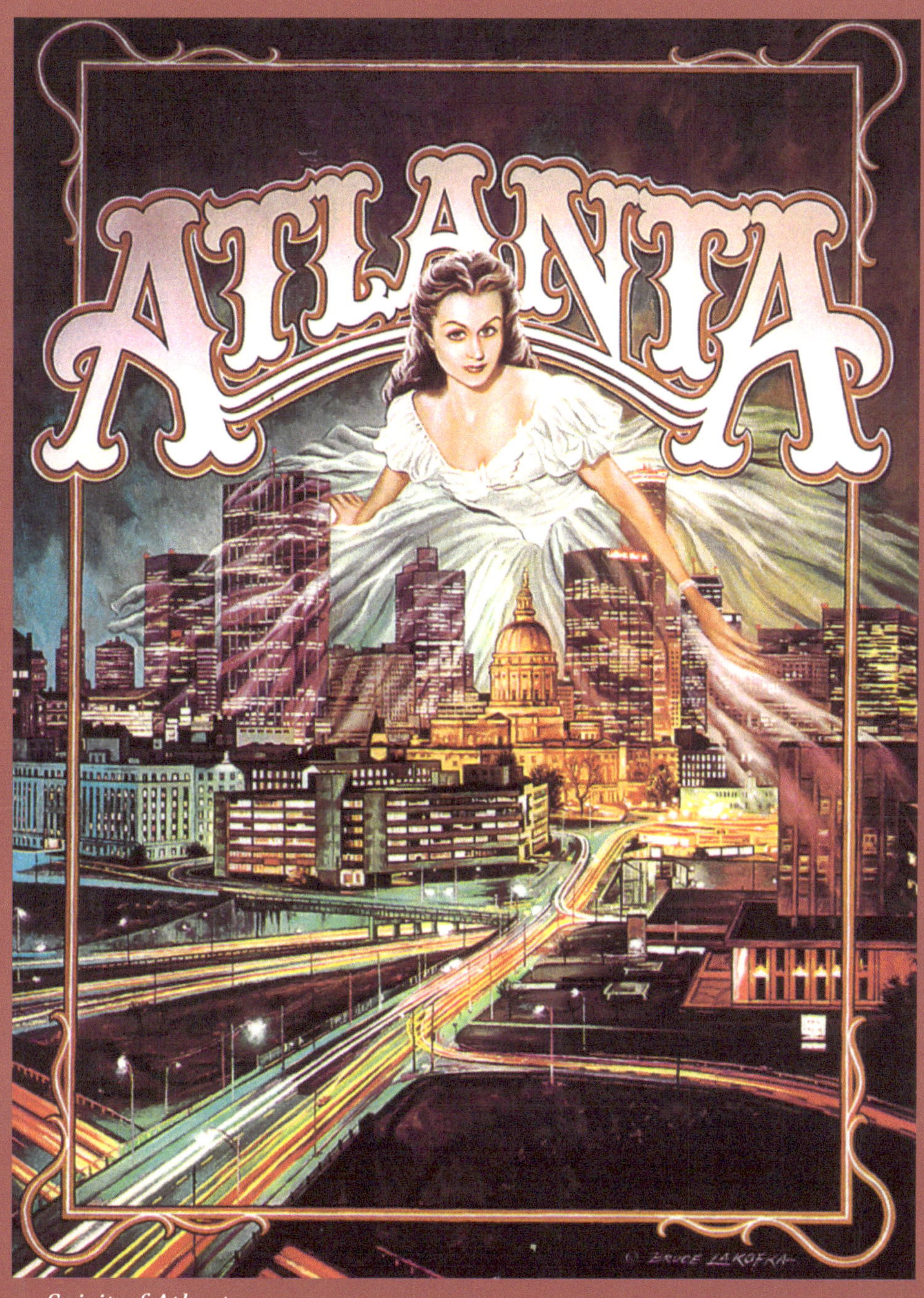

Spirit of Atlanta

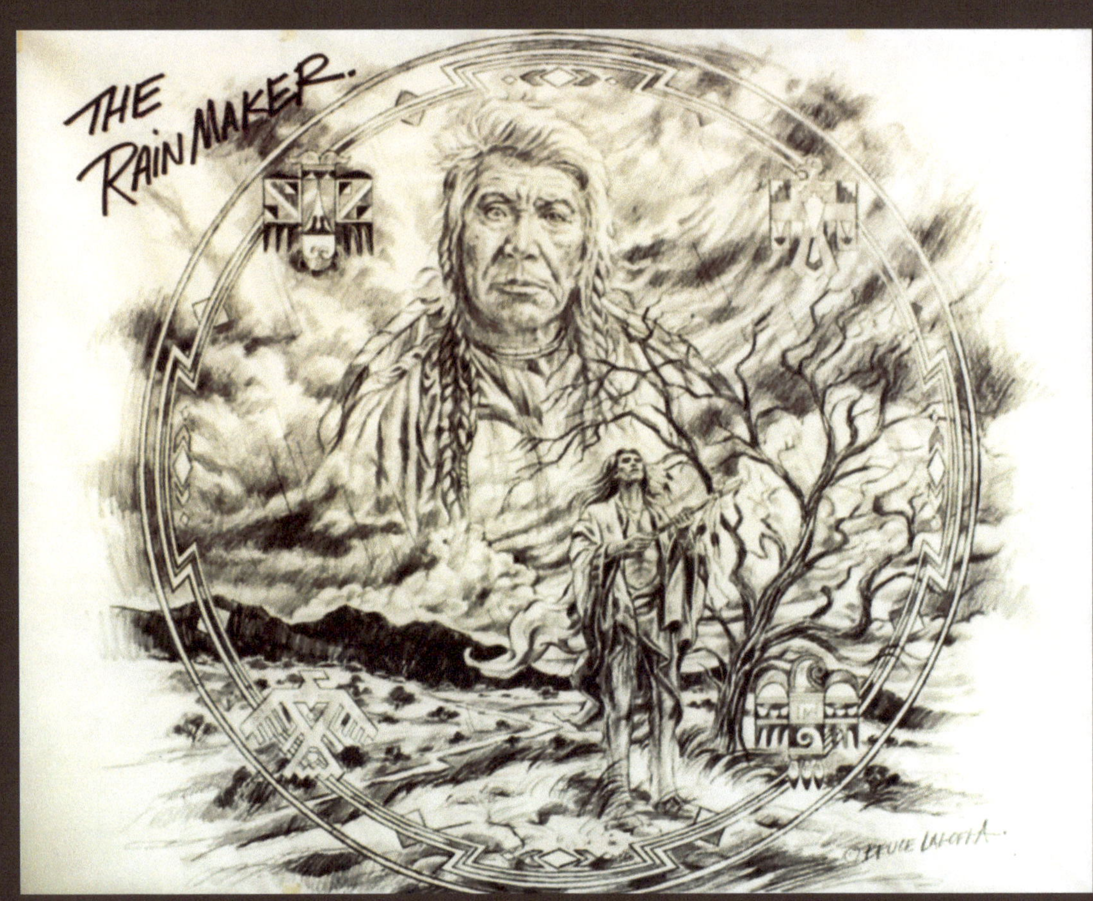

The Rainmaker

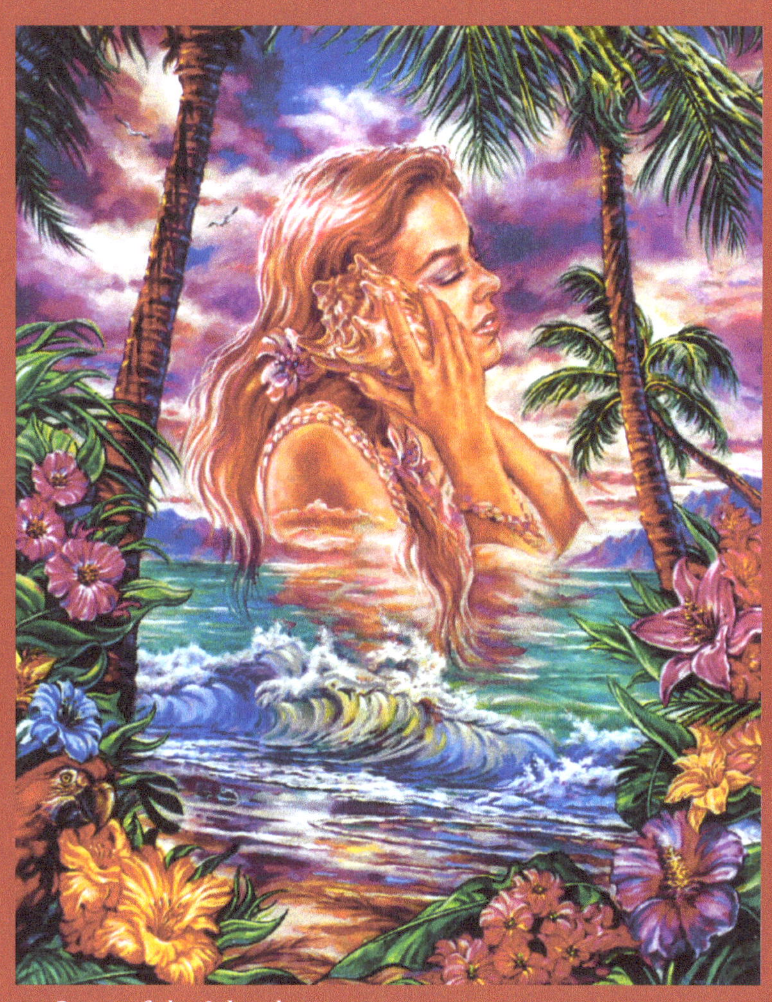

Song of the Islands

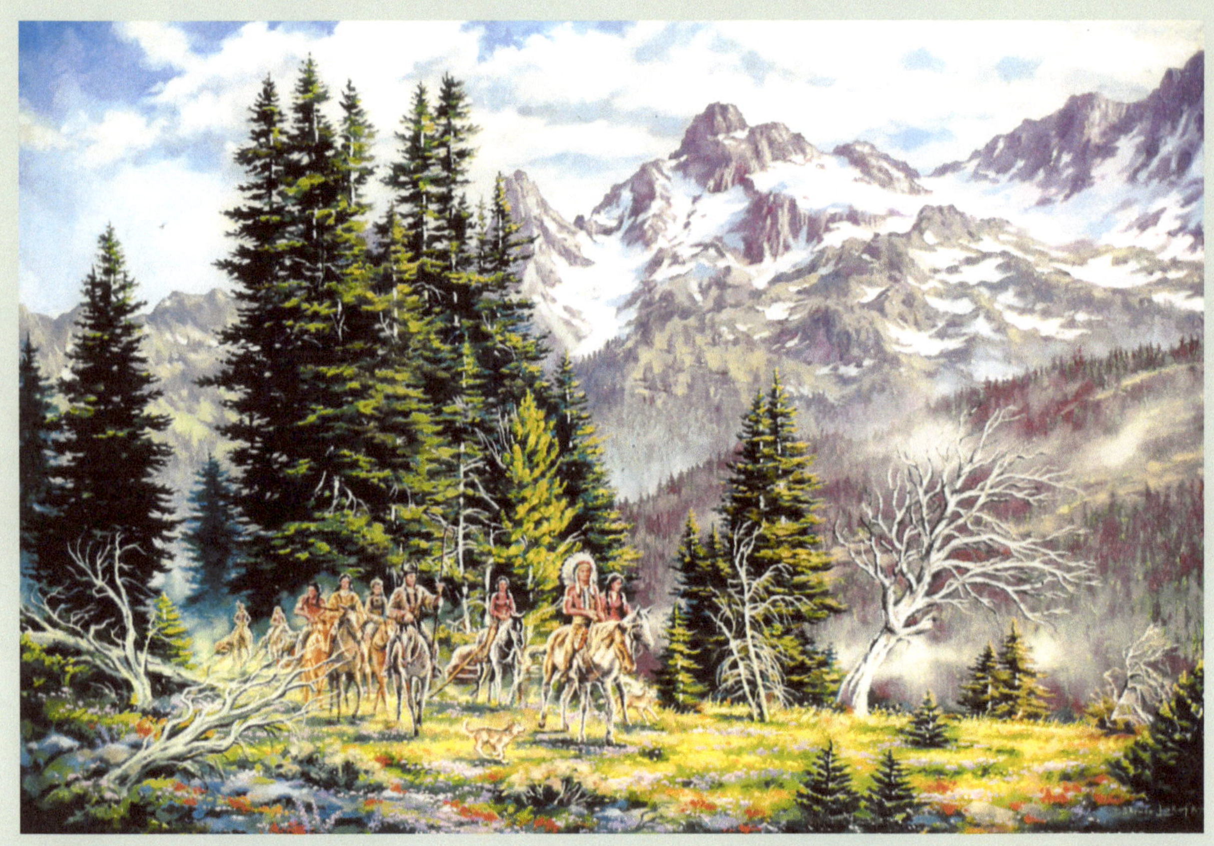

Back to the High Country

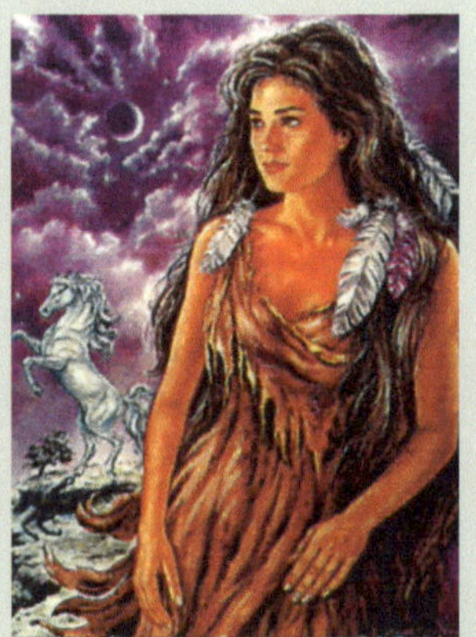

Crescent Moon

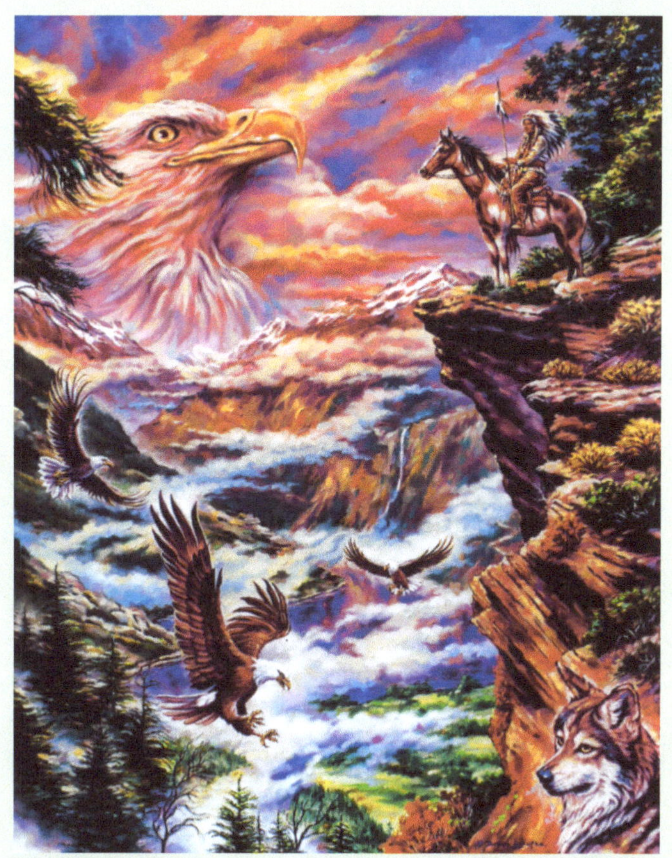

Above the Clouds

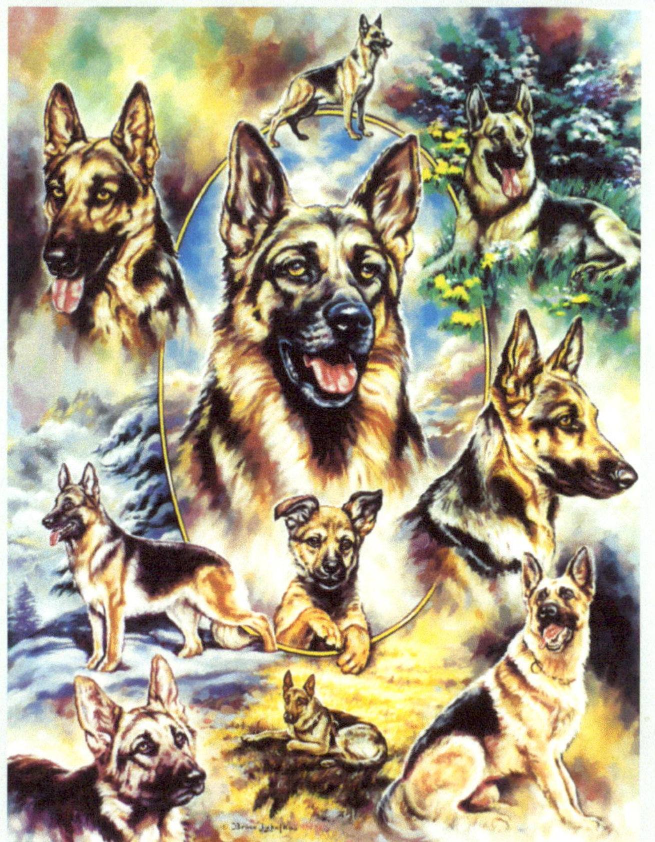

The German Shepherd

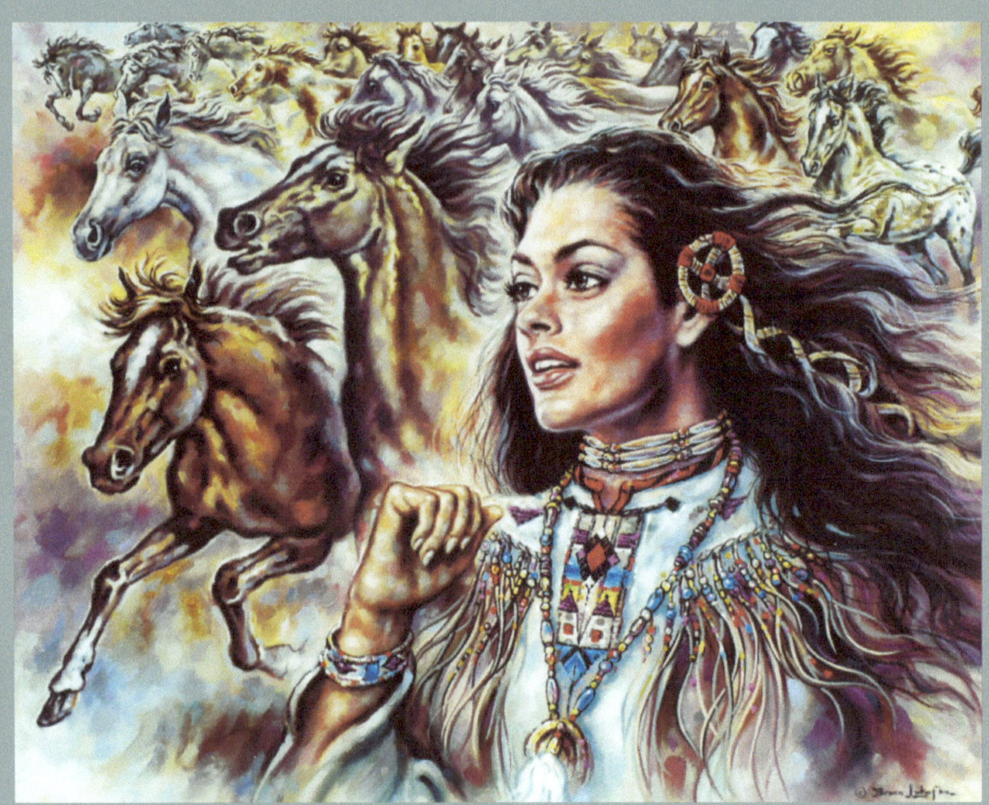

Stampede

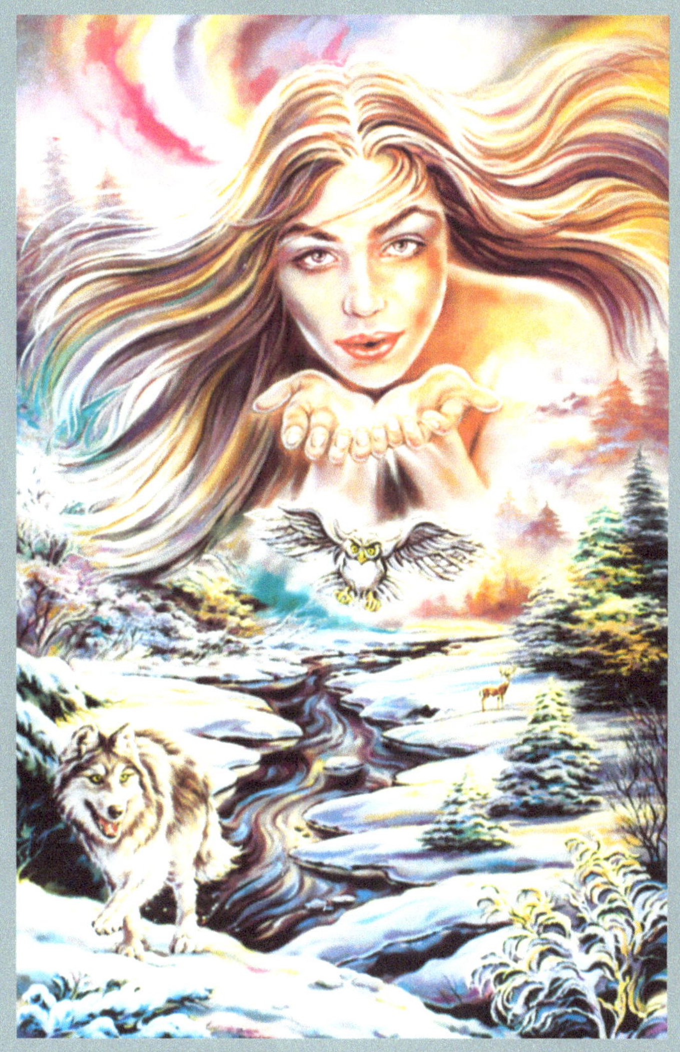

A Winter's Breath

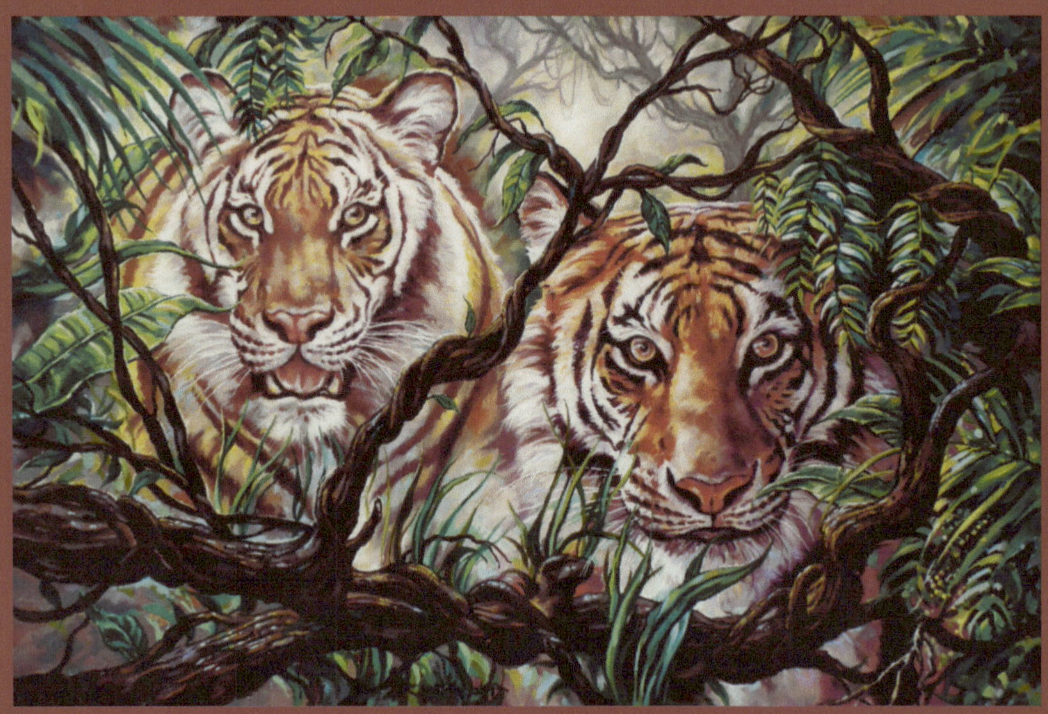

Eyes of the Jungle

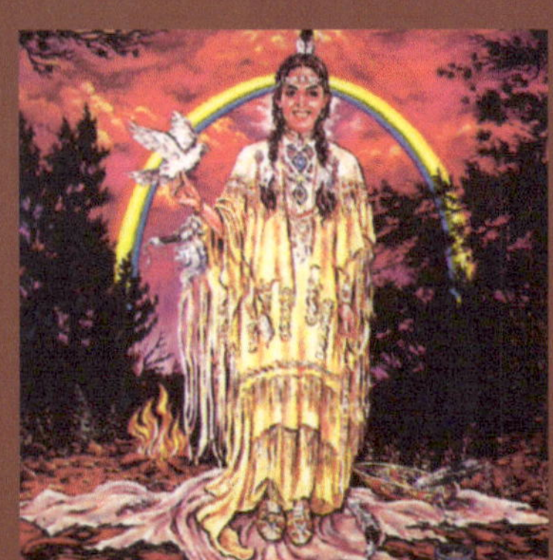

Rainbow Dove

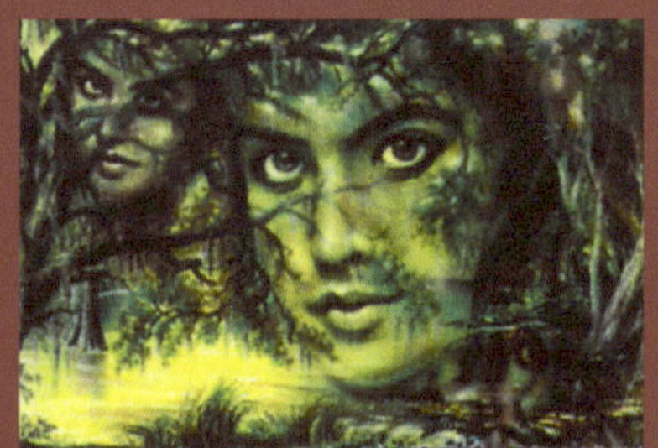

Seminole Spirits

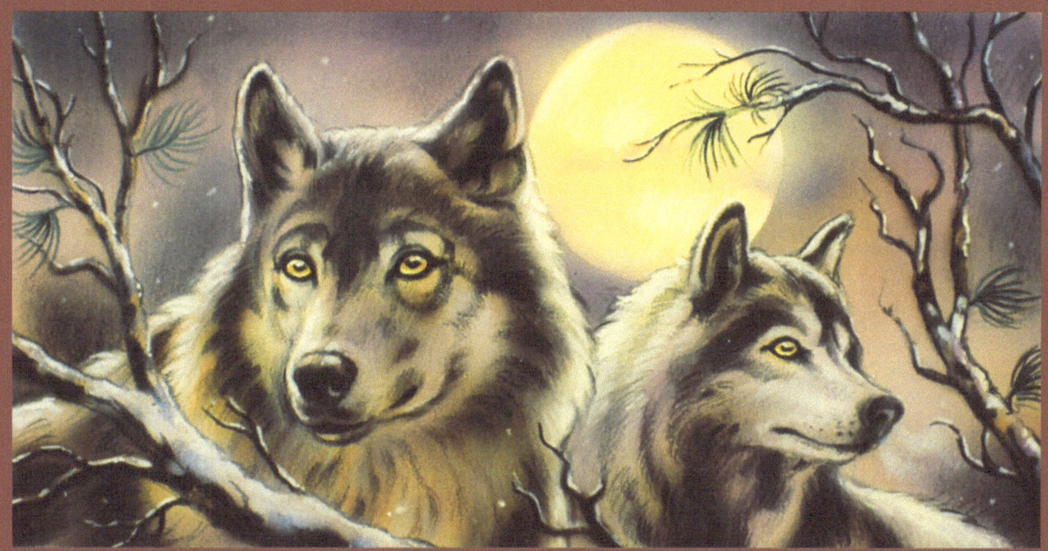

Moon Wolves

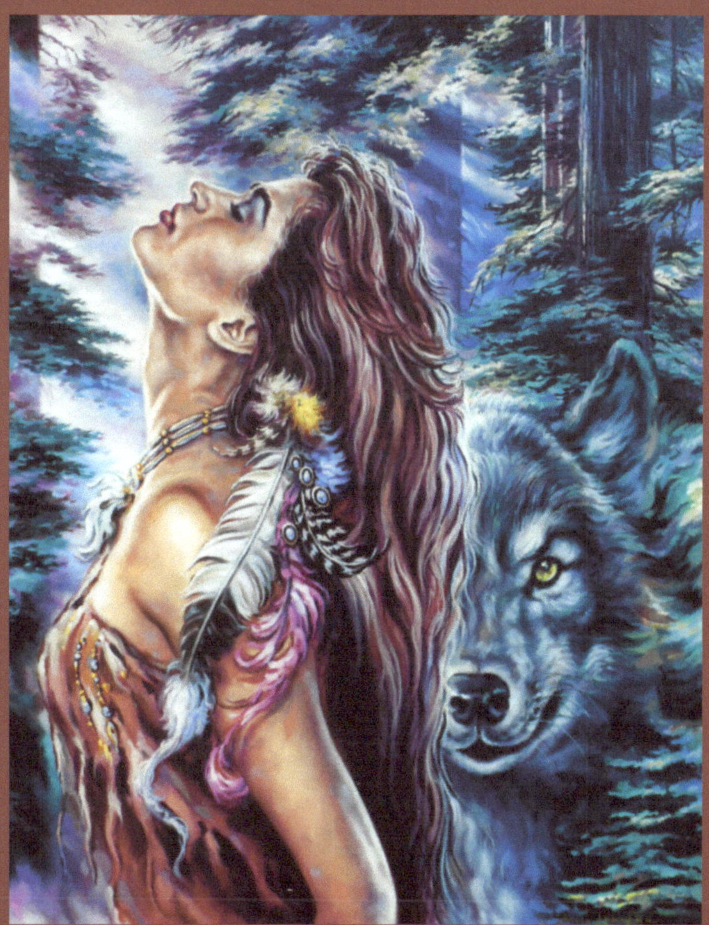

Drawn to the Light

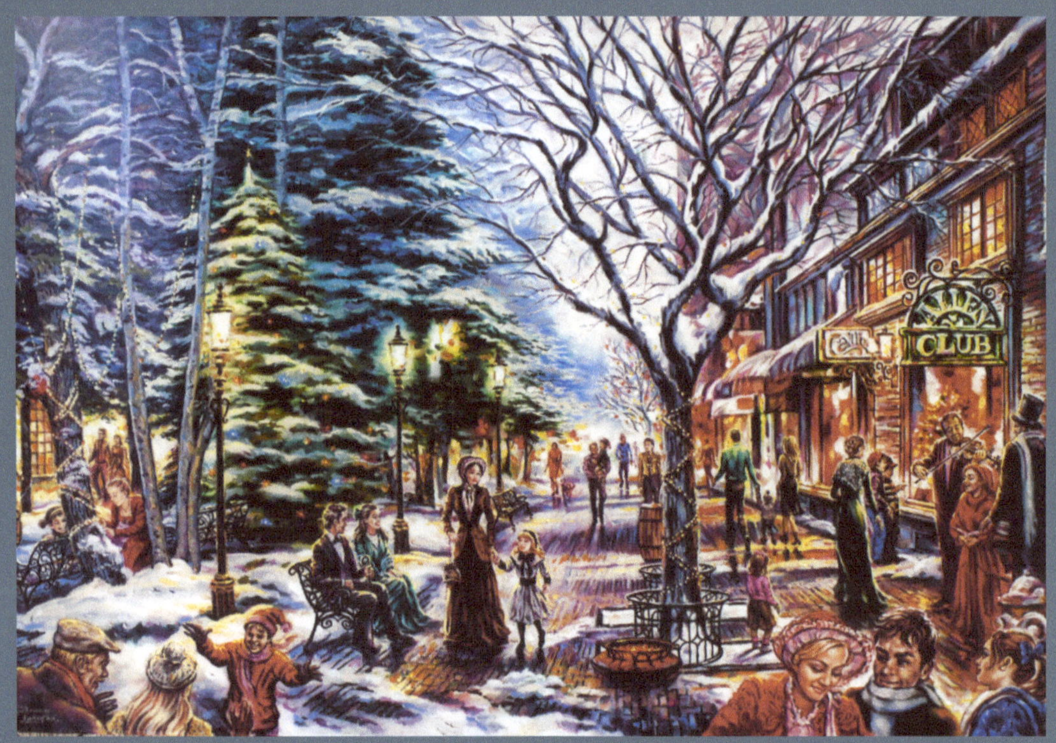

Village Lights

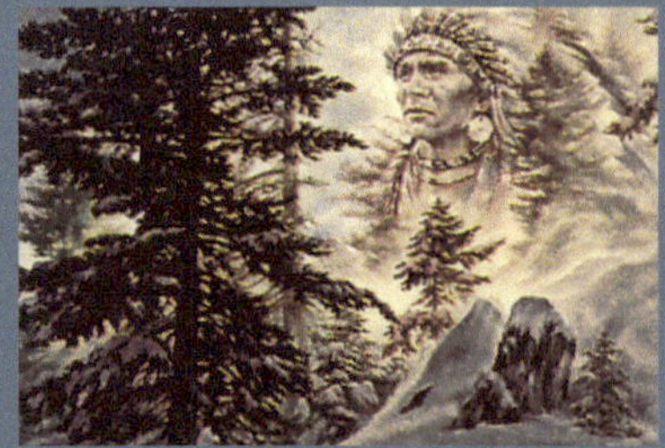

Return of the Snow Chief

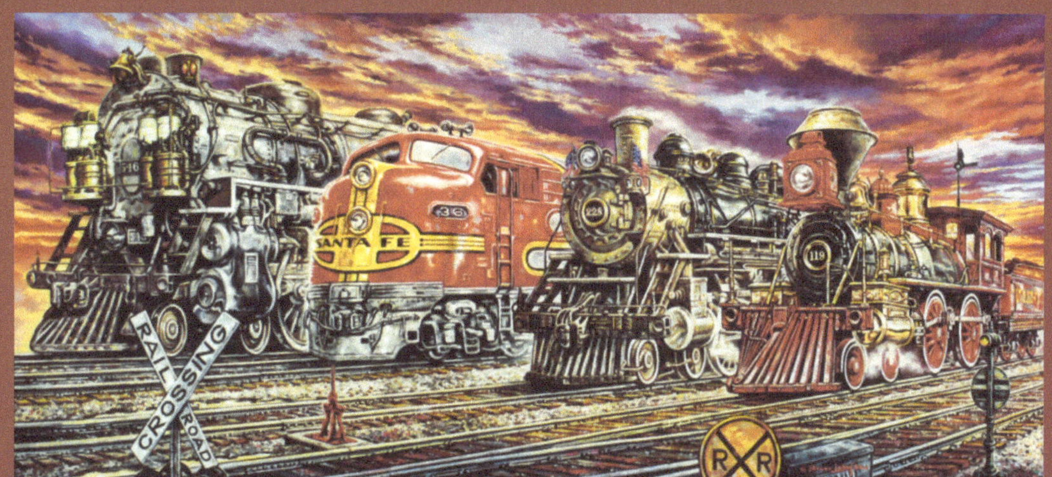

Heritage of the Rails

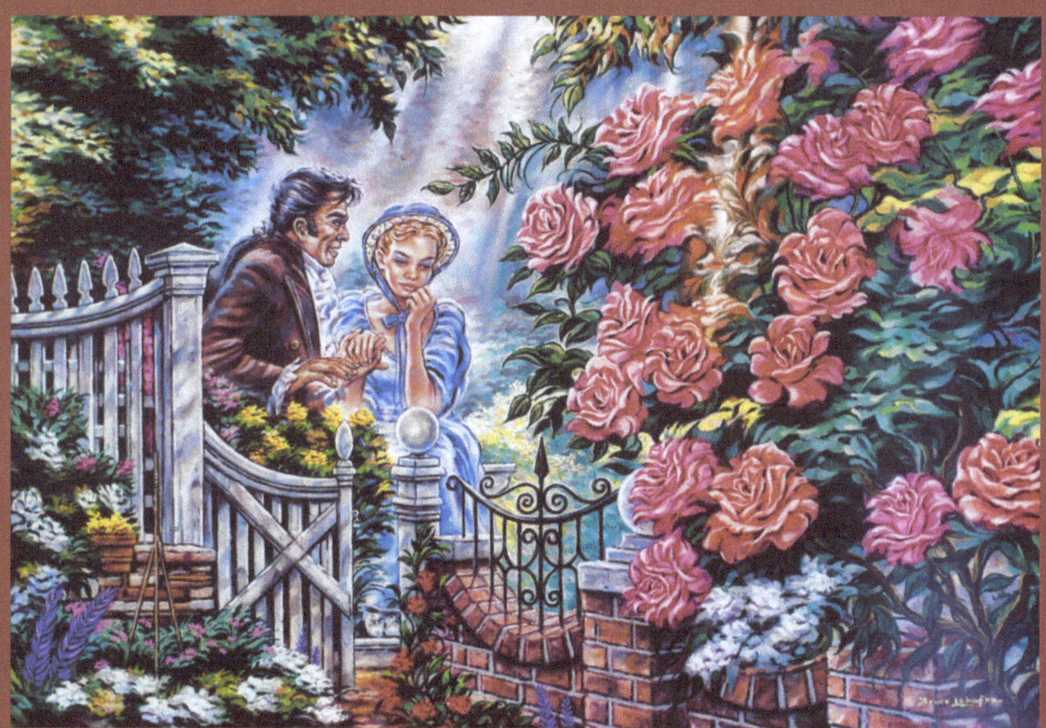

Beyond the Garden Gate

~ 5 ~

All Oil Paintings Listed by Category of Subject Matter

(Top 38 "Best" Paintings Indicated with an asterisk.)

A. Montage Paintings

*1 Las Vegas: The Rat Pack Years

*2 Be a Clown

*3 Sweet Dreams

*4 Wild Earth

*5 Meow: The Cat Family

*6 Iloni

B. Inspirational / Religious

*1 The Prayer

2 Heavenly Welcome

3 Peace Be Still

*4 Christ and the Children

*5 Israel

*6 Tradition

7 The Lion of the Tribe of Judah

*8 Fallen Comrade

*9 A Mother's Prayer

10 The Ascension

C. Indian Maidens

*1 Shenandoah

2 White Dove

*3 Morning Light

4 The Touch

5 Stampede

6 Drawn to the Light

7 Seminole Spirits

8 Rainbow Dove

9 Companions

10 Crescent Moon

11 The Guardian

12 Maiden of the Falls

13 Sundown

14 Native Tapestry

15 Snowfall

16 Cry of the Wolf

D. Sports

*1 Fourth Down and Inches

*2 Moonjumping

*3 Soccer Ballet

E. Indians

1 Fall River Camp

2 Under Silent Stars

3 Dance in the Sun

4 Journey's End

5 Back to the High Country

6 One in Spirit

*7 Dance of Tradition

*8 The Last Reservation

9 Home from the Winter Hunt

10 Ride the Wild Wind

11 Silent Encounter

12 In the Shadow of the Wolf

13 Under the Big Sky

14 Night Riders

*15 One with the Sky

16 Native Cathedral

17 Other Worlds

18 When Lightning Casts Shadows

19 Sunset and Glory

20 Return of the Snow Chief

21 Above the Clouds

22 Night Eyes

*23 Spirit of the Full Moon

24 The Rainmaker

25 Above the Superstitions

F. Multiple Images of One Subject

1 Eagle Dance

*2 Thanks for the Memories (Bob Hope)

3 The German Shepherd

4 Heritage of the Rails

5 Lions, Tigers and Bears...OH MY!

*6 Bouquet of Kittens

G. Humorous

*1 The Rival

*2 The Competitor

3 Moonbeams

H. Miscellaneous

1 Once Upon a Time

*2 The Dance

3 Angel Whispers

4 Leopard's Domain

5 The Girl on the Staircase

6 Afternoon Shade

7 Racing with the Moon

8 Into the Wind

9 Spirit of Atlanta

10 Spirit of Hollywood

11 Eyes of the Jungle

12 Song of the Islands

13 Village Lights

14 The Proposal

15 Beyond the Garden Gate

16 A Winter's Breath

17 Monument Valley

*18 Doll Friends

19 Desert Sunshine

*20 Southern Cross

21 Teacher Lady

22 Moon Wolves

23 The French Lady

I. Children

1 My Guardian Angel

*2 The Smell of Summer Flowers

*3 Wish Upon a Star

*4 Rain, Rain, Go Away

*5 The Tire Swing

*6 Children of the Great Spirit

*7 Wreath of Joy

*8 World of Imagination

*9 Back in the Fifties

J. Black and White (Book Illustrations)

1 Kudu the Witch Doctor

2 Madame Soufrah

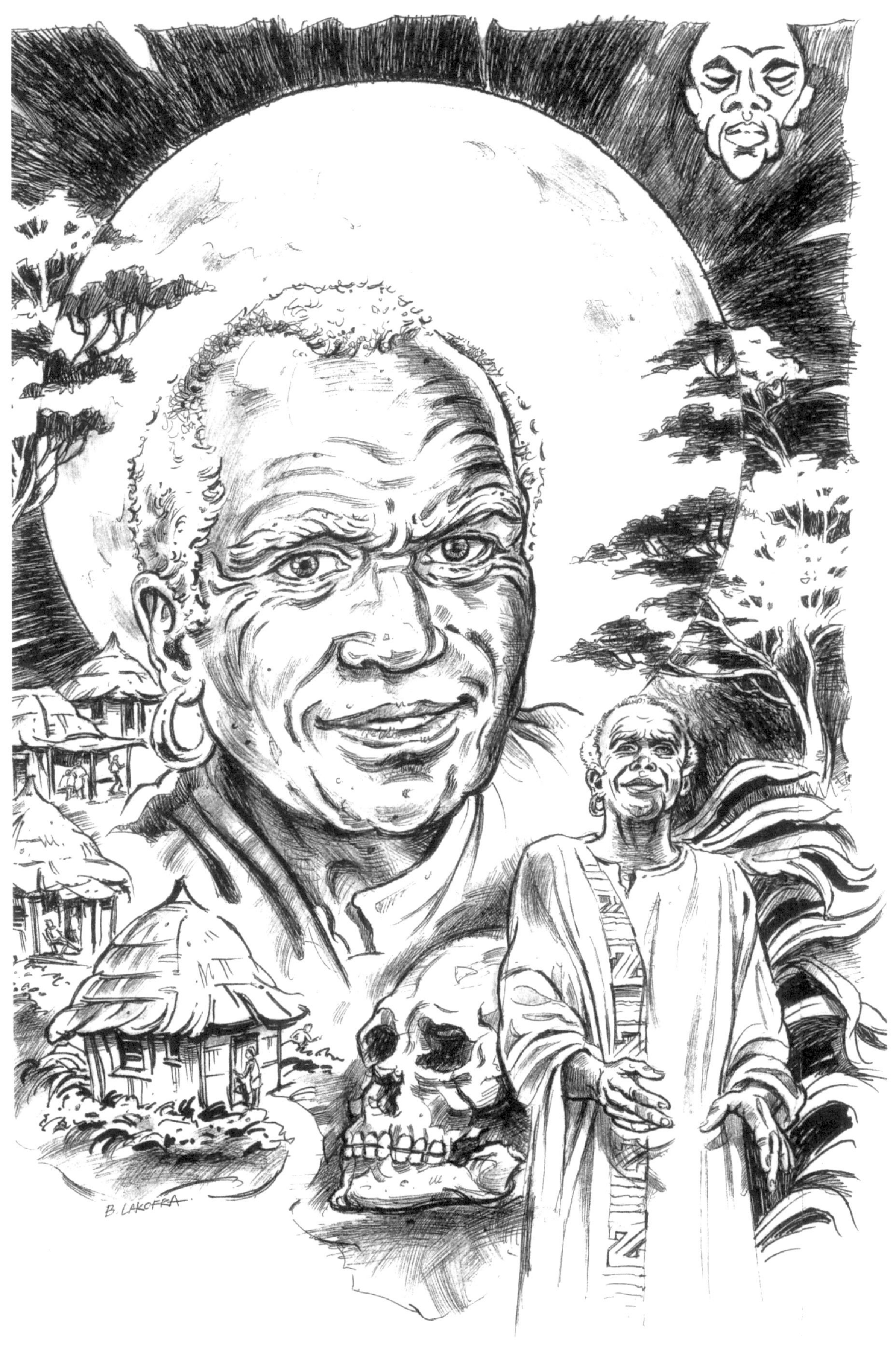

Kudu the Witch Doctor

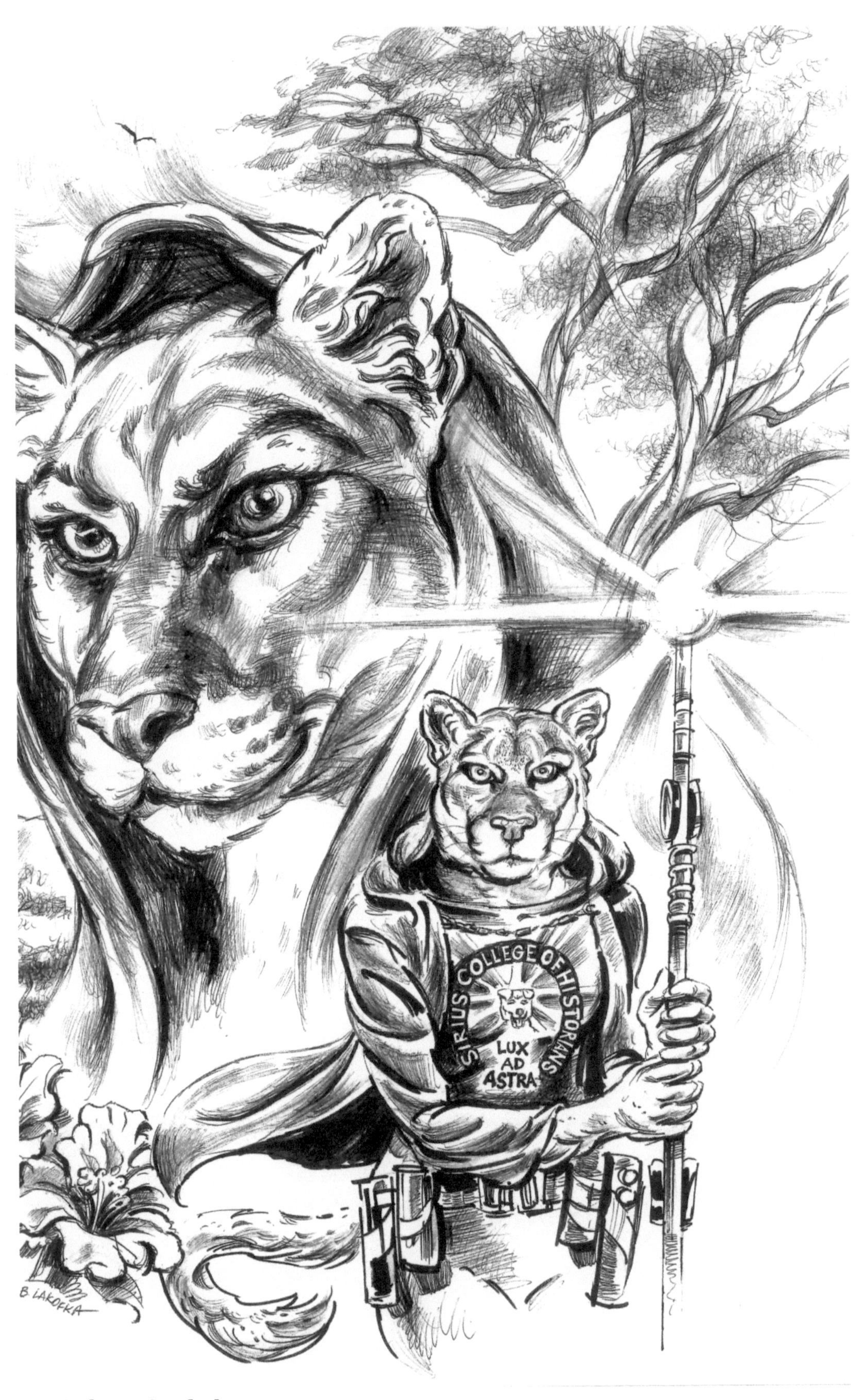

Madame Soufrah

~ 6 ~

Bruce Speaks for Himself

In this chapter I present you two items that will enable you to decide for yourself what kind of a person Bruce was.

The first item is an "Artist's Statement" which I developed after interviewing Bruce in the mid-nineties. Bruce assisted me with a re-write of my initial draft until it met his approval. He used it to further promote his painting career.

The second item is a personal letter dated June 3, 2010 addressed to me and my wife. In it are many of Bruce's views on life, art, and living your beliefs. The original letter (not a typed version) is here for you to see because his printing, I should almost say calligraphy, is both readable and beautiful for its own sake.

This is the last conversation I had with Bruce, because as so often happens in life when friends live hundreds or thousands of miles apart, bad health and family crises can temporarily cut off communication. By the time we came out of our crisis, we found to our grief that Bruce had passed away on October 21, 2015, two days short of his 69th birthday.

We miss him still. The world lost a great talent, a decent human being, and a Christian whose life was a shining endorsement of his faith.

Artist's Statement--- Bruce Lakofka

A photographer friend of mine asked me what I thought about photography vs. painting. We had been discussing the 19th century early American "wilderness painters". I told him that as far as the camera vs. the paintbrush in capturing nature, I think there's some tremendous artist's in both fields. It all comes from the soul and in that we are all related.

The artist's life is like this: you just try different things, serious research, get an idea here, a stroke of inspiration there. I like to have lots of input; sometimes you don't know what's going to work out until you try it.

Bruce thinks people are born with artistic talent which they can either develop (or not develop as they choose). He thinks his 9-year-old daughter, Machir has it. But he is not "pushing her into art", he feels " she needs her childhood and time to decide on her own what she wants to be or do". Bruce's sister has the gift too.

My family is very important in my life and we like to do things together. Whether hiking in the woods, or riding bikes, tennis, or walking through the Promenade in Santa Monica, we are a close family.

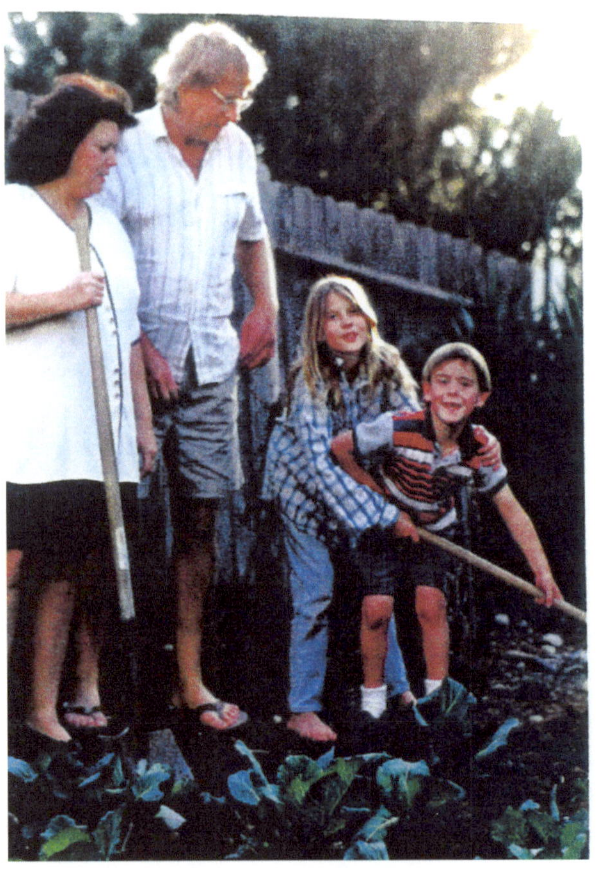

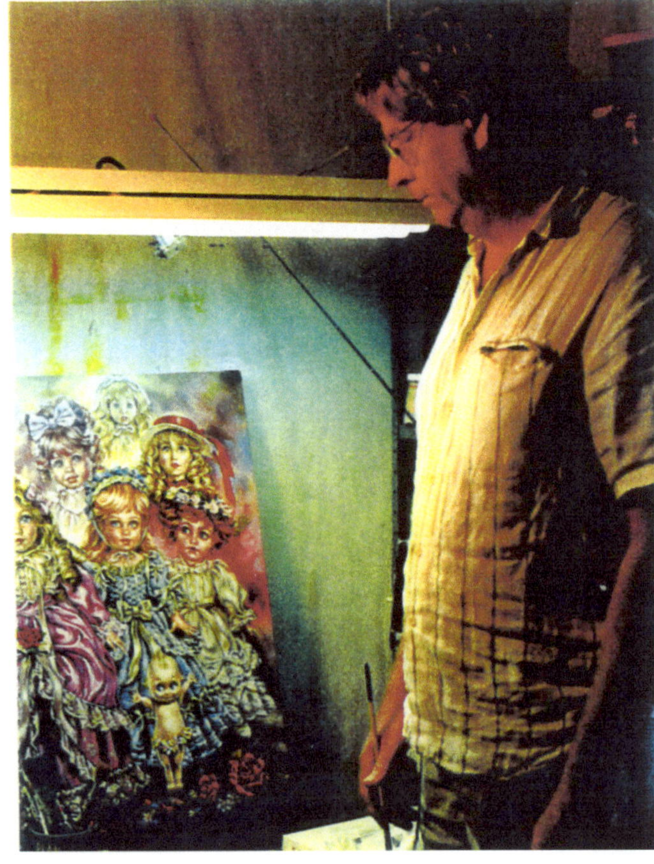

June 3, 2010

Hello Folks...
Got your post cards from Switzerland and Germany. The last was dated May 23 and we got it June 2, so that's the time it took to get here in the international mail. It's good of you to remember us when on your travels.

Back here on the home front, Brenda and I can see Moosh (21) and Jean (almost 19) growing into adulthood, with their own interests and friends... beginning to leave the nest as it were, as I'm sure you experienced with Damon. As parents all we can do is give them a firm foundation of support and love, guidance and stability. Machir has majored in graphic arts, design and all kinds of theater related endeavors... costume, sets, even some acting up at UC at San Bernadino. For a couple of weeks in late June she'll be attending a theater course at I think Cal Arts in Fresno. Practically speaking, one could argue you should study an occupation where the money is... health care, etc., but one follows one's heart and God has his future for her.

Jean is taking on manhood and responsibility, doing some paid part time work with kids and the local YMCA, also making appointments thru Cutco to sell cutlery.

Brenda does her nursing... she's such a faithful and good wife, and of course, I have the art.

We're both commited, Bible believing Christians, married since 1983. Just celebrated our 27th anniversary. Of course we've been living in this world, thru it's struggles and sorrows, always striving to follow Christ, or rather be held up and kept by him down thru the years, and He's been there every step of the way. It's been over 40 years now for me, since I came to know the Lord, but believe he had a hand in drawing me to His side long before that. Way back when I was selling art in Hollywood in 1967 and met you guys, I was serious about the painting and could have easily just have followed this career... but increasingly I had a nagging, searching soul, and the art wasn't enough. What was life all about, what's the purpose, what's the truth? You remember those day's of the '60s... a lot of young people were searching — some got into drugs, false religions, destructive behaviour — but God had a purpose and design in what He led me thru, for I heard the gospel message from a witness in the streets, responded to the q Biblical offer of salvation thru Jesus Christ and got saved, laying down my life for Him. I was "born again" to live a life following after the Spirit and not the flesh... my self will. Thru it all I've

3.

continued to pur sue the art, because I believe God gives us talents and abilities and we should use them, for our own sustenance and to glorify Him. As Christ-ians... followers of Christ... Brenda and I share the same beliefs. Joe and Joyce, you know me. I would never want to come off as preachey, or holier than thou, and a lot of these things you probably already know, but it occurred to me that I never really talk-ed to you about God and the hope we have in Christ and I didn't want any more time to go by, or be found an unfaithful witness for Christ and the true declar-ation of what he has freely offered to all of us thru the shed blood of calvary's cross.

Much Love...

† Bruce.

P.S. Your friendship and help down thru the years, and your kindness & hospitality, is much regarded.
Thank You.

www.ingramcontent.com/pod-product-compliance
Lightning Source LLC
LaVergne TN
LVHW070212110826
845147LV00003B/562
9781632933034